OBJECT ORIENTED ANALYSIS AND DESIGN WITH UML PATTERNS

Dr. Shivani Joshi
MCA, M.Tech., Ph.D.
Associate Professor
Guru Nanak Institute of Management, New Delhi
(Affiliated to Guru Gobind Singh Indraprastha University, Delhi)

S. CHAND
PUBLISHING
empowering minds

S. CHAND & COMPANY PVT. LTD.

(AN ISO 9001 : 2008 COMPANY)
RAM NAGAR, NEW DELHI - 110 055

S.CHAND PUBLISHING
empowering minds

S. CHAND & COMPANY PVT. LTD.

(An ISO 9001 : 2008 Company)
Head Office: 7361, RAM NAGAR, NEW DELHI - 110 055
Phone: 23672080-81-82, 9899107446, 9911310888 Fax: 91-11-23677446
Shop at: **schandgroup.com;** e-mail: **info@schandgroup.com**

Branches :

AHMEDABAD : 1st Floor, Heritage, Near Gujarat Vidhyapeeth, Ashram Road, **Ahmedabad** - 380 014, Ph: 27541965, 27542369, ahmedabad@schandgroup.com

BENGALURU : No. 6, Ahuja Chambers, 1st Cross, Kumara Krupa Road, **Bengaluru** - 560 001, Ph: 22268048, 22354008, bangalore@schandgroup.com

BHOPAL : Bajaj Tower, Plot No. 2&3, Lala Lajpat Rai Colony, Raisen Road, **Bhopal** - 462 011, Ph: 4274723, 4209587. bhopal@schandgroup.com

CHANDIGARH : S.C.O. 2419-20, First Floor, Sector - 22-C (Near Aroma Hotel), **Chandigarh** -160 022, Ph: 2725443, 2725446, chandigarh@schandgroup.com

CHENNAI : No.1, Whites Road, Opposite Express Avenue, Royapettah, **Chennai** - 600014 Ph. 28410027, 28410058, chennai@schandgroup.com

COIMBATORE : 1790, Trichy Road, LGB Colony, Ramanathapuram, **Coimbatore** - 6410045, Ph: 2323620, 4217136 coimbatore@schandgroup.com **(Marketing Office)**

CUTTACK : 1st Floor, Bhartia Tower, Badambadi, **Cuttack** - 753 009, Ph: 2332580; 2332581, cuttack@schandgroup.com

DEHRADUN : 1st Floor, 20, New Road, Near Dwarka Store, **Dehradun** - 248 001, Ph: 2711101, 2710861, dehradun@schandgroup.com

GUWAHATI : Dilip Commercial (Ist floor), M.N. Road, Pan Bazar, **Guwahati** - 781 001, Ph: 2738811, 2735640 guwahati@schandgroup.com

HALDWANI : Bhatt Colony, Talli Bamori, Mukhani, Haldwani -263139 **(Marketing Office)** Mob. 09452294584

HYDERABAD : Padma Plaza, H.No. 3-4-630, Opp. Ratna College, Narayanaguda, **Hyderabad** - 500 029, Ph: 27550194, 27550195, hyderabad@schandgroup.com

JAIPUR : 1st Floor, Nand Plaza, Hawa Sadak, Ajmer Road, **Jaipur** - 302 006, Ph: 2219175, 2219176, jaipur@schandgroup.com

JALANDHAR : Mai Hiran Gate, **Jalandhar** - 144 008, Ph: 2401630, 5000630, jalandhar@schandgroup.com

KOCHI : Kachapilly Square, Mullassery Canal Road, Ernakulam, **Kochi** - 682 011, Ph: 2378740, 2378207-08, cochin@schandgroup.com

KOLKATA : 285/J, Bipin Bihari Ganguli Street, **Kolkata** - 700 012, Ph: 22367459, 22373914, kolkata@schandgroup.com

LUCKNOW : Mahabeer Market, 25 Gwynne Road, Aminabad, **Lucknow** - 226 018, Ph: 4076971, 4026791, 4065646, 4027188, lucknow@schandgroup.com

MUMBAI : Blackie House, IInd Floor, 103/5, Walchand Hirachand Marg, Opp. G.P.O., **Mumbai** - 400 001, Ph: 22690881, 22610885, mumbai@schandgroup.com

NAGPUR : Karnal Bagh, Near Model Mill Chowk, **Nagpur** - 440 032, Ph: 2720523, 2777666 nagpur@schandgroup.com

PATNA : 104, Citicentre Ashok, Mahima Palace , Govind Mitra Road, **Patna** - 800 004, Ph: 2300489, 2302100, patna@schandgroup.com

PUNE : Sadguru Enclave, Ground floor, Survey No. 114/3, Plot no. 8 Alandi Road, Vishrantwadi **Pune** - 411015 Ph: 64017298 pune@schandgroup.com

RAIPUR : Kailash Residency, Plot No. 4B, Bottle House Road, Shankar Nagar, **Raipur** - 492 007, Ph: 2443142,Mb. : 09981200834, raipur@schandgroup.com **(Marketing Office)**

RANCHI : Shanti Deep Tower, Opp. Hotel Maharaja, Radium Road, **Ranchi** - 834001 Mob. 09430246440, ranchi@schandgroup.com

SILIGURI : 122, Raja Ram Mohan Roy Road, East Vivekanandapally, P.O., Siliguri, **Siliguri** - 734001, Dist., Jalpaiguri, (W.B.) Ph. 0353-2520750 **(Marketing Office)** siliguri@schandgroup.com

VISAKHAPATNAM : No. 49-54-15/53/8, Plot No. 7, 1st Floor, Opp. Radhakrishna Towers, Seethammadhara North Extn., **Visakhapatnam** - 530 013, Ph-2782609 (M) 09440100555, visakhapatnam@schandgroup.com **(Marketing Office)**

First Edition 2014

ISBN : 81-219-9769-0 **Code :** 10 559

PRINTED IN INDIA

By B.B. Press, A-37, Sector-67, Noida-201301 (U.P.)
and published by S. Chand & Company Pvt. Ltd., 7361, Ram Nagar, New Delhi -110 055.

Dedicated to

My Husband Mr. Rajiv Joshi

and

Loving Sons Vedant Joshi and Garv Joshi

PREFACE

This book *Object Oriented Analysis and Design with UML Patterns* is designed for undergraduate and postgraduate students of Computer Science and Engineering, Information Technology, and Master of Computer Applications (MCA).

Object Oriented Analysis and Design (OOAD) is a language which provides a powerful tool for building flexible and extensible software components. Software development is a team effort, and it is equally important that developers have a language for talking about analyses and designs. It is a language which is able to deal in requirements and high level design without being cluttered by the fine detail of program code. It refers to the application of object oriented modeling to the analysis of systems and designing object oriented systems fulfilling these requirements. The system may be virtually anything including an organization (e.g. a company), a business unit, a software system which exists or one for which the requirements specification are written, a data warehouse or even a hardware system.

OOAD in modern software engineering is best conducted in an iterative and incremental way. Iteration by iteration, the outputs of OOAD activities, analysis models for OOA and design models for OOD respectively, will be refined and evolved continuously driven by key factors like risks and business values.

This course will give IT professionals an in-depth understanding on using the Unified Modeling Language (UML) to define, model and specify requirements for new systems.

The course materials are based on best practices that have evolved since 1995 when UML became the de facto modeling language for object oriented systems analysis and design.

The techniques taught on this course focus on understanding, modeling and specifying requirements which can be implemented on object oriented platforms to produce application solutions

It will also benefit professionals who wish to sharpen their programming skills using UML.

Case studies, practical's at and review questions at the end of every chapter make the book reader-friendly.

Dr. Shivani Joshi

SYLLABUS

B.TECH.(CS)–SEMESTER V

CS1310 – Object Oriented Analysis and Design

Unit I

Fundamentals

An overview of object oriented systems development – Object basics – Object oriented systems development life cycle.

Unit II

Object Oriented Methodologies

Rumbaugh methodology – Booch methodology – Jacobson methodology – Patterns – Frameworks – Unified approach – Unified modeling language – Use case diagram – Class diagram – Interaction diagram – Package diagram – State diagram – Activity diagram – Implementation diagram.

Unit III

Object Oriented Analysis

Identifying use cases – Object analysis – Classification – Identifying object relationships – Attributes and methods.

Unit IV

Object Oriented Design

Design axioms – Designing classes – Access layer – Object storage – Object interoperability.

Unit V

Software Quality and Usability

Designing interface objects – Software quality assurance – System usability – Measuring user satisfaction .

MCA–SEMESTER IV

Object Oriented Modeling and Design using UML

Introduction

- An overview - Object basics - Object state and properties, Behavior, Methods, Messages.
- Object oriented system development life cycle.
- Benefits of OO methodology.

1. **Overview of Prominent OO Methodologies:** (a) The Rumbaugh OMT. (b) The Booch methodology. (c) Jacobson's OOSE methodologies. (d) Unified Process. (e) Introduction to UML. (f) Important views and diagram to be modelled for system by UML.

2. **Factional view(models):** Use case diagram: (a) Requirement capture with use case. (b) Building blocks of use case diagram - actors, use case guidelines for use case models. (c) Relationships between use cases - extend, include, generalize. Activity diagram (a) Elements of activity diagram - action state, activity state, object node, control and object flow, transition (fork, merge, join) (b) Guidelines for creating activity diagrams. (c) Activity diagram - Action decomposition (Rake). (d) Partition - swim lane.
3. **Static structural view (models):** (a) Classes, values and attributes, operations and methods, responsibilities for classes, abstract classes, access specification (visibility of attributes and operations). (b) Relationships among classes: associations, dependencies, inheritance – generalizations, aggregation. (c) Adornments on association: association names, association classes, qualified association, n-ary associations, ternary and reflexive association. (d) Dependency relationships among classes, notations (e) Notes in class diagram, extension mechanisms, metadata, refinements, derived , data, constraint, stereotypes, package and interface notation. (f) Object diagram notations and modeling, relations among objects (links).
4. **Class modeling and design approaches:** (a) Three approaches for identifying classes - using noun phrases, abstraction, use case diagram. II (b) Comparison of approaches. (c) Using combination of approaches. (d) Flexibility guidelines for class diagram: cohesion, coupling, forms of coupling (identity, representational, subclass, inheritance), class generalization, class specialization versus aggregation.
5. **Behavioral (dynamic structural view):** • State diagram: (a) State diagram notations, events (signal events, change events, Time events). (b) State diagram states (composite states, parallel states, history states), transition and condition, state diagram behavior(activity effect, do-activity, entry and exit activity), completion transition, sending signals. • Interaction diagrams: (a) Sequence diagram - Sequence diagram notations and examples, iterations, conditional messaging, branching, object creation and destruction, time constraints, origin of links, Activations in sequence diagram. (b) Collaboration diagram - collaboration diagram notations and examples, iterations, conditional messaging, branching, object creation and destruction, time constraints, origin of links, activations in sequence diagram.
6. **Approaches for developing dynamic systems:** (a) Top - down approach for dynamic systems. (b) Bottom - up approach for dynamic systems. (c) Flexibility guidelines for behavioral design - guidelines for allocating and designing behaviors that lead to more fexible design.
7. **Architectural view:** (a) Logical architecture: dependency, class visibility, sub systems. (b) Hardware architecture: deployment diagram notations, nodes, object migration between node (c) Process architecture: what are process and threads and their notations in UML, object synchronization, invocation schemes for threads (UML notations for different types of invocations). (d) Implementation architecture: component diagram notations and examples.

8. **Reuse:** Libraries, Frameworks components and patterns: (a) Reuse of classes. (b) Reuse of components. (c) Reuse of frameworks, black box framework, white box frame. (d) Reuse of patterns: architectural pattern and design pattern.

B.TECH.(IT AND CS)

Code No.: IT 309 **L:3 T/P:1 C: 4**

Paper ID: 15309 **Paper: Object Oriented Software Engineering**

Unit I

Introduction to Software Engineering: Software Engineering Development, Software Life Cycle Models, Standards for Developing Life Cycle Models.

Object Methodology and Requirement Elicitation: Introduction to Object Oriented Methodology, Overview of Requirements Elicitation, Requirements Model-Action and Use Cases, Requirements Elicitation Activities, Managing Requirements Elicitation.

Unit II

Architecture: Model Architecture, Requirements Model, Analysis Model, Design Model, Implementation Model, Test Model.

Unit III

Modeling with UMLZ: Basic Building Blocks of UML, A Conceptual Model of UML, Basic Structural Modeling , UML Diagram

System Design: Design Concepts and Activities, Design Models, Block Design, Testing

Unit IV

Testing Object Oriented Systems: Introduction, Testing Activities and Techniques, The Testing Process, Managing Testing.

Case Studies

CONTENTS

CHAPTER

1 Introduction

1.1 PROGRAM

A program is set of instructions. In a program set of instructions executes. A single program can have multiple files. Program is written for our knowledge and consists of coding.

1.1.1 Software

It is a collection of computer programs and related data that provide the instructions for telling a computer what to do and how to do it. In other words, software is a conceptual entity which is a set of computer programs, procedures, and associated documentation concerned with the operation of a data processing system.

In other words software is a set of **programs, procedures, operating manuals** and its **documentation**. Program software performs the function of the program it implements, either by directly providing instructions to the computer hardware or by serving as input to another piece of software. The term was coined to contrast to the old term hardware (meaning physical devices). In contrast to hardware, software is intangible, meaning it "cannot be touched".

1.1.2 Program vs. Software

Program	*Software*
Programs are developed by individuals. They are small in size and have limited functionality.	They are large in size.
Here, programmer is a sole user.	Many users are involved in the development.
It consists of single program or set of instructions.	It consists of number of programs.
Single interface may not be important.	Each and every interface is important, carefully handled and designed.
It requires small or little documentation.	It requires complete documentation and operating manual.
It can be developed by individual style.	It has to follow software or system development life cycle (SDLC).

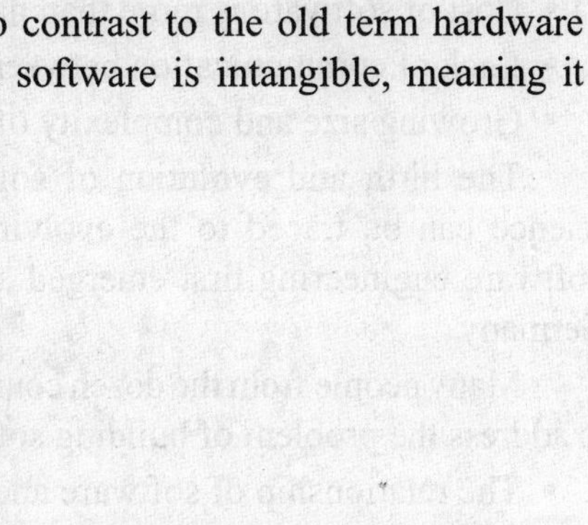

Fig. 1.1

1.1.3 Characteristics of Software

- Software is engineered.
- Software doesn't wear out.
- Software is complex.

1.2 SOFTWARE CRISIS

The software crisis means problem encountered during the software development. The software crisis has the following characteristic:

- Expensive delivery
- Extremely late.
- Unsatisfactory software system.
- Viability to complete.
- Over budget.
- Not according to the requirements of the user.

People in software industry bothered about the software crisis for last 25 years, but we have successfully avoided actual clap of doom until now.

1.2.1 Reason for Software Crisis

There are three main reasons occurs for the software crises. These are written below as:

- Cost of software is more than hardware.
- Lack of communication between software engineer and user.
- Growing size and complexity of the programs.

The birth and evolution of software engineering as a discipline within computer science can be traced to the evolving and maturing view of the programming activity Software engineering first emerged as a popular term in 1968 NATO conference held in Germany.

Many people from the dozen countries were invited to participate in this first conference to address the problem of building software application of computer in a large problem.

- The relationship of software and engineering intended to be provocative.
- The person in the software industry already facing a software crisis as no good software was developed.
- The developed software was not on time within budget and according to the requirement of the user the software engineering emerged as the organizing force to overcome these problems of the software industry.

The growing economic importance of software production and the enormous expansion of the data processing branch lead to the demand for improved programming techniques becoming an increasing hue of research interests in the field of computer science.

Software engineering conferences sponsored by NATO:

- Garmisch, Germany, in 1968
- Rome in 1969.

1.2.2 Software Applications

- System software.
- Application software's
- Engineering/scientific software.
- Embedded software.
- Product-line software.
- Web Apps (Web applications).
- AI software

1.2.3 Legacy Software

- Software must be adapted to meet the needs of new to computing environments or technology.
- Software must be enhanced to implement new to business requirements.
- Software must be extended to make it interoperable extended interoperable with other more modern systems or databases.
- Software must be re-architected to make it viable within a network environment.

1.2.4 Software Myths

Affect managers, customers (and other non technical stakeholders) and practitioners are believable because they often have elements of truth, **but** Invariably lead to bad decisions, **therefore** insist on reality as you navigate your way through software engineering.

1.2.5 Software Engineering

There are different definitions of the software engineering given by the different software researcher scientists, software developers and software development organizations. Some of the important definitions are:

"Software engineering is the establishment and use of sound engineering principles in order to obtain economically software that is reliable and work efficiently on real machines"

"Software Engineering is a systematic approach to development, operation, maintenance and retirement of software".

Or

"Software Engineering is the application of science and mathematics by which the capabilities of computer equipment are made useful to man via computer programs, procedures and associated with documentation".

The IEEE definition for software Engineering is:

Software Engineering

1. *"The application of a systematic, disciplined, quantifiable approach to the development, operation, and maintenance of software; that is, the application of engineering to software".*
2. *The study of approaches as in the above statement.*

1.2.6 Software Engineering is a Layered Technology

See Fig. 1.2 for detailed definition.

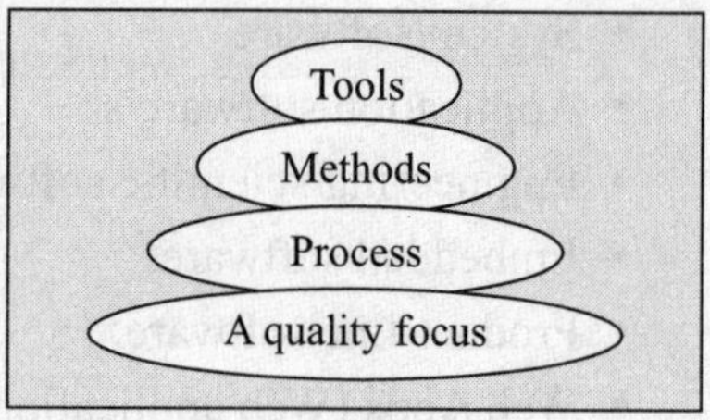

Fig. 1.2

Software Process

It is a set of activities whose goal is the development or evolution of software.

Generic activities in all software processes are:

- **Specification**—what the system should do and its development constraints.
- **Development**—production of the software system.
- **Validation**—checking that the software is what the customer wants.
- **Evolution**—changing the software in response to changing demands.

1.2.7 Software Process Models

A simplified representation of a software process, presented from a specific perspective.

Examples of process perspectives are:

- **Workflow perspective**—sequence of activities
- **Data-flow perspective**—information flow
- **Role/action perspective**—who does what
- Generic process models:
  - o Waterfall
  - o Evolutionary development
  - o Formal transformation
  - o Integration from reusable components

1.3 PURPOSES OF SOFTWARE LIFE CYCLE MODEL

For the development of software, the software life cycle model is the base model which has the following purposes:

1. Guideline to organize, plan, staff, budget, schedule and manage software project work over organizational time, space, and computing environments.
2. Prescriptive outline for what documents to produce for delivery to client.
3. Basis for determining what software engineering tools and methodologies will be most appropriate to support different life cycle activities.
4. Framework for analyzing or estimating patterns of resource allocation and consumption during the software life cycle.
5. Basis for conducting empirical studies to determine what affects software productivity, cost, and overall Quality.

1.4 TYPES OF SOFTWARE LIFE CYCLE MODELS

1.4.1 Strengths and Weaknesses

A comparison of the strengths and weaknesses of SDLC:

Strengths	*Weaknesses*
Control.	Increased development time.
Monitor Large projects.	Increased development cost.
detailed steps.	Systems must be defined up front.
Evaluate costs and completion targets.	Rigidity.
Documentation.	Hard to estimate costs, project overruns.
Well defined user input.	User input is sometimes limited.
Ease of maintenance.	
Development and design standards.	
Tolerates changes in MIS staffing.	

There are several different kinds of software lifecycle Models, but some of the important and mostly used models are discussed in detail below:

- Build and Fix Model
- Waterfall models
- V-Shaped Model
- Iterative Model
- Incremental Model
- Spiral Model
- Evolutionary Model
- Prototyping Model
- Object oriented Model
- Prototyping and Object oriented Model
- Rapid Application Development Model
- Component Assembly Model

1.4.2 Build-and-Fix Model

- This is short project model.
- This is known as Ad-hoc Model.
- It does not require specific requirements
- The software is build and fix for errors until it satisfies the client's requirements.

  Advantage: Appropriate for small projects.

  Disadvantages:

  1. It is not used for large projects.

  2. Cost is quiet high.

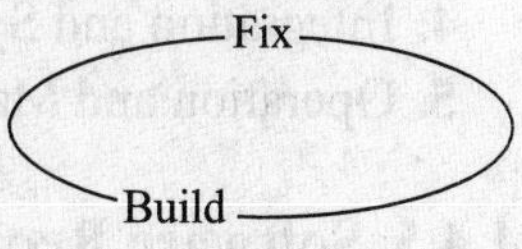

Fig. 1.3

3. It is difficult to maintain.
4. The risks factors are not considered.

1.4.3 When to use the Waterfall Model

- Requirements are very well known
- Product definition is stable
- Technology is understood
- New version of an existing product
- Porting an existing product to a new platform.

1.4.4 Waterfall Model

- The Waterfall Model is the most common and classic life cycle model, which is introduced by Winston Royce in 1970.
- It is used for large term projects.

Waterfall Model is one of the most widely used Software Development Process. It is also called as "**Linear Sequential model**" or the "classic life cycle" or iterative model. It is widely used in the commercial development projects. It is called so because here, we move to next phase (step) after getting input from previous phase, like in a waterfall, water flows down to from the upper steps.

In this iterative waterfall model Software Development process is divided into **five phases**:

1. SRS (Software Requirement Specifications)
2. System Design and Software Design
3. Implementation and Unit testing
4. Integration and System Testing
5. Operation and Maintenance (Fig. 1.4)

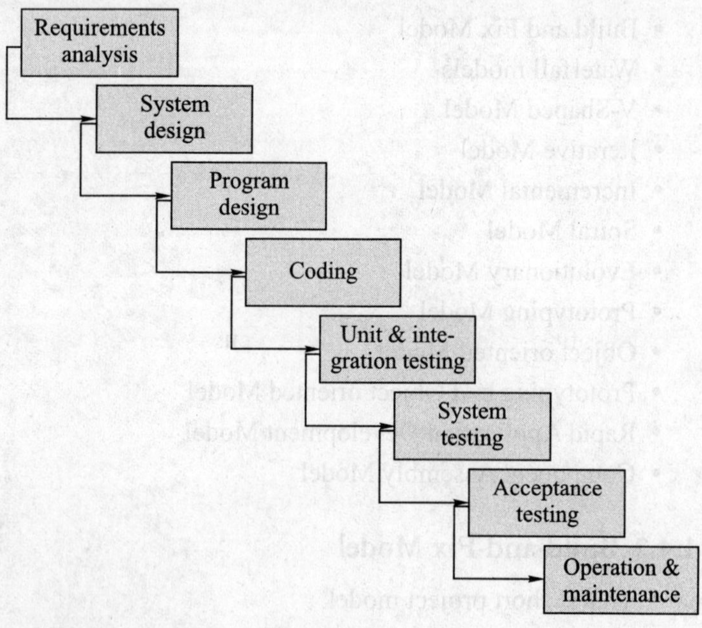

Fig. 1.4

1.4.5 Software Requirements Specifications

This phase is more critical. System analyst makes a complete outline of functional and non functional requirement. Make a brainstorming sessions uses FAST, QFD techniques to develop SRS. A small amount of top-level analysis and design is also documented. This document is verified and endorsed by the customer before starting the project. SRS serves as the input for further phases.

1.4.6 System Design and Software Design

According to the SRS, designing is done. It includes system design which includes designing of software and hardware. Various design for database and information flow is done. E.g. E-R diagram, context diagrams, DFDs.

1.4.7 Implementation and Unit Testing

After system design, code generation begins. Code generation is conversion of design into machine-readable form. If designing of software and system is done well, code generation can be done easily. Software modules are now further divided into units. A unit is a logically separable part of the software. Testing of units can be done separately. In this phase unit testing is done by the developers itself to ensure that there's no defect.

1.4.8 Integration and System Testing

Now the units of the software are integrated together and a system is built. So we have complete software at hand which is tested to check if it meets the functional and performance requirements of the customer. Testing is done, as per the steps defined in the test plan, to ensure defined input produces actual results which agree with the required results. A test report is generated which contains test results.

1.4.9 Operation & Maintenance

Now the software is being delivered to customer. Regular feedbacks are being taken and changes are done if required.

Advantages:

- Easy to understand, easy to use.
- Provides structure to inexperienced staff.
- Milestones are well understood.
- Sets requirements stability.
- Good for management control (plan, staff, and track).
- Works well when quality is more important than cost or schedule.

Disadvantages: Following are the disadvantage of the Water Fall Model:

- o All requirements must be known upfront.
- o Deliverables created for each phase are considered frozen—inhibits flexibility.
- o Can give a false impression of progress.
- o Does not reflect problem-solving nature of software development—iterations of phases.

- o Integration is one big bang at the end.
- o Little opportunity for customer to preview the system (until it may be too late).

1.4.10 V-Shaped Model

V-Model means Verification and Validation model. It is just like the waterfall model, the V-Shaped life cycle is a sequential path of execution of processes. Each phase must be completed before the next phase begins. Testing of the product is planned in parallel with a corresponding phase of development.

1.4.11 When to use the V-model

- The V-shaped model should be used for small to medium sized projects where requirements are clearly defined and fixed.

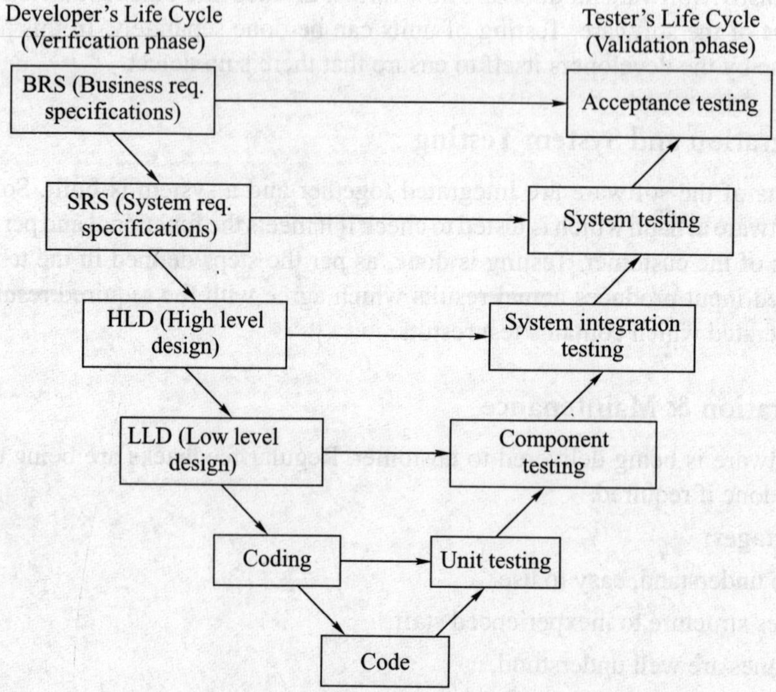

Fig. 1.5

- The V-Shaped model should be chosen when ample technical resources are available with needed technical expertise.
- Project and Requirements Planning—allocate resources.
- Product Requirements and Specification Analysis—complete specification of the software system.
- Architecture or High-Level Design—defines how software functions fulfill the design.
- Detailed Design—develop algorithms for each architectural component.
- Production, operation and maintenance—provide for enhancement and corrections.

- System and acceptance testing—check the entire software system in its environment.
- Integration and Testing—check that modules interconnect correctly.
- Unit testing—check that each module acts as expected.
- Coding—transform algorithms into software.

Advantages:

- Emphasize planning for verification and validation of the product in early stages of product development.
- Each deliverable must be testable.
- Project management can track progress by milestones.
- Easy to use.

Disadvantages:

- Does not easily handle concurrent events.
- Does not handle iterations or phases.
- Does not easily handle dynamic changes in requirements.
- Does not contain risk analysis activities.

1.4.12 Structured Evolutionary Prototyping Model

- Developers build a prototype during the requirements phase.
- Prototype is evaluated by end users.
- Users give corrective feedback.
- Developers further refine the prototype.
- When the user is satisfied, the prototype code is brought up to the standards needed for a final product.

1.4.13 When to Use

- Requirements are unstable or have to be clarified.
- As the requirements clarification stage of a waterfall model.
- Develop user interfaces.
- Short-lived demonstrations.
- New, original development.
- With the analysis and design portions of object-oriented development.

1.4.14 Structured Evolutionary Prototyping Model Steps

- A preliminary project plan is developed.
- A partial high-level paper model is created.
- The model is source for a partial requirements specification.
- A prototype is built with basic and critical attributes.
- The designer builds:
    - o The database.

- o User interface.
- o Algorithmic functions.

- The designer demonstrates the prototype, the user evaluates for problems and suggests improvements.
- This loop continues until the user is satisfied.

1.4.15 Strengths

- Customers can "see" the system requirements as they are being gathered.
- Developers learn from customers.
- A more accurate end product.
- Unexpected requirements accommodated.
- Allows for flexible design and development.
- Steady, visible signs of progress produced.

Interaction with the prototype stimulates awareness of additional needed functionality.

1.4.16 Weaknesses

- Tendency to abandon structured program development for "code-and-fix" development.
- Bad reputation for "quick-and-dirty" methods.
- Overall maintainability may be overlooked.
- The customer may want the prototype delivered.
- Process may continue forever (scope creep).

1.4.17 Rapid Application Model (RAD)

- Requirements planning phase (a workshop utilizing structured discussion of business problems).
- User description phase—automated tools capture information from users.
- Construction phase—productivity tools, such as code generators, screen generators, etc. inside a time-box ("Do until done").

Cutover phase: Installation of the system, user acceptance testing and user training.

1.4.18 When to use RAD

- Reasonably well-known requirements.
- User involved throughout the life cycle.
- Project can be time-boxed.
- Functionality delivered in increments.
- High performance not required.
- Low technical risks.
- System can be modularized.

1.4.19 RAD Strengths

- Reduced cycle time and improved productivity with fewer people means lower costs
- Time-box approach mitigates cost and schedule risk
- Customer involved throughout the complete cycle minimizes risk of not achieving customer satisfaction and business needs
- Focus moves from documentation to code (WYSIWYG).
- Uses modeling concepts to capture information about business, data, and processes.

1.4.20 Weaknesses

- Accelerated development process must give quick responses to the user.
- Risk of never achieving closure.
- Hard to use with legacy systems.
- Requires a system that can be modularized.
- Developers and customers must be committed to rapid-fire activities in an abbreviated time frame.

1.4.21 Spiral Model

- The spiral model is similar to the incremental model, with more emphases placed on risk analysis.
- In spiral development Process is represented as a spiral rather than as a sequence of activities with backtracking and each loop in the spiral represents a phase in the process there are no fixed phases such as specification or design loops in the spiral are chosen depending on what is required Risks are explicitly assessed and resolved in this model.
- The spiral model has four phases: **Planning, Risk Analysis, Engineering and Evaluation.**
- A software project repeatedly passes through these phases in iterations called Spirals in this model.
- The baseline of the spiral model is starting in the planning phase, then requirements are gathered and risk is assessed.
- Each subsequent spiral builds on the baseline spiral.
- It is as shown in the Fig. 1.6.

  Following are the phases of this model:

1. Planning Phase Requirements are gathered during the planning phase Specific objectives for the phase is also identified in this phase.
2. Risk Analyses Phase-In the risk analysis phase, a process is undertaken to identify risk and alternate solutions A prototype is produced at the end of the risk analysis phase Risks are assessed and activities put in place to reduce the key risks.

3. Engineering phase Software is produced in the engineering phase, along with testing at the end of the phase. A development model for the system is chosen which can be any of the generic models.

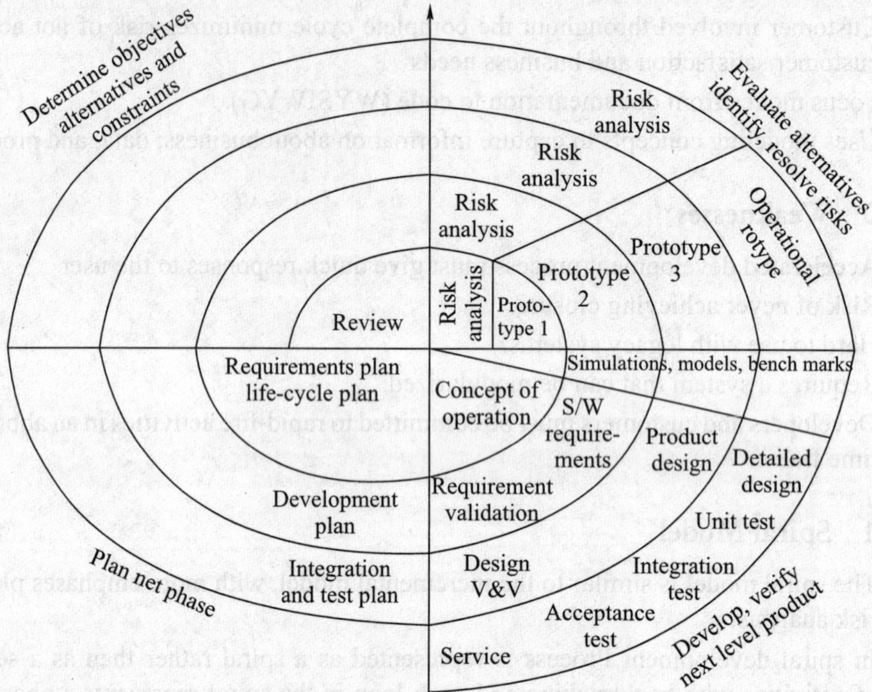

Fig. 1.6

4. Evaluation Phase the evaluation phase allows the customer to evaluate the output of the project to date before the project continues to the next spiral.

Advantages: Following are the advantage of the Spiral Model:

- There is high amount of risk analysis in this model.
- The model is good for large and mission-critical projects
- Software is produced early in the software life cycle.

Disadvantages: Following are the disadvantage of the Spiral Model:

- It can be a costly model to use.
- Risk analysis in the model requires highly specific expertise.
- Project s success is much dependent on the risk analysis phase
- It does not work well for smaller projects.

1.4.22 Prototype Model

Here, a prototype is made first and based on it final product is developed. A prototype is a model or a program which is not based on strict planning, but is an early approximation of the final product or software system. A prototype acts as a sample to test the process. From this sample we learn and try to build a better final product. Please note that this prototype may or may not be completely different from the final system we are trying to develop (Fig. 1.7).

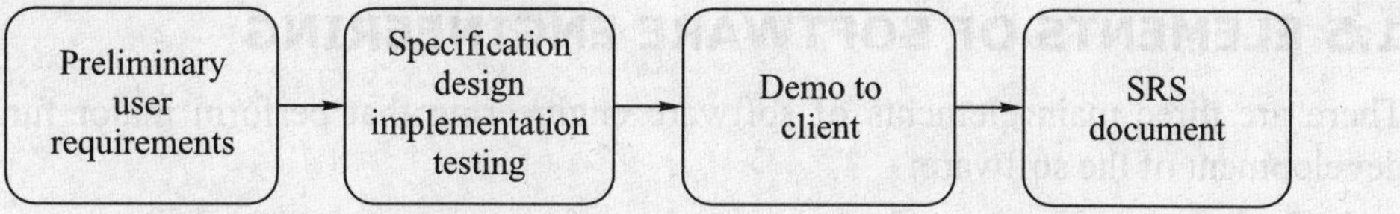

Fig. 1.7

1.4.23 When to use

While making the model, user keeps giving feedbacks from time to time and based on it, a prototype is made. Completely built sample model is shown to user and based on his feedback; the SRS (System Requirements Specifications) document is prepared. After completion of this, a more accurate SRS is prepared, and now development work can start using Waterfall Model.

Advantages of Prototyping Model:

1. When prototype is shown to the user, he gets a proper clarity and 'feel' of the functionality of the software and he can suggest changes and modifications.
2. This type of approach of developing the software is used for non-IT-literate people. They usually are not good at specifying their requirements, nor can tell properly about what they expect from the software.
3. When client is not confident about the developer's capabilities, he asks for a small prototype to be built. Based on this model, he judges capabilities of developer.
4. Sometimes it helps to demonstrate the concept to prospective investors to get funding for project.
5. It reduces risk of failure, as potential risks can be identified early and mitigation steps can be taken.
6. Iteration between development team and client provides a very good and conductive environment during project.
7. Time required to complete the project after getting final the SRS reduces, since the developer has a better idea about how he should approach the project.

Disadvantages of Prototyping Model:

1. Prototyping is usually done at the cost of the developer. So it should be done using minimal resources. It can be done using Rapid Application Development (RAD) tools. Please note sometimes the start-up cost of building the development team, focused on making prototype, is high.
2. Once we get proper requirements from client after showing prototype model, it may be of no use. That is why; sometimes we refer to the prototype as "Throw-away" prototype.
3. It is a slow process.
4. Too much involvement of client, is not always preferred by the developer.
5. Too many changes can disturb the rhythm of the development team.

1.5 ELEMENTS OF SOFTWARE ENGINEERING

There are three main elements of software engineering that perform major function in development of the software:

1. **Techniques:** These are formal procedures for producing some results.
2. **Tools:** Tools are an instrument for accomplishing something in a better way.
3. **Paradigms:** Paradigms represent approach or philosophy for building software.

1.6 TRADITIONAL vs. OBJECT-ORIENTED APPROACH

The systems development life cycle (SDLC) can be defined as a process of understanding how an information system can support business needs or requirements of an organization, modeling the business processes, designing the systems components, and building the system. A systems development project thus goes through a sequence of some fundamental phases such as planning, analysis, design, and implementation. Each of these phases can be divided into a series of steps or activities that rely on some models and techniques to produce required deliverables. Even though all projects cycle through some common phases or activities, but how they are approached by the systems development group can be different—the project team might move through the phases or steps logically, consecutively, incrementally, or iteratively (Dennis, *et al.*, 2002; Satzinger, *et al.*, 2004).

1.6.1 The Traditional Approach

The most common approach to SDLC is a structured methodology based on Waterfall model. It adopts a formal step-by-step approach to the SDLC phases and activities—the activities of one phase must be completed before moving to the next phase. At the completion of each activity or phase, a document is produced that must be approved by the stakeholders before moving to the next activity or phase. The structured approach looks at a system from a top-down view. The center of the structured approach is the process model, which depicts the business processes of a system, and the primary model that presents the processes is the data-flow diagram (DFD). The DFDs and their associated data dictionary contain information about the systems components (inputs, outputs, processes, and data storage) that need to be designed and ultimately built. The structured approach has been around for many years (Fig. 1.8).

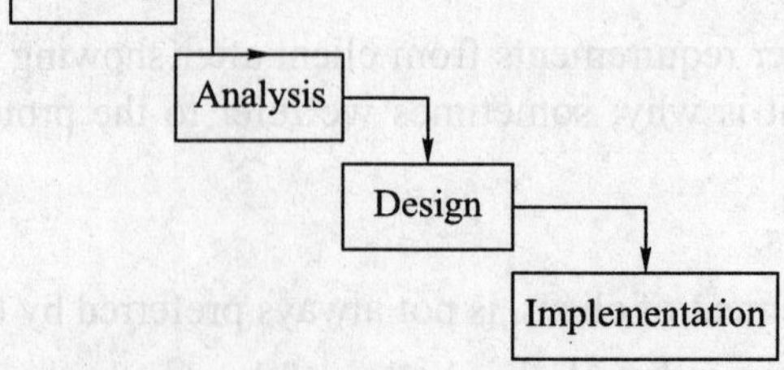

Fig. 1.8 Structured approach to SDLC (waterfall model).

1.6.2 The Object-Oriented Approach

Another approach to SDLC that is widely discussed in recent years is the object-oriented (OO) methodology (Booch, *et al.*, 1999; Brown, 2002; Dennis *et al.*, 2002; Schach, 2004). It is developed by the software engineering professionals who deal with large and complex systems in domains such as aerospace and process control (Schach, 2004). Failure of a business system may cost money but that of mission-critical systems such as that used in the airplanes and space shuttles might cost life. Business system is only one domain that is typically addressed in the SAD texts.

The object-oriented methodology views a system as a bottom-up approach to systems development. To start with, it describes the system through a set of business processes it performs as well the object classes that these processes deal with. It uses a set of diagrams or models to represent various views and functionality of a system and is commonly known as Unified Modeling Language or UML. When these models are used along with a particular method of systems development, the OO approach later became known as the Unified process. (Schach, 2004). Unified Process follows an iterative and incremental approach to systems development. The systems development life cycle is viewed as consisting of several increments or phases: inception, elaboration, construction, and transition (Booch, *et al.*, 1999; Dennis, *et al.*, 2002; Schach, 2004). In each increment or phase, the developers move through the activities of gathering requirements, analyzing the requirements, designing the system, implementing the design, and testing the system. Thus the Unified approach is a two dimensional model. As shown, the phases of the traditional systems development approach do not match with those of the Unified Process; but in each increment, all phases of the SDLC (requirements, analysis, design, implementation, and testing) are visited until the developers satisfy the requirements. However, in each increment, activities of one phase predominate over the others.

It is important to note that many authors use the terms Object-Oriented approach and UML interchangeably, as UML covers universally accepted OO models, notations, and steps to develop an information system. UML focuses on three architectural views of a system: functional, static, and dynamic. The functional view describes the external behavior of the system from the perspective of the user. Use cases and use-case diagrams are used to depict the functional view. The static view is described in terms of attributes, methods, classes, relationships, and messages. Class-responsibility-collaboration (CRC) cards, class diagrams, and object diagrams are used to portray the static view. The dynamic view is represented by sequence diagrams, collaboration diagrams, and state charts. All diagrams are refined iteratively until the requirements of a proposed information system are fully understood and the design is laid out. Finally, the information system is developed through a combination of traditional relational database and object-oriented programming. Because of the large number of models, the relationships of these models in various viewpoints of the systems architecture, a new approach to system development, and a large vocabulary—that are present in the UML, most authors present only a subset of UML knowledge in their texts and it is presented as object-oriented methodology (Fig. 1.9).

1.6.3 Which Approach is Better?

There is a common misunderstanding that the object-oriented approach is the latest methodology of systems analysis and design. The OO methodology promises many benefits such as reduction of development time, reduction of time and resources required to maintain existing systems, increase code reuse, and provide a competitive advantage to organizations that use it. While the potential benefits and advantages may be real, excessive hype has lead to unrealistic expectations among executives and managers (Shah, *et al.*, 2004). Even software developers often miss the subtle but profound differences between the OO methodology and the classic systems development approach. Thus, it is not clear whether we all should move towards the OO methodology of systems development or not. Some authors even argue that prior knowledge of structured methodology may be a hindrance to learn OO methodology (Shaft *et al.*, 2004).

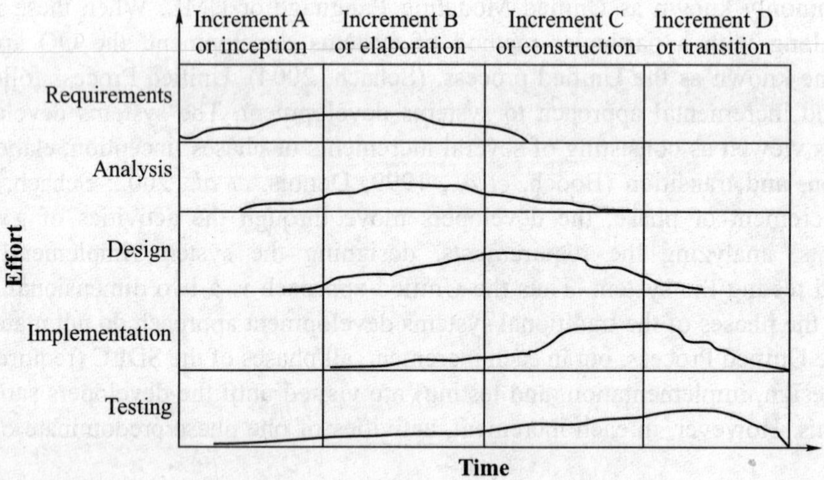

Fig. 1.9

According to a report by Sircar *et al.* (2001), IT managers revealed that 39% of organizations have adopted OO methodology in some form; nevertheless, only 5% of IT projects are developed in OO methodologies. The Unified Processes are intended for use in developing large and complex information systems; however, handling many intricacies of the UML might be far more complex than the development of the most information systems in business (Schach, 2004). There have been some studies on the use of OO methodology as compared to structured approach; although most of these were performed in the classroom setting. Johnson (2002) provides an excellent overview of 12 empirical studies that report advantages and disadvantages of using OO methodology as compared to structured methodology. These studies include subjects from both classroom setting as well as IT professional arena. Most studies show that OO methodology is difficult to learn than conventional methodology; however, it produces increased quality and productivity. Sim and Wright (2002) performed a study on a group of students regarding their understanding of basic OO concepts in three categories, namely the structural, behavioral, and modeling.

They concluded that the students can grasp the structural concepts such as objects and classes easily as compared to dynamic aspects of objects such as operations, message passing, object models, object interaction diagrams, and so on.

It is also important to mention that most of the studies mentioned above were performed only on the learning difficulty of OO concepts and models used for the analysis and design activities—not for the complete life cycle activities, such as implementing the OO design. These studies were also limited to a set of concepts and models—not all the concepts and models used in the OO paradigm were addressed. Most authors suggest that more research is necessary on the subject, especially in industrial settings with real-life projects rather than semester-long student projects. The following discussions focus on some of the intricacies of adapting the OO methodology as compared to the structured approach in a systems development project.

QUESTIONS

1. Difference between program and software.
2. Define software crisis. What are reason for software crisis.
3. What are the software development life cycle phases.
4. Define software engineering.
5. Compare and contrast different SDLC models.
6. Distinguish between traditional US. Object oriented approach of software engineering.

CHAPTER 2 The UML within a Development Process

2.1 THE UML AS A NOTATION

The Three Amigos, when developing the UML, made a very clear decision to remove any process based issues from the language. This was because processes are very contentious—what works for company A might be a disaster for company B. A defense company requires much more documentation, quality and testing than (say) an e-commerce company. So the UML is a generic, broad language enabling the key aspects of a software development to be captured on "paper".

In other words, the UML is simply a language, a notation, a syntax, whatever you want to call it. Crucially, it does not tell you *how* to develop software.

To learn how to use the UML effectively, however, we will follow a simple process on this course, and try to understand how the UML helps at each stage. To start with, let's have a look at some common software processes.

2.2 THE WATERFALL MODEL

The waterfall model prescribes that each stage must be complete before the next stage can commence (Fig. 2.1).

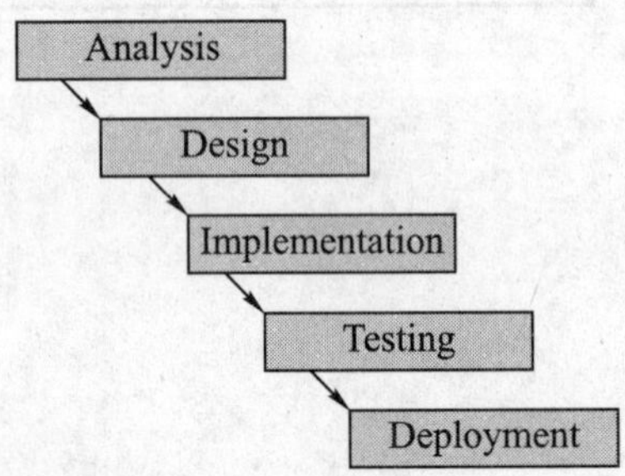

Fig. 2.1 The traditional "Waterfall" model.

This simplistic (and easy to manage) process begins to break down as the complexity and size of the project increases. The main problems are:

- Even large systems must be fully understood and analysed before progress can be made to the design stage. The complexity increases, and becomes overwhelming for the developers.
- Risk is pushed forward. Major problems often emerge at the latter stages of the process—especially during system integration. Ironically, the cost to rectify errors increase exponentially as time progresses.
- On large projects, each stage will run for extremely long periods. A two-year long testing stage is not necessarily a good recipe for staff retention!

Also, as the analysis phase is performed in a short burst at the outset of the project, we run a serious risk of failing to understand the customer's requirements. Even if we follow a rigid requirements management procedure and sign off requirements with the customer, the chances are that by the end of Design, Coding, Integration and Testing, the final product will not necessarily be what the customer wanted.

Having said all the above, there is *nothing wrong* with a waterfall model, providing the project is small enough. The definition of "small enough" is subjective, but essentially, if the project can be tackled by a small team of people, with each person able to understand every aspect of the system, and if the lifecycle is short (a few Months), then the waterfall is a valuable process. It is much better than chaotic hacking!

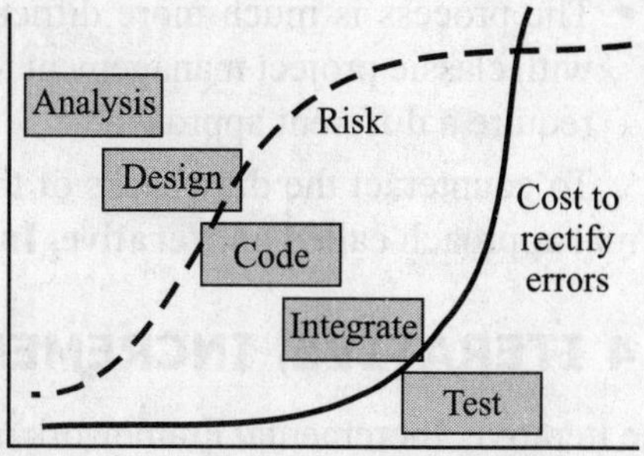

Fig. 2.2 Over time on the waterfall, both the risks and the cost to rectify errors increase.

In summary, the waterfall model is easy to understand and simple to manage. But the advantages of the model begin to break down once the complexity of the project increases.

2.3 THE SPIRAL MODEL

An alternative approach is the **spiral model**. In this approach, we attack the project in a series of short lifecycles, each one ending with a release of executable software (Fig. 2.3).

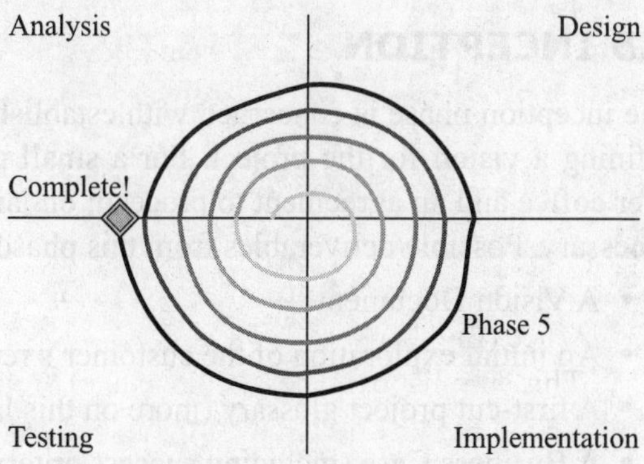

Fig. 2.3 A spiral process. Here, the project has been divided into five phases, each phase building on the previous one and with a running release of software produced at the end of each phase.

With this approach:

- The team is able to work on the entire lifecycle (Analysis, Design, Code Test) rather than spending years on a single activity.
- We can receive early and regular feedback from the customer, and spot potential Problems before going too far with development.
- We can attack risks up-front. Particularly risky iterations (for example, an iteration Requiring the implementation of new and untested technology) can be developed first.
- The scale and complexity of work can be discovered earlier.
- Changes in technology can be incorporated more easily.
- A regular release of software improves morale.
- The status of the project (*e.g.*,—"how much of the system is complete") can be assessed more accurately.

The drawbacks of a spiral process are:

- The process is commonly associated with Rapid Application Development, which is considered by many to be a hacker's charter.

- The process is much more difficult to manage. The Waterfall Model fits in closely with classic project management techniques such as Gantt charts, but spiral processes require a different approach.

To counteract the drawbacks of the spiral technical, let's look at a similar, but more formal approach called an **Iterative, Incremental Framework**.

2.4 ITERATIVE, INCREMENTAL FRAMEWORKS

The Iterative, Incremental Framework is a logical extension to the spiral model, but is more formal and rigorous. We will be following an Iterative, Incremental Framework through the rest of this course (Fig. 2.4).

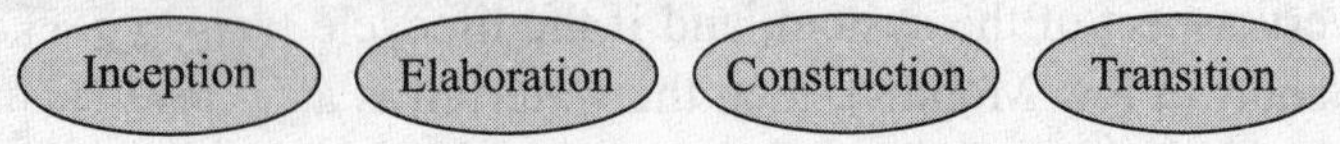

Fig. 2.4 The four phases of an Iterative, Incremental Framework.

The framework is divided into four major phases: **Inception**; **Elaboration**; **Construction** and **Transition**. These phases are performed in sequence, but the phases must not be confused with the stages in the waterfall lifecycle. This section describes the phases and outlines the activities performed during each one.

2.5 INCEPTION

The inception phase is concerned with establishing the scope of the project and generally defining a vision for the project. For a small project, this phase could be a simple chat over coffee and an agreement to proceed; on larger projects, a more thorough inception is necessary. Possible deliverables from this phase are:

- A Vision Document
- An initial exploration of the customer's requirements
- A first-cut project glossary (more on this later)
- A Business Case (including success criteria and a financial forecast, estimates of the Return on Investment, etc.)
- An initial risk assessment
- A project plan

We'll explore the inception phase in a little detail when we meet the case study in.

2.6 ELABORATION

The purpose of elaboration is to analyze the problem, develop the project plan further, and eliminate the riskier areas of the project. By the end of the elaboration phase, we aim to have a general understanding of the entire project, even if it is not necessarily a *deep* understanding (that comes later, and in small, manageable chunks).

Two of the UML models are often invaluable at this stage. The *Use Case Model* helps us to understand the customer's requirements, and we can also use the *Class Diagram* to explore the major concepts our customer understands.

2.7 CONSTRUCTION

At the construction phase, we build the product. This phase of the project is not carried our in a linear fashion—rather, the product is built in the same fashion as the spiral model, by following a series of iterations. Each iteration is our old friend, the simple waterfall. By keeping each iteration as short as possible, we aim to avoid the nasty problems associated with waterfalls (Fig. 2.5).

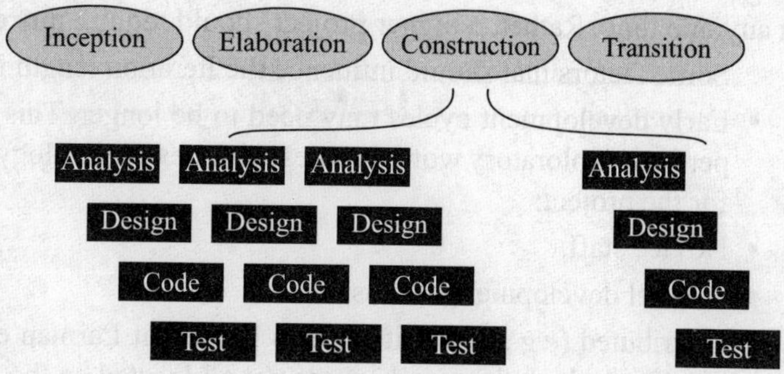

Fig. 2.5 The Construction Phase consists of a series of "mini waterfalls".

Note that at the increption and elaboation phases, prototypes can be built. These prototypes can be developed in exactly the same way—as a series of mini waterfall iterations. However, for this course, we will keep the inception and elaboration phases simple and use the waterfalls for construction only.

At the end of as many iterations as possible, we will aim to havę a running system (albeit, of course, a very limited system in the early stages). These iterations are called *Increments*, hence the name of the framework!

2.8 TRANSITION

The final phase is concerned with moving the final product across to the customers. Typical activities in this phase include:

- Beta-releases for testing by the user community.
- Factory testing, or running the product in parallel with the legacy system that the product is replacing.
- Data take on (*i.e.*, converting existing databases across to new formats, importing data, etc.).
- Training the new users.
- Marketing, Distribution and Sales.

The Transition phase should not be confused with the traditional test phase at the end of the waterfall model. At the start of Transition, a full, tested and running product should be available for the users. As listed above, some projects may require a beta-test stage, but the product should be pretty much complete before this phase happens.

2.9 HOW MUCH ITERATION? HOW LONG SHOULD THEY BE?

A single iteration should typically last between *2 weeks* and *2 months*. Any more than two months leads to an increase in complexity and the inevitable "big bang" integration stage, where many software components have to be integrated for the first time.

A bigger and more complex project should **not** automatically imply the need for longer iterations—this will increase the level of complexity the developers need to handle at any one time. Rather, a bigger project should require **more** iteration.

Some factors that should influence the iteration length include:.

- Early development cycles may need to be longer. This gives developers a chance to perform exploratory work on untested or new technology, or to define the infrastructure for the project.
- Novice staff.
- Parallel developments teams.
- Distributed (*e.g.*, cross site) teams [note that Larman even includes in this category any team where the members are not all located on the same floor, even if they are in the same building!].

To this list, I would also add that a *high ceremony* project will generally need longer iterations. A high ceremony project is one which might have to deliver a lot of project documentation to the customer, or perhaps a project which must meet a lot of legal requirements. A very good example would be any defense related project. In this case, the documentary work will extend the length of the iteration—but the amount of software development tackled in the iteration should still be kept to a minimum to avoid our chief enemy, complexity overload.

2.10 TIME BOXING

A radical approach to managing an iterative, incremental process is *Time Boxing*. This is a rigid approach which sets a fixed time period in which a particular iteration must be completed by.

If iteration is not complete by the end of the time box, the iteration ends anyway. The crucial activity associated with time boxing is the review at the end of iteration. The review must explore the reasons for any delays, and must reschedule any unfinished work into future iterations.

Larman gives details on how to implement time boxing. One of his recommendations is that the developers be responsible for (or at least, have a large say in) setting which requirements are covered in each iteration, as they are the ones who will have to meet the deadlines.

Implementing time boxing is difficult. It requires a culture of extreme discipline through the entire project. It is extremely tempting to forgo the review and overstep the time box if the iteration is "99%" complete when the deadline arrives. Once a project succumbs to temptation and one review is missed, the whole concept begins to fall apart. Many reviews are missed, future iterations planning become sloppy and chaos begins to set in.

Some managers assume that time boxing prevents slippage. It does not. If iteration is not complete once the time box has expired, then the unfinished work must be reallocated to later iterations, and the iteration plans are reworked—this could include slipping the delivery date or adding more iteration. However, the benefits of time boxing are:

- The rigid structure enforces planning and replanning. Plans are not discarded once the project begins to slip.

- If time boxes are enforced, there is less of a tendency for the project to descend into chaos once problems emerge, as there is always a formal time box review not too far away.
- If panic sets in and developers start to furiously hack, the hacking is stemmed once the review is held.

Essentially, time boxing allows the entire project to regularly "stand back" and take stock. It does not prevent slippage, and requires strong project management to work.

2.11 TYPICAL PROJECT TIMINGS

How long should each of the four phases last? This is entirely up to individual projects, but a loose guideline is 10% inception, 30% elaboration, 50% construction and 10% transition.

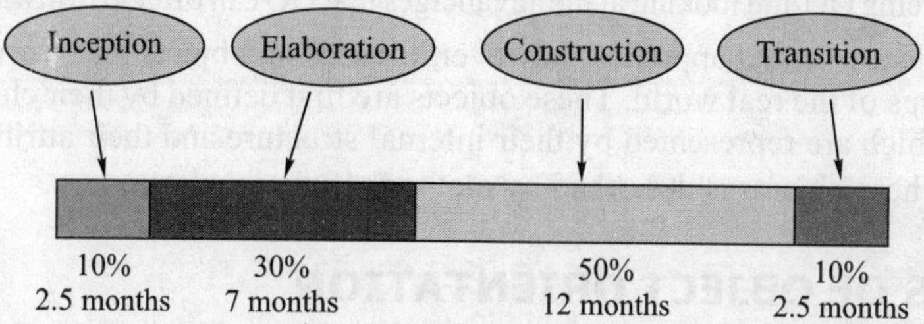

Fig. 2.6 Possible timings for each phase. This example shows the length of each phase for a two year project.

2.12 THE RATIONAL UNIFIED PROCESS

The Rational Unified Process (the RUP) is the most famous example of an Iterative, Incremental Lifecycle in use at the moment. The RUP was developed by the same "Three Amigos" that developed the UML, so the RUP is very complementary to the UML.

Essentially, Rational appreciate that every project is different, with different needs. For example, for some projects, a tiny Inception Phase is appropriate, whereas for defense projects, the Inception phase could last years.

To this end, the RUP is tailor able, and enables each phase of the process to be customized. The RUP also defines the roles of everyone on the project very carefully (in the shape of so-called *Workers*-again, these are tailor able to the project's needs).

The precise advantages and disadvantages of the RUP are beyond the scope of this course. However, the core of the RUP, the Iterative, and Incremental Lifecycle will be followed throughout this course to illustrate the key aspects of the UML models.

QUESTIONS

1. What is the use UML in different SDLC model?
2. What frameworks RAD model gives?
3. Explain time boxing.
4. What is RUP?

CHAPTER 3 Object Orientation

In this chapter we will look at the concept of Object Orientation (OO). The Unified Modeling Language has been designed to support Object Orientation, and we'll be introducing Object Oriented concepts throughout. Before we begin looking at the UML in depth, however, it is worth introducing OO and looking at the advantages that OO can offer to Software Development.

The object-oriented approach, however, focuses on objects that represent abstract or concrete things of the real world. These objects are first defined by their character and their properties which are represented by their internal structure and their attributes (data). The behavior of these objects is described by methods (functionality).

3.1 USES OF OBJECT ORIENTATION

Some of the advantages of object-oriented programming are:

1. Complex software systems become easier to understand, and provides a close representation of reality than any other programming techniques.
2. It is possible to implement changes at class level, without having to make alterations at other points in the system which reduces the overall amount of maintenance required.
3. Polymorphism and inheritance, allows to reuse individual components.
4. The amount of work involved in revising and maintaining the system is reduced, since many problems can be detected and corrected in the design phase.

To Achieve these goals requires:

- **Object-oriented programming languages:** Object-oriented programming techniques do not depend on object-oriented programming languages. The efficiency of object-oriented programming depends directly on techniques which are to be implemented in the system kernel.
- **Object-oriented tools:** Object-oriented tools allow you to create programs in object-oriented languages. They allow to model and store development objects and the relationships between them.
- **Object-oriented modeling:** The object-orientation modeling of a software system is the most important, most time-consuming, and most difficult requirement for attaining the above goals. It provides logical advantages that are independent of the actual implementation.

3.2 STRUCTURED PROGRAMMING

First of all, let's examine (in very rough terms) how software systems are designed using the Structured (sometimes called Functional) approach.

In Structured Programming, the general method was to look at the problem, and then design a collection of ***functions*** that can carry out the required tasks. If these functions are too large, then the functions are broken down until they are small enough to handle and understand. This is a process known as **functional decomposition**.

Most functions will require data of some kind to work on. The data in a functional system was usually held in some kind of database (or possibly held in memory as global variables).

As a simple example, consider a college management system. This system holds the details of every student and tutor in the college. In addition, the system also stores information about the courses available at the college, and tracks which student is following which courses.

A possible functional design would be to write the following functions:

```
add_student
enter_for_exam
check_exam_marks
issue_certificate
expel_student
```

We would also need a data model to support these functions. We need to hold information about Students, Tutors, Exams and Courses, so we would design a database schema to hold this data.

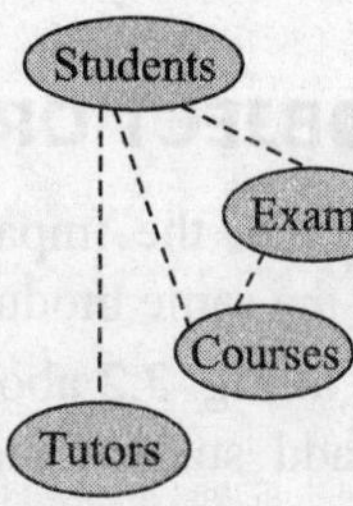

Fig. 3.1 Simple Database Schema. The dotted lines indicate where one set of data is dependent on another. For example, each student is taught by several tutors.

Now, the functions we defined earlier are clearly going to be dependent on this set of data. For example, the "add_student" function will need to modify the contents of "Students". The "issue_certificate" function will need to access the Student data (to get details of the student requiring the certificate), and the function will also need to access the Exam data.

The following diagram is a sketch of all the functions, together with the data, and lines have been drawn where a dependency exists:

The problem with this approach is that if the problem we are tackling becomes too complex, the system becomes harder and harder to maintain. Taking the example above, what would happen if a requirement changes that leads to an alteration in the way in which Student data is handled?

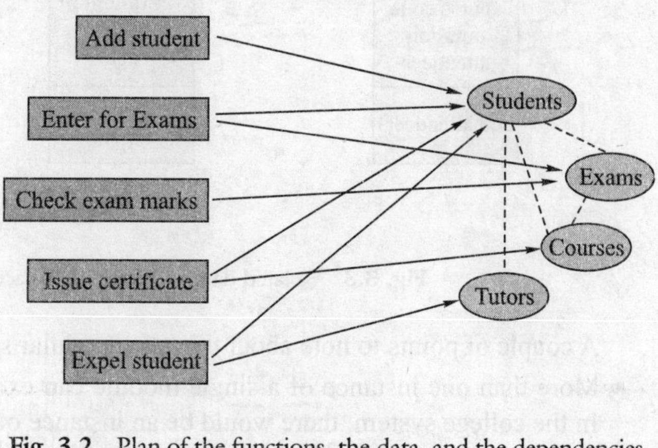

Fig. 3.2 Plan of the functions, the data, and the dependencies.

As an example, imagine our system is running perfectly well, but we realize that storing the Student's date of birth with a two digit year was a bad idea. The obvious solution is to change the "Date of Birth" field in the Student table, from a two-digit year to a four-digit year.

The serious problem with this change is that we might have caused unexpected side effects to occur. The Exam data, the Course data and the Tutors data all depend (in some way) on the Student data, so we might have broken some functionality with our simple change. In addition, we might well have broken the add_student, enter_for_exams, issue_certificate and expel_student functions. For example, add_student will certainly not work anymore, as it will be expecting a two digit year for "date of birth" rather than four.

So we have a large degree of potential knock-on problems. What is far, far worse is that in our program code, we cannot easily see what these dependencies actually are.

How many times have you changed a line of code in all innocence, without realizing that you've inadvertently broken apparently unrelated functionality?

3.3 THE OBJECT ORIENTATED APPROACH

OO tries to lessen the impact of this problem by simply combining related data and functions into the same module.

Looking at Fig. 3.2 above, it is apparent that the data and functions are related. For example, the add_student and expel_student functions are clearly very closely related to the Student data.

The following Fig. 3.3 shows the full grouping of the related data and functions, in the form of modules.

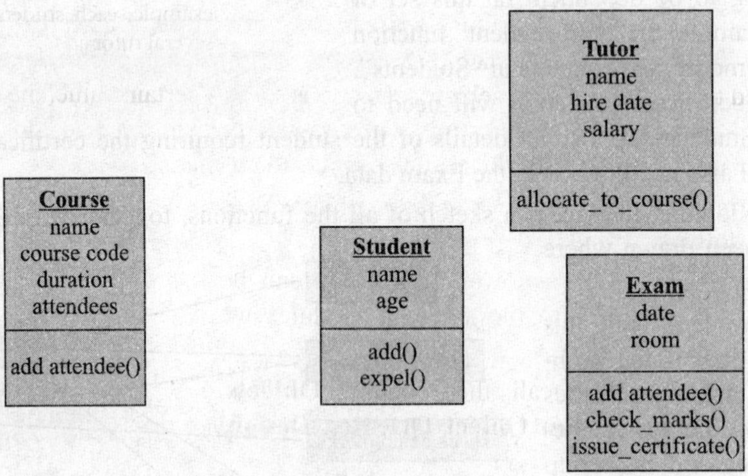

Fig. 3.3 Related data and functions placed in modules.

A couple of points to note about this new modular system of programming:

- More than one instance of a single module can exist when the program is running. In the college system, there would be an instance of "Student" for every student that belongs to the college. Each instance would have its own values for the data (certainly each would have a different name).

- Modules can "talk" to other modules by calling each other's functions. For example, when the "add" function is called in Student, a new instance of the Student module would be created, and then the "add_attendee" function would be called from the appropriate instances of the "Course" module.

3.4 ENCAPSULATION

Crucially, only the instance that owns an item of data is allowed to modify or read it. So for example, an instance of the Tutor module cannot update or read the "age" data inside the Student module.

This concept is called **Encapsulation**, and enables the structure of the system to be far more robust, and avoid the situation as described previously, where a small change to a data member can lead to rippling changes.

With Encapsulation, the programmer of (say) the Student module can safely make changes to the data in the module, and rest assured that no other modules are dependent upon that data. The programmer might well need to update the functions inside the module, but at least the impact is isolated to the single module.

3.5 OBJECTS

Throughout this chapter, I have referred to these collections of related data and functions as being "modules". However, if we look at the characteristics of these modules, we can see some real world parallels.

Objects in the real world can be characterized by two things: each real world object has **data** and **behavior**. For example, a television is an object and posses data in the sense that it is tuned to a particular channel, the scan rate is set to a certain value, the contrast and brightness is a particular value and so on. The television object can also "do" things. The television can switch on and off, the channel can be changed, and so on.

We can represent this information in the same way as our previous software "modules" (Fig. 3.4).

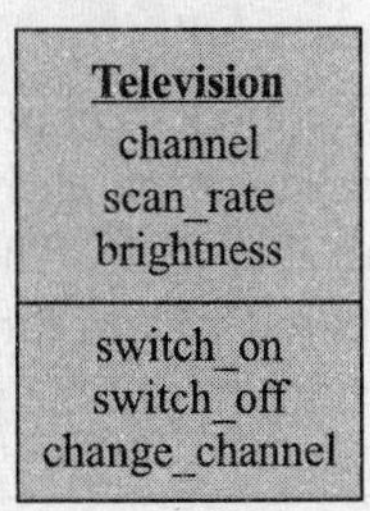

Fig. 3.4 The data and behavior of a television.

In some sense, then, real world "objects" can be modeled in a similar way to the software modules we discussed earlier.

For this reason, we call the modules **Objects**, and hence we have the term **Object Oriented Design/ Programming**.

Since our software systems are solving real world problems (whether you are working on a College booking system, a Warehouse Management System or a Weapons Guidance System), we can identify the objects that exist in the real world problem, and easily convert them into software objects.

In other words, *Object Orientation is a better abstraction of the Real World.* In theory, this means that if the problem changes (ie the requirements change, as they always do), the solution should be easier to modify, as the mapping between the problem and solution is easier.

3.6 TERMINOLOGY

The data for an object are generally called the **Attributes** of the object. The different behaviors of an object are called the **Methods** of the object. Methods are directly analogous to functions or procedures in programming languages.

The other big jargon term is **Class**. A class is simply a template for an object. A class describes what attributes and methods will exist for all instances of the class. In the college system we described in this chapter, we had a class called **Student**.

The attributes of the **Student Class** were name, age, etc. The methods were add() and expel(). In our code, we would only need to define this class once. Once the code is running, we can create instances of the class—*i.e.*, we can create objects of the class.

Each of these objects will represent a student, and each will have its own set of values of data.

3.7 THE OBJECT ORIENTED STRATEGY

Although this chapter has briefly touched on the benefits of Object Orientation (*i.e.*, more robust systems, a better abstraction of the real world), we have left many questions unanswered. How do we identify the objects we need when we're designing a system? What should the methods and attributes be? How big should a class be? I could go on! This course will take you through a software development using Object Orientation (and the UML), and will answer all these questions in full.

One significant weakness of Object Orientation in the past has been that while OO is strong at working at the class/object level, OO is poor at expressing the behaviour of an entire system. Looking at classes is all very well, but classes are very "low-level" entities and don't really describe what the system as a **whole** can do. Using classes alone would be rather like trying to understand how a computer works by examining the transistors on a motherboard!

The modern approach, strongly supported by the UML is to **forget** all about objects and classes at the early stages of a project, and instead concentrate on what the system must be able to do. Then, as the project progresses, classes are **gradually** built to realize the required system functionality. Through this course, we will follow these steps from the initial analysis, all the way through to class design.

QUESTIONS

1. Define object orientation.
2. What is structured programming?
3. Explain object oriented approach.
4. What is object oriented strategy?

CHAPTER 4

Benefits of Object Model

4.1 OBJECT-ORIENTED ANALYSIS

Emphasis is on finding and describing the objects or concepts of the problem domain. Focus on **what** the system must do. **Do the right thing**.

4.2 OBJECT-ORIENTED DESIGN

- Emphasis is on defining software objects and how they collaborate to fulfill requirements. Focus on **how** the system will do it. **Do the thing right**.
- A critical, fundamental ability in OOA/D is to skillfully assign responsibilities to software components.

4.3 ITERATION

- Is a short, time-boxed and risk-driven mini project whose outcome is a tested, integrated and executable system? Each iteration includes its own requirements analysis, design, and implementation and testing activities.
- An iteration length is recommended to be between two and six weeks unless the team size is massive.
- For a large team of developers (200) an iteration length is months instead of weeks.
- If it seems that it will be difficult to meet an iteration deadline, the recommended response is to remove tasks or requirements to a future iteration. Date slippage is discouraged.

4.4 REFACTORING

- Refactoring is about changing the internal structure of the system in order to make it easier to understand and work with.
- Refactoring is made easier by the following steps:
    - o Don't refractor a program and add functionality to it at the same time.
    - o Make sure you have a good test in place before you begin refactoring.
    - o Take short, delivered steps.
- During Refactoring is a good idea to keep an eye on the amount of code thrown away in each iteration.
- Be suspicious if less that 10 percent of the previous code is discarded each time.
- Full integration should be done daily.

4.5 ITERATIVE AND INCREMENTAL DEVELOPMENT

- During the iterative and incremental development the system grows incrementally over the time iteration by iteration.
- Feedback and Adaptation plus short iterations are the core drivers of iterative and incremental development.
- Early iterations are farther from the true path of the system. In late iterations a significant change in requirements is rare.
- While implementing code an early activity to do at the start of every iteration is to synchronize the design diagrams. The earlier diagrams of the iteration will not match the final code and they need to be synchronized before being extended with new design results.
- There can be iterations in all phases (inception, elaboration, construction and transition) but Construction is the key phase in which to iterate.

4.6 INCEPTION

- The intent of inception is to establish some initial common vision for the objectives of the project and decide if it is worthwhile to proceed doing deeper exploration that occurs in elaboration or stop.
- Inception is 1 week long for most projects.
- During inception lightweight use case analysis is performed at least the names of most use cases and actors should be identified.
- Most use cases are written in brief format.
- Most influential and risky quality requirements are identified.
- Technical proofs of concept prototypes of any tricky parts of the use cases are written.
- High-level architecture and components are proposed.
- Plan for the first iteration is written.
- Recommendations are made on what components to buy/build/reuse.

4.7 ELABORATION

- Build the core architecture, resolve the high-risk elements, define most requirements and estimate the overall schedule and resources.
- Adaptively design, implement and test the core and risky parts of the architecture during early iterations.
- Programming and testing should be started early.
- Adapt based on feedback from test, users and developers.
- Elaborations consist of between two and four iterations long and have heavy use case analysis.
- In elaboration 80–90% of the use cases are written in detail.
- Elaboration takes about a fifth (20%) of the total length of the project.

- Two events are key indicators that elaboration is complete:
  - o The developers can feel comfortable providing estimates to the nearest person-week of effort of how long it will take to build each use case.
  - o All the significant risks have been identified and the major ones are understood to the extent that you know how you intend to deal with them.

4.8 CONSTRUCTION

- Iterative implementation of the remaining lower risk and easier elements, and preparation for deployment.

4.9 TRANSITION

- Beta tests, deployment, performance tuning and user training.
- Optimization (performance improvement) should be left always at the end.
- During transition there is no development to add functionality unless is small and absolutely essential.

4.10 PLANNING AND PROJECT MANAGEMENT

- The criteria used to rank requirements as high, medium and low across iterations is based on:
  - o Risks are classified in requirements, technological, skill and political.
  - o Coverage implies that all major parts of the system are at least touched on in early iterations.
  - o Criticality refers to functions of high business value.
- Early iterations must implement high ranking scenarios
- Use Case implementation may be spread across iterations.
- The essence of building a plan involves setting up a series of iterations for construction and defining the functionality to deliver in each one.
- The customer should divide the use cases according to their business value into three piles: high, medium and low.
- The developers then divide the use cases according to the development risk.
- The next step is to estimate the length of the time each use case will require.
- To perform a calculation of how many iterations are needed for the project multiply the number of developers by the iteration length and the divide the result by the load factor, this will give you how much development you can do in an iteration, then add up your time for all use cases, divide the effort per iteration and add 1 for luck and this will give you the first estimate of how many iterations are needed. For example:
  - o 5 developers and iteration length is 2 weeks = 10 person-weeks
  - o Sum of use cases = 200 person-weeks
  - o 200/10 + 1 = 21 iterations (42 weeks elapse time)

- For transition allocate 10% to 35% of the construction time for tuning and packaging for delivery.
- Then add a contingency factor: 10 percent to 20 percent of the construction time depending how risky things look.
- Add this factor to the end of the transition phase. You should commit to deliver at the end of contingent time.

4.11 ARCHITECTURE: REQUIREMENT MODEL

4.11.1 Actor

- Is something with behavior such as person, computer system or organization?
- Actors are classified as:
  - o Primary actor has user goals fulfilled through using services of the system under development.
  - o Supporting actor provides a service to the system under development.
  - o Offstage actor has "somehow" an interest in the behavior of the use case.
- Actor is a role that a user plays with respect to the system.
- When dealing with actors is important to think about roles rather than people or job titles.
- Actors carry out use cases.
- A single actor may perform many use cases and many roles.

4.11.2 Scenario

- Is a specific sequence of actions and interactions between actors and the system.
- A scenario is also called use case instance.

4.12 USE CASE

- Is a collection of related success and failure scenarios that describe an actor using a system to satisfy a specific goal. It must return an observable result of value to a particular actor.
- Use cases drive the whole development process.
- Use cases are not object-oriented.
- Use cases represent an external view of the system.
- Use case types:
  - o **Fully Dressed:** The most elaborate.
  - o **Causal:** Informal paragraph format.
  - o **Brief:** One paragraph summary.
- Black-box Use cases are the most recommended type to write during analysis, they don't describe the internal workings of the system, its components or design. Rather the system is described as having responsibilities.

- Black-box behavior is a description of "what" the system does, without explaining "how" it does it.
- Use cases should be written and named at the domain level in requirements.
- EBP (elementary business processes) guideline:
  - o A task performed by one person in one place at one time, in response to a business event, which adds measurable business value and leaves the data in a consistent state.
  - o Higher-level user goals are discovered using the EBP guideline in order to define use cases.
  - o A common use case mistake is defining many use cases at too low level; that is as single step, sub-function, or subtask within the EBP.
  - o Many use cases can exist that fail the EBP test, they potentially exist at lower level.
- A use case should be defined for each user goal.
- A low-level user goal is called sub-function goal. Use cases should only occasionally be written for these sub-function goals.
- The system boundary can be found by defining what is outside (the external primary and supporting actors).
- The recommended procedure to write use cases is:
  - o Choose the system boundary.
  - o Identify the primary actors. Those that have user goals fulfilled through using services of the system.
  - o Identify user goals. Raise them to the highest user goal level that satisfies the EBP guideline.
  - o Define use cases that satisfy user goals.
- Use case names should start with a verb and should match the user's goal name.
- CRUD requirements should be in a single use case named Manage <X>.
- During early requirements work the use cases should be written in an "Essential Style" keeping the user interface out and focus on the actor's intent.
- During later steps use cases may be written in a "Concrete Style" embedding UI details in the use case text.
- The "SystemAnalyst" is responsible for requirements definition and the "Requirements Specified" who usually are end users and developers help writing use cases.
- Include Relationship represents some partial behavior that is common across several use cases. Use includes when you are repeating yourself in two or more separate use cases and you want to avoid repetition.
- Use Case Generalization occurs when you have one use case that is similar to another use case but does a bit more.

- Use Extend when you are describing a variation on normal behavior and you wish to use a more controlled form declaring extension points in your base use case. The extending use case can't be modified so is necessary to create a sub use case that extends it.
- Factor out sub-function use cases and use the include relationship when:
  - o They are duplicated in other use cases or a use case is very complex and long.
  - o And separating it into subunits adds comprehension.
- A System Use Case is an interaction with the software whereas a business use case discusses how a business responds to a customer or an event.
- The extending use case is divided in two sections:
  - o The name section and
  - o The extension points section. A <<extend>> stereotype may be used.
- Use Cases sections:
  - o **Preface Elements:** Contains preface elements.
  - o **Stakeholders (Actors) and Interests List:** Provides the interests of each Actor, *i.e.*, Salesperson: Wants sales commissions updated.
  - o **Preconditions:** State what must always be true before beginning a scenario in the use case? Preconditions are not tested within the use case, rather they are assumed to be true.
  - o **Success guarantees or Post conditions:** State what must be true on successful completion of the use case.
  - o **Main Success Scenario or basic flow:** Describes the typical success path that satisfies the interests of the stakeholders. It often does not include any conditions or branching.
  - o It is a common idiom to capitalize the actor names for ease identification.
- The scenario records the following steps:
  - o An interaction between actors.
  - o A validation (usually by the system).
  - o A state change by the system.
- Extension (or Alternate Flows):
  - o Extension scenarios are branches from the main success scenario. An extension has two parts the condition and the handling and is something that can be detected by the system or an actor.

4.13 SPECIAL REQUIREMENTS

- Contains any non-functional requirement, quality attribute or constraint that relates to a use case it must be recorded here.

4.14 TECHNOLOGY AND DATA VARIATIONS LIST

- Contains any technical variations in how something must be done.

4.15 OPERATION CONTACTS

- Contracts are defined for system operations and help define system behavior in terms of state changes to objects in the Domain Model.
- Contracts are helpful to record fine-grained details and complexity of required state changes that are awkward to capture in Use Cases.
- Contracts are written during elaboration phase.
- Contract sections are:
  - o **Operation:** Name of operation and parameters.
  - o **Cross References (optional):** Use cases this operation can occur within.
  - o **Preconditions:** Assumptions about the state of the system or objects in the Domain Model before execution of the operation. These will not be tested, are assumed to be true.
  - o **Post-conditions:** Describe changes in the state of objects in the Domain Model after the system operation was executed. Post-conditions are not actions to be performed during the operation; rather they are declarations about the Domain Model objects that are true when the operation has finished.
- **Guidelines:** Contracts:
  - o Identify system operations for the SSDs.
  - o For system operations that are complex and perhaps subtle in their results, or which are not clear in the use case, construct a contract.
  - o To describe the post-conditions use the following categories:
    - Instance creation and deletion.
    - Attribute modification.
    - Associations formed and broken.
    - Post-conditions must be written in past sense.

4.16 DESIGN BY CONTRACT

- An assertion is a Boolean statement that should never be false and therefore will only be false because of a bug.
- Design by Contract uses three kinds of assertions:
  - o Pre-condition is a statement of how we expect the world to be before we execute an operation.
  - o Post-condition is a statement of what the world should look like after the execution of an operation.
  - o An invariant is an assertion about a class. The invariant is always true for all instances of the class. In essence this means that the invariant is added to pre-conditions and post-conditions associated with all public operations of the given class.

4.17 GLOSSARY (DATA DICTIONARY)

Is a list of noteworthy terms and their definitions? The goal is not to record all possible terms but those that are unclear, ambiguous or which require some kind of noteworthy elaboration such as format information rules.

QUESTIONS

1. Different between object oriented analysis.
2. Benefits of object model design.
3. Where requirement model is used?

CHAPTER 5 Object Mapping

Object-relational mapping (ORM, **O/RM**, and **O/R mapping**) in computer software is a **programming** technique for converting data between incompatible **type systems in object-oriented** programming languages. This creates, in effect, a **"virtual object database"** that can be used from within the programming language. There are both free and commercial packages available that perform object-relational mapping, although some programmers opt to create their own ORM tools.

Data management tasks in object-oriented (OO) programming are typically implemented by manipulating objects that are almost always non-**scalar** values. For example, consider an address book entry that represents a single person along with zero or more phone numbers and zero or more addresses. This could be modeled in an object-oriented implementation by a **"Person object"** with **attributes/fields** to hold each data item that the entry comprises: the person's name, a list of phone numbers, and a list of addresses. The list of phone numbers would itself contain "PhoneNumber objects" and so on. The address book entry is treated as a single object by the programming language (it can be referenced by a single variable containing a pointer to the object, for instance). Various methods can be associated with the object, such as a method to return the preferred phone number, the home address, and so on.

However, many popular database products such as structured query language database management systems **(SQL DBMS)** can only store and manipulate **scalar** values such as integers and strings organized within **tables**. The programmer must either convert the object values into groups of simpler values for storage in the database (and convert them back upon retrieval), or only use simple scalar values within the program. Object-relational mapping is used to implement the first approach.

The heart of the problem is translating the logical representation of the objects into an atomized form that is capable of being stored on the database, while somehow preserving the properties of the objects and their relationships so that they can be reloaded as an object when needed. If this storage and retrieval functionality is implemented, the objects are then said to be **persistent** Comparison with traditional data access techniques.

Compared to traditional techniques of exchange between an object-oriented language and a relational database, ORM often reduces the amount of code that needs to be written.

Disadvantages of O/R mapping tools are in areas where proprietary or database-specific techniques have been highly optimized. Most O/R mapping tools do not perform well during bulk deletions of data or joins. **Stored procedures** may have better performance, but are not portable.

In addition, heavy reliance on ORM software has been pointed to as a major factor in producing poorly designed databases. Non-SQL databases.

Another solution is to use an **object-oriented database management system** (OODBMS) or **document-oriented databases** such as native **XML databases.** OODBMS systems are databases designed specifically for working with object-oriented values. Using an OODBMS eliminates the need for converting data to and from its SQL form, as the data is stored in its original object representation and relationships are directly represented, rather than requiring **join tables**/operations.

Document oriented databases also prevent the user from having to "shred" objects into table rows. Many of these systems also support the **XQuery** query language for fast retrieval of large datasets.

Object-oriented databases tend to be used in complex, niche applications. One of the arguments against using an OODBMS is that switching from an SQL DBMS to a purely object-oriented DBMS means that you may lose the capability to create application independent queries for retrieving ad-hoc combinations of data without restriction to access path. For this reason, many programmers find themselves more at home with an object-SQL mapping system, even though most object-oriented databases are able to process SQL queries to a limited extent.

5.1 GENERAL DBMS CONCEPTS

The **database management system** (DBMS) is a software system that enables users to define, create, maintain, and control access to the database. Physically, this database is stored in one, or more files.

There are many reasons for using a DBMS, some of which are:

1. Control of data redundancy.
2. Data consistency: by eliminating or controlling redundancy, the inconsistency in the data of database is reduced.
3. Sharing between users: multiple users can access the database at the same time.
4. Sharing between applications: multiple application programs can read and write data to the same database.
5. Improved data integrity: database integrity refers to the validity and consistency of stored data. A DBMS can control the quality of its data over and above facilities that may be provided by application programs.
6. Improved security: database security is the protection of the database from unauthorized users.
7. Improved backup and recovery services: the database is protected from hardware crashes, and disk media failures.
8. Extensibility: data may be added to the database without changing the existing programs.
9. Data distribution: the database may be partitioned across various sites, organizations, and hardware platforms.

10. Economy of scale: combining all the organization's operational data into one database and creating a set of applications that work on this one source of data can result in cost savings.

The lifecycle of the database applications includes the following steps:

1. Requirement analysis of the application.
2. Design of the application.
3. Devise a specific architecture for coupling the application to a database.
4. Selection of the desired DBMS depending upon the feasibility analysis.
5. Design of the database.
6. Write the application programs which provide a user interface, validate data, and perform computations.
7. Populate the database with the required data.
8. Execute the application and then query, insert, and update the database as needed.

There are two approaches to database design, **attribute driven** and **entity driven**.

- **Attribute driven:** Compile a list of attributes relevant to the application and normalize the groups of attributes that preserve functional dependencies.
- **Entity driven:** Discover entities that are meaningful to the application and describe them.

In a typical database design, there are few entities as compared to the attributes. Entity design is much more easily to manage. Object modelling is a form of entity design.

The three schema architecture on DBMS that was originally proposed by ANSI/SPARC committee is shown in Fig. 5.1. The database design consists of three layers, which are:

- External schema,
- Conceptual schema, and
- Internal schema.
- **External schema:** an external view is an abstract representation of some portion of the total database. An external schema is a definition of an external view. Each external schema is a database design from the perspective of a single application. The external schema isolates applications from most changes in the conceptual schema.
- **Conceptual schema:** The conceptual view is a logical representation of the database in its entirety. The conceptual schema is a definition of that conceptual view. It integrates related applications and hides the details of the implementation of the underlying DBMS.
- **Internal schema:** The internal schema is the database as it is physically stored. The internal schema is the definition of that internal view. The internal schema level consists of actual DBMS.

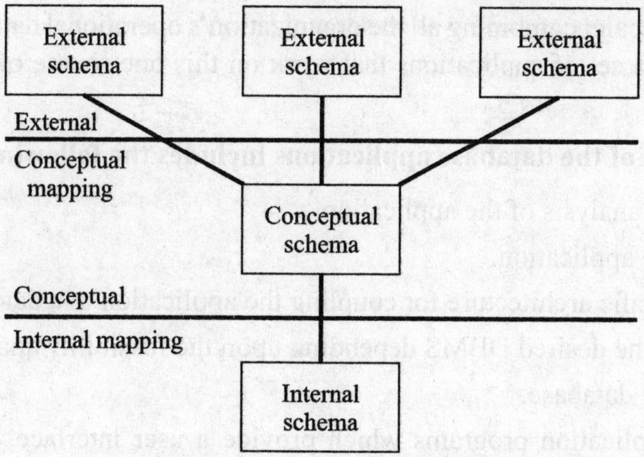

Fig. 5.1 ANSI-SPARC Three Level Architecture.

Object modelling is useful for designing both the **external** and **conceptual** schema. For this, **one should construct one object model for each external schema, and another object model for the conceptual schema.**

5.1.1 Relational DBMS Concepts

RDBMS, as defined by Codd, has three major parts:

1. Data that is presented as tables.
2. Operators for manipulating tables.
3. Integrity rules on tables.

Now, let us discuss the concepts covering these three parts.

5.1.2 RDBMS Logical Data Structure

A relational database logically appears **simply as a collection of tables**. Tables have a **specific number** of columns and an **arbitrary number** of rows. The columns of tables are called attributes and directly correspond to attributes in object models. The rows are called **tuples** and correspond to **object instances** and **links**. A value is stored at each table row and column intersection.

Each value in a table **must belong to the domain of its attribute** or **can be null**. Null means that an attribute value is unknown or indeterminate.

The RDBMS decides if tuning is required for processing a query, and if so, automatically uses it. The RDBMS automatically updates tuning information.

Object Mapping with Database whenever the corresponding tables are updated. Indexing, hashing, and sorting are common tuning techniques.

RDBMS Operators

SQL is the most popular language for RDBMS. It follows ANSI as well as ISO standards. SQL provides operators for manipulating tables. The SQL 'SELECT' statement queries tables.

The syntax of the select command looks something like:

SELECT attribute-list {as Alias}
FROM table-5.1, table-5.2, ...
WHERE predicate-is-true

Logically Table-5.1, Table-5.2, and any others are combined into one temporary table. The attribute list specifies which columns should be retained in the temporary table. The predicate expression specifies which rows should be retained.

SQL can be classified into two categories:

SQL DDL commands: for creating the tables.

SQL DML commands : for inserting,updating, deletion operations.

SQL commands create Tables, insert rows into tables, delete rows from tables, and perform other functions.

RDBMS Integrity

A primary key is a combination of one, or more attributes whose unique value locates each row in a table. The primary key is always a candidate key. In the table shown below, **emp_no** is the primary key of the employee table; dept_no is the primary key of the department table.

Table 5.1

Employee table emp_no	*Emp_name*	*Address*	*dept_no*
1	Ram Kumar	20/780, Hauz Khas, New Delhi	02
2	Shyam Kumar	2/462, Sector 62, Noida	01

Student Table

Table 5.2: Different views from Student Table

Name_id	*Course_no*	*Grade*	*Phone_no*	*Major_no*	*Major-elective*	*Prof.*
N1	C1	A	232456	M1	M1E1	Sanjay
N2	C2	B	256665	M1	M1E1	Ram
N3	C2	D	267677	M2	M2E1	Ram

View 1

Course_no	*Prof.*
C1	Sanjay
C2	Ram

View 2

Name_id	*Course_no*	*Grade*
N1	C1	A
N2	C2	B
N3	C2	D

View 3

Major_no	*Major-elective*
M1	M1E1
M2	M2E1

View 4

Name_id	*Phone_no*	*Major_no*
N1	232456	M1
N2	256665	M1
N3	267677	M2

5.2 OBJECT CLASSES TO DATABASE TABLES

Here, we will consider relational database design as RDBMS technology is gaining more acceptance among organization and companies and it dominates the marketplace.

5.2.1 Extended Three Schema Architecture for Object Models

First, we should formulate object models for the external and conceptual schema. Then we should translate each object model to ideal tables, that is, the table model. Views and interface programs connect external tables to conceptual tables. Conceptual tables convert these to the internal schema.

The object model focuses on logical data structures. Each object model consists of many classes, associations, generalizations, and attributes. Object models are effective for communicating with application experts and reaching a consensus about the important aspects of a problem. Object models help developers achieve a consistent, understandable, efficient, and correct database design.

Each table model consists of many ideal tables. These ideal tables are generic and DBMS independent. Ideal tables abstract the common characteristics of RDBMS implementations. The table model decouples DBMS from object model to table model mapping rules. (see Fig. 5.2)

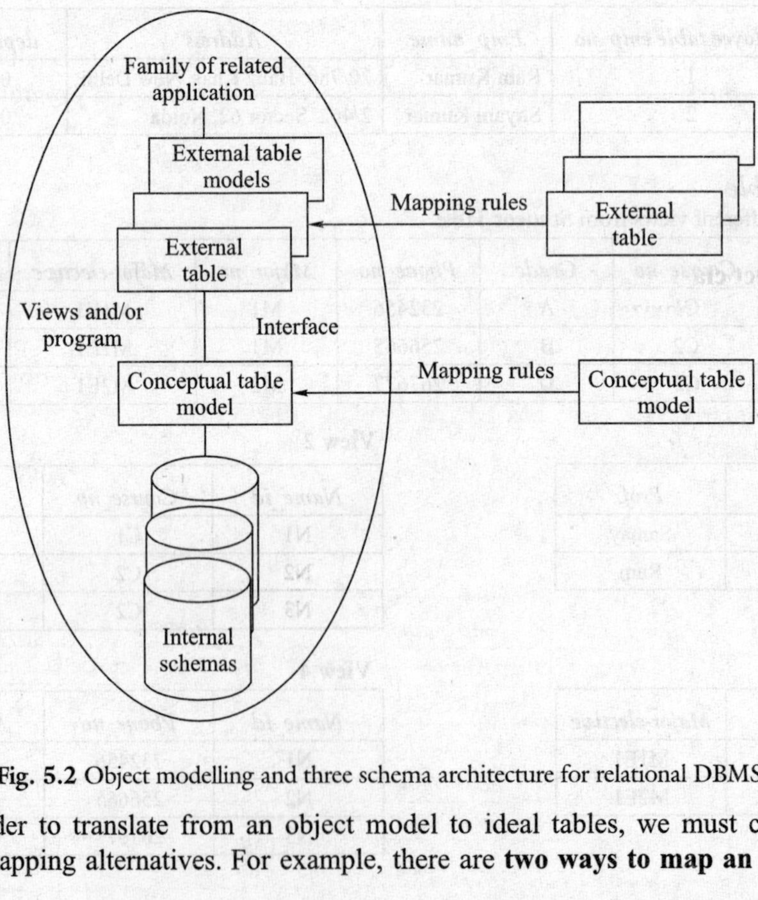

Fig. 5.2 Object modelling and three schema architecture for relational DBMS.

In order to translate from an object model to ideal tables, we must choose from different mapping alternatives. For example, there are **two ways to map an association**

to tables, and **four ways to map a generalization**. We must also supply details that are missing from the object model, such as the primary key and candidate keys for each table and whether each attribute can be null, or not null. Attributes in 27 **Implementation** candidate keys usually should not be null. You must assign a domain to each attribute and list groups of attributes that are frequently accessed.

The internal schema of the three-schema architecture consists of SQL commands that create the tables, attributes, and performance tuning structures.

5.2.2 The use of Object IDs

Each class-derived table has an ID for the primary key, one or more object IDs form the primary key for association derived tables. An ID is the equivalent database construct. There are benefits of using the IDs. IDs are never changing and completely independent of changes in data value and physical location. The stability of IDs is particularly important for associations since they refer to objects. A changing in a name requires update of many associations. IDs provide a uniform mechanism for referencing objects.

On the other hand, IDs have some disadvantages also. There is no support by the RDBMS for generating the IDs. For example, it is difficult to track previously allocated IDs, and to reclaim deleted IDs for reuse.

Object oriented programming uses IDs of many bits, so that reuse of IDs is avoided. We can define IDs as attributes, and adopt a mechanism for handling them.

IDs are not used in applications where users directly access the database. A user thinks in terms of descriptive properties such as names, and not in terms of numbers. The advantage of IDs may prevail when database access is restricted via programs. Restricted access often occurs because application software is needed to compensate for DBMS deficiencies, to enforce integrity, and to provide a user interface.

5.2.3 Mapping Object Classes to Tables

Each **object class** maps to **one**, or **more tables** in the database. The objects in a class may be **partitioned horizontally** and/or **vertically**. For instance, if a class has many instances from which a few are often referenced, then horizontal partitioning may improve efficiency by placing the frequently accessed objects in a table, and the remaining objects in another tables. Similarly, if a class has attributes with different access patterns, it may help to partition the objects vertically.

Employee Table

Table 5.3: Horizontal Partition

Emp_no	*Emp_name*	*Address*
1	Ram Kumar	20/780, Hauz Khas, New Delhi
2	Shyam Kumar	2/462, Sector 62, Noida

Emp_no	*Emp_name*	*Address*
3	Avinash Kumar	F32, Madangir, New Delhi

Table 5.4: Vertical Partition Horizontal and Vertical Partitioning of Tables

Emp_no	*Emp_name*
1	Ram Kumar
2	Shyam Kumar

Emp_no	*Address*
1	20/780, Hauz Khas, New Delhi
2	2/462, Sector 62, Noida

An object class is converted to one table. Class employee has attributes emp_name and address. The table model lists these attributes, and adds the implicit object ID. As part of formulating the table model, we also add details. We specify that emp_ID, ID cannot be null since it is a candidate key. Emp_name cannot be null name must be **Object Mapping with Database** entered for every employee. Attribute address can be null. We assign a domain to each attribute, and specify the primary key for each table. Finally, the SQL DDL statements create the employee table.

5.3 MAPPING ASSOCIATIONS TO TABLES

In this section, we will discuss the mapping of different kinds of associations into database tables.

5.3.1 Mapping Binary Associations to Tables

In general, an association may, or may **not map to** a table. It depends on the type and multiplicity of the association, and the database designer's preferences in terms of extensibility, number of tables, and performance tradeoffs. Let us see one example of mapping a binary association into tables.

Object Model

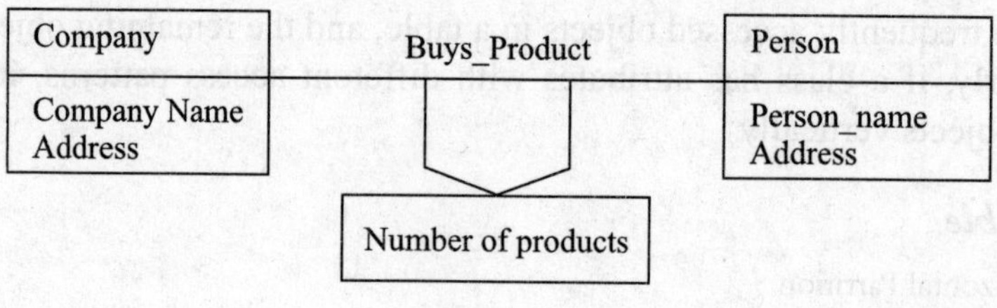

Fig. 5.3

Table Model

Attribute Name	*Nulls?*	*Domain*
person_ID	N	ID
person_name	N	Name
Address	Y	address

Person Table

Candidate key: (person_ID)

Primary key: (person_ID)

Frequently accessed: (person_ID)(person_name)

Attribute Name	*Nulls?*	*Domain*
company_ID	N	ID
company_name	N	Name
Address	Y	address

Company Table

Candidate key: (company_ID)

Primary key: (company_ID)

Frequently accessed: (company_ID)(company_name)

Attribute Name	*Nulls?*	*Domain*
company_ID	N	ID
person_ID	N	ID
Number_of_products	Y	product-count

Buys_products Table

Candidate key: (company_ID, person_ID)

Primary key: (company_ID, person_ID)

Frequently accessed: (company_ID, person_ID)

SQL Code

```
        Create TTABLE Person
        (person_ID              ID              not null,
        person_name             chart(20)       not null,
        address                 chart(20)
PRIMARY KEY (person_ID));

CREATE SECONDARY INDEX person-index-name
ON Person (person_name);
```

Similary, table and indexes can be created for company also

Create TABLE Buys_product

SQL Code

```
(company_ID             ID           not null,
person_ID               ID           not null,
number_of_products integer
PRIMARY KEY ((company_ID, person_ID)),
FOREIGN KEY (company_ID) references Company,
FOREIGN KEY (person_ID) references Person;,

CREATE SECONDARY INDEX buys_product-index-company
ON buys_product (company_ID);

CREATE SECONDARY INDEX buys_product-index-person
ON buys_product (person_ID);
```

5.3.2 Mapping Many-to-Many Association to Tables

A many too many association always maps to a distinct table. The primary keys for both related classes and any link attributes become attributes of the association table. Attributes company ID, and person ID combines to form the only candidate key for the Buys_product table. In general, an association may be traversed starting from either **Object Mapping with Database** class so that both company ID and Person ID could be frequently accessed. The foreign key clauses to the SQL code indicate that each Buys_product table tuples must reference a company and person that had been defined in their respective tables.

An association table always sets the foreign keys from the related objects to not null. If a given pair of objects does not have a link, we omit an entry in the association table.

Company Table (similar to the Company table in the last example)

Person Table (similar to Person table in the last example)

Attribute Name	*Nulls?*	*Domain*
company_ID	N	ID
person_ID	N	ID
Job_designation	Y	Designation

Works for Table

Candidate key: (person_ID)

Primary key: (person_ID)

Frequently accessed: (company_ID, person_ID)

Table Model for one-to-many Associations-distinct association table

Company Table (similar to the Company table in the last example)

Attribute Name	*Nulls?*	*Domain*
person_ID	N	ID
person_name	N	Name
Address	Y	Address
company_ID	Y	ID
Job_designation	Y	Designation

Person Table

Candidate key: (person_ID)

Primary key: (person_ID)

Frequently accessed: (person_ID) (person_name)(company_ID)

Table Model for one-to-many Associations-added association table

Figure 5.4, shows two options for mapping a one-to-many association to the tables. We can create a distinct table for the association, or add a foreign key in the table for much class. The advantages of merging an association into a class are:

1. Fewer tables.
2. Faster performance due to fewer tables to navigate.

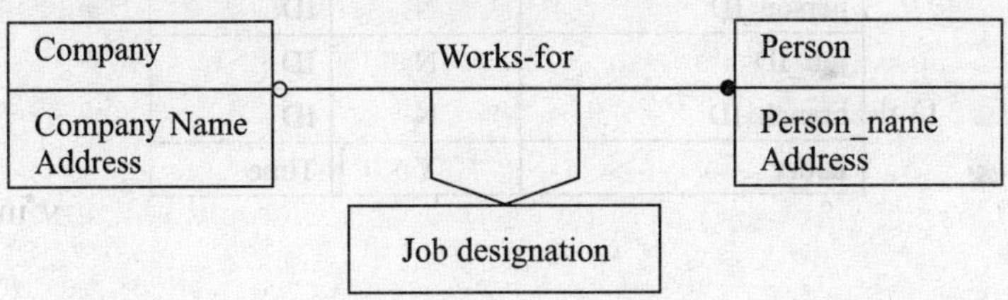

Fig. 5.4 Object Model for one-to-many Association.

The disadvantage of merging an association into a class is:

1. **Less design firmness:** associations are between independent objects of equal weight. In general, it seems inappropriate to mix objects with knowledge of other objects.
2. **Reduced extensibility:** it is difficult to get multiplicity right on the first few design passes. One-to-one and one-to-many associations may be externalized. Many-to-many associations must be externalized.
3. **Increased complexity:** an asymmetrical representation of the association complicates search and update.

The final decision on whether to merge an association into a related class depends on the application. For a one-to-many association you may also merge both classes and the association all into one table.

5.3.3 Mapping Ternary Associations to Tables

Whenever a ternary relationship is there between the different classes then each class is mapped to a table with the inclusion of object ID. Apart from this a new ternary table is also created which has attributes from the different classes involved in the relationship. The attributes will the object ID of all the classes involved in the relationship and the attributes of the relation. Let us look at one example of mapping a ternary association to the tables.

Object Model

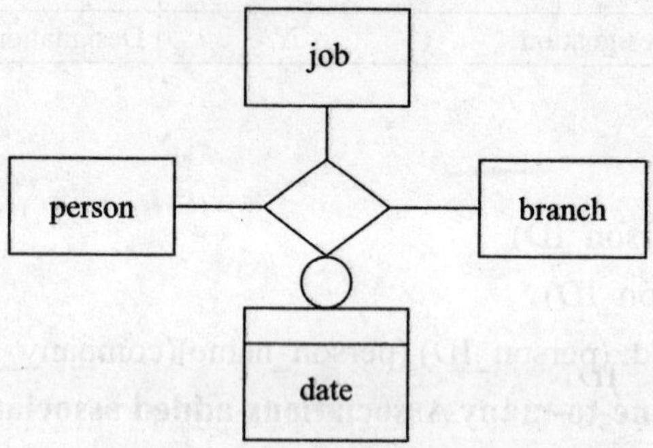

Candidate key: (person_ID, branch_ID, job_ID)

Fig. 5.5

Ternary Table

Attribute Name	*Nulls?*	*Domain*
person_ID	N	ID
job_ID	N	ID
branch_ID	N	ID
hours	Y	Time

Table Model

Candidate key: (person_ID, branch_ID, job_ID)
Primary key: (person_ID, branch_ID, job_ID)
Frequently accessed: (person_ID, branch_ID, job_ID)

Person Table

Attribute Name	*Nulls?*	*Domain*
person_ID	N	ID
person_name	N	Name
Address	Y	Address

Candidate key: (person_ID)
Primary key: (person_ID)
Frequently accessed: (person_ID)(person_name)

Similarly, the job and branch tables will have the required attributes.

SQL Code

```
          Create TTABLE Person
          (person_ID              ID            not null,
          person_name             chart(20)     not null,
          address                 chart(20)
    PRIMARY KEY (person_ID));
```

Similarly, create the other table for job and branch

```
          Create TTABLE Person-job-branch-ternary
          (person_ID              ID            not null,
          job_ID                  ID            not null,
          branch_ID               ID            not null,
          date                    date
    PRIMARY KEY (person_ID, branch_ID, job_ID),
    Foreign key (person_ID) references person,
    Foreign key (job_ID) references job,
    Foreign key (branch_ID) references branch);
```

Also, create the indexes in the same manner.

5.4 MAPPING GENERALIZATIONS TO TABLES

There are different approaches for mapping generalizations to table.

The first approach is shown in the Fig. 5.6. The super class and the subclass each map to a table. The identity of an object across a generalization is preserved through the use of a shared ID. Thus, vehicle car may have one row in the vehicle table with ID 1001, and another row in the Car table also with ID 1001.This approach is simple and extensible. However, it involves many tables, and super class to subclass navigation may be slow.

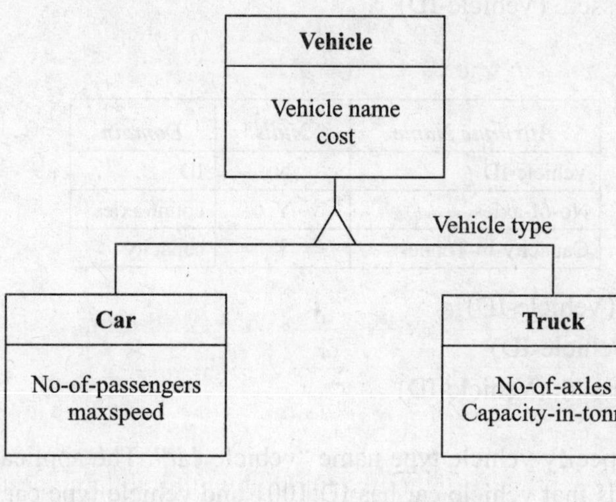

Fig. 5.6 Object Model for Generalization.

The navigation of the tables is as follows:

1. The user gives a vehicle name.
2. Find the Vehicle row that corresponds to vehicle name.
3. Retrieve the vehicle ID and vehicle type for this row.
4. Go to the subclass table indicated by vehicle type, and find the subclass row with the same ID as the Vehicle row.

Table: Model for Generalization Super class and Subclass Tables:

Vehicle Table

Attribute Name	*Nulls*	*Domain*
Vehicle-ID	N	ID
Vehicle-name	N	Name
Cost	Y	Money
Vehicle-type	N	Vehicle type

Candidate key: (Vehicle-ID, Vehicle-name)
Primary key: (Vehicle-ID)
Frequently accessed: (Vehicle-ID, Vehicle-name)

Car Table

Attribute Name	*Nulls*	*Domain*
Vehicle-ID	N	ID
No-of-passengers	Y	Person
Maxspeed	Y	speed

Candidate key: (Vehicle-ID)
Primary key: (Vehicle-ID)
Frequently accessed: (Vehicle-ID)

Truck Table

Attribute Name	*Nulls*	*Domain*
Vehicle-ID	N	ID
No-of-axles	Y	count-axles
Capacity-in-Tonnes	Y	capacity

Candidate key: (Vehicle-ID)
Primary key: (Vehicle-ID)
Frequently accessed: (Vehicle-ID)

The user may specify vehicle type name "vehicle car". The application looks in the vehicle table and finds that vehicle car has ID 1001 and vehicle type car. The application then searches the car table and retrieves additional data for ID 1001.

The SQL code for the generalization of the super-class and sub-class as mentioned above is as follows:

```
Create table vehicle
(Vehicle-ID ID not null,
Vehicle-name char (40) not null,
cost number,
Vehicle-type char (8) not null,
primary key (Vehicle-ID));
Create Secondary index vehicle-index-name on vehicle (vehicle-name);
Create table car
(Vehicle-ID ID not null,
no-of-passengers number,
maxspeed real,
primary key (Vehicle-ID),
foreign key (Vehicle-ID) references vehicle);
Create table truck
(Vehicle-ID ID not null,
no-of-axles number,
Capacity-in-Tonnes real,
primary key (Vehicle-ID),
foreign key (Vehicle-ID) references Vehicle);
```

Object Mapping with Database

In the other approach, the navigation from super class to subclass is eliminated and thus speed performance is achieved. The improved performance incurs a price by inserting the attributes of Vehicle table in both the subclasses.

Table Model for Generalization Many Subclass Tables :

Car Table

Attribute Name	*Nulls*	*Domain*
Vehicle-ID	N	ID
Vehicle-name	N	Name
Cost	Y	Money
No-of-passengers	Y	Person
Maxspeed	Y	Speed

Candidate key: (Vehicle-ID, Vehicle-name)
Primary key: (Vehicle-ID)
Frequently accessed: (Vehicle-ID, Vehicle-name)

Truck Table

Attribute Name	*Nulls*	*Domain*
Vehicle-ID	N	ID
Vehicle-name	N	Name
Cost	Y	Money
No-of-axles	Y	count-axles
Capacity-in-Tonnes	Y	Capacity

Candidate key: (Vehicle-ID, Vehicle-name)
Primary key: (Vehicle-ID)
Frequently accessed: (Vehicle-ID, Vehicle-name)

The above Table (Car Table, Truck Table) illustrates various subclass approaches. This approach eliminates the super class table and replicates all the super class attributes in each subclass table. We may use this approach if a subclass has many attributes, the super class has few attributes, and the application knows which subclass to search.

Table Model for Generalization one Super Class Table

Vehicle Table

Attribute Name	*Nulls*	*Domain*
Vehicle-ID	N	ID
Vehicle-name	N	Name
Cost	Y	Money
No-of-passengers	Y	Person
Maxspeed	Y	Speed
No-of-axles	Y	count-axles
Capacity-in-Tonnes	Y	Capacity

Candidate key: (Vehicle-ID, Vehicle-name)
Primary key: (Vehicle-ID)
Frequently accessed: (Vehicle-ID, Vehicle-name)

The one super class table approach shown above brings all subclass attributes up to the super class level. Each record in the super class table uses attributes present in one subclass, the other attribute values are null. The table in the above table (Vehicle table) violates third normal form. Vehicle-ID or vehicle-name is the primary key, but attributes values also depend on equipment type. This may be a useful approach if there are only two or three subclasses with few attributes.

The best way to handle generalization relationships that exhibits multiple inheritances from disjoint classes is to use **one table per super-class, one table per subclass**. The best way to handle multiple inheritances from overlapping classes is to use one table for the super class, one table for each subclass, and one table for the generalization relationship.

5.5 INTERFACING TO DATABASES

For many applications, the only adequate solution to providing persistency of large amounts of data is to make use of an existing database system. As well as being able to handle effectively unlimited amounts of data, databases provide a number of valuable services, such as support for multiple users, which cannot realistically be implemented again and again, for every application.

Object oriented databases provide seamless database support for applications designed using object oriented methods. However, affordable object oriented databases are not easily writable for object oriented applications. Object oriented applications may be written using backend relational database. However, this approach can create significant problems because the relational model of data is in some ways quite different from the object model.

Suppose that we have a class diagram describing the data model of an application, containing a number of persistent classes related by associations and generalization relationships. To provide database support for this application, we will have to create a relational database schema enabling the same information to be stored. This activity involves **translating one notation into another**, and is similar in principle to that of implementing a model in a programming language: we need to find a way of expressing each UML construct using the concepts and notations of the target environment.

5.5.1 Representing Associations

Associations can be translated into relational schemas in a number of ways. In the simplest case, a unidirectional link from object X to object Y can be implemented by storing the key value of Y in the row of the table corresponding to X. This is the relational equivalent of one object holding a reference to another; the embedded reference is known as a foreign key in relational database terminology.

5.5.2 Representing Generalization

Implementing generalizations in relational databases is slightly problematic, as there is no single feature or technique which provides the required semantics. The most straightforward approach is to represent both the super class and the subclass in the generalization relation as tables, with attributes of each class defined in the corresponding table.

5.5.3 Interfacing to Databases

Once an object oriented data model has been implemented as a relational database, it is necessary to write the code that provides the functionality of the system. This code must be able to read and write data from the database, interpreting it wherever necessary, in terms of the model used by the program.

To achieve this, programming environments typically support an interface that allows programmers to abstract away from the details of individual databases, and enables an application to work with a variety of databases, or data sources. A typical example of such an interface is the Java Database Connectivity (JDBC) API that enables Java programmers to write programs, which interface to relational databases.

Essentially, an API like JDBC enables programmers to manipulate a database by constructing commands in the database query language SQL, executing them on the database, and then dealing with the data that is returned as a result.

SUMMARY

In this unit, we have discussed mapping object classes to tables, *i.e.*, each class maps to one, or more tables. Mapping associations to tables, each many-to-many association maps to a distinct table.

We have also seen that each one-to-many association maps to a distinct table, or may be buried as a foreign key in the table for the many class.

- Each one-to-one association maps to a distinct table, or may be buried as a foreign key in the table for either class.
- For one-to-many, and one-to-one associations, if there are no cycles, you have the additional option of storing the association, and both related objects, all in one table. Be aware that this may introduce redundancy, and violate normal forms.
- Role names are incorporated as a part of the foreign key attribute name.
- N-ary (n > 2) associations map to a distinct table. Sometimes, it helps to promote an n-ary association to a class.
- A qualified association maps to a distinct table with at least three attributes, the primary key of each related class, and the qualifier.
- Aggregation follows the same rules as association.

Further, we have discussed mapping single inheritance generalizations to tables which includes:

- The super class and each subclass map to a table.
- No super class table, super class attributes are replicated for each subclass.
- No subclass tables bring all subclass attributes up to the super class level.

We have also seen that in mapping disjointed multiple inheritances to tables, the super-class and each subclass map to a table. In the mapping overlapping multiple inheritance to tables the super class and each subclass map to a table, the generalization relationship also maps to a table.

CHAPTER

6 Object–Oriented Methodologies

6.1 INTRODUCTION

A methodology is a systematic collection of techniques & guidelines for how to build, buy, maintain and/or enhance software products. A methodology provides a basis for communication. It is used for reliability and quality for software engineering. The term method means guidelines to perform activities.

The way something is done in systems analysis and design is usually called a **methodology**.

Methodologies is the approach to incorporate guidance for business analysis, project planning and management, project processes (e.g., estimation, metrics, risk management), quality assurance, testing, role and responsibilities, reuse and architect.

There are number of methodologies for developing information systems because most businesses prefer to create their own methodology for more utility to their own organizational culture.

General methodology classifications have evolved:

- Traditional,
- Structured analysis & design,
- Information (data) modeling, and
- Object-oriented.

6.1.1 The Traditional Methodology

If, a team, consisting of one member (developing a system for oneself) probably could use this methodology. The traditional methodology becomes much less effective as the size of the team grows or as the complexity of the information system grows. Tools used in a traditional methodology are system flowcharts and **Hierarchical Input Process Output charts (HIPO)**. This methodology has serious problems in most information systems development situations; however, the tools used to support it have applicability in certain development situations.

6.1.2 Structured Analysis and Design Methodology

The **structured analysis and design methodology,** also known as the **data flow modeling** methodology, came in mid1970s for structured programming, It is being utilized for business-oriented information systems development, done in **Management Information Systems (MIS)** departments within businesses and governmental agencies.

6.1.3 Information Modeling Methodology

The **information modeling methodology** also referred as the **data modeling** methodology or **information engineering** methodology came in the early 1980s used for database management systems. It approaches the development of information systems predominantly from an **information perspective** rather than a functional perspective, as does the structured analysis and design methodology.

6.1.4 Object Oriented Methodology

The objectoriented systems analysis and design methodology came in the mid to late 1980s for objectoriented-programming languages for developing and implementing systems. **Simula**, circa 1966, is the first objectoriented language, popular objectoriented (or object-enabled/enhanced) languages such as Smalltalk, C++, Objective C, and Eiffel came into their own in the 1980s and Java was introduced by Sun Microsystems in mid-1995. A few other object-enhanced products made their way to the marketplace in the 1990s—perhaps most notably Visual Basic, Delphi and PowerBuilder. All of these objectoriented languages approach programming from a significantly different paradigm than previous programming languages. These languages follow the approach from Simula based on **objects, attributes, responsibilities,** and **messages**.

The problemsolving strategy inherent in objectoriented programming is to approach the problem from an object (e.g., person, place, thing or concept) perspective rather than the functional perspective of traditional and structured methodologies or the information perspective of an information engineering methodology. Since object oriented programming's problem solving strategy is unique, the need for an object oriented systems analysis and design approach leading up to the programming task makes sense.

In 1990s, such as **Booch, Coad, Cox, Firesmith, HendersonSellers, Jacobson, Mellor, Meyer, Odell, Rumbaugh, Shlaer, WirfsBrock, and Yourdon** have made significant and documented contributions to the objectoriented methodology. Tools and the techniques that support them such as dynamic and static objectoriented models, sequence, collaboration and state diagrams, and use cases are the basis for object-oriented modeling. In November 1997 the **Unified Modeling Language (UML)** became a universally recognized standard of the Object Management Group (OMG). The UML is a set of models and notations that give software developers a standard way to visualize, specify, construct, document and communicate the artifacts of an information system. The UML will be used later in this book for object-oriented modeling. As we move through time the UML continues to evolve and be refined.

However, in 2nd approach, the main building block is the object or a class. To achieve these objectives—**Unified Modeling Language (UML)** is used as a standard language for writing software blueprints.

There are several authors who have given their won notations, to construct system models. Some of these scientists and there notations are as follows:

Rambaugh (1999) : OMT (Object Modeling Technique)
Booch (1986) : OOD (Object oriented design)

Jacobson (1994)	:	OOSE (Object Oriented software engineering)
Coad and Yourdan (1991)	:	OOA/OOD
Shleor and Mellor (1987)	:	OOSA/OOA
Coleman (1994)	:	Fusion
Delate& Robinson (1992)	:	HOOD (Hierarchical Object oriented Design)
Wirf (1989-2002)	:	CRC(Class Responsibility collaboration)/Responsibility driven Design (RDD)
Wasserman (1989)	:	OOSD
Reen (1992)	:	OORASS

6.1.5 OMT

The **Object Modeling technique (OMT)** given by Rambaugh in 1991.

- A method for analysis, design and implementation by an object oriented technique.
- Fast and intuitive approach for identifying and modeling all objects making up a system.
- Class attributes, methods, inheritance and association can be expressed easily.
- Dynamic behavior of objects can be described using the OMT dynamic model.
- Detailed specification of state transitions and their
- Descriptions within a system

It describes the software development process has four phases:

- **Analysis:** It consists of objects, dynamic and functional models
- **System Design:** It explains the basic architecture of the system.
- **Object Design:** It explains static, dynamic and functional models of objects.
- **Implementation:** It tells about reusable, extendible and robust code.

Most of the modeling is performed in the analysis phase. The recommended method incorporates the following activities:

1. Develop a Problem Statement. It is used to collect and gather all the requirements. It covers requirement engineering.
2. **Build an Object Model:**
   (*i*) Identify object classes.
   (*ii*) Develop a data dictionary for classes, attributes, and associations.
   (*iii*) Add associations between classes.
   (*iv*) Add attributes for objects and links.
   (*v*) Organize and simplify object classes using inheritance.
   (*vi*) Test access paths using scenarios and iterate the above steps as necessary.
   (*vii*) Group classes into modules, based on close coupling and related function.
3. **Build a Dynamic Model:**
   (*i*) Prepare scenarios of typical interaction sequences.

(*ii*) Identify events between objects and prepare an event trace for each scenario.
(*iii*) Prepare an event flow diagram for the system.
(*iv*) Develop a state diagram for each class that has important dynamic behavior.
(*v*) Check for consistency and completeness of events shared among the state diagrams.

4. Build a Functional Model:
(*i*) Identify input and output values.
(*ii*) Use data flow diagrams as needed to show functional dependencies.
(*iii*) Describe what each function does.
(*iv*) Identify constraints.
(*v*) Specify optimization criteria.

5. Verify, iterate, and refine the three models:
(*i*) Add most important operations to the object model.
(*ii*) Verify that classes, associations, attributes and operations are consistent and complete, check with problem statement.
(*iii*) Iterate steps to complete the analysis.

6.1.6 Notation

The symbols used are:

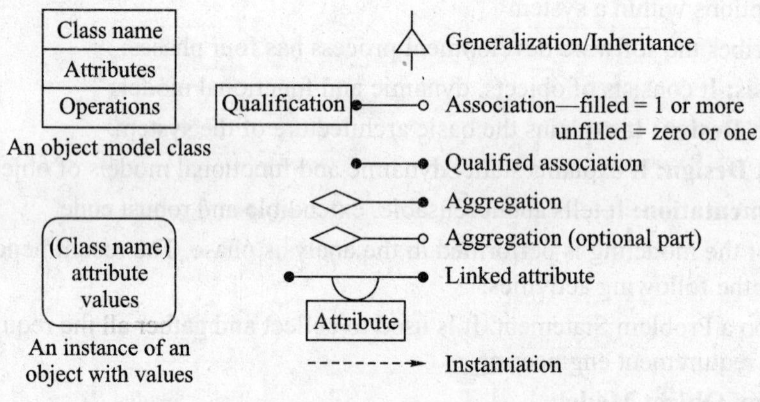

Fig. 6.1

A fundamental assumption of OMT is that object-oriented thinking represents a more natural and intuitive way for people to reason about reality.

The purposes of modeling according to Rumbaugh are:

- **Testing** physical entities before building them (simulation),
- **Communication** with customers,
- **Visualization** (alternative presentation of information), and
- Reduction of **complexity.**

Hence, **understanding** and **simulation** is at the core. As a general modeling approach, OMT may be used to model all types of work. OMT proposes three main types of models:

- **Object model**

  The object model represents the static and most stable phenomena in the modeled domain. Main concepts are **classes** and **associations,** with ***attributes*** and ***operations***. ***Aggregation*** and ***generalization*** (with multiple inheritances) are predefined relationships (Fig. 6.2).

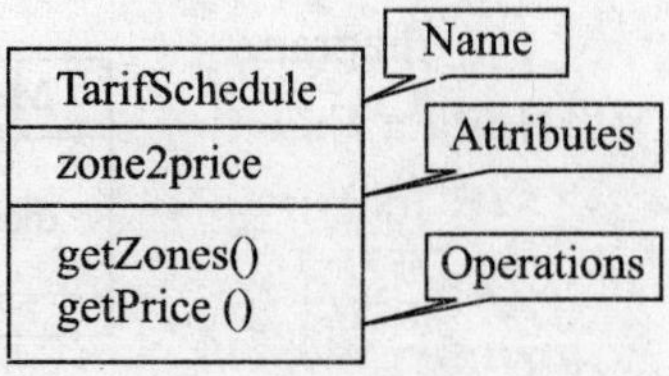

Fig. 6.2

- A **class** represents a concept.
- A class encapsulates state **(attributes)** and behavior **(operations).**
- Each attribute has a **type**.
- Each operation has a **signature.**

6.1.7 1-to-1 and 1-to-many Associations

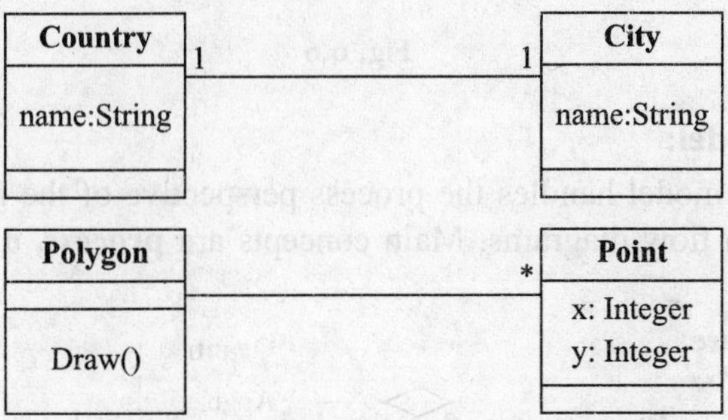

Fig. 6.3 Many-to-Many Associations

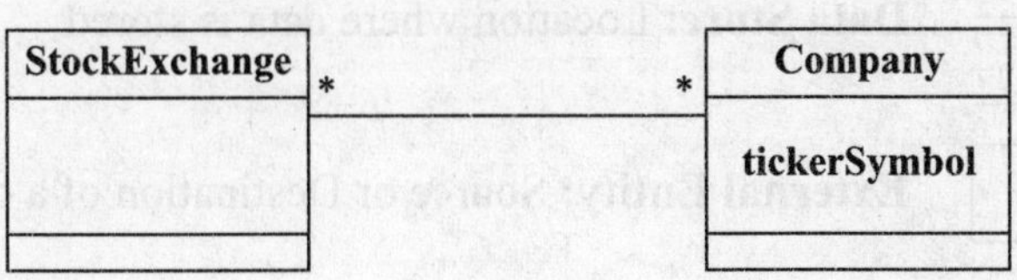

Fig. 6.4

- **Dynamic model:**

  The dynamic model represents a state/transition view on the model. Main concepts are **states, transitions** between states, and **events** to trigger transitions. **Actions** can be modeled as occurring within states. **Generalization and aggregation** (concurrency) are predefined relationships.

  An **aggregation** is a special case of association denoting a "consists-of" hierarchy. The *aggregate* is the parent class, the components are the children classes.

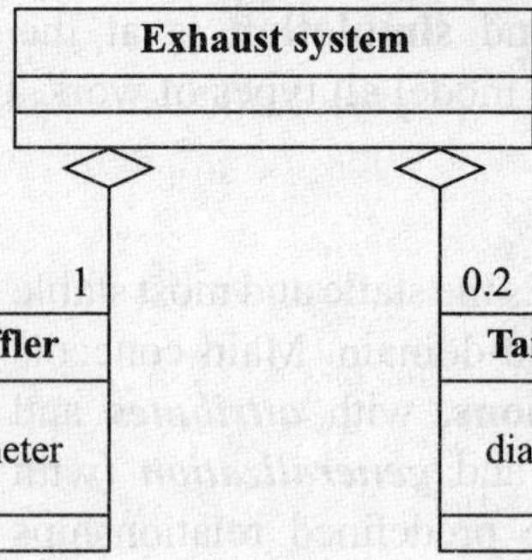

Fig. 6.5

State chart Diagram for Incident:

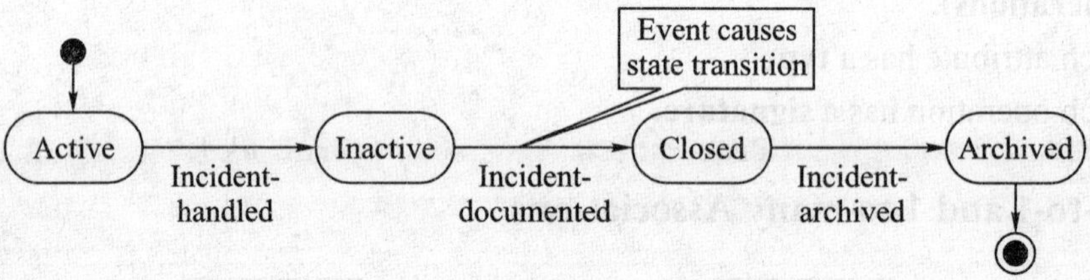

Fig. 6.6

- **Functional model:**

  The functional model handles the process perspective of the model, corresponding roughly to data flow diagrams. Main concepts are **process, data store, data flow,** and **actors.**

  The Notations are:

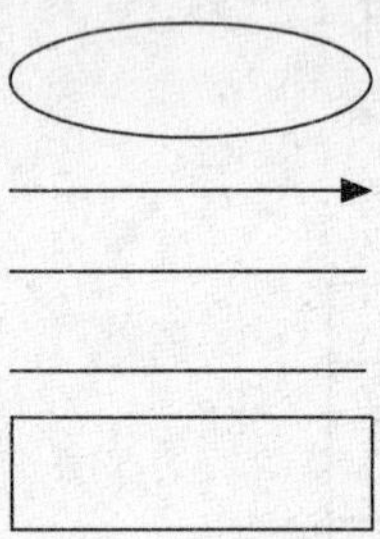

Process: any function being performed

Data Flow: Direction of data element movement

Data Store: Location where data is stored

External Entity: Source or Destination of a data element

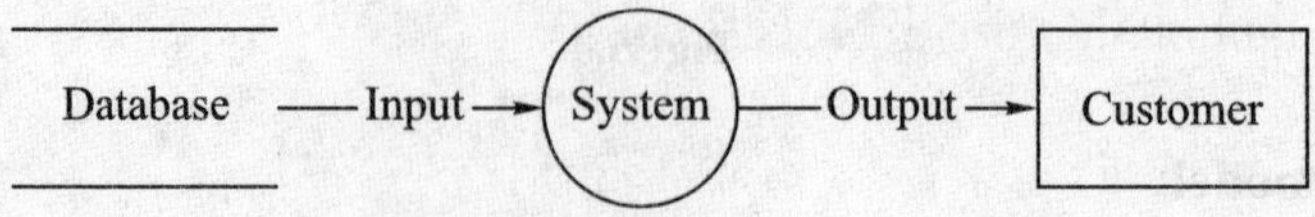

Fig. 6.7

6.1.8 OOD (Object Oriented Design)

Object oriented design was introduced by **Grady Booch** in 1991, is a widely used method in object-oriented analysis and design. It supersedes of UML.

The Booch method helps to design systems using the object paradigm. It covers the analysis- and design phases of an object-oriented system. The method defines different models to describe a system and it supports the iterative and incremental development of systems.

The Booch method includes **six types of diagrams**:

- **Class diagrams:** Describe roles and responsibilities of objects.
- **Object diagrams:** Describe the desired behavior of the system in terms of scenarios.
- **State transition diagrams:** State of a class based on a stimulus.
- **Module diagrams:** To map out where each class & object should be declared.
- **Process diagrams:** To determine to which processor to allocate a process.
- **Interaction diagrams:** Describes behavior of the system in terms of scenarios.

Booch method prescribes:

- Macro Development Process.
- Micro Development Process.

Macro Development Process: It is controlling framework for the micro process.

It is primary concern-technical management of the system.

Steps for macro development process:

1. Conceptualization
2. Analysis & Development of the model
3. Design or create the system architecture
4. Evolution or implementation
5. Maintenance

6.1.9 Micro Development Process

- Each macro process has its own micro development process.

Steps:

- Identify classes & objects.
- Identify class & objects semantics.
- Identify class & object relationship.
- Identify class & objects interface and implementation.

6.1.10 The Booch Method Notation

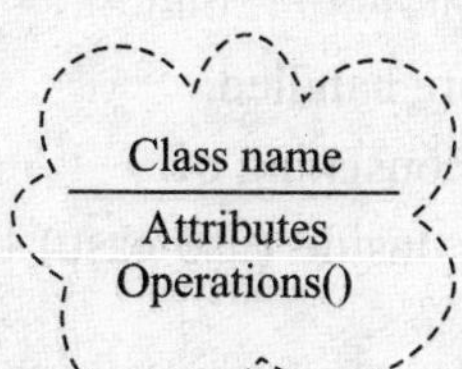

Fig. 6.8 A class diagram notation.

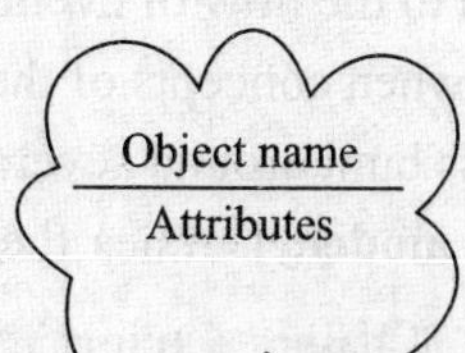

Fig. 6.9 A object diagram notation.

The dynamic nature of an application can be illustrated by state transition and interaction diagrams.

There are several Booch diagrams which are similar to UML diagrams. These Booch diagrams are state transition and interaction diagrams. The State transition diagram corresponds to UML's state chart diagram and the interaction diagram corresponds to UML's sequence diagram.

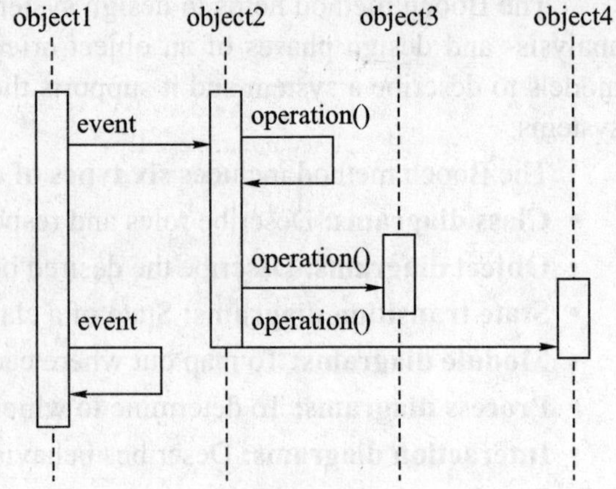

Fig. 6.10 An interaction diagram

Jacobson Methodologies et al.,

The OOSE methodology was discovered by Ivar Jacbson in year 1991.

- Object-oriented business engineering (OOBE).
- Object-oriented software engineering (OOSE).
- Object Factory for Software Development (Objectory).
- Cover entire life cycle.
- Stress traceability between phases—backward & forward.
- Enables reuse of analysis & design work.
- Use-case concepts used.

It is mainly used for real time systems. It includes four phases:

- Analysis Phase.
- Design Phase.
- Implementation Phase.
- Testing phase (Fig. 6.11).

Use Cases: It understands the system requirements and interacts between Users and Systems.

The use case description must contain:

- How and when the use case begins and ends.
- The Interaction between the use case and its actors, including when the interaction occurs and what is exchanged.
- How and when the use case will need data stored in the system.
- Exception to the flow of events.
- How and when concepts of the problem domain are handled.

Objector is built around several different models consisting of:

1. **Use case model:** Defines the outside (actors) & inside (use case) of the system's behavior.
2. **Domain model:** Maps real world object into the domain object model.
3. **Analysis object model:** How source code should be carried out & written.

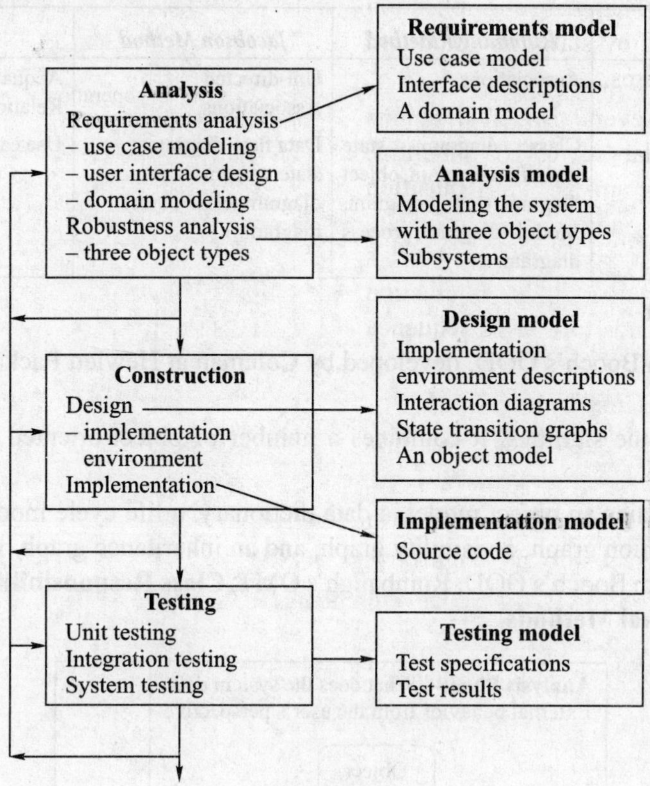

Fig. 6.11

4. **Implementation model:** Represents the implementation of the system.
5. **Test model:** Test plans, specifications & reports.

It is also known as:

Object-Oriented Business Engineering (OOBE): Object-oriented business engineering (OOBE) is a object model used at the enterprise level.

Booch Method	*Rumbaugh Method*	*Jacobson Method*	
Approach:	Object centered approach.	Object centered approach.	User centered approach.
Phases Covered:	Analysis, design and implementation phases.	Analysis, design and implementation phases.	All phases of life phase cycle.
Strength:	Strong method for producing detailed object oriented design models.	Strong method for producing object model static structure of the system.	Strong method for producing user driven requirements and object oriented analysis model.
Weakness:	Focus entirely on design and not on analysis.	Cannot fully express the requirements.	Do not treat OOP to the same level as other methods.
Uni-directional Relationship:	Uses.	Directed Association.	

Booch Method	*Rumbaugh Method*	*Jacobson Method*	
Bi-directional Relationship:	Associations.	Uni-directed Associations.	Acquaintance Relationships.
Diagrams used:	Class diagram, state transition diagram, object diagram, timing diagram, Module diagram, process diagram.	Data flow diagrams, state transmission diagram, class/object diagram.	Use case diagram.

6.1.11 Fusion

It is derived from Booch's OOD, developed by Coleman at Hewlett Packard Laboratories in 1994.

Like the name signifies, it combines a number of object-oriented approaches and diagrams.

Fusion contains an object model, a data dictionary, a life cycle model, an operation model, an interaction graph, a visibility graph, and an inheritance graph. Fusion notations were adopted from Booch's OOD, Rumbaugh's OMT, **Class Responsibility Collaborator (CRC)** and **Formal Methods.**

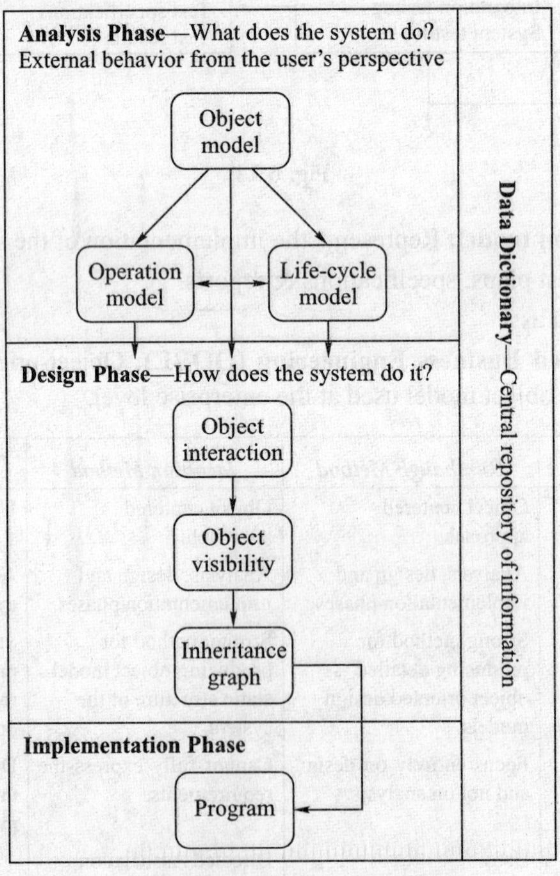

Fig. 6.12 Fusion diagrams

- **Create a Fusion Object:** Iit use the following notations:

Dynamic Reference

Permanent Reference

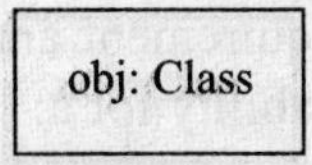

Shared server

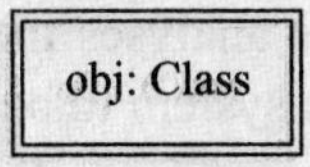

Exclusive reference to server

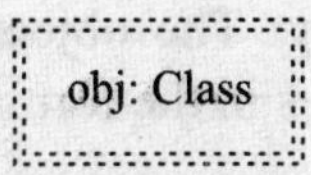

Exclusive reference to server collection

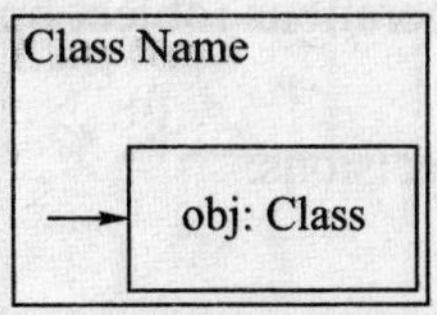

Server-Lifetime bound

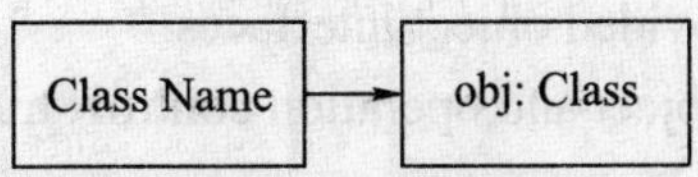

Server-Lifetime unbound

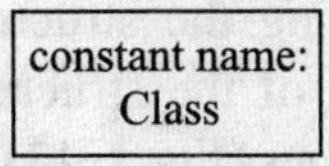

Constant server object

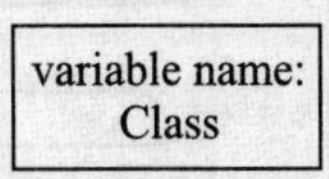

6.2 HIERARCHICAL OBJECT-ORIENTED DESIGN (HOOD)

It has been developed by Robinson in year 1992 for the European Space Agency as a design/notation method for Ada. This method is used for data flow diagrams starting from a context diagram which shows all the external interfaces with one central process. This process is then elaborated into other processes with data flows and control flows. It is used to develop the design as a set of objects which together provide the functionality of the program.

The main process is called as Basic Design Step. It shows child objects of a given parent object, and of their individual relationships to other existing objects, or the refinement of a terminal object to the level of the code. This is based on the identification of objects by means of object-oriented design techniques. It is divided into four phases:

1. **Problem definition:** The main object is designed with its goal of organizing and structuring the data from the requirement analysis phase. This provide a complete check on requirements and traceability for a:
   - o A clear and precise definition of the problem.
   - o The context of the system to design.

   Analysis of data: It gathers and analyses the information relevant to the problem, including the environment of the system to be designed.
2. **Development of solution strategy:** The outline solution of the problem stated above is described in terms of objects at a high level of abstraction.
3. **Formalizations of the strategy:** The objects and their associated operations are defined. There are five sub phases in the formalization of the strategy:
   - o Object identification.
   - o Operation identification.
   - o Grouping objects and operations (object operation table).
   - o Graphical description.
   - o Justification of design decisions.

6.2.1 Formalization

The solution is formalized through:

- Formal definition of provided object interfaces.
- Formal description of object and operation control structures.

6.2.2 Notation

The main diagram used for describing the structure of a system is the HOOD object diagram, which shows a static view of the structure in the hierarchical object oriented design. The symbols used are as follows (Fig. 6.13).

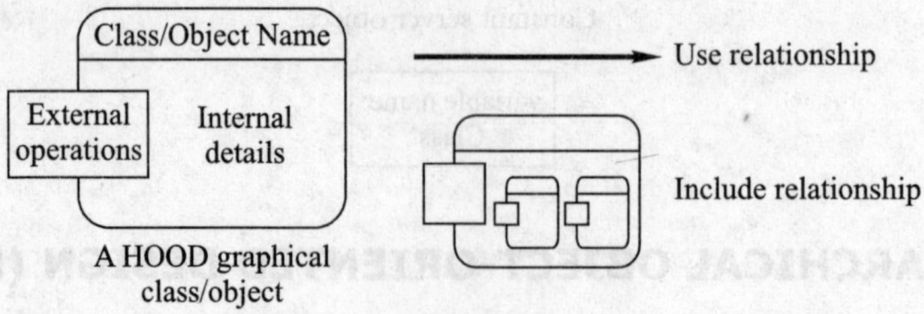

Fig. 6.13

6.2.3 Coad & Yourdon (OOA)

It gives two-phase introduction: Object-Oriented Analysis (OOA) in 1989, and Object-Oriented Design (OOD) in 1991. Yourdon and Constantine had studied effective designs in order to derive a method for structured design.

The analysis (OOA) phase of the methodology consists of five principal activities:

- Finding **"Classes"** (abstract classes) and "Class-&-Objects" (concrete classes).
- Identifying **"Structures"** (generalization-specialization and whole-part relationships between classes).
- Identifying **"Subjects"** (partitions/subsystems).
- Defining attributes, and **"Instance-Connections"** (association relationships between classes).
- Defining **"Services"** (class operations) and **"Message-Connections"** (invocations of operations).

OOA/OOD Results are reflected in a special Class-&-Object Diagram. The diagram consists of five layers:

- **Subject layer:** showing the overall partitions of the system
- **Class-&-Object layer:** showing the abstract and concrete classes of the system
- **Structure layer:** showing the generalization-specification and whole part relationships between the classes.
- **Attribute layer:** showing the attributes of the classes and the association relationships between classes.
- **Service layer:** showing the operations of the classes and the potential message-passing between the objects

During the design phase of the methodology (OOD) the system is designed in four components:

- **Problem Domain Component (PDC):** initially contains the results of the analysis phase. During OOD, it is improved and enriched with implementation detail.
- **Human Interaction Component (HIC):** handles sending and receiving messages to and from the user.
- **Task Management Component (TMC):** for systems needing to implement multiple threads of control; defines the multi-task processing classes, coordinates the tasks (processes) and provides means for inter task communication.
- **Data Management Component (DMC):** provides the infrastructure to store and retrieve objects; may be a simple file system, a relational database management system, or even an object-oriented database management system.

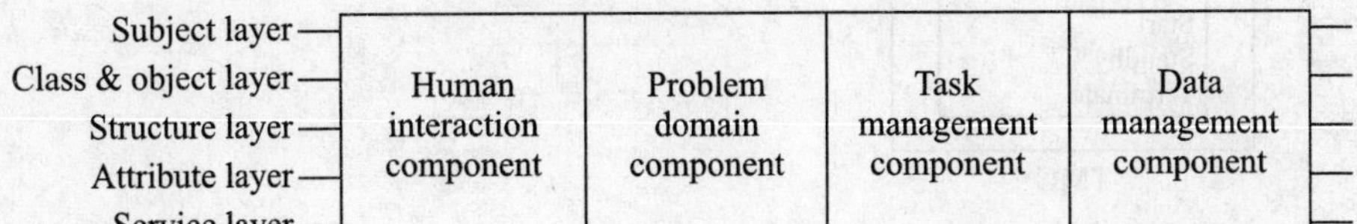

Fig. 6.14

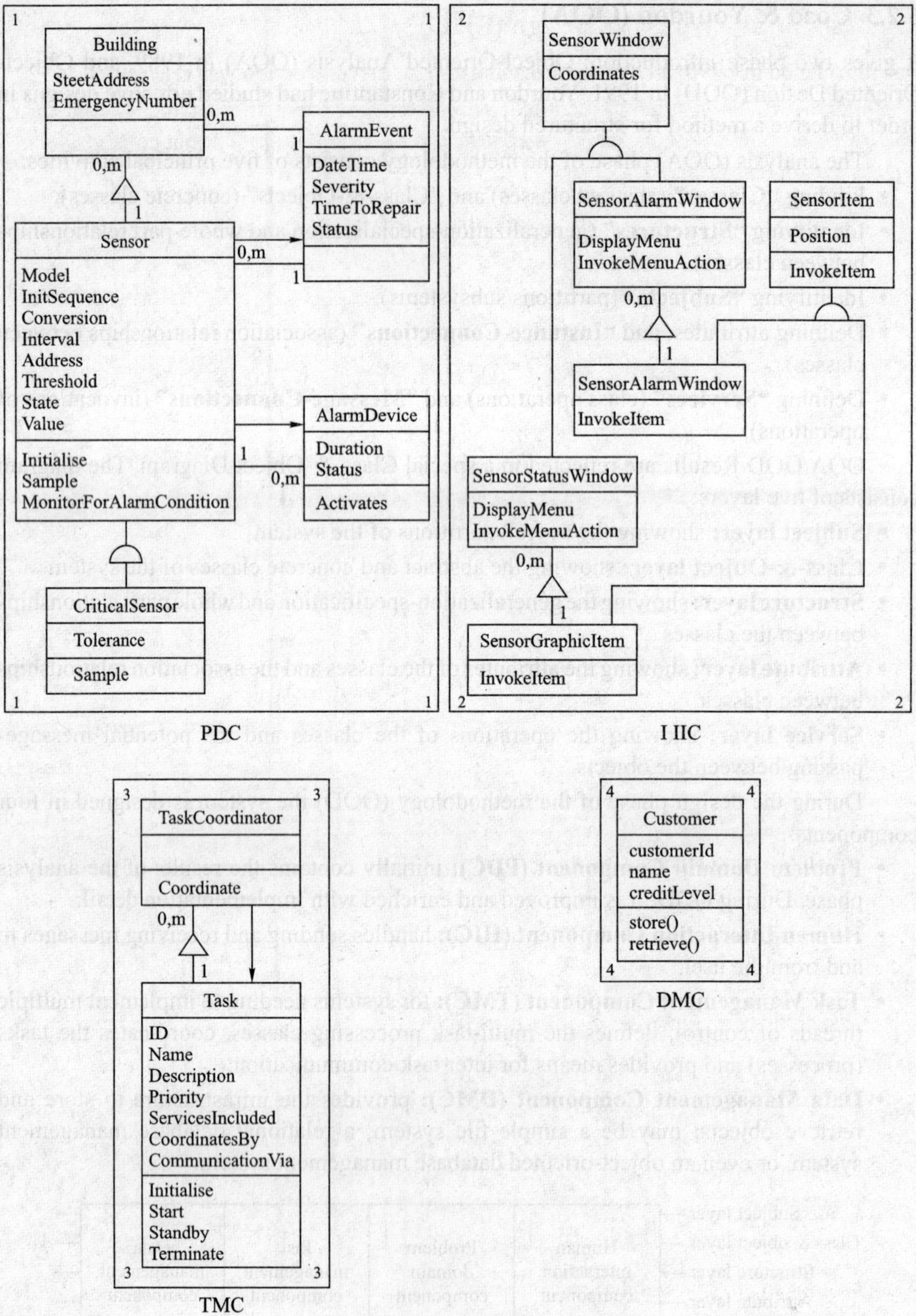
Building
SteetAddress
EmergencyNumber
AlarmEvent
DateTime
Severity
TimeToRepair
Status
Sensor
Model
InitSequence
Conversion
Interval
Address
Threshold
State
Value
Initialise
Sample
MonitorForAlarmCondition
AlarmDevice
Duration
Status
Activates
CriticalSensor
Tolerance
Sample
0,m
1
PDC
SensorWindow
Coordinates
SensorAlarmWindow
DisplayMenu
InvokeMenuAction
SensorItem
Position
InvokeItem
SensorAlarmWindow
InvokeItem
SensorStatusWindow
DisplayMenu
InvokeMenuAction
SensorGraphicItem
InvokeItem
I IIC
TaskCoordinator
Coordinate
Task
ID
Name
Description
Priority
ServicesIncluded
CoordinatesBy
CommunicationVia
Initialise
Start
Standby
Terminate
TMC
Customer
customerId
name
creditLevel
store()
retrieve()
DMC

Fig. 6.15

6.2.4 Responsibility-Driven Design (RDD)

It was introduced in 1990; a UML-based and use-case driven version was released in 2002.

The process starts when a detailed requirements specification of the system has already been provided. The system is modeled as a collection of objects that collaborate to fulfill their responsibilities.

Responsibilities include two key items:

- The knowledge an object maintains.
- Actions an object can perform

6.2.5 RDD: Process

The process is divided into two phases:

- **Exploratory Phase:** Classes and their responsibilities and collaborations are identified.
- **Analysis Phase:** Subsystems and class details are specified (Fig. 6.16).

Exploratory Phase: The major tasks to be iteratively performed in this phase are:

- Discovering the classes required to model the application.
- Determining what behavior the system is responsible for and assign these responsibilities to specific classes.
- Determining what collaborations must occur between classes of objects to fulfill the responsibilities.
- Results are modeled in CRC (Class-Responsibility-Collaborator) cards.

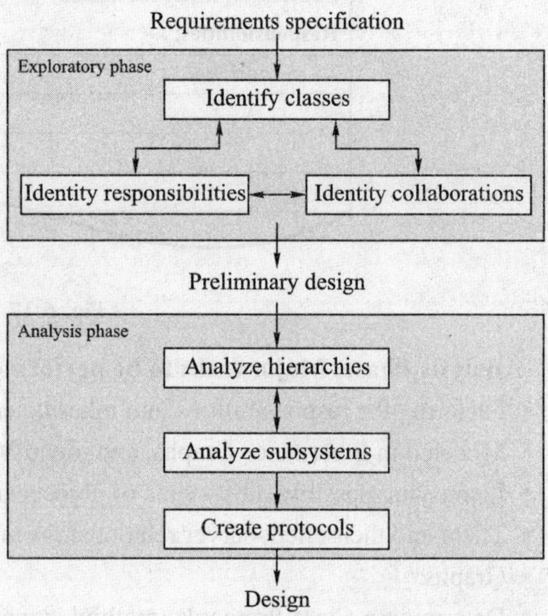

Fig. 6.16

6.2.6 Classes

Extract noun phrases from the specification and build a list:

- Identify candidate classes from the noun phrases.
- Identify candidates for abstract super classes.
- Use categories to look for missing classes.
- Write a short statement for the purpose of each class.

6.2.7 Responsibilities

- Find responsibilities.
- Assign responsibilities to classes.
- Find additional responsibilities by looking at the relationships between classes.

6.2.8 Collaborations

- Find and list collaborations by examining responsibilities associated with classes.
- Identify additional collaborations by looking at relationships between classes.
- Discard and classes that take part in no collaboration (as client or server).

CRC Card

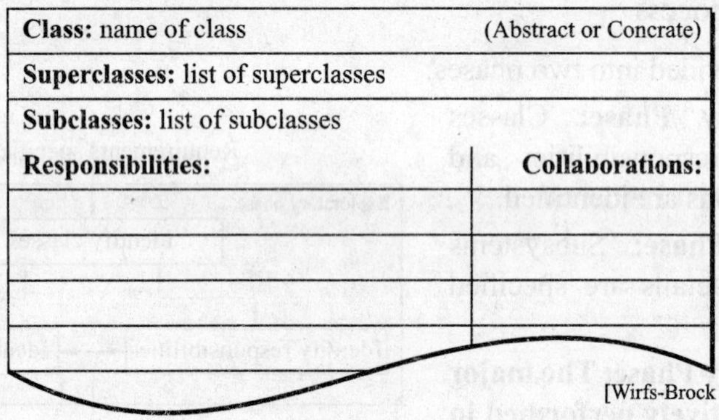

Fig. 6.17

Analysis Phase: Major tasks to be performed in this phase:

- Factoring the responsibilities into inheritance hierarchies.
- Modeled in Inheritance Graphs, and identifying class contracts.
- Identifying possible subsystems of objects and modeling.
- Them and their client-server relationships in Collaboration.
- Graphs.
- Determining Class Protocols (method signatures) and completing a specification of classes, subsystems of classes, and client-server contracts.

6.2.9 Hierarchies

- Draw inheritance hierarchy graphs.
- Identify which classes are abstract/concrete.
- Draw Venn diagrams showing how responsibilities are shared between classes.
- Refine class hierarchy, checking the allocation of responsibilities.
- Define how responsibilities are clustered into contracts, and which classes support which contracts.

6.2.10 Subsystems

Draw a complete collaborations graph for the system.

- Identify possible subsystems.
- Simplify the collaborations between and within subsystems.

6.2.11 Protocols

- Define protocols for each class, by refining responsibilities into sets of method signatures.
- Write a specification for each class.
- Write a specification for each subsystem.
- Write a specification for each contract.

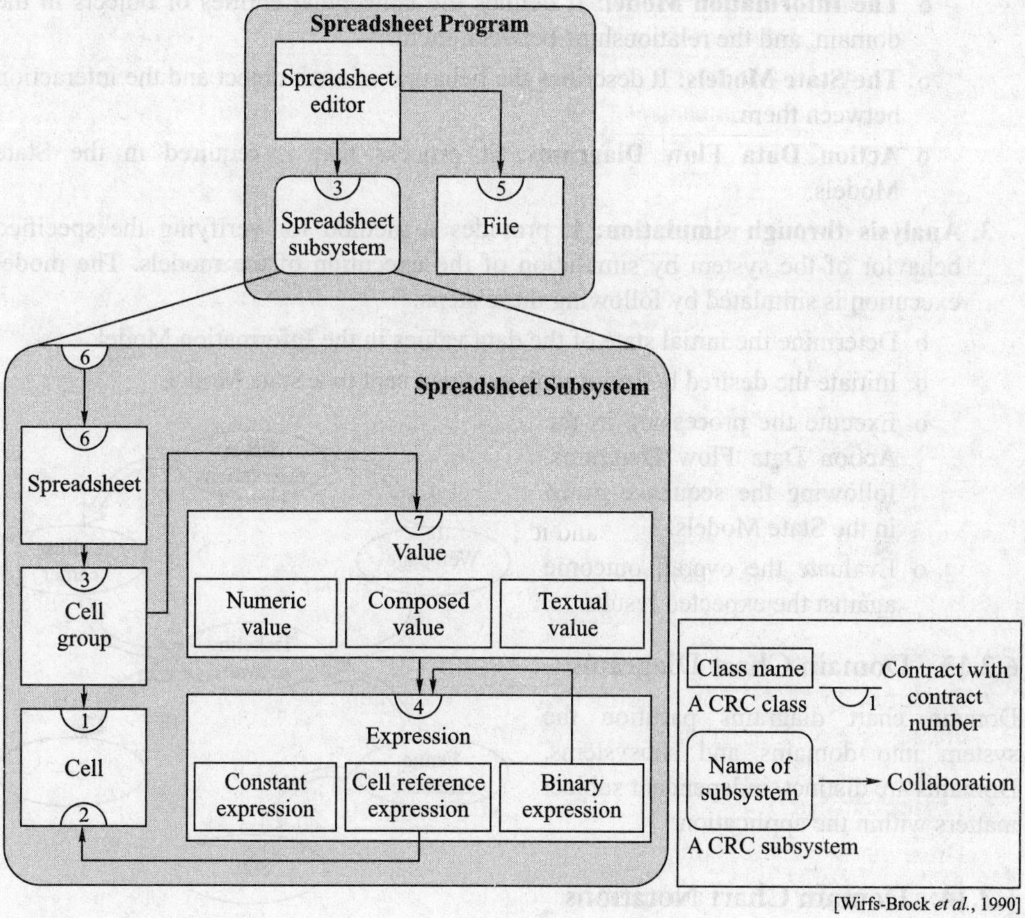

[Wirfs-Brock *et al.*, 1990]

Fig. 6.18

6.2.12 Shlaer-Mellor Method Object Oriented Structured Analysis (OOSA)

It is a method of software design describes a set of integrated models and diagrams that are used to analyze large software application projects. This is also known as the Object-Oriented Systems Analysis (OOSA). OOSA contains a wide variety of diagrams including: a domain chart diagram, object information model diagram, state transition model, an action data flow diagram, a class diagram, and a class structure chart.

1. **Domain Chart Diagram:** It includes user interface and other external interfaces of the system. The architectural domain covers the hardware and software which will be used to build and run the desired system. It includes the operating systems and programming languages used to build the system. A Domain Chart is used to depict these domains, and the interrelationships between them.
2. **Application domain:** It is integrated set of Object-Oriented Analysis (OOA) models. This produces a set of formal models which are depicted in three related diagrams:
   - o **The Information Model:** It defines the conceptual entities or objects in the domain, and the relationships between them.
   - o **The State Models:** It describes the behavior of each object and the interaction between them.
   - o **Action Data Flow Diagrams:** It process that is required in the State Models.
3. **Analysis through simulation:** It provides a method for verifying the specified behavior of the system by simulation of the execution of the models. The model execution is simulated by following these steps:
   - o Determine the initial state of the data values in the Information Model.
   - o Initiate the desired behavior with an event sent to a State Model.
   - o Execute the processing in the Action Data Flow Diagrams, following the sequence given in the State Models.
   - o Evaluate the overall outcome against the expected results.

6.2.13 Domain Chart Diagrams

Domain chart diagrams partition the system into domains and subsystems. Domains are distinct, independent subject matters within the application.

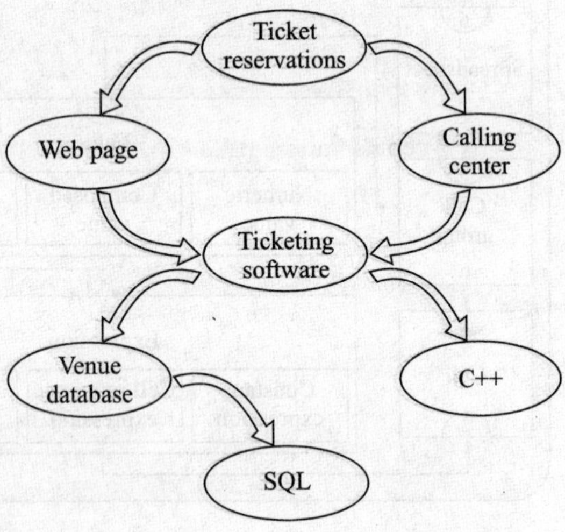

Fig. 6.19 A domain chart

6.2.14 Domain Chart Notations

6.2.14.1 Domains

There are four types of domains identified by Shlaer and Mellor. These are: application, service, architectural, and implementation.

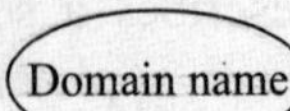

6.2.14.2 Relationships

Domains are connected by thick arrows that symbolize client-server relationships or bridges. The head of the arrow points to the server in the relationship.

6.2.15 Object-Oriented Structured Design (OOSD)

It is as described by Wasserman in 1989, and the "goal of OOSD is to provide a single architectural design notation that can support every software design."

This is described independent methodology. It is expected that designers will develop and use their own design esthetics and design metrics within the framework of OOSD, which simply carries a valid design notation.

The main entities in OOSD are:

- **A system:** It consists of a set of units, which are classes, modules and monitors.
- **A class:** It can inherit from other classes. A class can be public or private, and can raise exceptions.
- **A module:** It is a data-object or an operation.
- **A monitor:** It is used to define and use asynchronous processes.

OOSD strengths are:

- Keeping modularity as the main component of the design method.
- Building on a familiar notation.
- Attempting to target a wide variety of applications and development languages, while supporting development from a wide range of analysis methods.

6.2.16 Object Oriented Role Analysis, Synthesis and Structuring (OORASS)

This methodology was discovered by Reen in year 1992. It is an analysis and design method which emphasizes on the role played by objects in the system. Analysis is performed as a top down, but not hierarchical, process until the model is stable and the analysts fully understand the areas of concern. Types of objects are categorized on the roles required. Categorization is based on the process of creating new objects which are inherited from simpler objects.

The goals of **OORASS** are:

1. **Total lifecycle support:** It cover analysis, design, implementation, testing and maintenance of object oriented programs in a seamless fashion.

2. **Integrated description:** It supports an integrated representation of all kinds of informal documentation as well as source code and formal descriptions of the design.
3. **Separation of concerns:** It allows different concerns to be treated independently, to allow the whole system to be understood in parts.
4. **Reuse:** It supports the notion of reusable ideas, specifications, designs, code and compiled programs.
5. **Tool support:** It is supported by an integrated support environment for the complete system lifecycle.

QUESTIONS

1. Define HIPO.
2. What do you mean by object oriented methodology?
3. What is work of OMT in Dynamic model?
4. Distinguish OOD & OOA.
5. Explain Jacbson methodologies.
6. Compare and contrast Booch method, Rambargh and Jacbson method.
7. What is the use of CRC? How is it differ from RDD?
8. Explain notation of HOOD.
9. Explain Shaler method or OOSA.
10. Differ OOSE/POAD/OOSA/OORASS.

CHAPTER

7 Requirement Engineering

7.1 DEFINITION

The tools and techniques to collect the information for a system is called requirement engineering. It is the first or initial step of **software development life cycle (sdlc).** This requires 60 to 80% effort. Based on this, software becomes successful. This is the most important phase of the **sdlc**.

The process of establishing the services that the customer requires from a system and the constraints under which it operates and is developed. The requirements themselves are the descriptions of the system services and constraints that are generated during the requirements engineering process.

"Requirements are the things we should discover early stages of the software development life cycle." This is the branch of system engineering.

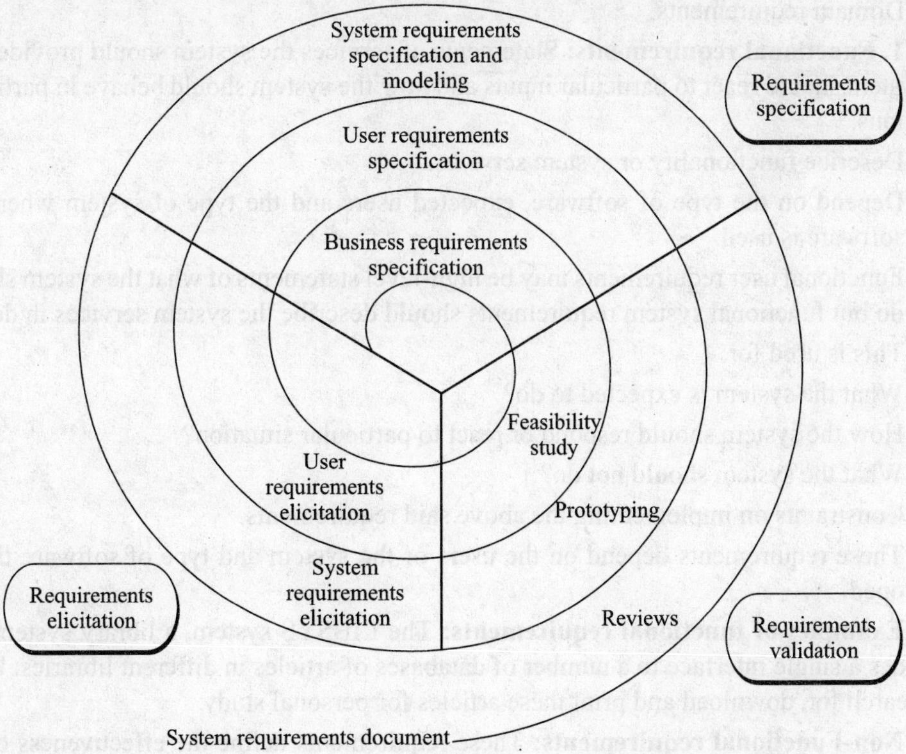

Fig. 7.1

Requirements are of two types:

1. User Requirements 2. System Requirements

1. User Requirements: It is the expected services required from the system. It is written in such a manner that person can easily understands who is not having technical background. This is the main foundation written in clear, precise language that common person can understands. This requirement generally covers the external activities and behavior of the system (*i.e.* functionality of the system). User requirements are defined using natural language, tables and diagrams as these can be understood by all users.

Problems arises using natural language:

- **Lack of clarity:** Precision is difficult without making the document difficult to read.
- **Requirements confusion:** Functional and non-functional requirements tend to be mixed-up.
- **Requirements amalgamation:** Several different requirements may be expressed together.

2. System Requirements: A structured document setting out detailed descriptions of the system's functions, services and operational constraints. Defines what should be implemented so may be part of a contract between client and contractor.

It is used to design system architecture. This is used for implementation proposed into the system. It is classified into different types:

1. Functional requirements. 2. Non-Functional requirements.
3. Domain requirements.

1. Functional requirements: Statements of services the system should provide how the system should react to particular inputs and how the system should behave in particular situations.

- Describe functionality or system services.
- Depend on the type of software, expected users and the type of system where the software is used.
- Functional user requirements may be high-level statements of what the system should do but functional system requirements should describe the system services in detail.

This is used for:

- What the system is expected to do?
- How the system should respond or react to particular situation?
- What the system should not do?
- Constraints on implementing the above said requirements.

These requirements depend on the users of the system and type of software that is developed.

Examples of functional requirements: The LIBSYS system, a library system that provides a single interface to a number of databases of articles in different libraries. Users can search for, download and print these articles for personal study.

Non-Functional requirements: These requirements define the effectiveness of the functions provided by the system. They are not provided by the system but they affect the functions provided by the system. These form the basis for quality of the system. Failure of non functional requirement leads to failure of the whole system.

These define system properties and constraints *e.g.* reliability, response time and storage requirements. Constraints are I/O device capability, system representations, etc.

Process requirements may also be specified mandating a particular CASE system, programming language or development method.

Non-functional requirements may be more critical than functional requirements. If these are not met, the system is useless.

This includes:

- Safety and security measures provided by the system.
- Reliability and efficiency of the system.
- Portability and integrity of the system.
- Memory used and cost effectiveness of the system.
- Budget and scheduling of the system.

2. Non-Functional classification:

Product requirements: Requirements which specify that the delivered product must behave in a particular way *e.g.* execution speed, reliability, etc.

Organisational requirements:

- Requirements which are a consequence of organisational policies and procedures *e.g.* process standards used, implementation requirements, etc.

External requirements:

- Requirements which arise from factors which are external to the system and its development process *e.g.* interoperability requirements, legislative requirements, etc.

Non-functional requirement types:

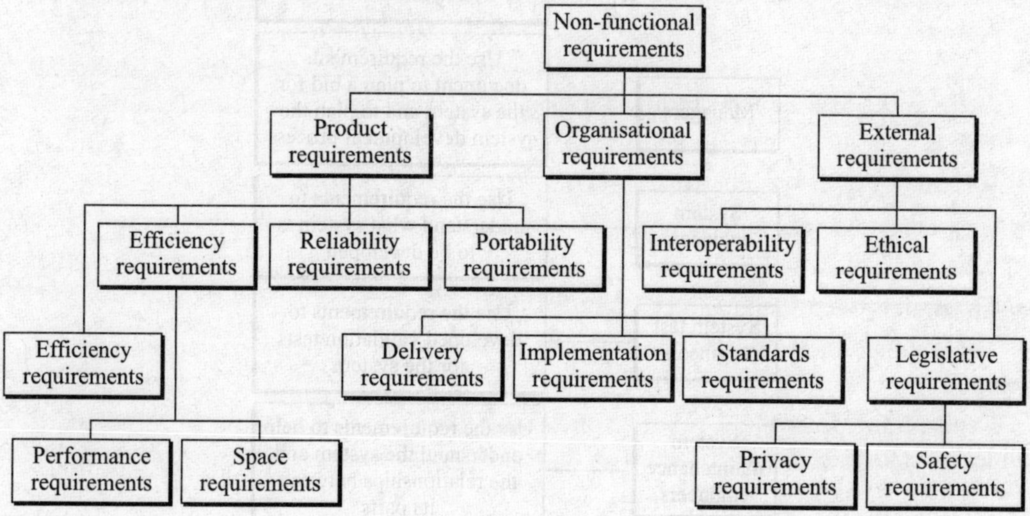

Fig. 7.2

3. Domain requirements:

- Derived from the application domain and describe system characteristics and features that reflect the domain.
- Domain requirements be new functional requirements, constraints on existing requirements or define specific computations.
- If domain requirements are not satisfied, the system may be unworkable.
- Requirements that come from the application domain of the system and that reflect characteristics of that domain.

Domain requirements problems: Understand ability:

- Requirements are expressed in the language of the application domain;
- This is often not understood by software engineers developing the system.
- Implicitness
- Domain specialists understand the area so well that they do not think of making the domain requirements explicit.

Guidelines for writing requirements:

- Invent a standard format and use it for all requirements.
- Use language in a consistent way. Use shall for mandatory requirements, should for desirable requirements.
- Use text highlighting to identify key parts of the requirement.
- Avoid the use of computer jargon.

Users of a requirements document:

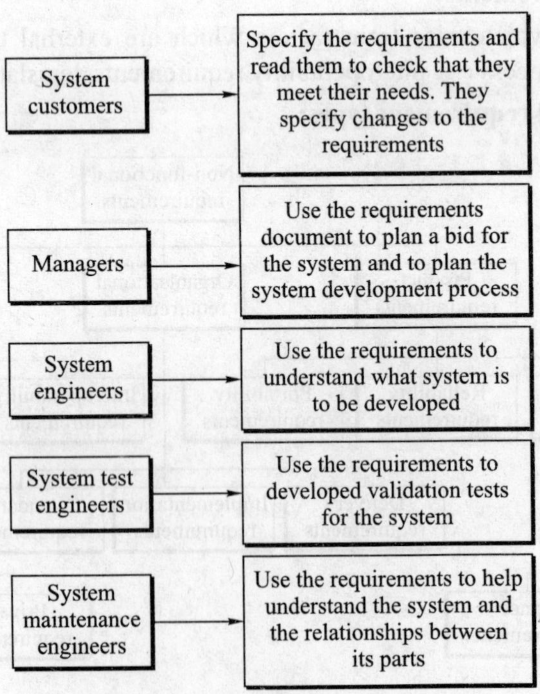

Fig. 7.3

The Requirements Document: Official statement of what is required of the system developers should include both a definition and a specification of requirements which are:

- Specify external system behaviour.
- Specify implementation constraints.
- Be easy to change (but changes must be managed).
- Serve as a reference tool for maintenance.
- Record forethought about the life cycle of the system (*i.e.* predict changes).
- Characterise responses to unexpected events.

It is not a design document it should state what the system should do rather than how it should do it.

IEEE requirements standard: It defines a generic structure for a requirements document that must be instantiated for each specific system.

- Introduction.
- General description.
- Specific requirements.
- Appendices.
- Index.

Requirements document structure: the structure of document is:

- Preface
- Introduction
- Glossary
- User requirements definition
- System architecture
- System requirements specification
- System models
- System evolution
- Appendices
- Index

Requirements Engineering Processes: It is used to describe the principal requirements engineering activities and their relationships. It involves the techniques for requirements elicitation and analysis and describes requirements validation and the role of requirements reviews. It also discusses the role of requirements management in support of other requirements engineering processes which are:

- Requirements elicitation
- Requirements analysis
- Requirements validation
- Requirements documentation
- Requirement review

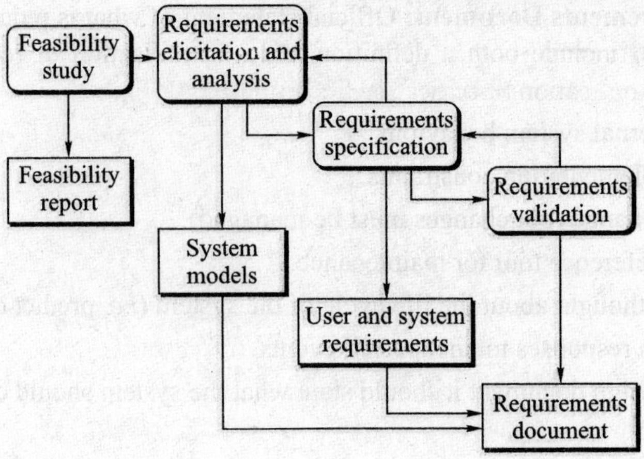

Fig. 7.4

7.1.1 Feasibility Study

Before starting with any project we go for feasibility study which means can project be successful and how much effort, time and manpower is required for the project. A feasibility study decides whether or not the proposed system is worthwhile.

A short focused study that checks:

- If the system contributes to organisational objectives.
- If the system can be engineered using current technology and within budget.
- If the system can be integrated with other systems that are used.

Based on technical, economical feasibility questionnaire is prepared for the organisation whether it will be worthwhile or not:

- What if the system wasn't implemented?
- What are current process problems?
- How will the proposed system help?
- What will be the integration problems?
- Is new technology needed? What skills?
- What facilities must be supported by the proposed system?

Requirement elicitation: Elicitation means information gathering or requirement discovery. It involves technical staff working with customers to find out about the application domain, the services required for the system, system's operational constraints. It also includes end-users, managers, engineers involved in maintenance, domain experts, trade unions, etc. These are called **stakeholders.**

Information can be collected by end users. Information can be collected and assessed in various manners:

1. Questionnaires.
2. Brainstorming session.

3. Interviews.
4. Facilitated Application Specification Technique (FAST).
5. Quality Function Deployment (QFD).
6. The Use case approach.

Interview: It is being conducted when:

- Requirements are detailed.

  Requirements cover many areas of knowledge that have specific individuals who are the experts.
- Differing opinions are likely or are sought.

Questionnaire: What? , Why? , When? , Where? Who? How? Is being asked. This is also called as WWWWWH principle.

7.1.2 Brainstorming Sessions

It is a group technique that may be used during requirement elicitation to understand the requirements. Group discussions may lead to new ideas and help to promote creative thinking. The group technique may be carried out with specialized groups like actual users, middle level managers etc, or with total stakeholders.

7.1.3 Facilitated Application Specification Technique

This is similar to brainstorming session and its objective to find the difference and gap between what developers think they are supposed to build and what customers think they are going to get. The basic guidelines are:

- Arrange a meeting at neutral site for developers and customers.
- Establishment of rules for preparation and participation.
- Prepare an informal agenda that encourages free flow of ideas.
- Appoint a facilitator to control the meeting.
- Participants should not criticize or debate.
- Prepare a definition mechanism-board, flip charts, worksheets, etc.

Quality Function Deployment: It helps to incorporate the voice of customer and then translated into technical requirements. They are further translated into design requirements and the requirements discovered are:

(i) **Normal requirements:** the objectives and goals are discussed with the customer.

(ii) **Expected requirements:** They are implicit to the customer but may not be clear to the customer explicitly.

(iii) **Exciting requirements:** Some features beyond the customer expectations and prove to be very satisfying when present.

The Use case approach: A use case is a specification of sequences of actions, including variant sequences and error sequences, that a system, subsystem, or class can perform by interacting with outside actors.

An actor is **an entity that interacts with the system and/or needs to exchange information with the system.** The actor is *not* part of the system itself and should be included to represent anyone or anything that interacts with the system in the following ways:

- Supplies input information to the system.
- Receives information from the system.
- Both supplies input information to and receives information from the system The total set of actors in a use case model includes everyone and everything that needs to exchange information with the system.

7.1.4 Identifying the Actors

- Who uses the system?
- Who installs the system?
- Who starts up the system?
- Who maintains the system?
- Who shuts down the system?
- What other systems use this system?
- Who gets information from this system?
- Who provides information to the system?
- Does anything happen automatically at a present time?

7.1.5 Identifying the Use Cases

The following questions can be asked to identify use cases:

- What functions will the actor want from the system?
- Does the system store information? What actors will create, read, update or delete this information?
- Does the system need to notify an actor about chances in the internal state?
- Are there any external events the system must know about? What actor informs the system of those events?

7.1.6 Identifying the Boundary

It is important to clearly define the boundary of your system. Things inside the boundary of the system are things you need to worry about creating. In a UML use case diagram, the **system boundary** is denoted by a rectangle.

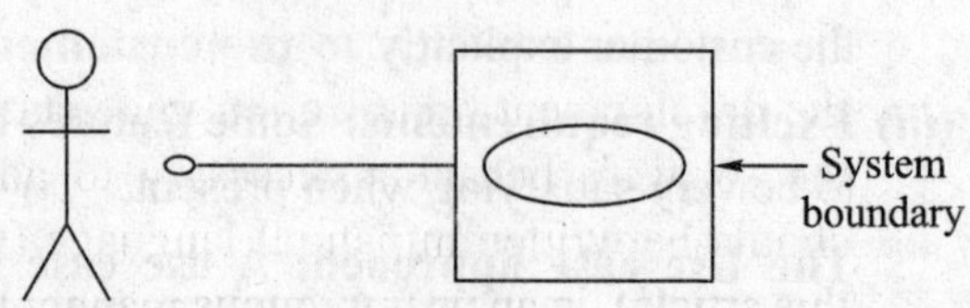

Fig. 7.5

7.1.7 Requirement Analysis

It is very important and essential activity after requirement elicitation. It refines and scrutinizes the gathered requirements and gives the graphical view of the entire system. The various step of RA are:

(*i*) **Draw the context diagram:** This identifies the input and output entities of the proposed system.

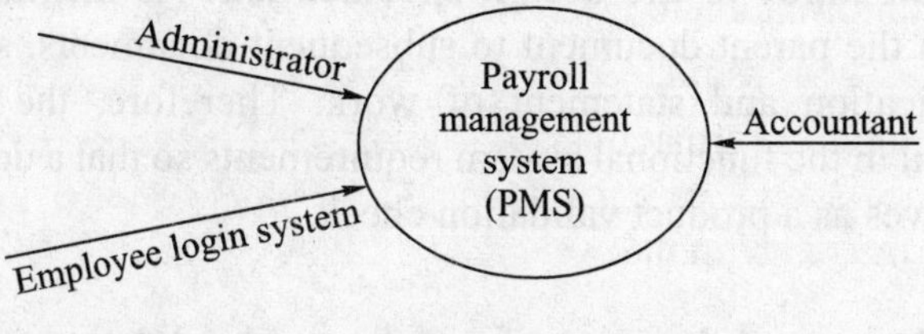

Fig. 7.6

(*ii*) **Development of a prototype:** Prototype helps the client to visualize the proposed system and increase the understanding of requirements. It helps in the feedback of the customers and prototype is the dummy which helps to give complete functionality of the system. Through this dummy, customer can give their opinion which helps in the success of the project.

(*iii*) **Model the requirements**: This consists of graphical representations of the functions, data entities, external entities and the relationships between them.

(*iv*) **Finalize the requirement:** It helps to understand the system behavior. The inconsistencies and ambiguities have been identified and correct. Flow of data amongst various models are been analyzed.

This consists of data dictionaries, entity relationship diagram and data flow diagram etc.

Requirements Documentation: It is also called as **Software Requirements Specification (SRS).** An SRS is basically an organization's understanding (in writing) of a customer or potential client's system requirements and dependencies **at a particular point in time** (usually) prior to any actual design or development work. It's a two-way insurance policy that assures that both the client and the organization understand the other's requirements from that perspective at a given point in time.

The SRS also functions as a blueprint for completing a project with as little cost growth as possible. The SRS is often referred to as the "parent" document because all subsequent project management documents, such as design specifications, statements of work, software architecture specifications, testing and validation plans, and documentation plans, are related to it.

It's important to note that an SRS contains functional and nonfunctional requirements only a well-designed, well-written SRS accomplishes four major goals:

- **It provides feedback to the customer:** An SRS is the customer's assurance that the development organization understands the issues or problems to be solved and the software behavior necessary to address those problems. Therefore, the SRS should be written in natural language (versus a formal language, explained later in this article), in an unambiguous manner that may also include charts, tables, data flow diagrams, decision tables, and so on.

- **It decomposes the problem into component parts:** The simple act of writing down software requirements in a well-designed format organizes information, places borders around the problem, solidifies ideas, and helps break down the problem into its component parts in an orderly fashion.
- **It serves as an input to the design specification:** As mentioned previously, the SRS serves as the parent document to subsequent documents, such as the software design specification and statement of work. Therefore, the SRS must contain sufficient detail in the functional system requirements so that a design solution can be devised. It serves as a product validation check.

  The SRS also:
- **It serves as the parent document** for testing and validation strategies that will be applied to the requirements for verification.

Software requirements specifications are typically developed during the first stages of "Requirements Development," which is the initial product development phase in which information is gathered about what requirements are needed–and not.

7.2 SOFTWARE REQUIREMENTS SPECIFICATION

7.2.1 Purpose

Specify the purpose of this Software Requirements Specification (SRS) and its intended audience.

7.2.2 Business Context

Provide an overview of the business organization sponsoring the development of the software application, including the mission statement and organizational objectives of the business unit.

7.2.3 Scope

Describe the scope of the software application to be produced.

7.2.4 User Characteristics

Identify each type of user of the software by function, location, and type of device. Specify the number of users in each group and the nature of their use of the software.

7.3 ASSUMPTIONS, DEPENDENCIES, CONSTRAINTS

7.3.1 Assumptions

Describe the assumptions that can affect the requirements specified in this SRS.

7.3.2 Dependencies

Describe the dependencies that can affect the requirements specified in this SRS.

7.3.3 Constraints

Describe the constraints that can affect the requirements specified in this SRS.

7.4 REQUIREMENTS

7.4.1 Business Requirements

Describe all business requirements for the software.

7.4.2 Functional Requirements

Customize this sub function to contain the sub functions necessary to comprehensively define the fundamental actions that must take place within the software to accept and process the inputs and to process and generate the outputs.

Sub function templates for each of the means of specifying functional requirements are provided below.

3.2.xf—Function X: When functional decomposition is used as the means of specifying the functional requirements provide a sub function for each function. Each 3.2.xf sub function should be labeled and titled appropriately for a specific function, where xf is the appropriate sequential sub function number and X is the name of the specific function.

3.2.xf.1—Function X Purpose: Describe the intent of the function.

3.2.xf.2—Function X Inputs: Describe the inputs to the function.

3.2.xf.3—Function X Operations: Describe the operations to be performed within the function.

3.2.xf.4—Function X Outputs: Describe the outputs from the function.

3.2.xu—*Use Case* Y: When use cases are used as the means of specifying the functional requirements, provide a 3.2.xu sub function for each use case. Each 3.2.xu sub function should be labeled and titled appropriately for a specific use case, where xu is the appropriate sequential sub function number and Y is the name of the specific use case.

Within each use case sub function, specify the use case information, including the actor, pre-conditions, post-conditions, scenarios, and alternate scenarios.

7.4.3 Logical Data Requirements

Describe the logical data requirements for the software.

7.4.4 User Requirements

Describe the user requirements for the software.

7.4.5 Information Management Requirements

Describe the information management requirements for the software.

7.4.6 Systems Requirements

7.4.6.1 Performance Requirements

Describe the performance conditions and their associated capabilities.

7.4.6.2 Quality Requirements

Describe requirements for the quality characteristics of the software.

7.4.7 Interfaces

Describe the logical characteristics of each interface between the application and other hardware, software, and communication protocols.

7.4.8 Other Requirements

Identify any other requirements that do not fit appropriately into the preceding requirement sections.

7.5 REQUIREMENTS TRACEABILITY MATRIX

Provide reference to the location of the Requirements Traceability Matrix that indicates traceability from the system requirements documented in the System Requirements Specification to the design elements documented in the System Design Description to the software requirements documented in this Software Requirements Specification (SRS).

7.6 REFERENCES

Provide a list of all documents and other sources of information referenced in the SRS and utilized in developing the SRS. Include for each the document number, title, date, and author.

Document No.	*Document Title*	*Date*	*Author*

7.7 GLOSSARY

Define of all terms and acronyms required to interpret the SRS properly.

7.8 REVISION HISTORY

Identify changes to the SRS.

Version	*Date*	*Name*	*Description*

7.9 APPENDICES

Include any relevant appendices.

Requirements Validation: After the completion of SRS document and check the document for:

- Completeness and consistency.
- Conformance to standards.
- Requirements conflicts.
- Technical errors.
- Ambiguous requirements.

Validation is to check the constraints and correctness of the requirement document. It helps to find errors and improves the quality of the software development process. It checks the standards and quality for the organizational knowledge. It helps in corrective actions of the document.

Requirements Reviews: Problems are identified and rectified and final review is prepared. The review process includes:

1. **Plan review:** Team is selected and meeting is fixed.
2. Distribute SRS document.
3. Organize review meeting.
4. Follow up actions.
5. Revise SRS document.

Requirements Management: It is adopted by the industry. It is the process of understanding and controlling changes to system understandings. Requirements are not independent.

It makes the tasks much more difficult and challenging:

Enduring and volatile requirements: It is broadly into two categories:

(i) **Enduring requirements:** Core requirements are related to main activity of the organization.

(ii) **Volatile requirements:** This is likely to change during software development life cycle. There are many reasons:

- Changes to the environment.
- Changes in technology.
- Changes in policies.
- Changes in customer's expectations.

7.10 A CASE STUDY ON AN ELECTRONIC EXAMINATION SYSTEM

7.10.1 Problem Description

This case study comprises an electronic examining system. A teacher makes use of the system to give an examination to her/his students. We assume that creating an examination is a separate task performed out of the scope of the examining system. This system should be made available on the web, so that both the teacher and the students have remote access to it.

A teacher creates a test and stores this test into a test repository. Afterwards the teacher can assign this test to a group of students. There can be different types of tests but all of them must have a deadline defined by the teacher. So, for example the teacher may propose an examination in which the students are requested to write an essay about a certain subject or to solve some questions. The former activity may take several days to be completed while the latter may take only a limited number of minutes. The teacher also evaluates a student's test answer by attaching comments and grading it.

When a student access the system, this student can consult his/her personal profile and do a test. A student personal profile contains his/her personal information, the list of tests to be done and the answers, grades and comments of completed tests. A student does a test by submitting the answers for this test. Once an answer is submitted it can not be resubmitted. All the student personal profiles are stored in a profile repository; however the access of a student is limited to his/her personal profile.

7.10.2 Problem Modelling

This section reports the results of our case study modelling activities. Each of the following subsections presents some of the results of these activities, viz., requirements capturing and analysis. We have performed neither implementation nor test activities because the execution of such activities is not the intent of this case study. Ideally some design activities should have been performed as well. However, due to the shortage of time this activity was not performed either. The development of this case study was performed making use of Rational Rose as a modelling support tool.

7.10.3 Requirements Capturing

The requirements of the electronic examining system were captured by means of a use case diagram according to the following steps:

1. Identification of the actors.

2. Identification of the use cases.

3. Description of each use case.

The identification of the actors of the system was straightforward. We simply identified the roles of the potential users of the system. The identified actors are the following:

- **Student**, who is a person who takes exams and consults some personal and test related information that are, stored in his/her profile. The student has limited access rights to the system;
- **Teacher**, who is a person that assigns tests to groups of students and grade the assigned tests. The teacher has full rights to the system.

The identification of the use cases was more complex. As a rule of thumb to identify a use case we considered the following criteria: a use case should represent a sequence of related actions that provide some functionality to the actor when successfully executed. Whenever a variation on a normal behaviour or a repetition of a separate use case were identified, the **extends** and *uses* relationships between use cases were used. The identified use cases are the following:

- **Access Student Profile**, which is used to access the student profiles. All student profiles are kept in a profile repository ordered according to the student groups that the student belongs. The teacher reads and writes the student profile, while the student reads the student profile. The student can write to his/her profile only the test results.
- **Access Test Repository**, which is used to access the test repository. The teacher can read and write to the test repository, while the student can read from the test repository only the tests that are assigned to his/her profile.
- **Assign Test**, which is used to select a test from the test repository and assign the selected test to a group of students.
- **Consult Profile**, which is used to consult a student personal profile. The student profile contains the student personal information, the tests to be done, the test answers and the grades received so far. The student profiles are stored in a profile repository. A student has access rights only to his/her personal profile.
- **Do Test**, which is used to do a test. The student selects one of the tests from his/her profile. The student retrieves this test from the test repository. Then, the student does the test and submits the test answers, which are stored in his/her profile.
- **Evaluate Test**, which is used to evaluate a performed test. The evaluation of a test consists of making comments concerning the answers provided and grading the test. The teacher first selects a test to be evaluated and then retrieves from the student profiles some or all the answers provided for that test.
- **Register Test**, which is used to register and store one test in the test repository.

Each use case was described briefly, by means of few sentences that summarises the actions (see previous use case descriptions), and in a step-by-step manner, by means of a detailed description of what the system needs to do when interacting with its actors. The detailed description of the identified use cases is presented in Appendix A.

Figure 7.7 depicts the use case diagram of the electronic examining system.

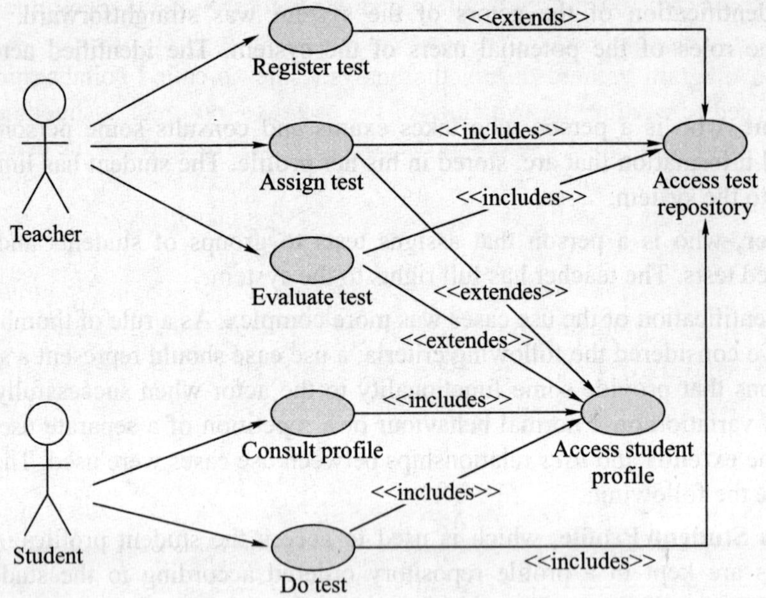

Fig. 7.7 Use case diagram.

7.10.4 Analysis

The analysis of the electronic examining system was performed based on the use cases identified previously. Such activity is called use case realisation-analysis and as a result of this activity an analysis model of the system is obtained. In the use case realisation-analysis three activities were performed:

1. Creation of a class diagram for each use case.
2. Creation of at least one collaboration diagram for each use case, and
3. Creation of a conceptual diagram for the overall system.

The creation of a class diagram for each use case is the first step towards obtaining an analysis model of the electronic examining system. To create a class diagram in the analysis phase, the so-called class diagram analysis, we primarily identify object classes and associations among these classes (including aggregation). Depending on the abstraction level of the diagram, attributes should be identified as well.

The identification of object classes is carried out by first selecting some candidate classes. Candidate classes can be selected by looking for nouns in the use case description plus adding some other classes according to the knowledge of the application domain. Then we remove any candidate class that is redundant, irrelevant or vague. Candidate classes that also resemble attributes, operations, roles or implementation constructs are also discarded.

The identification of associations if carried out by looking for any kind of dependency between two or more classes. Again, depending on the abstraction level of the diagram, the identification of association roles and multiplicity is optional.

The second step towards obtaining an analysis model of the electronic examining system is the development of at least one collaboration diagram of each use case. Each collaboration diagram created during the analysis, the so-called collaboration diagram analysis, is used to capture the dynamics of the use case in a high abstraction level. The elaboration of a collaboration diagram is based on the class diagram of the use case and on the use case description. The types of objects in the collaboration diagram come from the classes identified in the class diagram of the use case, while the messages exchanged comes from the use case detailed description.

Due to the impossibility of combining independent interactions into a collaboration diagram without compromising the understanding of the diagram, a separate collaboration diagram was created to capture each independent interaction in the use case.

Last but not least, the final step of the analysis of the electronic examining system is the development of its conceptual class diagram. A conceptual class diagram is a class diagram in which no operations are defined. The purpose of such a diagram is merely to capture and represent the concepts present in a problem domain. In order to build the conceptual class diagram we just combined the class diagrams of the different use cases into one big diagram.

In the sequel we present some of the results of the analysis of our case study. The use cases presented are a good example of a generic use case, *i.e.*, an use case that is used by other use cases, a use case related with the teacher and a use case related with the student, respectively. Additionally, the presented diagrams are illustrative of different and complementary insights of the performed analysis.

7.10.5 Access Student Profile Use Case

We started the analysis with the use case realisation of the generic use cases, viz., Access Student Profile and Access Test Repository. In this section, we briefly describe the realisation of the former use case, but the reasoning presented here is the same for both use cases.

Besides the object classes that we identified through the use case description (nouns) we added some classes to represent the interfaces of the system (application domain knowledge). For each use case that makes use of the Access Student Profile use case and that is related with one of the users (actors) of the system, one object class is created to represent such user interface. In later stages of the development process two or more of these classes can be combined into one. However, during the analysis this is not relevant.

Figure illustrates the class diagram of the Access Student Profile use case. In order to avoid representing in the class diagram of a generic use case the same object classes as in the class diagram of use cases that make use generic ones, we represented only those classes and that are directly related with the intent of the use case. In this particular case, the object class Profile Repository and directly related classes. According to this criterion, the representation of the object class Test List is optional because this class is not directly associated with Profile Repository.

Because the Access Student Profile use case is a generic use case, it contains several interactions, each one initiated by a different user interface. Further, under the point of view of the use case itself it is not possible to know whether or not two or more interactions originated from the same interface are in fact dependent of each other. So, we decided to create a separate collaboration diagram for each interaction either independent or not.

Figure depicts one of the collaboration diagrams of the Access Student Profile use case. Once more and corroborating the idea of representing only objects directly related to the purpose of the use case, we avoided the complete representation of a same collaboration in both the generic use case collaboration diagram and the use case collaboration diagrams that make use of it.

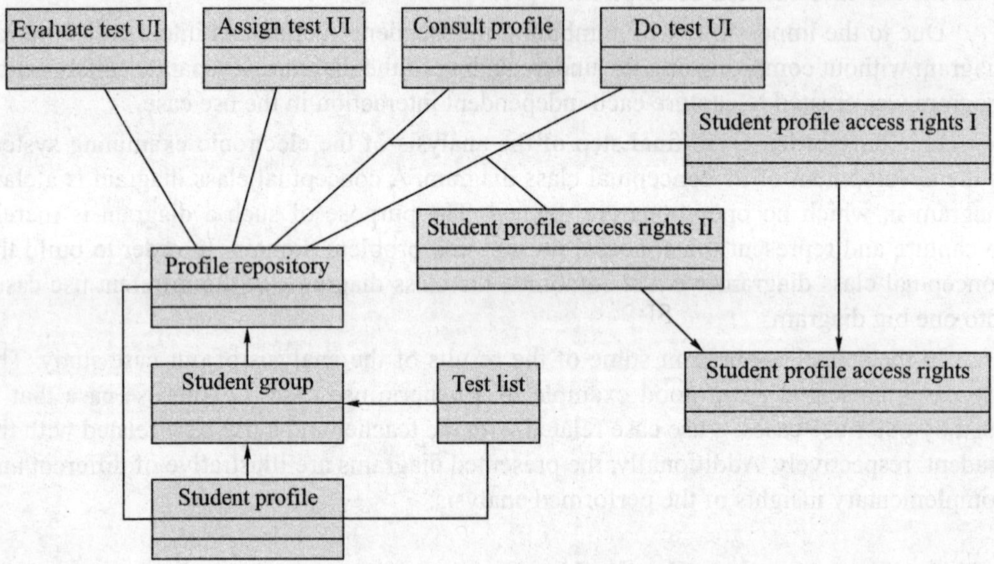

Fig. 7.8 Access Student Profile class diagram.

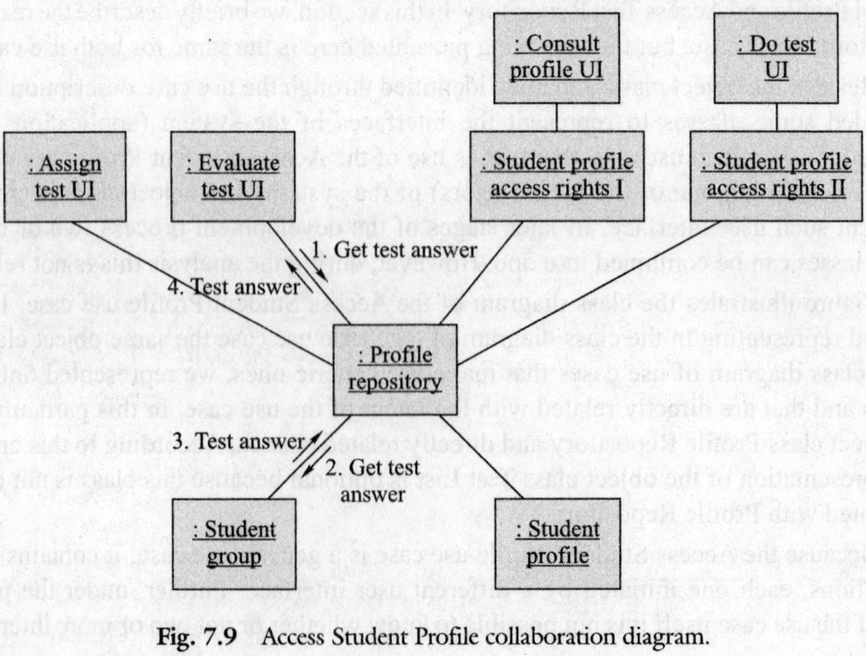

Fig. 7.9 Access Student Profile collaboration diagram.

7.10.6 Evaluate Test Use Case

Figure shows the class diagram of the Evaluate Test use case. This diagram illustrates well the differences between a generic use case and a "specific" one. While the class diagram of a generic use case shows only the object classes related with the main purpose of the use case, the class diagram of a "specific" use case shows all the object classes that are relevant to the use case.

QUESTIONS

1. What is requirement? Explain its types.
2. What are functional & non-functional requirements?
3. Explain requirement engineering process.
4. What are parts of requirement engineering?
5. Explain FAST & QFD techniques.
6. Define is SRS. Explain SRS for payroll management system.
7. What is use case diagram?

CHAPTER

8 Architecture

8.1 INTRODUCTION

Architecture means **"Construction"**. It denotes the activity, which balances functional requirements, available technologies, interests of involved stakeholders and desired system qualities.

According to **Rechtin** and **Maier**:

"Architecting is the art and science of designing and building systems".

Another definition:

"The architecture style of a system is the denotation of the modeling languages used when modeling that system".

After developing a SRS (Software Requirement Specification), a contract is being signed by the customer and developer. Customer or end user understands the functionality and quality of the system. After delivering SRS to the end user, a laid plan out is being designed for the construction of the software. The architecture of software is just similar how we construct a house.

It follows the same guidelines:

- What will be the layout plan?
- Which methods to be used?
- Which platform and methods will be used? What will be the process?
- What are the tools available?

Table 8.1: Key Differences between Structured and Object-Oriented Analysis and Design:

Phase	*Structured*	*Object-Oriented*

Analysis	**Structuring Requirements**
	• DFDs
	• Structured English
	• Decision Table/Tree
	• ER Analysis
		Requirement Engineering
		• **Use Case Model** (find Uses Cases, Flow of Events, Activity Diagram)
		• **Object Model**
		  • Find Classes & Class Relations
		  • Object Interaction: Sequence & collaboration Diagram, State Machine Diagram
		  • Object to ER Mapping

Design	**DB Design** • (DB normalization)	• **Physical DB Design** • **Design Elements**

Phase	Structured	Object-Oriented
	GUI Design • (forms & reports)	• **Design system Architecture** • **Design classes:** Checking The Model, Combine Classes, Splitting Classes, Eliminate Classes • Design components • GUI design

OOSE means maintenance and development of existing project and new project. For the development and maintenance of the system, OOSE use three techniques:

1. OOP.
2. Conceptual modeling.
3. Block Design.

8.1.1 OOP

It is a programming paradigm that represents concepts as "objects" that have data fields called as objects and associated procedure is known as methods. Objects are instances of classes used to interact with one another to design applications and computer programs. It uses the concepts of inheritance, reuse, encapsulation etc. It is useful for developing Graphical user interface (GUI) applications.

8.1.2 Conceptual Modeling

It is a model which gathers ideas from problem domain. This model came in 1970 for analysis of information systems. It represents E-R diagram (entity-relationship). It is also known as domain model for independent design. It helps to discuss problem and find the relationship between different concepts. It is used for mapping physical design. It gives good system architecture and form the basis for the actual system design. It uses various UML notations like class diagram.

8.1.3 Block Design

This is hardware-inspired software design. It is similar to component-based design. It originated from Swedish telecommunication Company-Ericsson. It able to collect program and data into modules (blocks) and describe their mutual communication through interfaces. The ideas was developed how hardware should be designed. By encapsulating program and data, these programs have lesser effect and it become easier to change or introduce the new functionality during operation. It can also change the implementation easily by changing the blocks. Concepts like blocks, with encapsulation of data and behavior, signals between these blocks are called as service packages.

It is a bottom up approach. Jacobson believes that building construction can be used as an analogy to software development. It helps to guide all the work in the different activities of a building project. The Fig. 8.1 illustrates this.

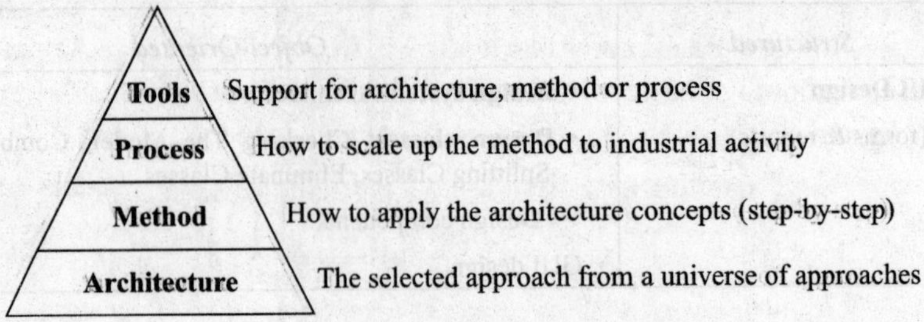

Fig. 8.1

8.2 SYSTEM DEVELOPMENT IN MODEL BUILDING

8.2.1 Architecture

It is the constructive approach for the foundation of concepts and techniques which characterize the structure of all buildings designed. The architecture is selected from a universe of potential foundations. For example, the architecture can be based solely on building blocks and components. For each possible approach, several different methods can be used to describe how to work with these constructs. A method can be defined as the step-by-step procedures to be followed in applying the architecture for projects. A method could for instance describe how to use appropriate combinations of building blocks. The method that is used must be scaled-up and related to other activities. Roughly speaking, a process is the use of a method in a certain case. This leads to various possible processes for each method defined. Different tools can then be used to support these processes.

System development includes the development of different models of a software system. The main aim is to find out a powerful modeling language for each of these models. These set of modeling techniques is called the **architecture** which depends upon development method used.

A modeling technique is normally described by means of syntax, semantics and pragmatics. Syntax means how it looks; Semantics is what it means and Pragmatic means heuristics and other rules of thumb for using the modeling technique. To build these models we require a method to show us how to work with modeling techniques in order to develop systems. The result of application of method is a specific system's architecture.

Before the actual production occurs, implementation details need to be defined. Providing implementation details together with production (or building) is called construction. The production might take advantage of developed prototypes and models. Since large-scale building projects are often placed in the hands of an entrepreneur, the importance of using methods, processes and tools is vital for documenting and defining work procedures.

Building construction projects must take account of the fact that the products should exist for many years. Life-cycle requirements for maintenance, alteration and extension must be considered. In the software industry it is essential to allow flexibility for altering the products. In all the phases of development, it is important to keep up-to-date documentation. This documentation must also be understandable for involved parties. The ability to reuse. Technology has evolved and has proven to be profitable. To be able to reuse building blocks and components, sophisticated documentation is needed.

System development includes the development of different models of a software system. In OOSE, the goal is to find a powerful modeling language (notation). A modeling language can be seen as a collection of modeling techniques. Such a set of modeling techniques (one for each model) defines the **architecture** upon which the system development method is based. A more formal way to express this is as follows: The architecture of a method is the denotation of its set of modeling technique.

The denotation of a language construct is what the construct stands for—the semantics of the construct. You can think of architecture as the set of all models you can build using a method. To build the models we need a method that describes how we can create models of different systems.

8.2.1.1 *A Method*

It is a planned procedure by which a goal is approached step-by-step. Most work descriptions for system development are method descriptions. They describe, often in a very abstract manner, how one should think and reason in developing a software system. Most methods indicate the sequence of steps to be followed. The description of the method is formulated in terms of the concepts of the architecture to be realized. A basic requirement is that a method simplifies the development of system of a particular architecture.

8.2.1.2 *A Process*

It is the natural scaling up of a method. Methods are typically described in a waterfall model (a step-by-step procedure). In other words a method is described as a system development project for one, often the first, version of a software product. However, a process focuses on a specific system and describes how such a product is handled during its entire lifetime. The process will continue to exist as long as the developed system is in operation, whereas a project only exists for a limited period of time.

A development organization has not only projects for developing the first version of a system, but also for several other kinds of projects with properties similar to those of maintenance projects. These other projects include *e.g.*, changing of an existing system, tendering projects, and error handling projects etc. All these different project types include activities for analysis, construction, testing and so on. These can be seen as the main processes in system development. System development iterates over these processes. This is one of several essential differences between a method and a process.

Activity descriptions in system development should be reusable in an organization ready to develop systems in an industrial manner. A development process defines these activities and can thus offer more than one project type. Different activities are combined for different project types, and the process should offer all the project types required by the organization using it. These different types can all be regarded as different development cases offered by the same process. To summarize, a process expresses more than a method.

During SDLC, we transform our requirements model to a design model and then write source code using some paradigms. The paradigms are of two types:

1. Operational Paradigm.
2. Transformational paradigm.

The difference between these paradigms is:

	Operational Paradigm	*Transformational Paradigm*
1.	It converts the SRS into a problem-oriented operational specification which the users can test.	It is performed on a lower level.
2.	Once this is complete and accepted, it can proceed to the implementation factor affecting development.	Each transformation should be proved correct so that the final result is correct.
3.	Design and implementation of the system take place	All transformations are saved for administration of the system
4.	Larger systems can be developed	Similar systems can be developed as it is difficult to define the correct transformations.
5.	It is an informal approach.	It is a formal approach.

8.2.1.3 *Tools*

The system development work needs computer-based tools. These tools are often referred to as **Computer-Aided Systems Engineering tools (CASE-tools)**. In large projects, it is very important that documentation is consistent. CASE-tools can support this, and thus simplify documentation. Tools can be used to automate a large number of tasks. E.g., a tool might allow information to be viewed in different ways. Each developer can receive precisely and only the information he or she needs when using a sophisticated tool. A project manager can for instance be interested in only overall descriptions of a system, whereas a designer might need all details. The process can be integrated into the tool as an extension, for example, by supporting decisions or handling change proposals.

The use of CASE-tools can lead to increased productivity, but are only part of a greater whole. The choice of a development technique has its roots in the architecture chosen to govern the system development project. In addition to this come a method and a process, and finally, CASE.

All systems change during their life cycles. This must be born in mind when developing systems expected to last longer than the first **version**. This is the case for most systems. However, most system development methods focus mainly on new development. A system normally develops through changes incorporated in new versions. New development is, from this point of view, only a special case—the first version. That is, new development constitutes a change from nothing to something.

All the models created in system development can be seen as **delta models**. A model is a delta model if it is a changed version of an existing model, *e.g.*, a new version of an analysis model. In most cases it is better to develop a system step-by-step. That is, working on the most critical parts of the system at first. As a 'correct' path becomes clear and a better understanding of the system functionality evolves, new functions can be added. This way the system is **incrementally** enlarged until the desired level is reached (when the finished product is available). All subsequent releases (versions) of the system are developed as a series of incremental stages.

Since it is often difficult to determine how a system is supposed to work, prototypes are often developed. A prototype often highlights certain functions in the system and can work as means of communication with users. A common desire in all development work is to reuse results from earlier development work. Therefore there is a need for a technique for building good components that can be reused. Another important thing is to develop applications in a way so they are easy to modify.

System development is a complex activity. Several different aspects must be taken into consideration which aims to achieve a reliable computer program that performs its tasks properly. System development is a difficult task with many different requirements to fulfill. Typically we cannot cope very well with handling so many requirements simultaneously. The complexity has to be handled in an organized way. We accomplish this by working with different *models*. Each model focuses on a certain aspect of the system. By introducing the complexity gradually, in a specific order in successive models, we can handle this complexity.

OOSE consists of five different models. The first model shows the customer requirements and the last model is a fully tested program:

1. Requirement Model.
2. Analysis Model.
3. Design Model.
4. Implementation Model.
5. Testing model.

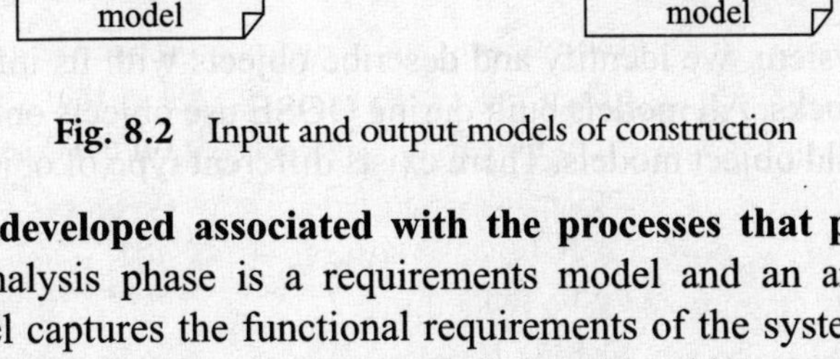

Fig. 8.2 Input and output models of construction

The models developed associated with the processes that produce them. The outcome of the analysis phase is a requirements model and an analysis model. The requirements model captures the functional requirements of the system, and the analysis model aims to give the system a robust and changeable object structure. Construction consists of the sub processes design and implementation. In the design phase, a design model and an implementation model is produced. The design model 'expands' the analysis model and takes implementation dependent issues such as database management systems and user interfaces into consideration. The separate programs (blocks) identified in the design are then coded, that is implemented. Basically, the implementation model aims to build the system. The testing phase results in a test model, which aims to verify the system.

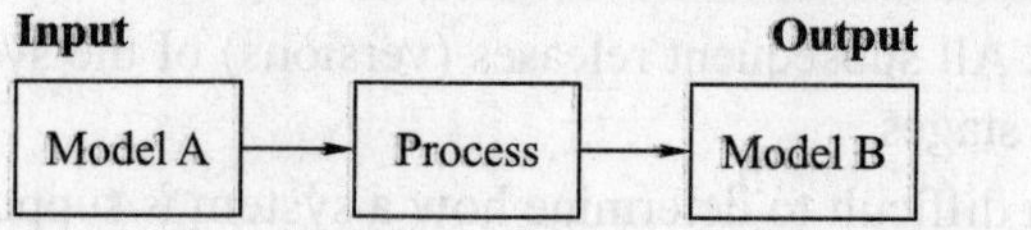

Fig. 8.3 Transformation of process from one model to another model

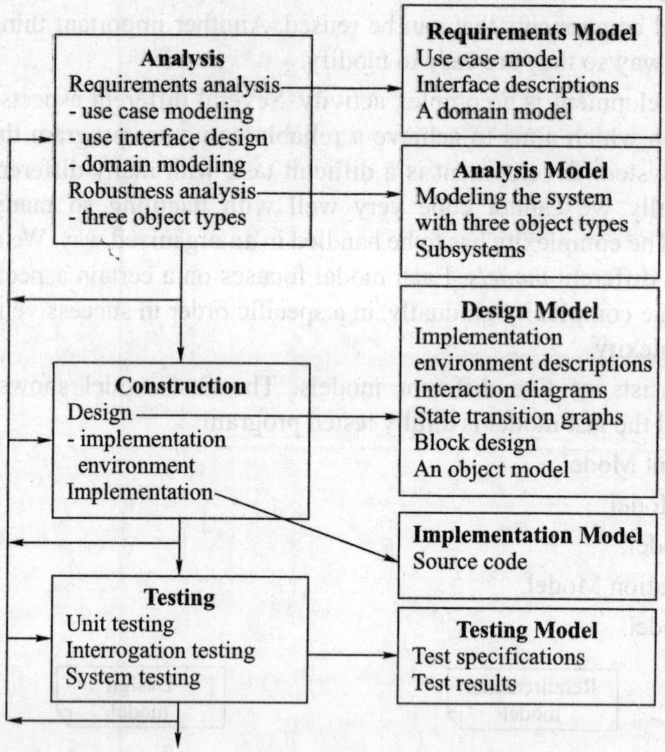

Fig. 8.4

8.2.2 Model Architecture

While developing system, we identify and describe objects with its information behavior and their building blocks. All models built during OOSE use objects only. With the help of these objects, we build object models. There exists different type of object which provides many benefits like:

- Encapsulation.
- Reusability.
- Locality of changes.

During OOA and OOD and other methodologies we are able to find a good object. Good object does not exist on its own. An object can be preferable good for one model. The characteristics of good object are as follows:

1. They should have interpretation in reality.
2. They should be obvious, tangible things.

3. Able to focus on things.
4. It should not exist on its own.

We need a good object model which should be robust against modification and should help in easy understanding of the system. We must create a robust model structure and understand how modifications will affect the system. After working we can develop a stable structure from the system.

8.2.3 Requirement Model

The requirements model is produced in the analysis phase, and aims to delimit the system and define the functionality it should offer. This model could function as a contract between the developer and the company of the system and thus formalizes the developer's view of what the customer wants. The requirements model consists of:

- A use case model.
- Interface descriptions.
- A problem domain model.

8.2.3.1 *Use Case Model*

It describes actors and use cases. Actors define roles that users can play in exchanging information with the system and use cases represent functionality inside the system. It's a complete course of events specifying all the actions between the user and the system (*e.g.*, when an operator wants to generate a daily report, the operator is an actor and 'generate a daily report' is a use case).This use case can also be expanded or defined in more detail using several associations between use cases:

- **Extends**, which defines alternative course of events.
- Optional parts of use cases.
- Complex and alternative courses which seldom occur.
- Separate sub-courses which are executed only in certain cases.
- Situation where several different use case can be inserted into a special use case.

Uses, which identifies a use case as a part of another use case definition.

A Use Case Model describes the proposed functionality of a new system. A Use Case represents a discrete unit of interaction between a user (human or machine) and the system. This interaction is a single unit of meaningful work, such as Create Account or View Account Details. Each Use Case describes the functionality to be built in the proposed system, which can include another Use Case's functionality or extend another Use Case with its own behavior (see Fig. 8.5).

Before defining a domain object model, the difference between object and domain model is:

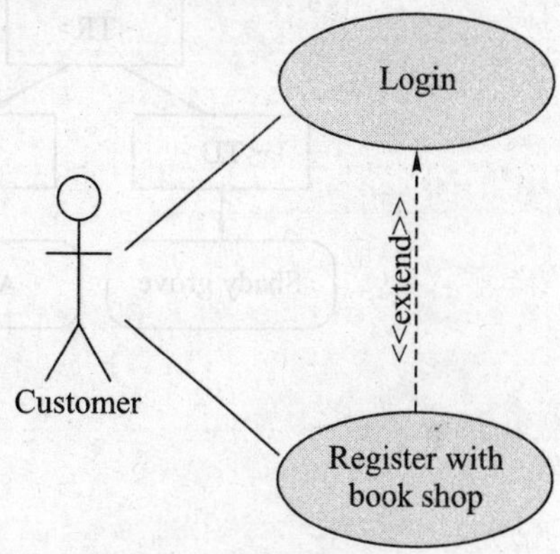

Fig. 8.5

An Object Model of a system is a collection of classes and objects describing the relationships between them and the properties and methods contained within, in terms of the Object Oriented principles: Abstraction, Encapsulation, Inheritance and Polymorphism.

A Domain Model is an Object Model describing the problem domain. They include the domain objects in the problem domain and describe the attributes, behavior and relationships between them.

8.2.3.2 *Problem Domain Object Model*

A domain model captures the most important types of objects in the context of the business. "The domain model represents the 'things' that exist or events that transpire in the business environment."

—I. Jacobsen

It is used for developing a logical view of the system that can be used for making a noun list which can be supportive for specifying the use cases. The model is the identification of the objects that have a direct counterpart in the application environment and that the system must know about. The refinement of the problem domain objects can be obtained in different possible degrees:

- Object name
- Logical attributes
- Static instances associations
- Inheritance
- Dynamic instance associations
- Operations

In a table form, it can be represented as (see Fig. 8.6):

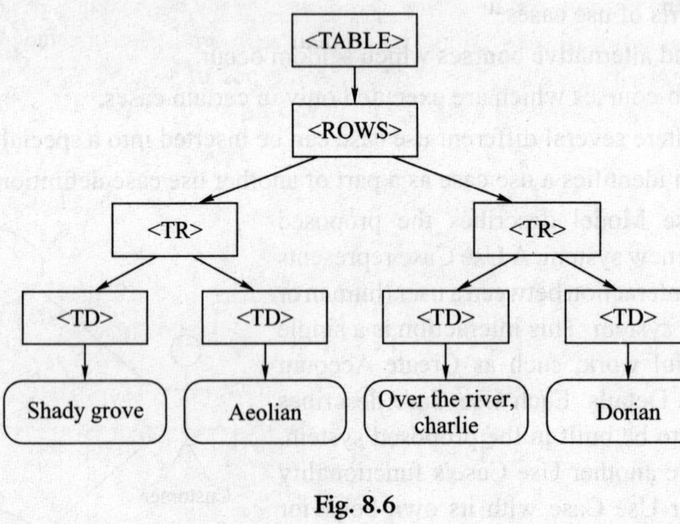

Fig. 8.6

8.2.3.3 *Simple Domain Model*

See Fig. 8.7.

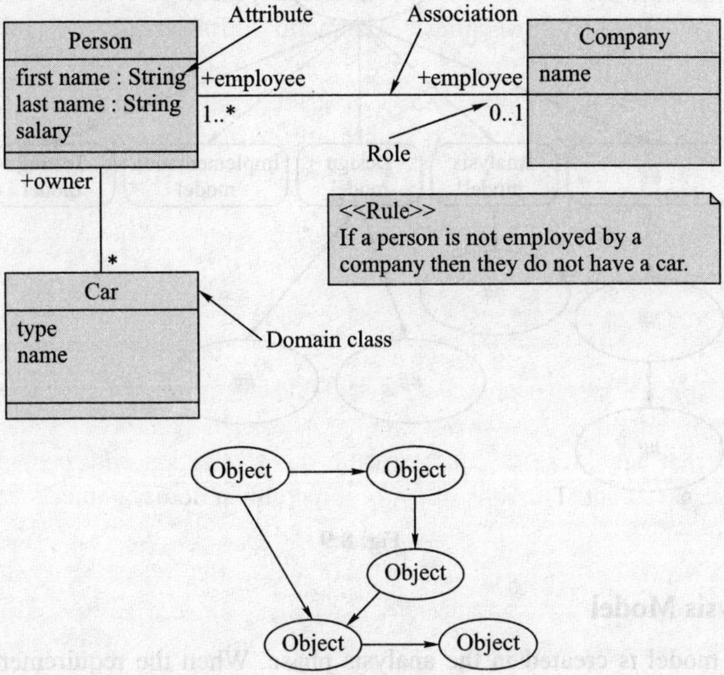

Fig. 8.7

8.2.3.4 *Interface Descriptions*

It is important that users are involved in making detailed interface descriptions. Therefore these descriptions should be made in an early stage. The interface has to capture the user's logical view of the system, because the main interest is the consistency of this logical view and the actual behavior of the system. It can deal with both user interfaces and interfaces with other systems by creating sketches or prototypes of what the user will see on the screen when performing the use case (see Fig. 8.8 and 8.9).

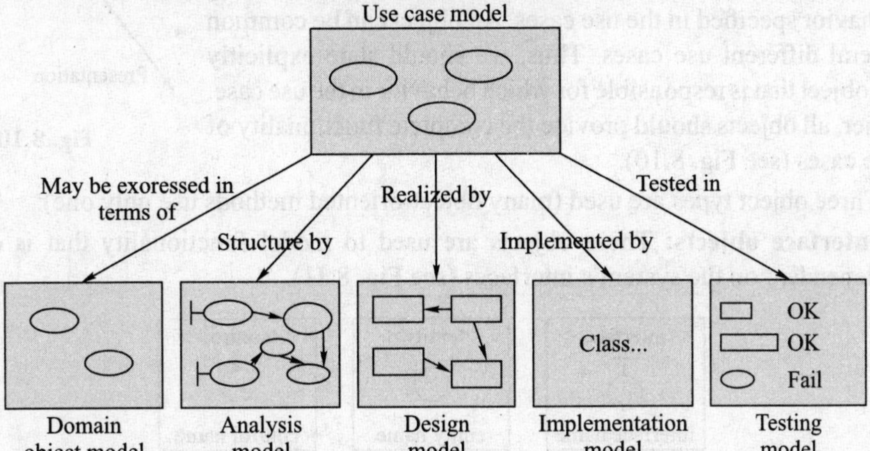

Fig. 8.8

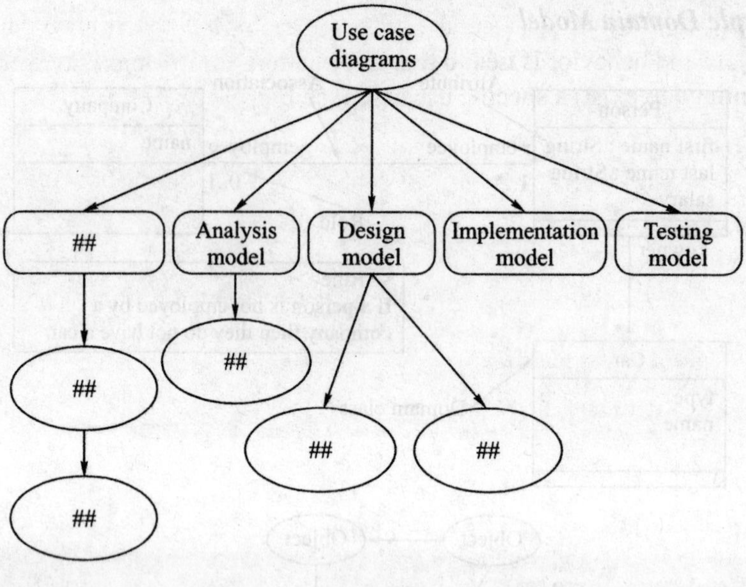

Fig. 8.9

8.2.4 Analysis Model

The analysis model is created in the analysis phase. When the requirements model has been created, the development of the actual system can begin. This starts with development of the *analysis model*. The analysis model aims to structure the system independently of the actual implementation environment. This means focus is on the logical structure of the system. Since many future changes in the system will come from changes in the implementation environment, it is good to have an analysis model that is not affected by such modifications. The analysis model captures the **information**, **behavior** and **presentation** of the system. The work in developing the analysis model really entails distributing the behavior specified in the use cases. An object can be common to several different use cases. Thus, we should state explicitly which object that is responsible for which behavior in the use case. Together, all objects should provide the complete functionality of the use cases (see Fig. 8.10).

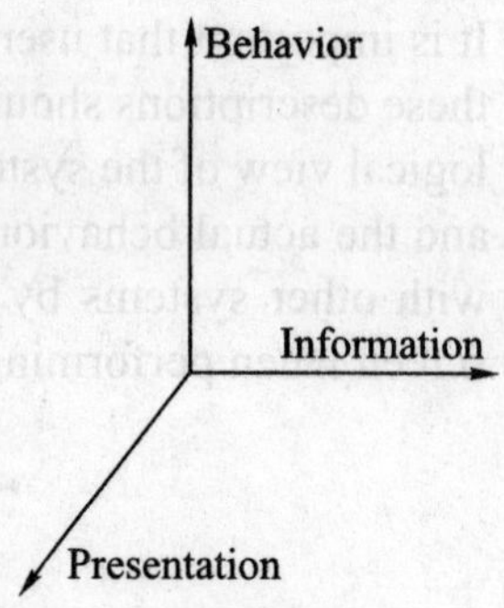

Fig. 8.10

Three object types are used (many object-oriented methods use only one):

- **Interface objects:** These objects are used to model functionality that is directly dependent on the system's interfaces (see Fig. 8.11).

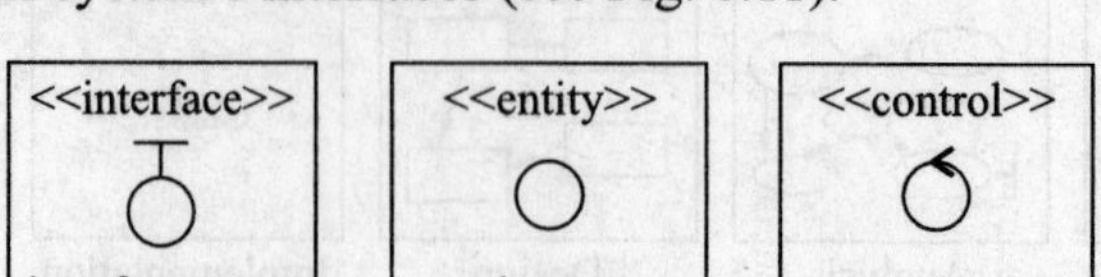

Fig. 8.11

- **Entity objects:** These objects model information that the system should manage for a longer time and behavior is tied to this information. Entity objects typically 'survive' (will continue to exist) a specific use case (see Fig. 8.12).

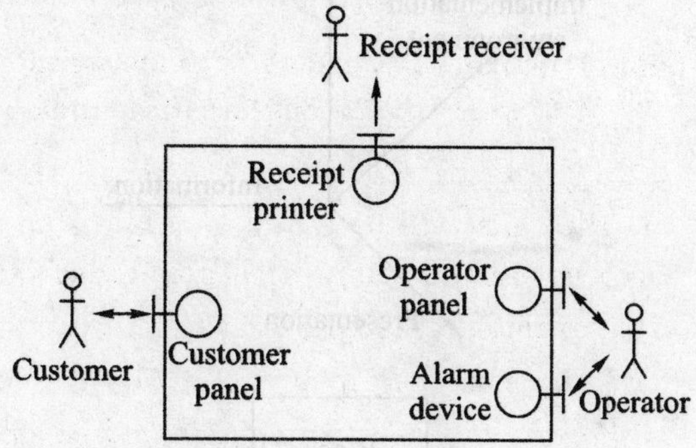

Fig. 8.12

- **Control objects:** These objects should model functionality which is transaction oriented for a specific use case and that should be kept together for maintainability purposes. Typically they do not 'survive' a use case. The reason for these three object types is that changes should preferably be local to one object only (see Fig. 8.13).

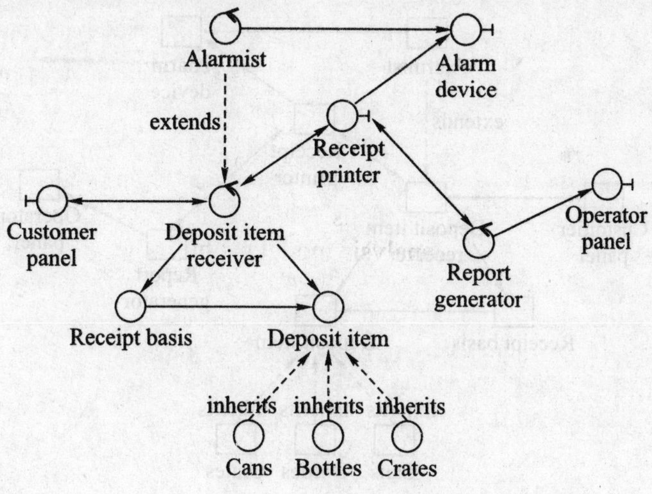

Fig. 8.13

8.2.5 Design Model

This is the first model to be produced in the construction phase. The initial work when developing the design model is to adapt to the actual implementation environment. The logical analysis model will now be adapted to reality—the implementation environment. The analysis model forms the basis for the design model. However, the analysis model will be modified when for instance introducing a relational DBMS, a specific programming language etc. This is why a new model—the design model is created (note that the analysis model is kept for documentation (see Fig. 8.14).

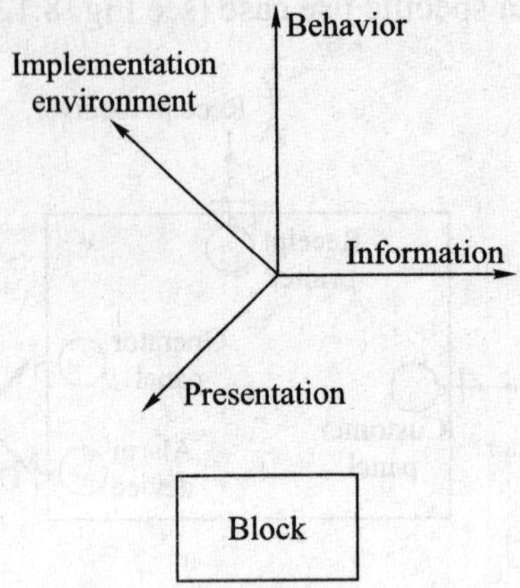

Fig. 8.14

Even if the structures used in the design model are practically the same as in the analysis model, the view is changed towards implementation. The concept of block is used to describe the intention of how the system should be produced (see Fig. 8.15).

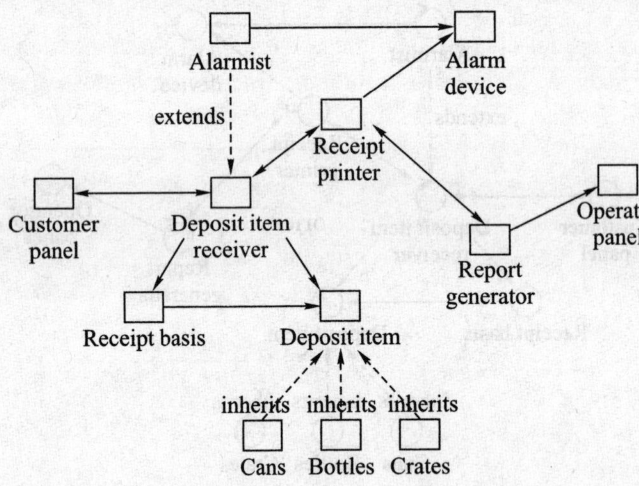

Fig. 8.15

The blocks will group the source code, but to know how to implement the blocks, we need to refine the design model further. This is done by modeling **stimuli**—how blocks communicate and interact. The sequence of the stimuli can be modeled in **interaction diagrams**. At this stage, it is appropriate to work at a subsystem level. This way, we only need to specify the interfaces between subsystems, since it is unnecessary for all team members to know the internal structure of each subsystem (see Fig. 8.16).

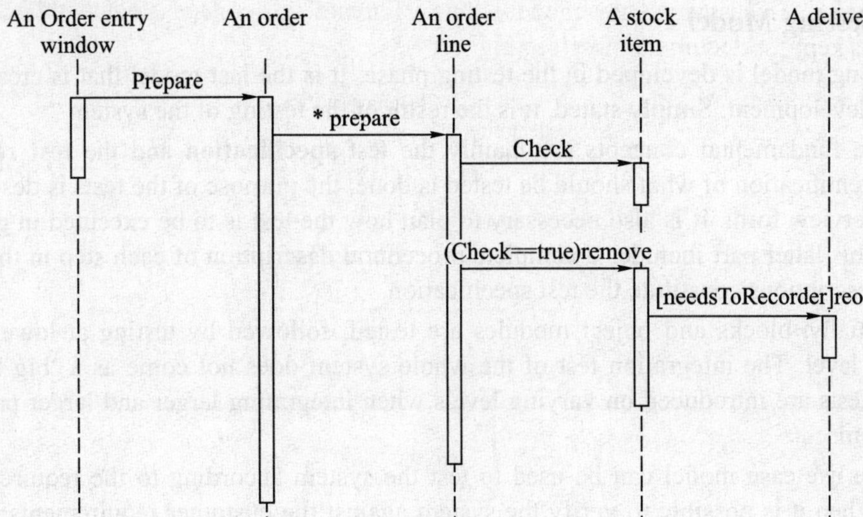

Fig. 8.16

An example of an interaction diagram shows how stimuli are sent between the blocks.

8.2.6 Implementation Model

The implementation model is created in the construction phase and consists of the actual source code in the system. The basis for the implementation is the design model. Here we have specified the interface for each block and the behavior of what is expected behind this interface. Note that we do not require an object-oriented programming language—the technique may be used with any programming language to obtain an object-oriented structure of the system. However, an object-oriented programming language is desirable, since all fundamental object-oriented concepts can easily be mapped onto language constructs (see Fig. 8.17).

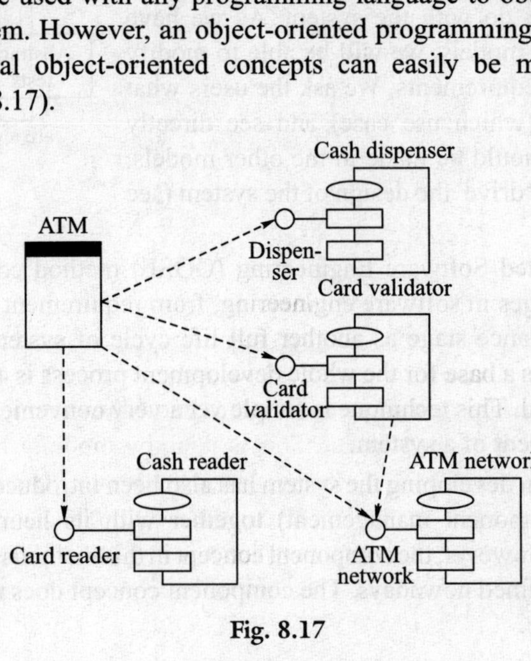

Fig. 8.17

8.2.7 Testing Model

The testing model is developed in the testing phase. It is the last model that is created in system development. Simply stated, it is the result of the testing of the system.

The fundamental concepts are mainly the test **specification** and the **test results.** When identification of what should be tested is done, the purpose of the tests is described in an overview form. It is also necessary to plan how the test is to be executed in greater detail. This latter part includes a complete procedural description of each step in the test. These descriptions constitute the test specification.

Initially, blocks and object modules are tested, followed by testing at lower sub-systems level. The integration test of the whole system does not come as a 'big bang'. Instead tests are introduced on varying levels when integrating larger and larger parts of the system.

The use case model can be used to test the system according to the requirements model. Then it is possible to verify the system against the customer requirements of the system. There are several tests that can be made, and the outcome of the tests is called test results. Jacobson means that testing can be done in an object-oriented manner. To accomplish this, the test specification can be seen as the test's class, and thus we can inherit common parts or compose them from several test specifications. Such an approach is valuable when writing and thus reusing the specifications. Doing it this way, we view a test execution as an instance of this class.

To begin the modeling in system development with use case modeling in the analysis process, is called **use case driven design**. When the system behavior is to be changed, the appropriate use cases and actors are remodeled. This way the whole system architecture will be controlled by what the users wish to do with the system. As we have traceability through all models, we will be able to modify the system from new requirements. We ask the users what they want to change (which use case) and see directly where these changes should be made in the other models. This way the use cases 'drive' the design of the system (see Fig. 8.18).

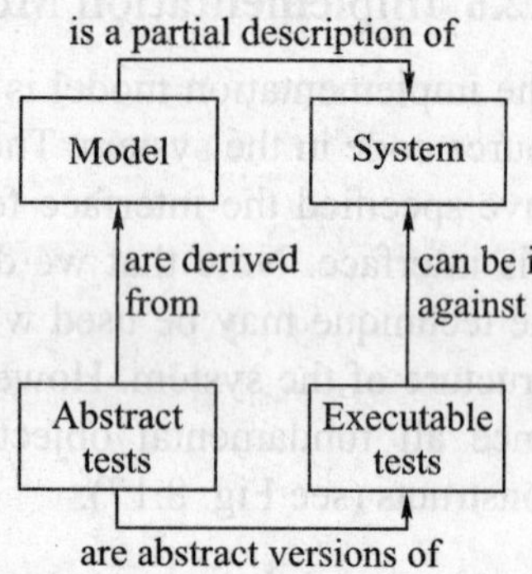

Fig. 8.18

The Object-oriented Software Engineering (OOSE) method considers a full range of the development stages in software engineering, from requirement gathering to testing. Jacobson treat maintenance stage as another full life cycle of system development. The idea of using use case as a base for the whole development process is a breakthrough in the world of object-oriented. This technique is simple yet a very convenient way of describing the functional requirement of a system.

The reuse aspect in developing the system has also been introduced and is represented as a full process (component management) together with its heuristic to support the Construction Process. However, the component concept in this method is not as sophisticated as the reuse concept defined nowadays. The component concept does not distinguish types and granularity of reuse.

The notation used in this method is basically simple, except for the state transition graphs, but they use different notation in different model to represent objects. Although the transformation between model (and pragmatic aspect) of the method is provided, the use of these notations in this manner may confuse the user.

8.3 ROUND-TRIP ENGINEERING

The capability of a modelling tool to generate template source code from a model for a specific programming language is called forward engineering. The capability of a product to process source code and extract partial model information is called reverse engineering. Support for forward and reverse engineering throughout the software development process is called round-trip engineering.

Round-trip engineering can also include cyclic repetitions of forward and reverse engineering, thus enhancing the iterative design and development process. This feature is essential for the collaboration between designers and developers, as developers might change the source code (*e.g.*, speed of execution optimisations) and the modellers should incorporate these minor changes (if any) in the model through reverse engineering. The same applies to changes in the model and their reflection on the source code templates. Another essential usage of round-trip engineering is when incorporating legacy code into new models.

At least, the modelling tool should support round-trip engineering for Java, C++ and IDL (for interfaces stereotypes and interfaces in component descriptions). The Java technology is one of the main choices in AMIDST with respect to the prototyping platform. Thus, any additional support for Java and related technologies in the surveyed products is considered a "good-to-have" feature.

Furthermore, we can distinguish two aspects in the forward engineering: code generation from static UML diagram and from dynamic UML diagrams. Since it is a generally difficult task to generate source code from dynamic diagrams, this is considered as a "good-to-have" feature.

One of the areas of research in AMIDST is design and implementation of middleware extensions, where reverse engineering will be essential, *e.g.*, when building on the source code of free ORB implementations.

8.3.1 Case Study

This is brief case study on the Banking system. It generally holds three types of accounts:

- Passbook savings,
- Checking and
- Bonus savings.

A number of different transactions are valid on each account type, but in a real application there may be many more. It shows,

1. **Structured chart (analysis/design):** Each transaction processing module deals with distinct variations for each account types. Each module is decomposed into sub modules for reuse purpose (see Fig. 8.19).

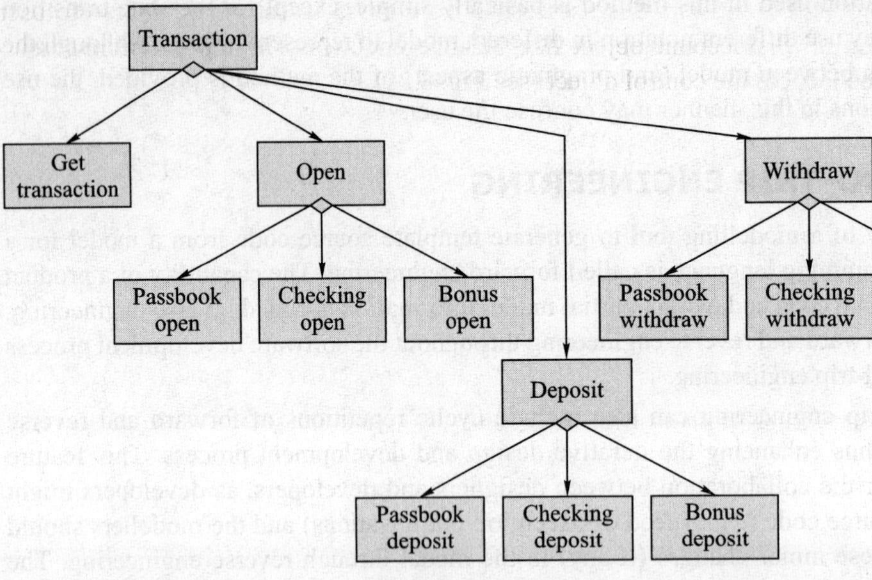

Fig. 8.19 A function/data solution for banking application

2. **Object oriented solution:** Various account types will now be modeled as descendents of the abstract call **Account**. The operations (Open, deposit & withdraw) are inherited. It required adding of one new descendant of the Account class. The interface will be same but need to implement the variations in the operations. We need to modify the objects that distinguish the various accounts. one object added and one modified versus three modules added and three modified in the functional solution (see Fig. 8.20).

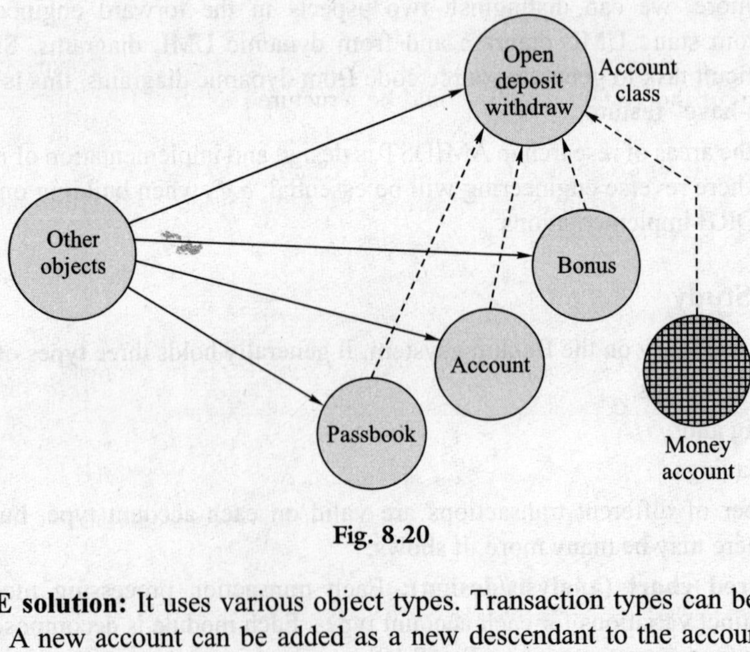

Fig. 8.20

3. **OOSE solution:** It uses various object types. Transaction types can be map to use cases. A new account can be added as a new descendant to the account class. The report use case would not be spread out over the entity objects. So we add a new

control object to support this use case. This control object would reuse the basic operation on the account object like balance enquires. The report-specific issued would be local to the control object (see Fig. 8.21).

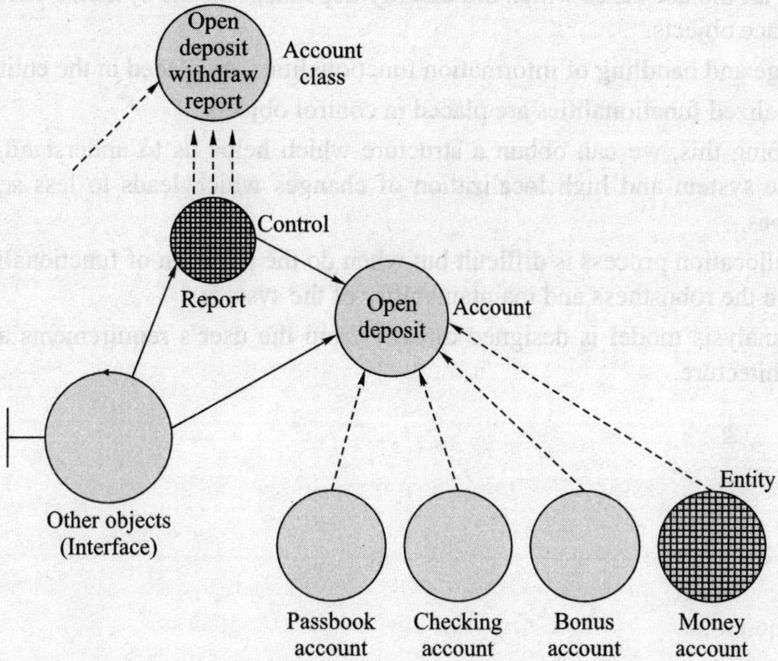

Fig. 8.21 OOSE solution

8.3.2 Case Model to Analysis Model

Each use case is divided into objects of three types. Requirement model specifies the entire functionality of the system which should be structured to obtain a robust and extendible structure. Use case is divided into analysis object and functionality in the use cases is allocated to different objects. Objects can be common to several use cases and it gives objects that are reusable in different use cases. This means reusability can be used for future changes in the system (see Fig. 8.22).

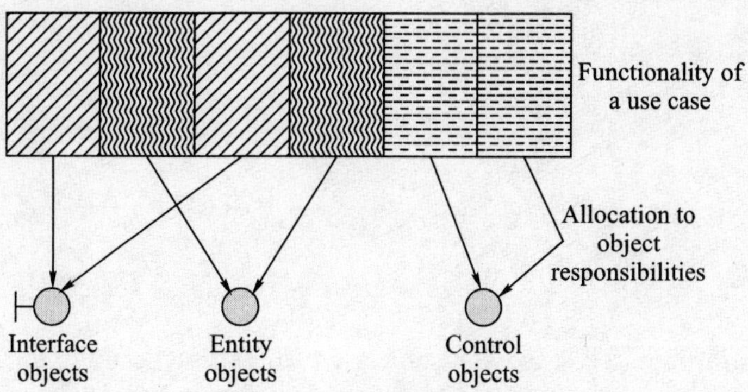

Fig. 8.22

8.3.3 Rule to Partition the Use Case

The following rules are to be followed to partition a use case:

1. Place all the use cases which are directly dependent on the system's environment in interface objects.
2. Storage and handling of information functionalities are placed in the entity object.
3. Specialized functionalities are placed in control objects.

By doing this, we can obtain a structure which helps us to understand the logical view of the system and high localization of changes which leads to less sensitivity to modifications.

The allocation process is difficult but when do the partition of functionality, then we decide upon the robustness and maintainability of the system.

The analysis model is designed directly from the user's requirements and specific system architecture.

CHAPTER

9

Analysis

9.1 INTRODUCTION

It is used to analyze, specify and define the system. The model will describe what the system is to do. It is easier for use to understand the system. The models that are developed during analysis are application-oriented. The purpose is to formulate the problem and to build models able to solve the problem under ideal conditions.

Two different models are developed in analysis: **the requirement model and analysis model.**

Requirement model is used to define the functionality. For this, conceptual picture of the system is developed using problem domain object and interface descriptions.

Analysis model gives a conceptual configuration of the system, consisting of control objects, entity object and interface objects. The purpose of this model is to develop a robust and extensible structure. It comprises a total functional specification of the system we wish to develop, without any reference to the implementation environment. In construction process, we construct the system from the analysis model. An object in one model can be directly traced an object in other model, called as traceability.

9.2 REQUIREMENT MODEL

It acts as an intermediary between the developer and customer. It is not very technical. It forms the developer's view of what customer wants. It governs the development of all other models. It is structured by analysis model, realized by design model and implemented by implementation model and tested by testing model. The requirement model functions as a basis for the development of operational instructions and manuals, anything that the system described from a user's perspective.

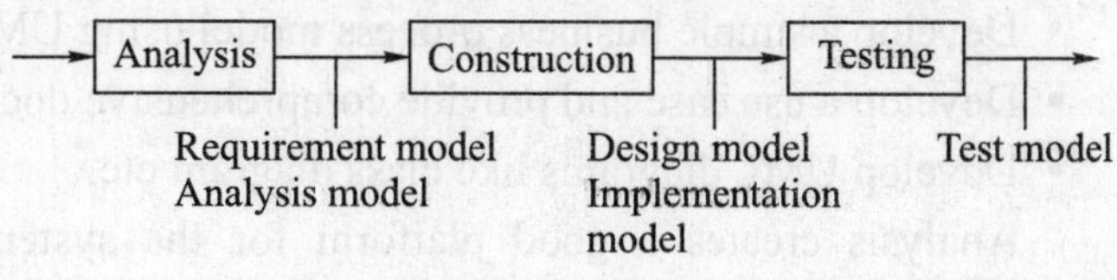

Fig. 9.1

Requirement model consists of:

1. **Use case Model:** It specifies the functionality the system has to offer from a user's perspective and we define that should take place inside the system. This model uses actors to represent roles the users can play, and use cases to represent what the user should be able to do with the system.

2. **Problem domain object model:** For better understanding of the system, we use objects which will serve as a common foundation for the developers and users.
3. **User Interface descriptions:** This specify in detail what the user interface will look like when the use cases are performed.

9.3 ACTORS

We have already discussed use case and actors. Here we will tell that actor is of two types:

1. Primary actors 2. Secondary actors

Like, Photostat shop is a primary actor and person consuming it is a secondary actor. Secondary actor exists because primary actor can use the system. So, only primary actor is the main who governs the system structure and changes to our system will come basically from these actors. Here Photostat machine is not an actor. Actor is a user type or category.

Actors can model human users, but they can also model other systems communicating with our system. To find out the difference between the actor and user, actor act as class and description as a behavior.

9.4 USE CASES

We can define the functionality inside the system. We do this by specifying use cases. Each use case constitutes a complete course of events initiated by an actor and it specifies the interaction that takes place between an actor and the system.

To understand use cases we can view their descriptions as state transition graphs. Each stimulus sent between an actor and the system performs a sate change in this graph. We can view a use cases existing in different states. By defining actors and their use cases we can completely understand the functionality of the system.

The use cases are identified through the actors. For every event, there is an actor which tells us which activity will be performed. This helps in requirement specification for actors and helps in understanding the following:

- Identify the actors of the system.
- Main tasks of the actors.
- Develop a simple business process model using UML.
- Develop a use case and provide comprehensive documentation of the system.
- Develop UML diagrams like class diagram etc.

Analysis creates a good platform for the system design. So, we can say that ***requirement model is structured by the analysis model.***

9.5 EXTENSION

It is used to structure and relate use case descriptions. It specifies how one use case description may be inserted into another use case description. It can be described in a simple way where changes and additions to the functionality are made easily.

By means of extension association the system will be given a good and modifiable structure. Example is when you want to collect statistics in a specific use case. Every time you execute this use case, you want to measure and collect some statistics in this process. This can be described by using use case collect statistics as an extension use case to control use case.

Extension is thus used to model extensions of other, complete use cases.

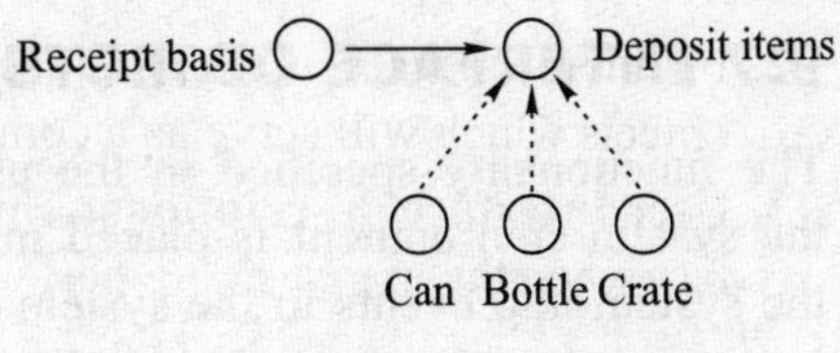

Fig. 9.2 Problem domain model

9.6 THE ANALYSIS MODEL

It focuses on the structuring of the system. Here, three different type of objects are being defined:

- Interface objects
- Entity objects
- Control objects

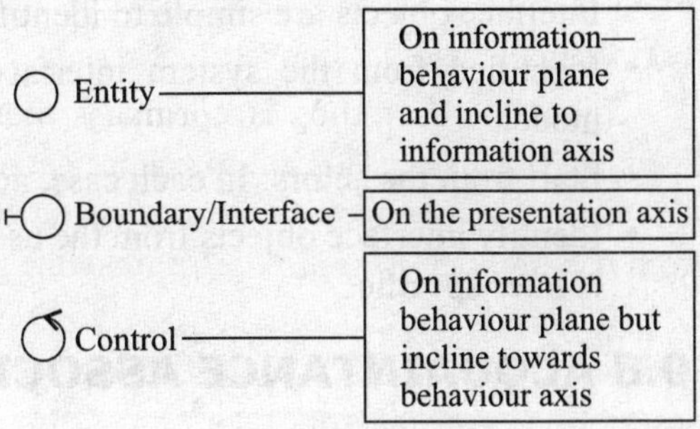

We also group these objects into subsystems to manage units. It creates a good platform for the system design and form the basis of the design.

An object can be common to several different use cases. We describe which object is responsible for which behavior in the use case. We write verbal descriptions of the responsibilities of roles played by each object.

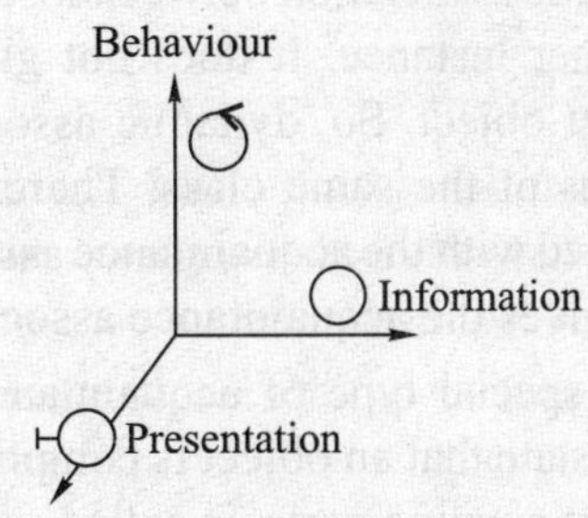

Fig. 9.3

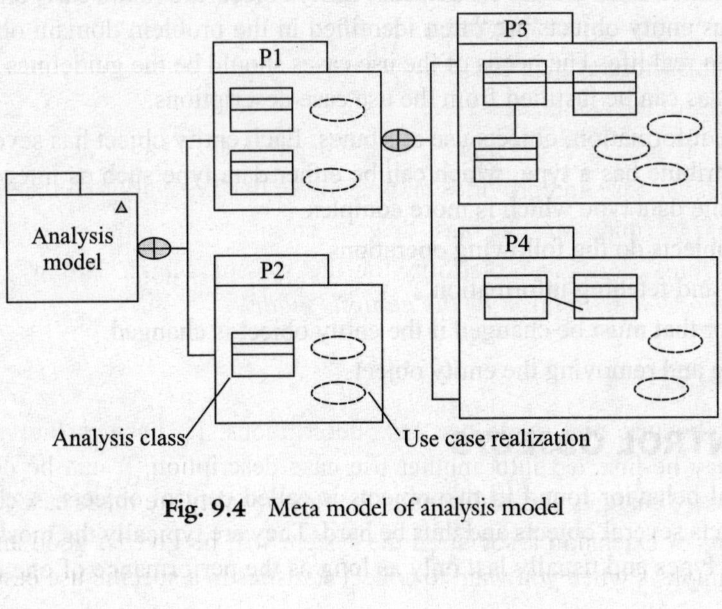

Fig. 9.4 Meta model of analysis model

9.7 INTERFACE OBJECTS

The functionality specified in the use case descriptions that is directly dependent on the system environment is placed in interface objects. It translates the actor's input to the system into events in the system that the actor is interested in into something which is presented to the actor. It is bidirectional communication between the system and its users.

Interface objects are simple to identify and divided into three strategies:

- Identified from the system interface descriptions accompanying the requirement model.
- Start from the actors: In each case, actors may need several interface objects.
- Identify interface objects from the use case descriptions that extract functionality that is inter-specific.

9.8 ACQUAINTANCE ASSOCIATIONS

It is a static association between instances and means that an instance knows of the existence of another instance. It does not give the object the right to exchange information with the other object. So, dynamic association is used. An object may associate several other instances of the same class. Therefore, we should describe how many instances cab be associated with the acquaintance association. This is done by cardinality to each association. It also gives the acquaintance association a name clarifying what the relationship entails.

A special type of acquaintance association is the consists-of association, which is used to state that an object is composed of other objects. The uniting object has association with participating parts, is called as an aggregate.

9.9 ENTITY OBJECT

They are identified from the use cases. Most entity objects are found early and are obvious. These obvious entity objects are often identified in the problem domain object model. It corresponds to real life. The needs of the use cases should be the guidelines and only such entity objects as can be justified from the use case descriptions.

- To store information, objects use attributes. Each entity object has several attributes. Each attribute has a type, which can be either data type such as integer or string or composite data type which is more complex.
- Entity objects do the following operations.
- Storing and fetching information.
- Behavior that must be changed if the entity object is changed.
- Creating and removing the entity object.

9.10 CONTROL OBJECTS

The unnatural behavior found in two objects is called control objects. A change in such behavior affects several objects and thus be hard. They are typically the most ephemeral of all the object types and usually last only as long as the performance of one use case lasts.

Control objects are normally found directly from the use cases. Each use case normally involves interface objects and entity objects. Thus behavior that remains after the interface objects and entity objects have been assigned their behavior will be placed in the control objects. They have limited tasks and will be simpler to understand and describe. Control objects are transaction-related behavior or control sequences specific to one or few use cases that separate the entity objects from the interface objects.

9.11 WORKING WITH THE ANALYSIS OBJECTS

We are working with one use case at a time and for one specific case we identify interfaced objects, entity objects and control objects. The specification of the objects should be written in a textual form. The simplest way of doing this is just to copy the text from the use cases and paste it into the object descriptions. It is better to describe each object's role and responsibilities bearing in mind those of the other objects.

9.12 SUB SYSTEM

When the analysis objects have been identified the system will contain a large number of objects. For medium-sized project typically between 30 and 100 objects will be specified. For clear overview of the number of objects, objects need to be placed in groups. Such groups of objects are called subsystems. They are thus the way of structuring the system for further development and maintenance. The lowest level of subsystem is to be viewed as a change unit. We call these units service package. The division into subsystem should also be based on the functionality of the system. All objects have a strong mutual coupling will be placed in same subsystem. There are several criteria which can be used to decide whether two objects are strongly functionally related. There follow a list few of them:

- Will changes in one object lead to changes in other object?
- Do they communicate with same actor?
- Are both of them dependent on a third object such as an interface object or entity object?
- Does one object perform several operations on the other?
- The aim is to have strong functional coupling within a subsystem and a weak coupling between subsystems.

Example and Case Study

9.13 OBJECT ORIENTED ANALYSIS (OOA)

It helps in:

- **Identifying objects**: Using concepts, CRC cards, stereotypes, etc.
- **Organizing the objects**: classifying the objects identified, so similar objects can later be defined in the same class.
- **Identifying relationships between objects**: this helps to determine inputs and outputs of an object.

- **Defining operations of the objects**: the way of processing data within an object.
- **Defining objects internally**: information held within the objects.

The Three ways to do Object Oriented Analysis:

- Conceptual model (Larman) Produce a "light" class diagram.
- CRC cards (Beck, Cunningham) Index cards and role playing.
- Analysis model with stereotypes (Jacobson) Boundaries, entities, control.

A good analyst knows more than one strategy and even may mix strategies.

9.14 CONCEPTUAL MODEL—OVERVIEW

- Representation of concepts in a problem domain.
- In UML it is basically a "class diagram without operations".

It may show:

- Concepts
- Associations of concepts
- Attributes of concepts

9.14.1 Strategies to Identify Concepts

Finding Concepts with the:

- Concept Category List.
- Noun Phrase Identification.

A central distinction between object oriented and structures analysis: division by concepts (Objects) rather than division by functions.

9.14.2 The Concept Category List

- Physical or tangible objects.
- Specifications, designs, descriptions of things.
- Places
- Transactions
- Transaction line items
- Roles of people
- Containers of other things
- Things in a container
- Abstract noun concepts
- Organizations
- Events
- Processes
- Rules and policies
- Catalogues

- Records
- Services
- Manuals, books

Noun Phrase Identification:

- Identify the noun and noun phrases in textual descriptions of a problem domain.
- Consider them as candidate concepts or attributes.
- Care must be applied with this method.
- Mechanical noun-to-concept mapping isn't possible.
- Words in natural languages are ambiguous (especially English).

The "return item" Use case-Exercise: Find the Nouns

- The system controls a recycling machine for returnable bottles, cans and crates. The machine can be used by several customers at the same time and each customer can return all three types of item on the same occasion.

The system has to check, for each item, what type has been returned. • The system will register how many items each customer returns and when the customer asks for a receipt, the system will print out what was deposited, the value of the returned items and the total return sum that will be paid to the customer.

- An operator also … (not in "return item" Use Case)

9.15 CASE STUDY: FIND THE NOUNS

- The **system** controls a **recycling machine** for returnable **bottles**, **cans** and **crates**. The **machine** can be used by several **customers** at the same time and each **customer** can return all three **types** of **item** on the same occasion. The **system** has to check, for each **item**, what type has been returned.
- The **system** will register how many items each **customer** returns and when the **customer** asks for a **receipt**, the **system** will print out what was deposited, the value of the **returned items** and the total **return sum** that will be paid to the **customer**.
- An operator also … (not in "return item" Use Case).

9.15.1 Nouns Found in the Description

- Recycling machine
- Bottles, cans, and crates
- Machine
- Customers, customer
- Types of item, item, type, returned items
- System
- Receipt
- Return sum

9.15.2 Discussion of "Recycling Machine"

- Recycling machine
- Bottles, cans and crates
- Machine
- Customers, customer
- Types of item, item, type, returned
- Items
- System
- Receipt
- Return sum
- This concept is the "overall system"
- As we consider only one single use case,
- Better to name this concept in the context of this use case, *e.g.* **Deposit item receiver.**

9.15.3 Discussion of "Bottles, Cans, and Crates"

- Deposit item receiver
- Bottles, cans, and crates
- Machine
- Customers, customer
- Types of item, item, type returned
- Items
- System
- Receipt
- Return sum
- Usually better to use singular and multiplicities instead of plural.
- As **bottle**, **can** and **crate** have much in common (they are processed as items),
- They could be generalized to an "item". We should remember this for later (**inheritance**).

9.15.4 Discussion of "Machine" and "System"

- Deposit item receiver
- Bottle, can, crate
- Machine
- Customers, customer
- Types of item, item, type, returned items
- System
- Receipt
- Return sum

- "Machine" and "System" mean here the same, namely the "Recycling machine", *i.e.*, the **Deposit item receiver.**

9.15.5 Discussion of "Customers" and "Customer"

- Deposit item receiver
- Bottle, can, crate
- **Customers, customer**
- Types of item, item, type, returned
- Items
- Receipt
- Return sum
- The customer has already been identified as an actor.
- They are outside of the system.
- We establish a concept, that interfaces with the customer (and is inside the system):
- Deposit item receiver.

9.15.6 Discussion of "Item" (etc.)

- Deposit item receiver
- Bottle, can, crate
- Customer panel
- Types of item, item, type, returned items
- Receipt
- Return sum
- The items that are inserted in the machine.
- Good candidate as super class for bottle, can, crate.
- Let's call it : **Deposit item.**

9.15.7 Discussion of "Receipt"

- Deposit item receiver
- Bottle, can, crate
- Customer panel
- Deposit item
- **Receipt**
- Return sum
- The concept that "remembers" all items inserted in the machine.
- To distinguish it from the piece of paper returned to the customer, call it: **Receipt basis**.

9.15.8 Discussion of "Return Sum"

- Deposit item receiver
- Bottle, can, crate
- Customer panel
- Deposit item
- Receipt basis
- Return sum
- The sum that it is returned to the customer is actually computed by adding up all values of the items stored in the receipt basis.
- The sum itself is only a **primitive data value,** and may therefore not be considered as a concept.

9.15.9 Discussion of Other Concepts

- Deposit item receiver
- Bottle, can, crate
- Customer panel
- Deposit item
- Receipt basis
- These are the concepts identified by nouns. Did we forget something?
- Check the "Concept Category List"!
- The system "**interfaces**" with the physical object "printer", so we add an interface concept : **Receipt printer**.

9.15.10 Summary of Concepts Identified in the Analysis

- Deposit item receiver
- Bottle, can, crate
- Customer panel
- Deposit item
- Receipt basis
- Receipt printer
- So far we have identified:
    - o Concepts
    - o A generalization relationship.
- Next step: Finding associations.

9.15.11 How to Make a Conceptual Model?

- Find the concepts.
- Draw them in a conceptual model.
- Add associations.
- Add attributes.

9.15.12 Drawing of Concepts

See Fig. 9.5.

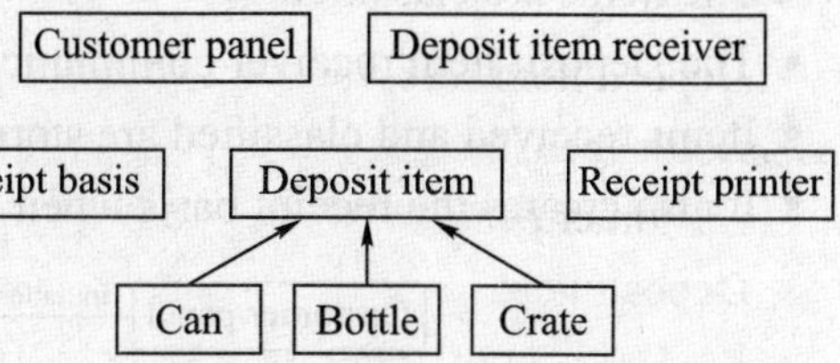

Fig. 9.5

9.15.13 Adding Associations

- If one concept needs to know of a another concept for some duration they should be linked by an association.
- Also use the Common Association list in order to identify associations.

9.15.14 Common Association List

- A is a part of B
- A is contained in B
- A is a description for B
- A is a line item of a transaction or report B
- A is known or reported in B
- A is a member of B
- A is a organizational subunit of B
- A uses or manages B
- A communicates with B
- A is related to a transaction B
- A is a transaction related to another transaction B
- A is next to B
- A is owned by B

9.15.15 Adding Associations

- The Customer panel communicates to the receiver when an item is inserted.
- Also when the receipt is requested.

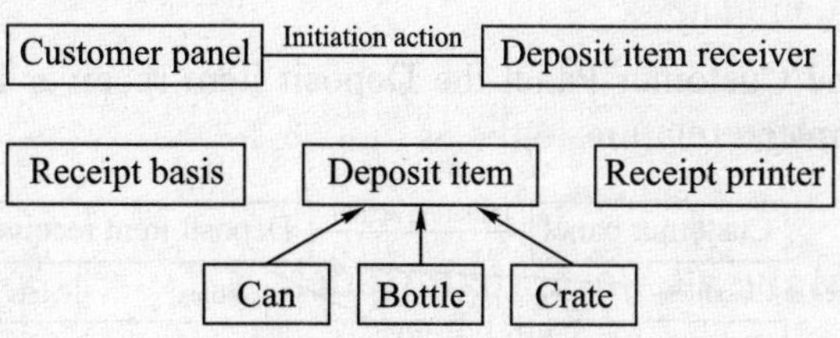

Fig. 9.6 The Deposit item receiver manages deposit items.

The items are classified:

- The Deposit item receiver communicates to Receipt basis.
- Items received and classified are stored.
- It also creates the receipt basis when it is needed for the first time.

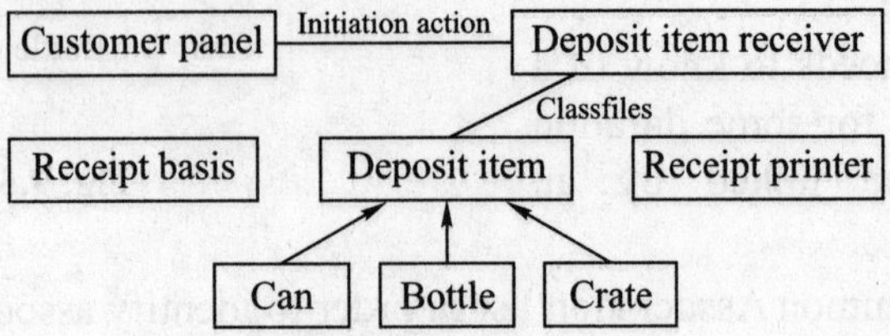

Fig. 9.7

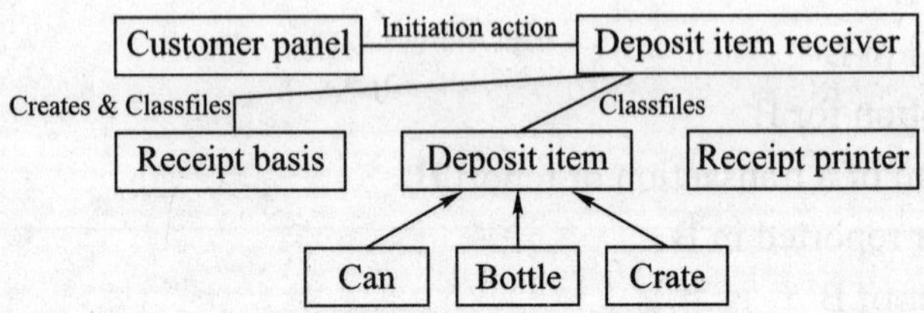

Fig. 9.8

9.15.16 The Receipt Basis Collects Deposit Items

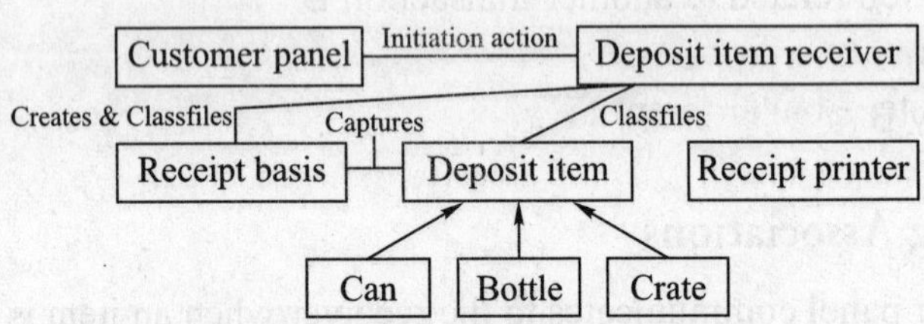

Fig 9.9

- On request by the Customer Panel the Deposit item receiver initiates printing of a receipt on the printer.

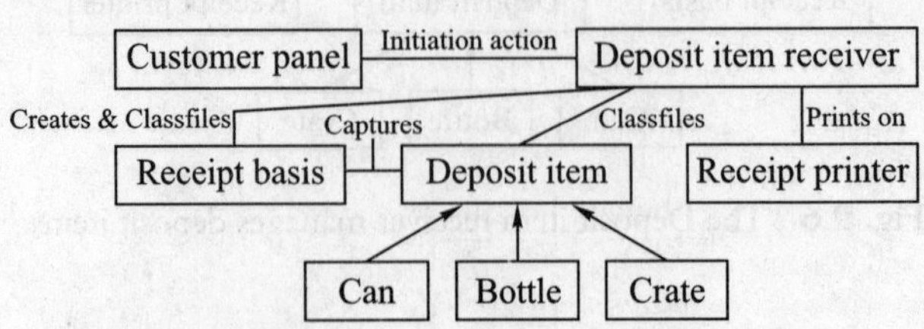

Fig. 9.10

9.16 ADDING ASSOCIATIONS

- Adding multiplicities
  Only one association here is a 1 to many relationships
- All others are 1 to 1.

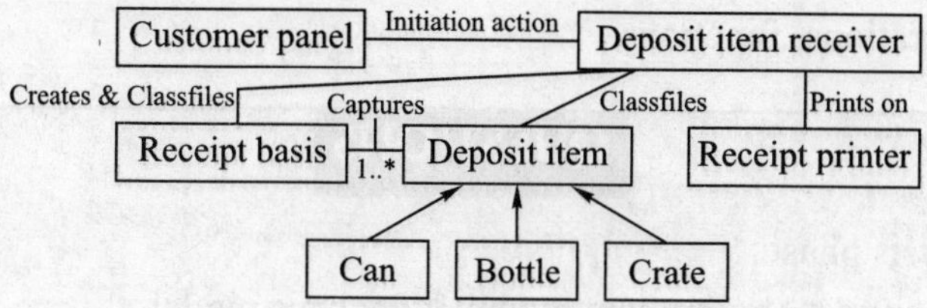

Fig. 9.11

- An attribute is a logical data value of an object.
- Attributes in a conceptual model are **simple data values.**
- As Boolean, Date, Number, String (Text), Time, Address, Color, Price, Phone Numbers, Product Codes, etc.
- Sometimes it is difficult to distinguish between attributed and concepts *e.g.* Concept "Car" vs. attribute "Reg. Number".
- The Deposit item has a value.
- Also it will be assigned a number that shows later on the receipt (Fig. 9.12).

In order to be classified by the Deposit item receiver each item has also a weight and a size.

- However this is the same for each type of item, but different *between* the types.

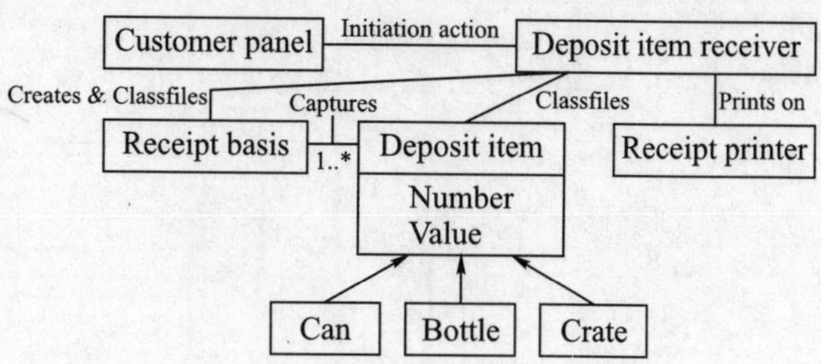

Fig. 9.12

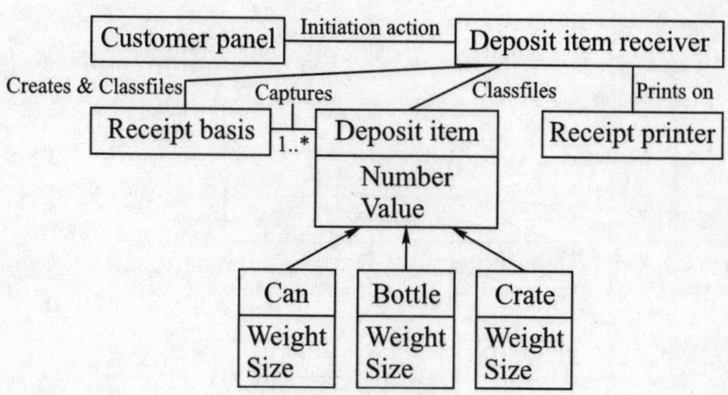

Fig. 9.13

Summary

NOT in a conceptual model:

- Arrows.
- Dotted lines.
- Methods, operations, functions.

QUESTIONS

1. Explain analysis phase.
2. Compare & contrast requirement model & analysis model.
3. Explain interface, entity & control objects.
4. Explain conceptual model.
5. How we find the nouns in the case study?

CHAPTER

10 Construction

There are two ways of constructing a software design:

- Make it so simple that there are obviously no deficiencies.
- Make it so complicated that there are no obvious defi.ciencies.

Specification is about **what**, and Design is the start of the how inputs to the design process.

- Specification document, including models etc.

Outputs of the design process:

- A design document that describes how the code will be written. Includes design models.
- What subsystems, modules or components are used?
- How these integrate (*i.e.*,, work together) Qualities of a good design.
- Correct, Complete, Changeable, Efficient, Simple.
- **Correctness:** It Should Lead To a Correct Implementation.
- **Completeness:** It Should Do Everything. Everything? It should follow the specifications.
- **Changeable:** It should Facilitate Change—Change Is Inevitable.
- **Efficiency:** It Should Not Waste Resources. But:

  Better a Working Slow Design Than A Fast Design That Does Not Work.
- **Simplicity:** It Should Be As Understandable As Possible.

10.1 LEVELS OF DESIGN

There are three possible levels:

- System Design, if appropriate Part of Systems Engineering
- High-level Software Design Architecture, architectural design
- Low-level Software Design Detailed Design, Module Design

Systems Engineering: Large combinations of hardware and software.

- Decompose system into subsystems
- Determine which subsystems are HW, which are SW
- Software Engineering activities thus become a part of a larger activity.

In the construction phase, we build the system based on the models developed during requirement and analysis phase. The construction process is used for coding and where coding is being implemented. The purpose of construction is basically to adapt the analysis models to the prevailing implementation conditions.

Construction can be divided into two sub processes, design and implementation, and produces two models:

- The Design Model and
- Implementation Model.

The construction process starts with examining the actual implementation environment. Everything that affects the realization of the system must be taken into account. Technical issues such as how the DBMS should be integrated, how distribution should be handled, constraints in the programming language.

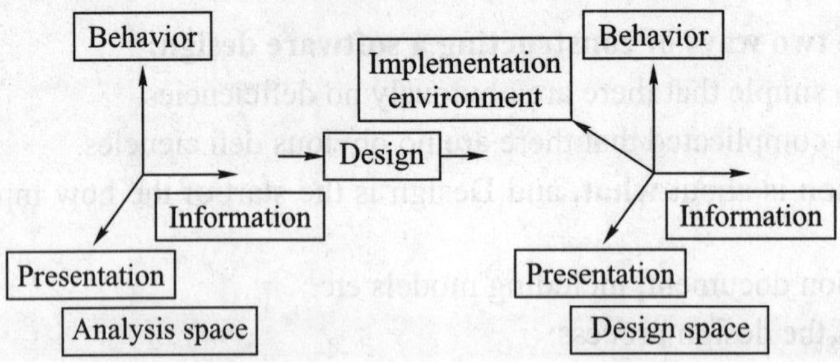

Fig. 10.1

10.2 DESIGN MODEL

It refines the analysis model and formalized to get design model. The design model basically cover one new dimension *i.e.*, implementation environment. This means that we want to adopt our analysis model to fit in the implementation model as the same time we refine. This helps to write the software easily.

Design model basically into implementation environment:

- Define interface of the objects.
- Define semantics of the operation.

Decide how different issues such as DBMS, programming language features, and distribution will be handled

The design model is composed of blocks which are the design objects

- The block will abstract the actual implementation

The implementation of the blocks may be: one specific class in the source code several different classes

10.3 OBJECT MODULE

These modules form the actual classes' *e.g.*, class in an OO language or package in Ada.

10.4 TRANSITION

Transition from analysis to design model should be made must be decided for each specific application. If there are no problem with adaptation with DBMS, distributed environment, real-time application etc., then it is fine to be quite formal in the analysis model. A design model is the specialization of analysis model for a specific implementation environment.

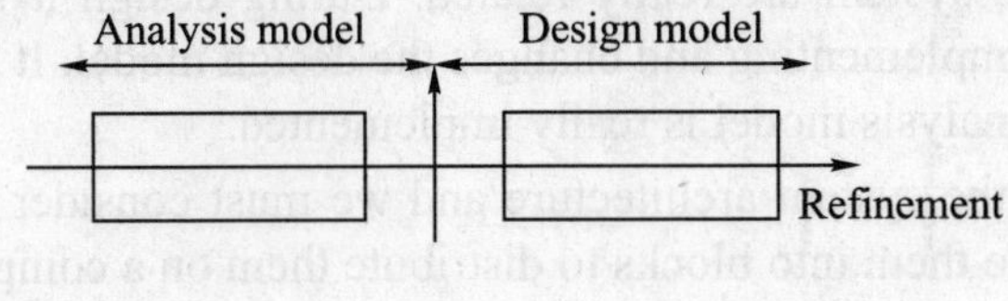

Fig. 10.2

10.4.1 How to Building a Design Model

First attempt can be made mechanically *i.e.*,,

- It is based on the analysis model.
- Obtain a clear traceability to the analysis model.

  The Analysis Model vs The Design Model:
- **The Analysis model:** It is developed in logical terms and is only a conceptual picture of the system to be built.
- **The design model:** It is an abstraction of how the actual system really is built.

  The final structure should reflect how the implementation:
- Environment has affected construction
- For example, if the programming language does not support inheritance, the model must reflect how the inheritance is really implemented.

  Create design models before **coding so that we can:**
- Compare different possible design solutions.
- Evaluate efficiency, ease of modification, maintainability, etc.

Identify the actual technical constraints under which the system should be built including:

- The target environment.
- Programming language.
- Existing products that should be used (DBMSs, etc).
- **Strategies:** As few objects as possible should be aware of the constraints of the actual implementation environment.

10.4.2 Traceability

Based on the analysis model we can now mechanically and seamlessly find the first attempt at a design model. The first attempt is analysis model. To differentiate between these two models, we use different notations. The semantics of the design model is somewhat different from analysis model. The analysis model is developed in logical terms and is only a conceptual picture of the system to be built. The design model, however, is an abstraction of how the actual system really is built.

The semantics of the block should thus reflect the semantics of the objects existing in the actual system and likewise the associations between the objects should also reflect how the objects in the system are really related. During design it is decided how this association should be implementing and changes the design model. It also reflects on how the inheritance in the analysis model is really implemented.

This is good for the system architecture and we must consider the implementation environment. We divide them into blocks to distribute them on a computer system.

The design model reduces the complexity of the system. The blocks are actually an abstraction mechanism for the source code. It is easier to build a correct system that will avoid errors caused by complexity.

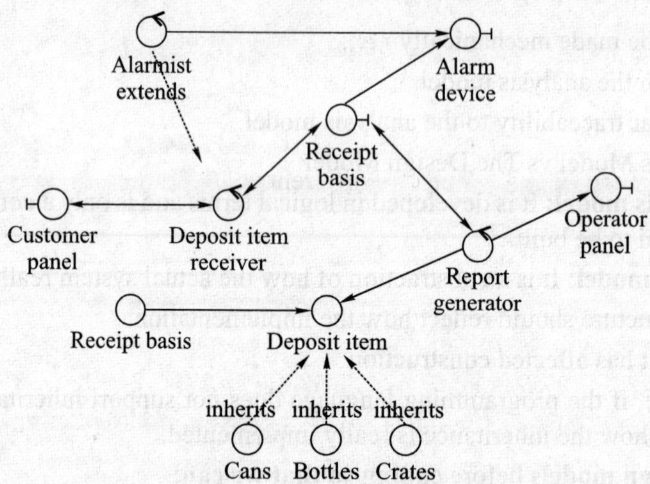

Fig. 10.3 Analysis model of the recycling machine.

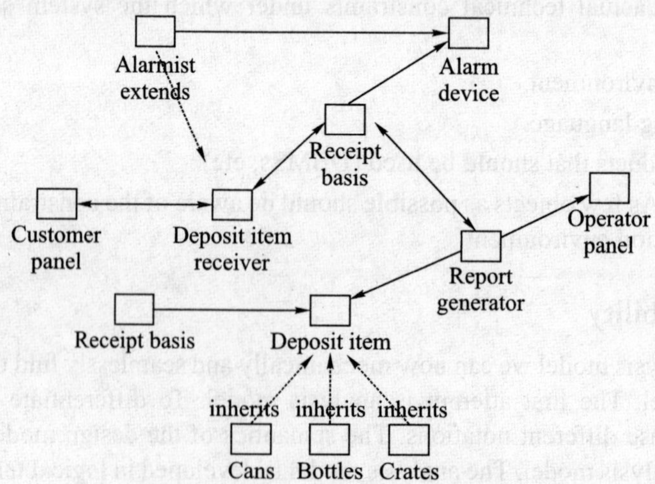

Fig. 10.4 First attempt to design the structure of the recycling machine.

10.5 THE IMPLEMENTATION ENVIORNMENT

The implementation environment identifies the actual constraints and emphasized on where and how the analysis model should be developed and refined. Before going to the target environment we check for the following:

- Target Environment
- Programming languages
- Existing products that should be used (DBMS etc.)

Strategies: Constraints are put on the few objects for the implementation environment.

10.5.1 Target Environment

- It creates new blocks that represent occurrences of the changed parts in the target environment and interfaces the application's file handling and the operating system's file.
- Block offer operations such as Create file to the application objects. This block may have different implementations for different configurations of the system.
- Specifies an abstract class for interface.
- Polymorphism
- The object can check the platform at run-time.
- CASE statement in the source code.
- Checks when the system is to be delivered.
- Provide several different modules which should be produced in final product.
- Investigate whether the target environment will execute in a distributed way.
- It checks on a different processors or different processes.

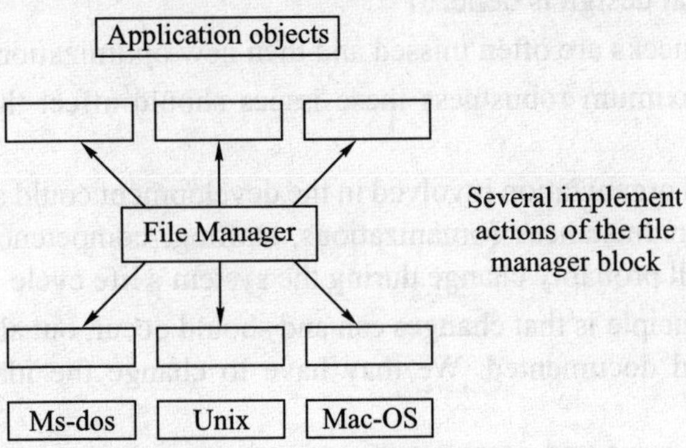

Fig. 10.5

10.5.2 Programming Language

- It checks which programming language is used which affects the design and concept.

- It check for the basic properties of the language and its environment are fundamental for the design:
    - o Inheritance and Multiple inheritances.
    - o Typing.
    - o Standard.
    - o Portability.
- Memory management strategy chosen for handling errors during run-time in:
    - o Exception (Ada)
    - o Assertions (Eiffel)
    - o None (C++ ver 2)
- It checks for automatic garbage collection.
- The use of component.
- Component library, such as interface objects.

  Often existing products are used when developing new systems. Examples are:
- DBMS
- UIMS (User Interface Management System).
- Network facilities.
- Internally or externally developed applications that should be incorporated.
- Products used during development affect the design. Products include Compilers, debuggers, preprocessor and other tools.
- Other considerations includes requirement for performance or limitations of memory which may also affect the design.
- To investigate potential optimizations early simulation or prototyping may be used before the actual design is done.
- The real bottlenecks are often missed and then new optimizations are necessary
- To achieve maximum robustness these issues should affect the design as little as possible.
- The people and organization involved in the development could also affect the design because the circumstances (organizations, staffing, competence areas) that are in effect today will probably change during the system's life cycle.
- The overall principle is that changes can and should occur, but all the changes should be justified and documented. We may have to change the ideal design model in various ways:
    - o Introduce new blocks in the design model which do not have any representation in the analysis model.
    - o To delete blocks from the design model. It is more suspicious as Changing the logical structure of the system should be made in the analysis model first.
    - o To change blocks in the design model. It is also suspicious as it decrease the robustness of the system.
    - o To change the associations between the blocks in the design model.

The synchronization and communication between processes helps the implementation environment in:

- Actual implementation of association.
- Extension association has no direct implementation technique.
- Inheritance associations.

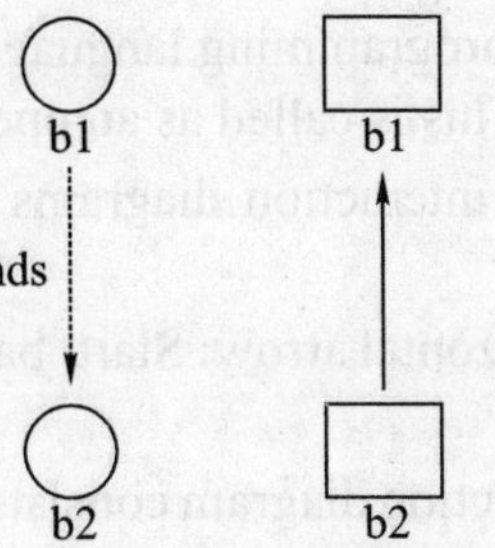

Fig. 10.6 Behavior b1 extends behavior b2. This will be implemented with a stimulus being sent from b2 to b1.

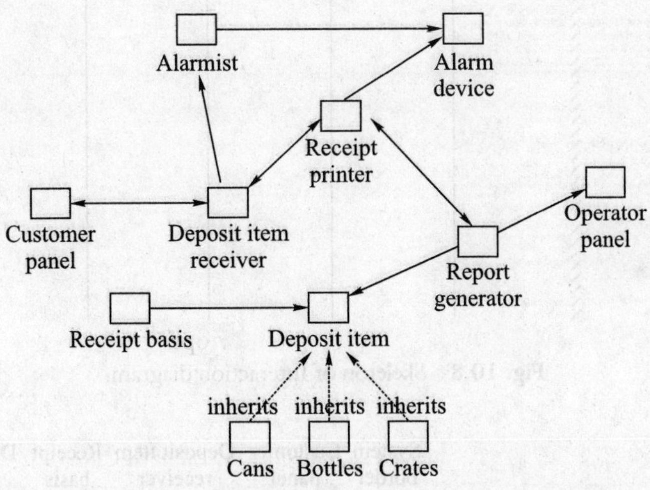

Fig. 10.7 The refined design model for the recycling machine.

10.5.3 Interaction Diagram

It identifies the system architecture and describes how the blocks are to communicate by designing the use case. For each use case, we draw an interaction diagram. The main purpose of the use case design is to define the protocols of the blocks. The interaction diagram describes how each use case is offered by communicating objects. The diagram shows how the participating objects realize the use case through their interaction. The blocks send stimuli between one another. All stimuli are defined including their parameters. For each concrete use case, draw an interaction diagram.

To build an interaction diagram: It is used in telecommunication. To build the interaction diagram:

- First identify blocks in the design model.
- Draw skeleton, consist of: System border, Bars for each block that participates.
- Describes the sequences at the left edge. Mark the bar to which operations belongs with a rectangle representing operation and describes the sequences in structured text or pseudo-code used for programming language. Text describes what is happening in the part of the use case. This is called as an operation.
- **Define a stimulus:** The interaction diagrams are controlled by events. Events are stimuli.
- Draw a stimulus as a horizontal arrow: Start: bar of the sending block, End: bar of the receiving block.
- The structure of the interaction diagram consists of **fork diagram** and **Stair diagram.**

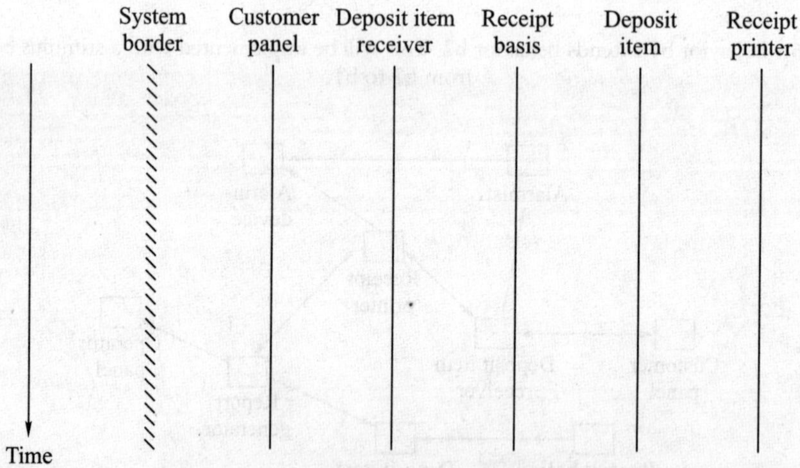

Fig. 10.8 Skeleton of Interaction diagram.

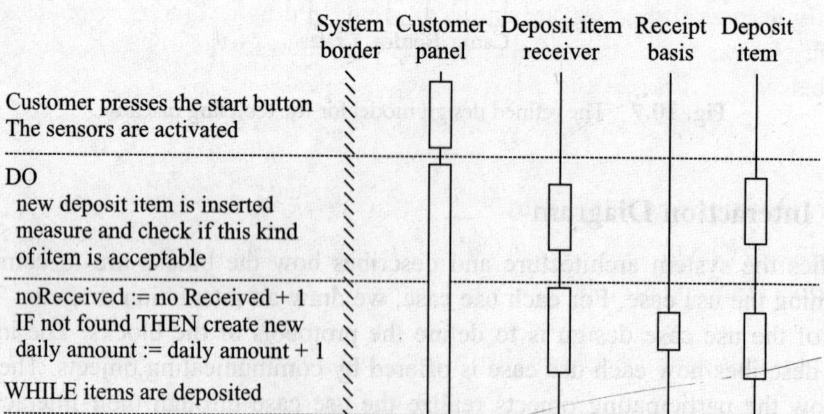

Fig. 10.9 Interaction diagram of Use Case Returning item.

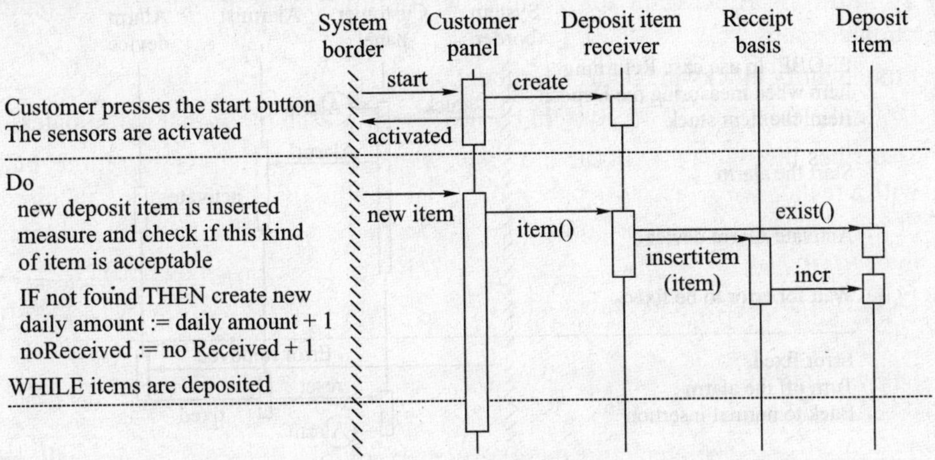

Fig. 10.10 Interaction diagram of Use Case Returning item.

10.5.4 Interaction Diagram Structure

The structure tells us about the realization characteristics of the use case. It validates the structure of the use case defined in analysis model. The use case is based on a real application. To build a structure it can be of two types:

10.5.4.1 Fork

It indicates a centralized structure and is characterized by the fact that it is an object controls the other objects interacted with it. This structure is best when:

- The operations can change order
- New operations could be inserted

10.5.4.2 Stair

It indicates decentralized structure and is characterized by delegated responsibility. Each object only knows a few of the other objects and knows which objects can help with a specific behavior. This structure is best when:

- The operation has a strong connection. Strong connection exists if the objects:
- Form a 'consist-of' hierarchy.
- Form an information hierarchy.
- Form a fixed temporal relationship.
- Form a (conceptual) inheritance relationship.

10.5.5 Use Case with Extension

It is described by a probe position in the interaction diagram and indicates a position in the use case to be extended. It is often accompanied by a condition which indicates under what circumstances the extension should take placed.

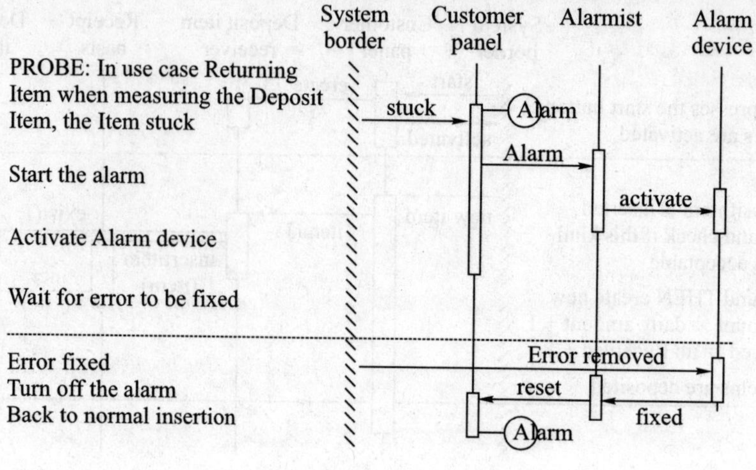

Fig. 10.11 Probe position

10.5.6 Homogenization

In parallel design process, several stimuli with the same purpose or meaning are defined by several designers working more or less independently of one another. These stimuli should be consolidated to obtain as few stimuli as possible which is called as **homogenization.** The example of homogenization is

What_is_your_phone_number?

Where_do_you_live?

Get_address

Get_address_and_phone_number

Which can be homogenized into

Get_address

Get_phone_num

QUESTIONS

1. What are the best methods to construct a software design?
2. Explain levels of design.
3. Explain traceability.
4. How we analyze & construct a model?
5. What is Homogenization?

CHAPTER 11

Testing

Testing is used to verify that all project deliverables and components are complete and to demonstrate and track project progress.

Testing is the phase after designing phase of the system development life cycle (SDLC). Before starting with the testing, software comes with few terminologies in this phase:

- ***Software Fault***: A static defect in the software.
- ***Software Error***: An incorrect internal state that is the manifestation of some fault.
- ***Software Failure***: External, incorrect behavior with respect to the requirements or other description of the expected behavior.
- ***Testing***: Evaluating software by observing its execution.
- ***Test Failure***: Execution that results in a failure.
- ***Debugging***: The process of finding a fault in given software.

11.1 VERIFICATION AND VALIDATION

Validation: The process of evaluating software at the end of software development to ensure compliance with intended usage.

Verification: The process of determining whether the products of a given phase of the software development process fulfill the requirements established during the previous phase.

Verification can be conducted through **Reviews**. Quality reviews provides visibility into the development process throughout the software development life cycle and help teams determine whether to continue development activity at various checkpoints or milestones in the process. They are conducted to identify defects in a product early in the life cycle.

Each level is characterized by the goal of the test engineers. The following material is adapted:

Level 0: There's no difference between testing and debugging.

Level 1: The purpose of testing is to show that the software works.

Level 2: The purpose of testing is to show that the software doesn't work.

Level 3: The purpose of testing is not to prove anything specific, but to reduce the risk of using the software.

Level 4: Testing is a mental discipline that helps all IT professionals develop higher quality software.

11.1.1 Why Testing is Done?

- Define the expected output or result.
- Don't test your own programs.
- Inspect the results of each test completely.
- Include test cases for invalid or unexpected conditions.
- Test the program to see if it does what it is not supposed to do as well as what it is supposed to do.
- Avoid disposable test cases unless the program itself is disposable.
- Do not plan tests assuming that no errors will be found.

11.1.2 Some Definitions

Expected Results: The result that will be produce when executing the test if and only if the program satisfies its intended behavior.

Two common practical problems associated with software testing are how to provide the right values to the software and observing details of the software's behavior. These two ideas are used to refine the definition of a test case.

Software Observability: How easy it is to observe the behavior of a program in terms of its outputs, effects on the environment and other hardware and software components.

Software Controllability: How easy it is to provide a program with the needed inputs, in terms of values, operations and behaviors.

A test case is the combination of all these components (test case values, expected results, prefix values and postfix values). When it is clear from context, however, we will follow tradition and use the term "test case" in place of "test case values".

Test Case: A test case is composed of the test case values, expected results, prefix values and postfix values necessary for a complete execution and evaluation of the software under test. We provide an explicit definition for a test set to emphasize that coverage is a property of a set of test cases, rather than a property of a single test case.

Test Plan: It is a logical collection of Test Cases. Lets say you have some test cases that test the Authentication functionality of a website, then you can group all those Test Cases under an Authentication Test Plan.

Test Suite: It is an execution unit such as Functional Test, User Acceptance Testing (UAT), Integration Test or Regression Test. These Test Suite can have any combination of Test Cases which are required for the corresponding Testing phase. So, Test Suites can actually have the same or widely different Test Cases.

Test Scenario: It is a sequence of events writing the test scenario in detailed is test case.

So Test Plan and Test Suite have very different purposes and the only reason Test Suite is linked to Test Plans to have a context of the Plan for which the Test Suite is executed. As Test Plan is the umbrella that helps to estimate, track and bill all testing activities so Test Suites and Test Cases need to be associated with a Test Plan.

Test Set: A test set is simply a set of test cases.

***Test Driver*:** Class or utility program that applies test cases.

***Test Harness*:** system of test drivers and other tools that support test execution.

***Test Strategy*:** Algorithm or heuristic to create test cases from a representation, implementation, or a test model.

***Oracle*:** means to check the output from a program is correct for the given input.

***Stub*:** partial temporary implementation of a component (usually required for a component to operate).

***Executable Test Script*:** A test case that is prepared in a form to be executed automatically on the test software and produce a report.

***Test Requirement*:** A test requirement is a specific element of a software artifact that a test case must satisfy or cover.

***Coverage Criterion*:** A coverage criterion is a rule or collection of rules that impose test requirements on a test set.

Software testing process:

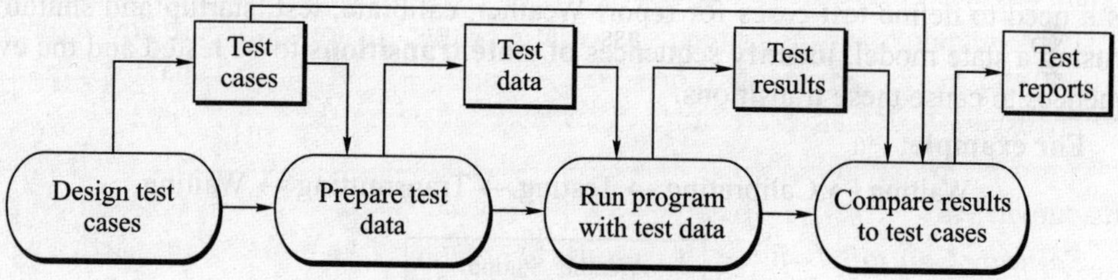

Fig. 11.1

11.1.3 Effectiveness *vs.* Efficiency

Test Effectiveness: Relative ability of testing strategy to find bugs in the software.

Test Efficiency: Relative cost of finding a bug in the software under test.

Testing Categorization: Fault-directed testing:

- o Unit testing
- o Integration testing

Conformance-directed testing:

- o System testing
- o Acceptance testing

11.2 CLASSIFICATION OF TESTING METHODS

- **Dynamic Testing:** Software component is executed with concrete input values (in a real environment).
- **Structural Testing (white-box testing):** Test cases derived from control flow or data flow of the component. Deriving tests from the source code internals of the software, specifically including branches, individual conditions and statements.

- **Functional Testing (black-box testing):** test cases derived from (formal) component specification. Deriving tests from external descriptions of the software, including specifications, requirements and design.
- **Static Testing:** Code analysis (components are not executed) by code inspections, code reviews, walkthroughs.
- **Symbolic Execution:** (abstract interpretation) execution of source code with abstract symbolic input values by interpreter; intermediate between testing and verification.
- **Object Class Testing:** It is complete **test coverage** of a class which involves the testing of all **operations** associated with an object. It is setting and interrogating all object **attributes** and exercising the object in all possible **states**. The inheritance makes it more difficult to design object class tests as the information to be tested is not localized.

11.3 AN EXAMPLE OF OBJECT CLASS TESTING

It is a need to define test cases for report Weather, calibrate, test, startup and shutdown. By using a state model, identify sequences of **state transitions** to be tested and the event sequences to cause these transitions.

For example:

Waiting → Calibrating → Testing → Transmitting → Waiting

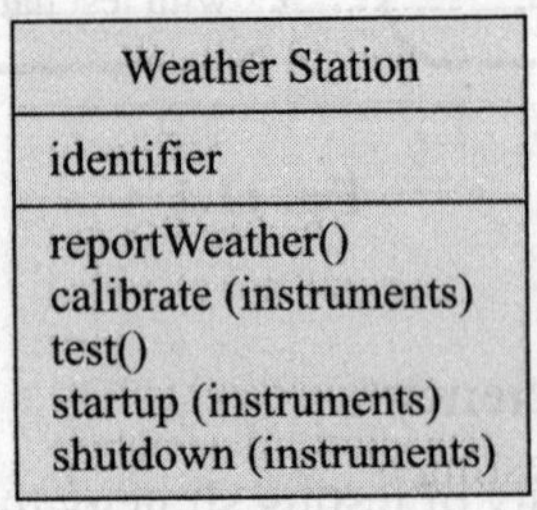

Fig. 11.2

Interface Testing: The objectives are to detect faults due to interface errors or invalid assumptions about interfaces. It is particularly important for object-oriented development as objects are defined by their interfaces.

11.3.1 Interface Types

Parameter interfaces (Data passed from one procedure to another).

Shared memory interfaces (Block of memory is shared between procedures or functions).

Procedural interfaces (Sub-system encapsulates a set of procedures to be called by other sub-system.

Message passing interfaces (Sub-systems request services from other sub-systems).

Interface misuse. A calling component calls another component and makes an error in its use of its interface *e.g.*, parameters in the wrong order.

Interface misunderstanding. A calling component embeds assumptions about the behavior of the called component which are incorrect.

Timing errors. The called and the calling component operate at different speeds and out-of-date information is accessed (see Fig. 11.3).

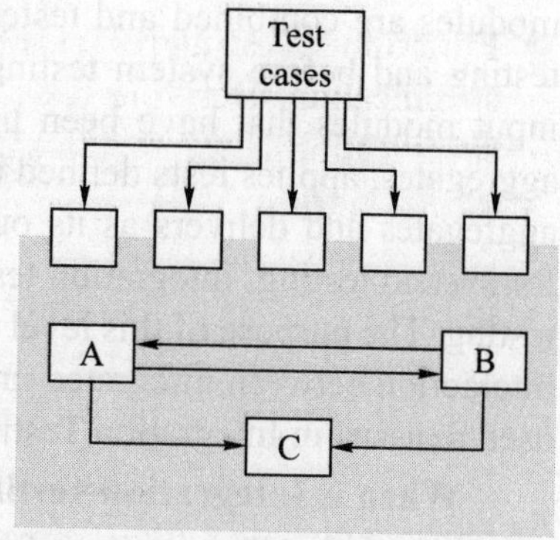

Fig. 11.3

Unit Testing: Unit testing is designed to assess the units produced by the implementation phase and is the "lowest" level of testing. In some cases, such as when building general-purpose library modules, unit testing is done without knowledge of the encapsulating software application. It is exercising the smallest individually executable code units. It is a defect testing process. Component or unit testing is the process of testing individual components in isolation. As with module testing, most software development organizations make unit testing the responsibility of the programmer. It is straightforward to package unit tests together with the corresponding code through the use of tools such as JUnit for Java classes.

Objectives: Its objectives are:

- Finding faults.
- Assure correct functional behavior of units.
- Usually performed by programmers.

Its components may be:

- Individual functions or methods within an object;
- Object classes with several attributes and methods and
- Composite components with defined interfaces used to access their functionality.

Regression testing: It is a standard part of the maintenance phase of software development. *Regression testing* is testing that is done after changes are made to the software and its purpose is to help ensure that the updated software still possesses the functionality it had before the updates. Mistakes in requirements and high-level design wind up being implemented as faults in the program; thus testing can reveal them. Unfortunately, the software faults that come from requirements and design mistakes are visible only through testing months or years after the original mistake. The effects of the mistake tend to be dispersed throughout multiple software components; hence such faults are usually difficult to pin down and expensive to correct. On the positive side, even if tests cannot be executed, the very process of defining tests can identify a significant fraction of the mistakes in requirements and design. Hence, it is important for test planning to proceed concurrently with requirements analysis and design and not be put off until late in a project. Fortunately, through techniques such as use-case analysis, test planning is becoming better integrated with requirements analysis in standard software practice.

11.4 INTEGRATION TESTING

It involves building a system from its components and testing it for problems that arise from component interactions. It is the phase in software testing in which individual software modules are combined and tested as a group. It occurs after unit testing and before system testing. Integration testing takes as its input modules that have been unit tested, groups them in larger aggregates, applies tests defined in an integration test plan to those aggregates and delivers as its output the integrated system ready for system testing. Integration testing is a logical extension of unit testing. The purpose of this level of testing is to expose faults in the interaction between integrated units. Test drivers and test stubs are used to assist in Integration Testing (see Fig. 11.4).

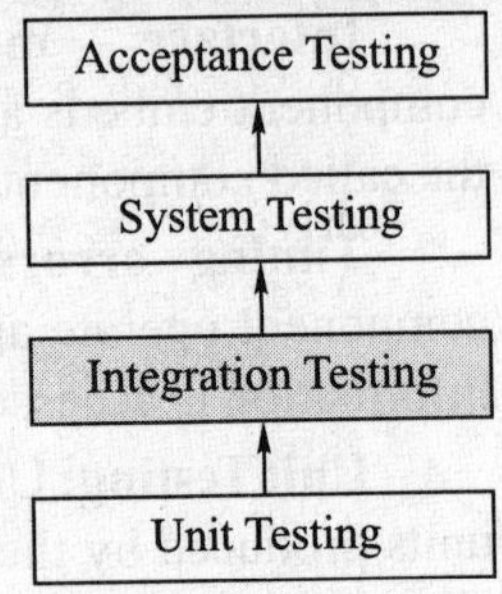

Fig. 11.4

When is Integration Testing performed?

Integration Testing is performed after Unit Testing and before System Testing.

Who performs Integration Testing?

Either Developers themselves or independent Testers perform Integration Testing.

11.4.1 Integration Testing Strategies

The larger the project, the more importance we need to place on the integration strategy. Very small systems are often assembled and tested in one phase. For most real systems this is impractical for two major reasons: First, the system would fail in so many places at once that the debugging and retesting effort would be impractical. Second, satisfying any white box testing criterion would be very difficult because of the vast amount of detail separating the input data from the individual code modules. Most integration testing has been traditionally limited to "black box" techniques. Large systems may require many integration phases, beginning with assembling modules into low-level subsystems, then assembling subsystems into larger subsystems and finally assembling the highest level subsystems into the complete system.

- ***Big Bang*** is an approach to Integration Testing where all or most of the units are combined together and tested at one go. This approach is taken when the testing team receives the entire software in a bundle. So what is the difference between Big Bang Integration Testing and System Testing? Well, the former tests only the interactions between the units while the latter tests the entire system.
- ***Top Down*** is an approach to Integration Testing where top level units are tested first and lower level units are tested step by step after that. This approach is taken when top down development approach is followed. Test Stubs are needed to simulate lower level units which may not be available during the initial phases.
- ***Bottom Up*** is an approach to Integration Testing where bottom level units are tested first and upper level units step by step after that. This approach is taken when bottom up development approach is followed. Test Drivers are needed to simulate higher level units which may not be available during the initial phases.
- ***Sandwich/Hybrid*** is an approach to Integration Testing which is a combination of Top Down and Bottom Up approaches.
- ***Umbrella Approach***: The umbrella approach requires testing along functional data and control-flow paths. First, the inputs for functions are integrated in the bottom-up pattern discussed above. The outputs for each function are then integrated in the top-

down manner. The primary advantage of this approach is the degree of support for early release of limited functionality. It also helps minimize the need for stubs and drivers. The potential weaknesses of this approach are significant, however, in that it can be less systematic than the other two approaches, leading to the need for more regression testing.

- ***Black Box Testing*:** Black box testing takes an external perspective of the test object to derive test cases. These tests can be functional or non-functional, though usually functional. The test designer selects valid and invalid inputs and determines the correct output. There is no knowledge of the test object's internal structure. This method of test design is applicable to all levels of software testing: unit, integration, functional testing, system and acceptance. The higher the level and hence the bigger and more complex the box, the more developers are forced to use black box testing to simplify. While this method can uncover unimplemented parts of the specification, one cannot be sure that all existent paths are tested.

  Integration Testing typically involves the following Steps:

  Step 1: Create a Test Plan.

  Step 2: Create Test Cases and Test Data.

  Step 3: If applicable create scripts to run test cases.

  Step 4: Once the components have been integrated execute the test cases.

  Step 5: Fix the bugs if any and re-test the code.

  Step 6: Repeat the test cycle until the components have been successfully integrated.

11.4.2 System Testing

System testing is the testing of behavior of a complete and fully integrated software product. It checks for the input values, output values, internal and external logical files and enquiries based SRS document. This is black box type of testing where external working of the software is evaluated with the help of requirement documents & it is totally based on Users point of view. This testing is to be carried out only after *System Integration Testing* is completed where both Functional & Non-Functional requirements are verified.

In the integration testing testers are concentrated on finding bugs/defects on integrated modules. But in the ***Software System Testing*** testers are concentrated on finding bugs/defects based on software application behavior, software design and expectation of end user.

Why system testing is important:

(*a*) In Software Development Life Cycle the *System Testing* is perform as the first level of testing where the System is tested as a whole.

(*b*) In this step of testing check if system meets functional requirement or not.

(*c*) *System Testing* enables you to test, validate and verify both the Application Architecture and Business requirements.

(*d*) The application/System is tested in an environment that particularly resembles the effective production environment where the application/software will be lastly deployed.

Generally, a separate and dedicated team is responsible for **system testing**. And, *System Testing* is performed on staging server which is similar to production server. So this means you are testing software application as good as production environment.

In Software System Testing following steps needs to be executed:

Step 1: First & important step is preparation of *System Test Plan*:

The what all points to be cover in **System Test** plan may vary from organization to organization as well as based on project plan, test strategy & main test plan. Nevertheless, here is list of standard point to be considered while creating *System Test Plan*:

- Goals & Objective
- Scope
- Critical areas Area to focus
- Test Deliverable
- Testing Strategy for System testing
- Testing Schedule
- Entry and exit criteria
- Suspension & resumption criteria for system testing
- Test Environment
- Roles and Responsibilities
- Glossary

Step 2: Second step is to creation Test Cases:

It is very much similar functional test case writing. In test case writing you should write the test scenarios & use cases.

Here you should consider different type of testing like Functional testing, Regression testing, Smoke testing, Sanity testing, Ad-hoc testing, Exploratory testing, Usability testing, GUI software testing, Compatibility testing, Performance testing, Load testing, Stress testing, Volume testing, Error handling testing, Scalability testing, Security testing, Capacity testing, Installation testing, Recovery testing, Reliability testing, Accessibility testing etc.

While writing test case you need to check that test cases are covering all functional, non-functional, technical & UI requirements or not.

Sample Test Case Format:

Test Case ID	Test Suite Name	How to Test?	Test Data	Expected Result	Actual Result	Pass/ Fail

Step 3: Creation of test data which used for System testing.

Step 4: Automated test case execution.

Step 5: Execution of normal test case & update test case if using any test management tool (if any).

Step 6: Bug Reporting, Bug verification & Regression testing.

Step 7: Repeat testing life cycle (if required).

11.5 TYPES OF SYSTEM TESTING

1. **Accessibility Testing:** Type of testing which determines the usability of a product to the people having disabilities (deaf, blind, mentally disabled, etc.). The evaluation process should be conducted by persons with disabilities.
2. **Active Testing:** Type of testing consisting in introducing test data and analyzing the execution results. This testing process is usually conducted by the testing teams.
3. **Agile Testing:** A software testing practice that follows the principles of the agile manifesto, emphasizing testing from the perspective of customers who will utilize the system. This type of testing is usually performed by QA teams.
4. **Age Testing:** Type of testing which evaluates a system's ability to perform in the future. The evaluation process is conducted by testing teams.
5. **Ad-hoc Testing:** Testing performed without planning and documentation—the tester tries to 'break' the system by randomly trying the system's functionality. This testing process is performed by testing teams.
6. **Alpha Testing:** Type of testing a software product or system conducted at the developer's site. This testing process is usually performed by the end user.
7. **Assertion Testing:** Type of testing consisting in verifying if the conditions confirm the product requirements. This type of testing is performed by the testing teams.
8. **API Testing:** Testing technique similar to unit testing in that it targets the code level. API testing differs from unit testing in that it is typically a QA task and not a developer task.
9. **All-pairs Testing:** Combinatorial testing method that tests all possible discrete combinations of input parameters. This testing process is usually performed by the testing teams.
10. **Automated Testing:** Testing technique that uses automation testing tools to control the environment set-up, test execution and results reporting. This testing process is performed by a computer and is used inside the testing teams.
11. **Backward Compatibility Testing:** A testing method which verifies the behavior of the developed software with older versions of the test environment. This testing process is performed by testing teams.
12. **Beta Testing:** Final testing before releasing application for commercial purpose. This testing process is typically done by end-users or others.
13. **Benchmark Testing:** Testing technique that uses representative sets of programs and data designed to evaluate the performance of computer hardware and software in a given configuration. This testing process is performed by testing teams.
14. **Binary Portability Testing:** Technique that tests an executable application for portability across system platforms and environments, usually for conformation to an ABI specification. This testing process is performed by the testing teams.
15. **Branch Testing:** Testing technique in which all branches in the program source code are tested at least once. This is done by the developer.
16. **Breadth Testing:** A test suite that exercises the full functionality of a product but does not test features in detail. This testing process is performed by testing teams.

17. **Code-driven Testing:** Testing technique that uses testing frameworks (such as x Unit) that allow the execution of unit tests to determine whether various sections of the code are acting as expected under various circumstances. This testing process is performed by the development teams.
18. **Compatibility Testing:** Testing technique that validates how well a software performs in a particular hardware/software/operating system/network environment. This testing process is performed by the testing teams.
19. **Comparison Testing:** Testing technique which compares the product strengths and weaknesses with previous versions or other similar products. Can be performed by tester, developers, product managers or product owners.
20. **Component Testing:** Testing technique similar to unit testing but with a higher level of integration—testing is done in the context of the application instead of just directly testing a specific method. Can be performed by testing or development teams.
21. **Configuration Testing:** A testing technique which determines minimal and optimal configuration of hardware and software and the effect of adding or modifying resources such as memory, disk drives and CPU. This testing process is performed by the performance testing engineers.
22. **Condition Coverage Testing:** Type of software testing where each condition is executed by making it true and false, in each of the ways at least once. This testing process is typically made by the automation testing teams.
23. **Compliance Testing:** Type of testing which checks whether the system was developed in accordance with standards, procedures and guidelines. This testing process is usually performed by external companies which offer "Certified OGC Compliant" brand.
24. **Concurrency Testing:** Multi-user testing geared towards determining the effects of accessing the same application code, module or database records. This testing process is usually done by performance engineers.
25. **Conformance Testing:** The process of testing that an implementation conforms to the specification on which it is based. This testing process is usually performed by testing teams.
26. **Context Driven Testing:** An Agile Testing technique that advocates continuous and creative evaluation of testing opportunities in light of the potential information revealed and the value of that information to the organization at a specific moment. This testing process is usually performed by Agile testing teams.
27. **Conversion Testing:** Testing of programs or procedures used to convert data from existing systems for use in replacement systems. This testing process is usually performed by the QA teams.
28. **Decision Coverage Testing:** Type of software testing where each condition/decision is executed by setting it on true/false. This testing process is typically made by the automation testing teams.
29. **Destructive Testing:** Type of testing in which the tests are carried out to the specimen's failure, in order to understand a specimen's structural performance or

material behavior under different loads. This testing process is usually performed by QA teams.

30. **Dependency Testing:** Testing type which examines an application's requirements for pre-existing software, initial states and configuration in order to maintain proper functionality. It is usually performed by testing teams.
31. **Domain Testing:** White box testing technique which contains checks that the program accepts only valid input. This testing process is usually done by software development teams and occasionally by automation testing teams.
32. **Error-Handling Testing:** Software testing type which determines the ability of the system to properly process erroneous transactions. This testing process is usually performed by the testing teams.
33. **End-to-end Testing:** Similar to system testing, involves testing of a complete application environment in a situation that mimics real-world use, such as interacting with a database, using network communications, or interacting with other hardware, applications, or systems if appropriate. This testing process is performed by QA teams.
34. **Endurance Testing:** Type of testing which checks for memory leaks or other problems that may occur with prolonged execution. This testing process is usually performed by performance engineers.
35. **Exploratory Testing:** Black box testing technique performed without planning and documentation. This testing process is usually performed by manual testers.
36. **Fault Injection Testing:** Element of a comprehensive test strategy that enables the tester to concentrate on the manner in which the application under test is able to handle exceptions. This testing process is performed by QA teams.
37. **Formal Verification Testing:** The act of proving or disproving the correctness of intended algorithms underlying a system with respect to a certain formal specification or property, using formal methods of mathematics. This testing process is usually performed by QA teams.
38. **Fuzz Testing:** Software testing technique that provides invalid, unexpected, or random data to the inputs of a program—a special area of mutation testing. Fuzz testing is performed by testing teams.
39. **Gorilla Testing:** Software testing technique which focuses on heavily testing of one particular module. This testing process is performed by quality assurance teams, usually when running full testing.
40. **GUI Software Testing:** The process of testing a product that uses a graphical user interface, to ensure it meets its written specifications. This is normally done by the testing teams.
41. **Globalization Testing:** Testing method that checks proper functionality of the product with any of the culture/locale settings using every type of international input possible. This testing process is performed by the testing team.
42. **Install/uninstall Testing:** Quality assurance work that focuses on what customers will need to do to install and set up the new software successfully. It may involve

full, partial or upgrades install/uninstall processes and is typically done by a software testing engineer in conjunction with the configuration manager.

43. **Internationalization Testing:** The process which ensures that product's functionality is not broken and all the messages are properly externalized when used in different languages and locale. This testing process is usually performed by the testing teams.

44. **Inter-systems Testing:** Testing technique that focuses on testing the application to ensure that interconnection between application functions correctly. This testing process is usually done by the testing teams.

45. **Keyword-driven Testing:** Also known as table-driven testing or action-word testing, is a software testing methodology for automated testing that separates the test creation process into two distinct stages: a Planning Stage and an Implementation Stage. It can be used by either manual or automation testing teams.

46. **Load Testing:** Testing technique that puts demand on a system or device and measures its response. It is usually conducted by the performance engineers.

47. **Localization Testing:** Part of software testing process focused on adapting a globalized application to a particular culture/locale. This testing process is normally done by the testing teams.

48. **Loop Testing:** A white box testing technique that exercises program loops. This testing process is performed by the development teams.

49. **Manual Scripted Testing:** Testing method in which the test cases are designed and reviewed by the team before executing it. It is done by manual testing teams.

50. **Manual-support Testing:** Testing technique that involves testing of all the functions performed by the people while preparing the data and using these data from automated system. This testing process is conducted by testing teams.

51. **Model-based Testing:** The application of Model based design for designing and executing the necessary artifacts to perform software testing. This testing process is usually performed by testing teams.

52. **Mutation Testing:** Method of software testing which involves modifying programs' source code or byte code in small ways in order to test sections of the code that are seldom or never accessed during normal tests execution. This testing process is normally conducted by testers.

53. **Modularity-driven Testing:** A software testing technique which requires the creation of small, independent scripts that represent modules, sections and functions of the application under test. This testing process is usually performed by the testing team.

54. **Non-functional Testing:** Testing technique which focuses on testing of a software application for its non-functional requirements. Can be conducted by the performance engineers or by manual testing teams.

55. **Negative Testing:** Also known as "test to fail"—testing method where the tests' aim is showing that a component or system does not work. This testing process is performed by manual or automation testers.

56. **Operational Testing:** Testing technique conducted to evaluate a system or component in its operational environment. This testing process is performed by testing teams.

57. **Orthogonal Array Testing:** Systematic, statistical way of testing which can be applied in user interface testing, system testing, regression testing, configuration testing and performance testing. This testing process is performed by the testing team.
58. **Pair Testing:** Software development technique in which two team members work together at one keyboard to test the software application. One does the testing and the other analyzes or reviews the testing. This can be done between one Tester and Developer or Business Analyst or between two testers with both participants taking turns at driving the keyboard.
59. **Passive Testing:** Testing technique consisting in monitoring the results of a running system without introducing any special test data. This testing process is performed by the testing team.
60. **Parallel Testing:** A testing technique which has the purpose to ensure that a new application which has replaced its older version has been installed and is running correctly. This testing process is conducted by the testing team.
61. **Penetration Testing:** A testing method which evaluates the security of a computer system or network by simulating an attack from a malicious source. This testing process is conducted by specialized penetration testing companies.
62. **Performance Testing:** Functional testing conducted to evaluate the compliance of a system or component with specified performance requirements. This testing process is usually conducted by the performance engineer.
63. **Qualification Testing:** Testing against the specifications of the previous release, usually conducted by the developer for the consumer, to demonstrate that the software meets its specified requirements.
64. **Ramp Testing:** Type of testing consisting in raising an input signal continuously until the system breaks down. This testing process may be conducted by the testing team or the performance engineer.
65. **Recovery Testing:** Testing technique which evaluates how well a system recovers from crashes, hardware failures, or other catastrophic problems. This testing process is performed by the testing teams.
66. **Requirements Testing:** Testing technique which validates that the requirements are correct, complete, unambiguous and logically consistent and allows designing a necessary and sufficient set of test cases from those requirements. This testing process is performed by QA teams.
67. **Security Testing:** A process to determine that an information system protects data and maintains functionality as intended. It can be performed by testing teams or by specialized security-testing companies.
68. **Sanity Testing:** A testing technique which determines if a new software version is performing well enough to accept it for a major testing effort. This testing process is performed by the testing teams.
69. **Scenario Testing:** Testing activity that uses scenarios based on a hypothetical story to help a person think through a complex problem or system for a testing environment. This testing process is performed by the testing teams.

70. **Scalability Testing:** Part of the battery of non-functional tests which tests a software application for measuring its capability to scale up—be it the user load supported, the number of transactions, the data volume, etc. This testing process is conducted by the performance engineer.
71. **Statement Testing:** A white box testing which satisfies the criterion that each statement in a program is executed at least once during program testing. It is usually performed by the development team.
72. **Stability Testing:** Testing technique which attempts to determine if an application will crash. This testing process is usually conducted by the performance engineer.
73. **Smoke Testing:** Testing technique which examines all the basic components of a software system to ensure that they work properly. Typically, smoke testing is conducted by the testing team, immediately after a software build is made.
74. **Storage Testing:** Testing type that verifies the program under test stores data files in the correct directories and that it reserves sufficient space to prevent unexpected termination resulting from lack of space. This testing process is usually performed by the testing team.
75. **Stress Testing:** A testing technique which evaluates a system or component at or beyond the limits of its specified requirements. This testing process is usually conducted by the performance engineer.
76. **Thread Testing:** A variation of top-down testing technique where the progressive integration of components follows the implementation of subsets of the requirements. This testing process is usually performed by the testing teams.
77. **Upgrade Testing:** Testing technique that verifies if assets created with older versions can be used properly and that user's learning is not challenged. This testing process is performed by the testing teams.
78. **User Interface Testing:** A type of testing which is performed to check how user-friendly the application is. This testing process is performed by testing teams.
79. **Usability Testing:** Testing technique which verifies the ease with which a user can learn to operate, prepare inputs for and interpret outputs of a system or component. This testing process is usually performed by end users.
80. **Volume Testing:** Testing which confirms that any values that may become large over time (such as accumulated counts, logs and data files), can be accommodated by the program and will not cause the program to stop working or degrade its operation in any manner. This testing process is usually conducted by the performance engineer.
81. **Vulnerability Testing:** A type of testing which regards application security and has the purpose to prevent problems which may affect the application integrity and stability. This testing process can be performed by the internal testing teams or outsourced to specialized companies.
82. **Workflow Testing:** A scripted end-to-end testing technique which duplicates specific workflows which are expected to be utilized by the end-user. This testing process is usually conducted by testing teams.

11.6 ACCEPTANCE TESTING

Acceptance Testing is a level of the software testing process where a system is tested for acceptability.

The purpose of this test is to evaluate the system's compliance with the business requirements and assess whether it is acceptable for delivery.

Acceptance tests are different from Unit Tests in that Unit Tests are modeled and written by the developer of each class, while the acceptance test is at least modeled and possibly even written by the customer. Hence the even-newer name, Customer Test.

The customer specifies scenarios to test when a user story has been correctly implemented. A story can have one or many acceptance tests, whatever it takes to ensure the functionality works.

Acceptance tests are black box system tests. Each acceptance test represents some expected result from the system. Customers are responsible for verifying the correctness of the acceptance tests and reviewing test scores to decide which failed tests are of highest priority. Acceptance tests are also used as regression tests prior to a production release.

Acceptance tests should be automated so they can be run often. The acceptance test score is published to the team. It is the team's responsibility to schedule time each iteration to fix any failed tests.

The name acceptance tests was changed from functional tests. This better reflects the intent, which is to guarantee that customers requirement have been met and the system is acceptable.

11.7 FUNCTIONAL TESTING

Due to its nature, functional testing is often called black box testing. The basic for deciding test cases in functional testing is the requirements or specifications of the system or module.

Black box testing involves looking at the specifications and does not require examining the code of a program. Black box testing is done from the customer's viewpoint. The test engineer engaged in black box testing only knows the set of inputs and expected outputs and is unaware of how those inputs are transformed into outputs by the software.

Black box testing is done without the knowledge of the internals of the system under test (see Fig. 11.5).

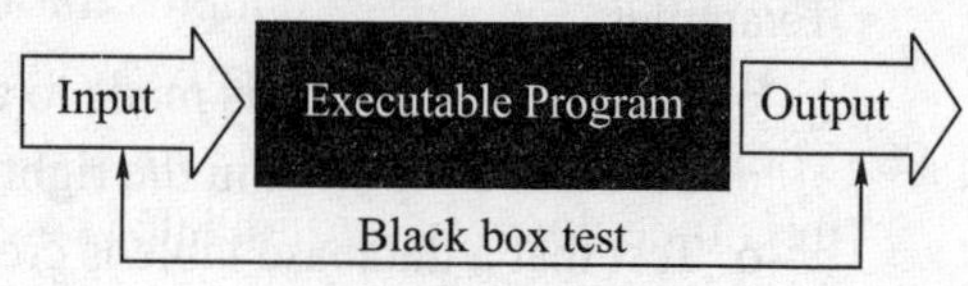

Fig. 11.5

11.8 WHY BLACK BOX TESTING?

Black box testing helps in the overall functionality verification of the system under test.

Black box testing is done based on requirements. It helps in identifying any incomplete, inconsistent requirement as well as any issues involved when the system is tested as a complete entity.

11.8.1 When to do Black Box Testing?

Black box testing activities require involvement of the testing team from the beginning of the software project life cycle, regardless of the software development life cycle model chosen for the project.

Testers can get involved right from the requirements gathering and analysis phase for the system under test. Test scenarios and test data are prepared during the test construction phase of the test life cycle, when the software is in the design phase.

11.8.1.1 *Types of Testing Criteria for Functional Requirements*

Demonstration:

- Demonstrate the operation of the function to the system owner to show that the requirement has been met.

Inspection:

- Sometimes used in combination with demonstration, it requires visual examination of the code documentation, table dumps, scans, etc.

Analysis/Special Qualification: The processing of accumulated data obtained from other methods, or any special tools, techniques, procedures, facilities and acceptable limits. This type of testing usually affects critical parts of the system and/or interfaces.

Demonstration:

- Demonstrate the operation of the function to the system owner to show that the requirement has been met.
- Examples:
  - o Test that a screen navigates to the correct next screen
  - o Test that a field is displayed
  - o Test that an inquiry can be made on a database.

Inspection:

- Sometimes used in combination with demonstration, it requires visual examination of the code documentation, table dumps, scans, etc.
- Examples:
  - o Test that an update is made to a database
  - o Test that a report is in the right format
  - o Test that a database table is created

Analysis/Special Qualification: The processing of accumulated data obtained from other methods, or any special tools, techniques, procedures, facilities and acceptable limits. This type of testing usually affects critical parts of the system and/or interfaces.

Black-box testing includes the following testing approaches:

- Equivalence Partitioning
- Boundary Value Analysis
- Decision Table Testing
- Error Guessing
- State Transition Testing

11.8.1.2 *Equivalence Partitioning*

Equivalence Partitioning is based on evaluation of business functions by evaluating the input and/or output data that falls into categories where the system responds in a similar manner.

To keep down our testing costs, we don't want to write several test cases that test the same aspect of our program. A good test case uncovers a different class of errors (*e.g.*, incorrect processing of all character data) than has been uncovered by prior test cases. Equivalence partitioning is a strategy that can be used to reduce the number of test cases that need to be developed. Equivalence partitioning divides the input domain of a program into classes. For each of these equivalence classes, the set of data should be treated the same by the module under test and should produce the same answer. Test cases should be designed so the inputs lie within these equivalence classes. For example, for tests of "Go to Jail" the most important thing is whether the player has enough money to pay the $50 fine.

Equivalence Partitioning Process:

Look at functions that require input

Select input and output data that is representative of all other data that would likely invoke the same process for that particular condition.

These should include:

- o All valid input/output data for a given condition
- o All invalid input/output data

Example: If a business rule stated that discounts were given to senior citizens (over 62) of 5%.

We would have test cases such as

One person over 62

(all others over in this equivalence class)

One person under 62

(all others over in this equivalence class)

11.8.1.3 *Boundary Value Analysis*

The purpose of boundary value testing is to evaluated a functions based on the boundaries of conditions. *Boundary value is defined as a data value that corresponds to a minimum or maximum input, internal, or output value specified for a system or component*. In an example, the boundary of the class is at 50, We should create test cases for the Player 1 having $49, $50 and $51. These test cases will help to find common off-by-one errors, caused by errors like using > = when you mean to use >.

11.8.1.4 *Decision Table Testing*

Decision tables are used to record complex business rules that must be implemented in the program and therefore tested. A sample decision table is found in table. In the table, the conditions represent possible input conditions. The actions are the events that should trigger, depending upon the makeup of the input conditions. Each column in the table is a unique combination of input conditions (and is called a rule) that result in triggering the action(s) associated with the rule. Each rule (or column) should become a test case.

If a Player (A) lands on property owned by another player (B), A must pay rent to B. If A does not have enough money to pay B, A is out of the game.

	Rule 1	*Rule 2*	*Rule 3*
Conditions			
A lands of B's property	Yes	Yes	No
A has enough money to pay rent	Yes	No	—
Actions			
A stays in game	Yes	No	Yes

11.8.1.5 *Error Guessing*

The purpose of error guessing is to focus the testing activity on areas that have not been handled by the other more formal techniques, such as equivalence partitioning and boundary value analysis. Error guessing is the process of making an educated guess as to other types of areas to be tested. Examples of areas where error guessing might be used:

- initialization of data,
- wrong kind of data (*e.g.*, negative numbers, non-numeric versus numeric),
- restart/recovery and
- proper handling of concurrent processes.

11.8.1.6 *State Transition Testing*

State transition testing focuses on the testing of transitions from one state (*e.g.*, open, closed) of an object (*e.g.*, an account) to another state. A good technique to test screen navigation.

11.8.2 Structural Testing

Also known as *glass box*, *structural*, *clear box* and *open box testing*. Software testing technique, whereby explicit knowledge of the internal workings of the item being tested are used to select the test data.

Structural testing techniques are systematic procedures that help testers design effective tests more efficiently when analyzing the program's source code to improve code coverage. But we would never advocate structural testing as the initial or the only approach to testing software. Structural testing techniques are designed to support and enhance other testing approaches and methods. Structural testing can also provide more in-depth information and reduce risk exposure by designing and executing tests to evaluate paths through the code that were not traversed by other testing approaches. This is important because logic errors are inversely relational to a path's probability of execution. If we don't execute a path through code, we must assume 100 per cent risk. If we execute that path, our risk is reduced by some per centage and the more we successfully traverse a path through code, especially with different data, the more we reduce our overall exposure to risk.

Behavioral testing approaches, systematic functional testing methods and structural testing methods are each intended to provide different types of information and evaluate the software from different perspectives. Complex problems require a plethora of perspectives to provide the qualified information the decision makers require to better assess risk and make informed business decisions. Structural testing simply provides a different perspective to a complex problem. But structural testing is an organizational investment. This level of testing costs more in terms of time and skills needed by testers to design white box structural tests. However, structural testing can prove invaluable in reducing long-term costs and minimizing risk for highly critical or complex systems that require a high degree of reliability.

- Structural testing methods are very amenable to:
    - o Rigorous definitions
- Data flow, control flow, objectives, coverage criteria, relation to programming language semantics:
    - o Mathematical analysis
- Graphs, path analysis:
    - o Precise measurement
- Metrics, coverage analysis

The best known form of structural testing is based on a construct known as a ***decision-to-decision path***.

A DD-Path is a *chains* obtained from a program graph, where a chain is a path in which the initial and terminal nodes are distinct and every interior node has indegree = 1 and outdegree = 1. We show in the next slide on selecting the nodes from a program graph to form a DD-Path chain. DD-Paths are used to create *DD-Path Graphs*.

Note that the initial node is 2-connected to every other node in the chain and there are no instances of 1- or 3-connected nodes.

An example of a chain is shown in Fig. 11.6:

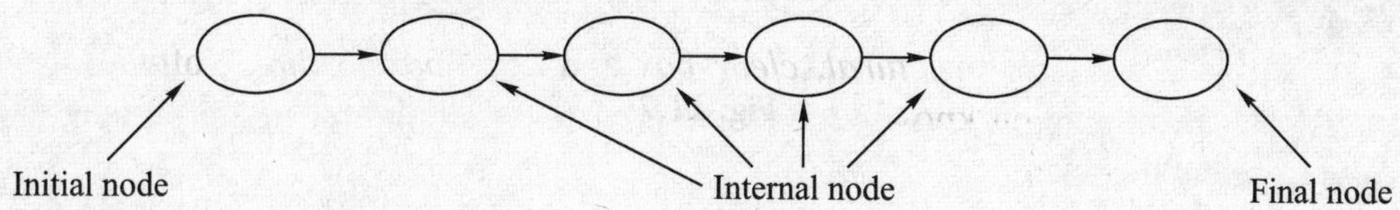

Fig. 11.6

More formally a DD-Path is a chain obtained from a program graph such that:

- Case 1: it consists of a single node with indeg = 0.
- Case 2: it consists of a single node with outdeg = 0.
- Case 3: it consists of a single node with indeg ≥ 2 or outdeg ≥ 2.
- Case 4: it consists of a single node with indeg = 1 and outdeg = 1.
- Case 5: it is a maximal chain of length ≥ 1.

DD-Path Formation—Example:

Program Graph Nodes	*DD-Path Name*	*Case #*
4	first	1
5–8	A	5

Program Graph Nodes	*DD-Path Name*	*Case #*
9	B	4
10	C	4
11	D	3
12–14	E	5
15	F	4
16	G	3
17	H	4
18	I	3
19	J	4
20	K	3
21	L	4
22	last	2

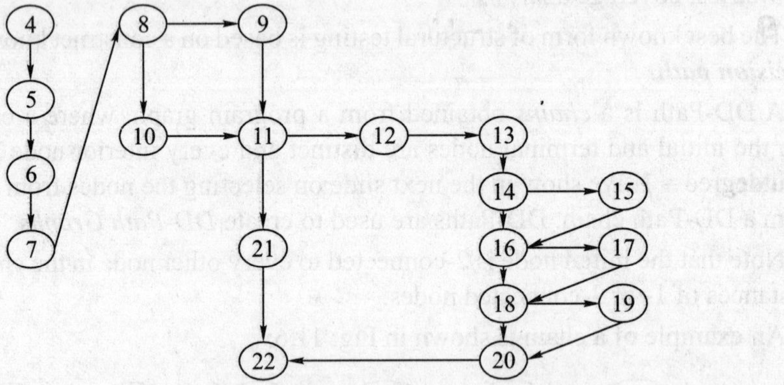

Fig. 11.7

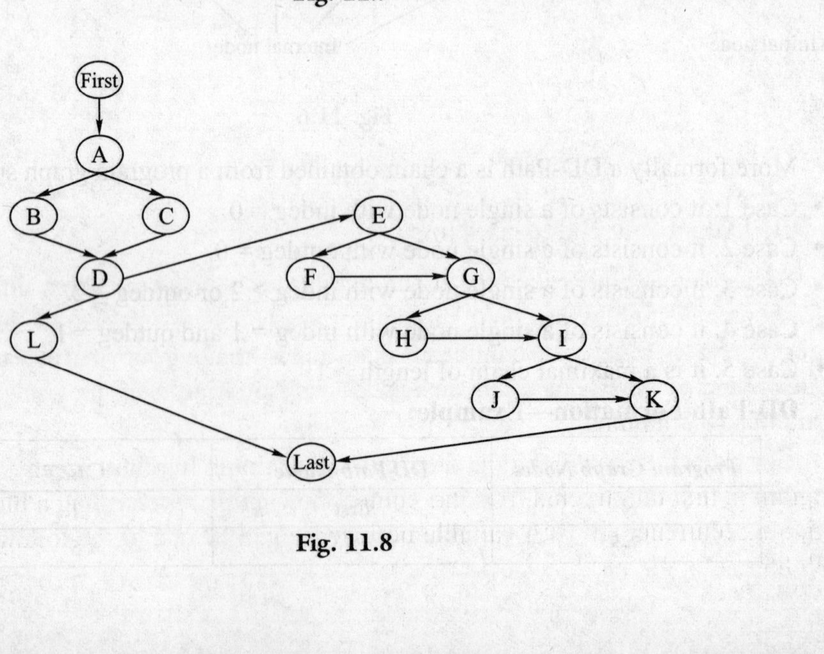

Fig. 11.8

- **Path Testing:** We can apply McCabe's Cyclomatic Complexity metric:
  - o gives an upper bound on number of test cases to ensure edge coverage is satisfied.
  - o in practice, it is usually the "lower bound" of the number of test cases due to the presence of loops.

McCabe Algorithm to Determine Basis Paths

- The algorithm is straightforward:
  - o The method begins with the selection of a "baseline path", which should correspond to a normal execution of a program (from start node to end node and has as many decisions as possible).
  - o The algorithm proceeds by retracing the paths visited and flipping the conditions one at a time.
  - o The process repeats up to the point all flips have been considered.
- The objective is to generate test cases that exercise these "basis" paths.

11.9 FLOW GRAPHS—USE IN DETERMINING PATHS FOR TESTING- REVISITED

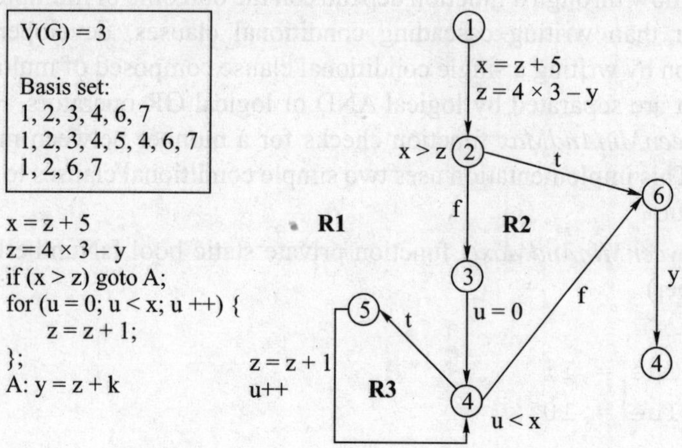

Fig. 11.9 Example of a simple control flowgraph

11.9.1 Data Flow-Based Testing

The basic idea behind data flow based testing is to make sure that during testing the definitions of variables and their subsequent use is tested. Just like the all nodes and all edges criteria try to generate confidence in testing by making sure that at least all statements and all branches have been tested the data flow testing tries to ensure some coverage of the definitions of variables.

For data flow based criteria a definition use graph (de flues graph for short) for the program is first constructed from the control flow graph representing a block of code has variable occurrences in it. A variable occurrence can be one of the following three types (RW 85):

- Def represents the definition of a variable. The variable on the left hand side of an assignment is the one getting defined.
- C-use represents computational use of a variable. Any statement (*e.g.*, read write an assignment) that uses the value of variables for computation purposes is said to be making c-use of the variables. In an assignment statement all variables on the right hand side have a c-use occurrence. In a read and a write statement all variable occurrences are of this type.
- P-use represents predicate use. These are all the occurrences of the variables in a predicate (*i.e.*, variables whose values are used for computing the value of the predicate), which is used for transfer of control.

In control flow based and data flow based testing the focus was on which paths to execute during testing. Mutation testing does not take a path-based approach. Instead it takes the program and creates many mutants of it by making simple changes to the program. The goal of testing is to make sure that during the course of testing each mutant produces an output different from the output of the original program.

11.9.2 Condition Testing

Sometimes control flow through a function depends on the outcome of multiple conditional clauses. But rather than writing cascading conditional clauses, developers can often simplify the function by writing a single conditional clause composed of multiple Boolean subexpressions that are separated by logical AND or logical OR operators. For example, the *IsNumberBetweenMinAndMax* function checks for a number between minimum and maximum values. This implementation uses two simple conditional clauses to return either a true or false output.

IsNumberBetweenMinAndMax() function private static bool IsNumberBetweenMin AndMax (int number)

```
{
int minValue = 1;
int maxValue = 10;

if !(number < minValue)
 {
  if !(number > maxValue)
  {
   return true;
  }
 }
 return false;
}
```

QUESTIONS

1. Define Fault, error, failure, debug and testing.
2. Different between verification and validation.
3. Explain types of testing.
4. What do you mean by regression testing?
5. What are testing strategies?
6. Explain types of system testing.
7. Difference between white box and black box testing.
8. Explain types of functional testing.

CHAPTER

12 An Overview of The UML

12.1 WHAT IS THE UML?

The *Unified Modelling Language*, or the *UML*, is a graphical modelling language that provides us with syntax for describing the major elements (called *artifacts* in the UML) of software systems. In this course, we will explore the main aspects of the UML, and describe how the UML can be applied to software development projects.

Through to its core, UML leans towards object oriented software development, so in this course, we will also explore some of the important principles of object orientation.

In this chapter, we'll look at the origins of the UML, and we'll discuss the need for a common language in the software industry. Then we will start to look at how to exploit the UML on a software project.

12.2 A COMMON LANGUAGE

Other industries have languages and notations, which are understood by every member of that particular field.

$$\int_{0}^{\infty} 1/x^2 dx$$

Fig. 12.1 A Mathematical Integral.

Although the picture above is a fairly simple drawing (a stylised "∫" figure), mathematicians the world over recognize instantly that I am representing an integral. Although this notation is simple, it masks a very deep and complicated topic (though perhaps not as deep as the concept represented by the figure of eight on its side!). So the notation is simple, but the payoff is that mathematicians all around the world can clearly and unambiguously communicate their ideas using this, and a small collection of other symbols. Mathematicians have a *common language*. So do musicians, electronic engineers, and many other disciplines and professions.

To date, Software Engineering has lacked such a notation. Between 1989 and 1994, aperiod referred to as the "method wars", more than 50 software modelling languages were in common use—each of them carrying their own notations! Each language contained syntax peculiar to itself, whilst at the same time, each language had elements which bore striking similarities to the other languages.

To add to the confusion, no one language was complete, in the sense that very few software practitioners found complete satisfaction from a single language!

In the mid 1990's, three methods emerged as the strongest. These three methods had begun to converge, with each containing elements of the other two. Each method had its own particular strengths:

- **Booch** was excellent for design and implementation. Grady Booch had worked extensively with the Ada language, and had been a major player in the development of Object Oriented techniques for the language. Although the Booch method was strong, the notation was less well received (lots of cloud shapes dominated his models—not very pretty!)
- **OMT** (Object Modelling Technique) was best for analysis and data-intensive information systems.
- **OOSE** (Object Oriented Software Engineering) featured a model known as **Use Cases**. Use Cases are a powerful technique for understanding the behaviour of an entire system (an area where OO has traditionally been weak).

In 1994, Jim Rumbaugh, the creator of OMT, stunned the software world when he left General Electric and joined Grady Booch at Rational Corp. The aim of the partnership was to merge their ideas into a single, unified method (the working title for the method was indeed the "Unified Method").

By 1995, the creator of OOSE, Ivar Jacobson, had also joined Rational, and his ideas (particularly the concept of "Use Cases") were fed into the new Unified Method—now called the Unified Modelling Language[1]. The team of Rumbaugh, Booch and Jacobson are affectionately known as the "Three Amigos".

Despite some initial wars and arguments, the new method began to find favour amongst the software industry, and a UML consortium was formed. Heavyweight corporations were part of the consortium, including Hewlett-Packard, Microsoft and Oracle.

The UML was adopted by the OMG[2] in 1997, and since then the OMG have owned and maintained the language. Therefore, the UML is effectively a public, non-proprietary language.

Before we begin to look at the theory of the UML, we are going to take a very brief run through some of the major concepts of the UML.

The first thing to notice about the UML is that there are a lot of different diagrams (models) to get used to. The reason for this is that it is possible to look at a system from many different viewpoints. A software development will have many stakeholders playing a part—for example:

- Analysts
- Designers
- Coders
- Testers
- QA
- The Customer
- Technical Authors

All of these people are interested in different aspects of the system, and each of them requires a different level of detail. For example, a coder needs to understand the design of the system and be able to convert the design to a low level code. By contrast, a technical writer is interested in the behaviour of the system as a whole, and needs to understand how the product functions. The UML attempts to provide a language so expressive that all stakeholders can benefit from at least one UML diagram.

Here's a quick look at some of the most important diagrams. Of course, we will look in detail at each of them as the course progresses:

12.3 THE USE CASE DIAGRAM

A Use Case is a description of the system's behaviour from a user's viewpoint. This diagram is a valuable aid during analysis—developing Use Cases helps us to understand requirements.

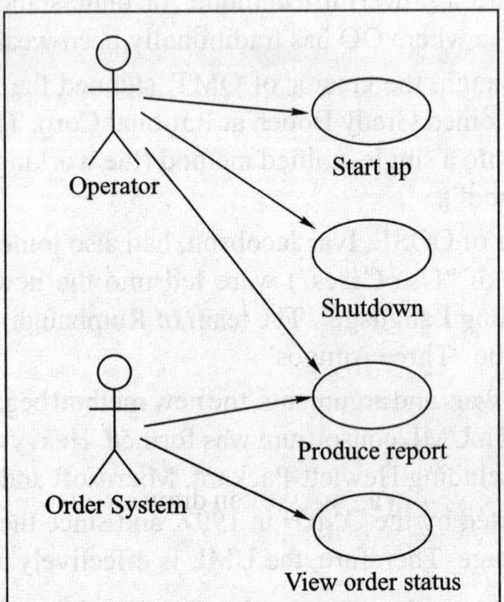

Fig. 12.2 The Use Case Diagram.

The diagram is deliberately simple to understand. This enables both developers (analysts, designers, coders, tests) *and* the customer to work with the diagram.

However, do not be tempted to overlook Use Cases as being "too simple to bother with". We shall see that Use Cases can drive an entire development process, from inception through to delivery.

12.3.1 The Class Diagram

Drawing Class Diagrams is an essential aspect of any Object Oriented Design method, so it isn't surprising that the UML provides us with the appropriate syntax. We'll see that we can use the Class Diagram at the analysis stage as well as design—we'll use the Class Diagram syntax to draw a plan of the major concepts our customer understands (and we'll call this the *Conceptual Model*). Together with Use Cases, a Conceptual Model is a powerful technique in requirements analysis.

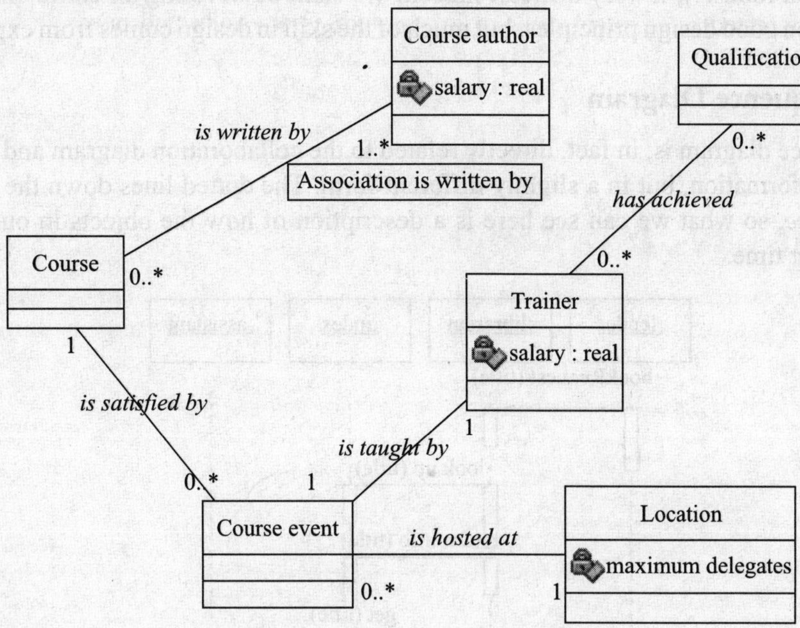

Fig. 12.3 The UML Class Diagram.

12.3.2 Collaboration Diagrams

As we are developing object-oriented software, anything our software needs to do is going to be achieved by objects **collaborating**. We can draw a **collaboration diagram** to describe how we want the objects we build to collaborate.

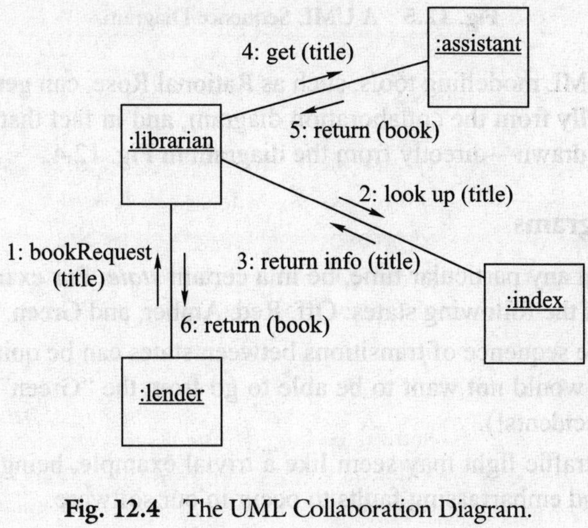

Fig. 12.4 The UML Collaboration Diagram.

Here is a good example of why the UML is "just" syntax rather a true software development process. We will see that the UML notation for the diagram is simple enough, but designing effective collaborations, (that is to say "designing software which is easy to maintain and robust"), is very difficult indeed. We shall be devoting an entire chapter for guidelines on good design principles, but much of the skill in design comes from experience.

12.3.3 Sequence Diagram

The sequence diagram is, in fact, directly related to the collaboration diagram and displays the same information, but in a slightly different form. The dotted lines down the diagram indicate *time*, so what we can see here is a description of how the objects in our system interact over time.

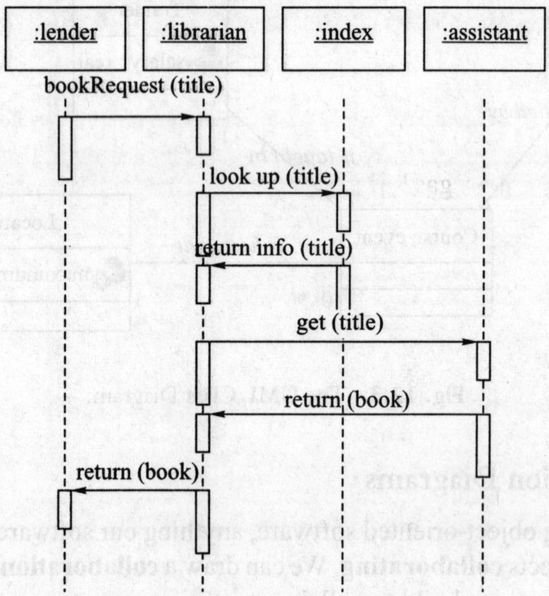

Fig. 12.5 A UML Sequence Diagram.

Some of the UML modelling tools, such as Rational Rose, can generate the sequence diagram automatically from the collaboration diagram, and in fact that is exactly how the diagram above was drawn—directly from the diagram in Fig. 12.4.

12.3.4 State Diagrams

Some objects can, at any particular time, be in a certain *state*. For example, a traffic light can be in any one of the following states: Off, Red, Amber, and Green.

Sometimes, the sequence of transitions between states can be quite complex—in the above example, we would not want to be able to go from the "Green" state to the "Red" state (we'd cause accidents!).

Although the traffic light may seem like a trivial example, being sloppy with states can cause serious and embarrassing faults to occur in our software.

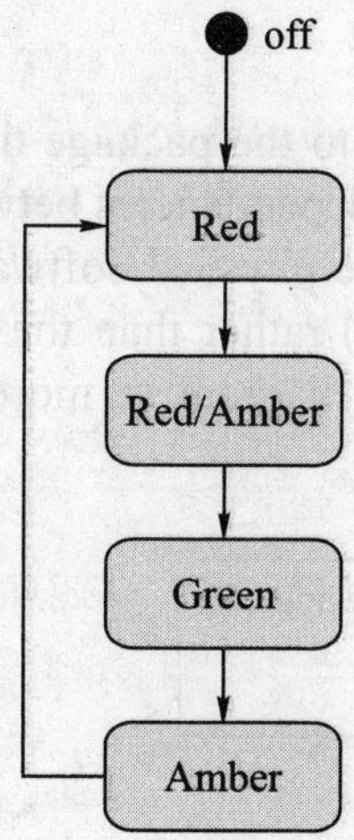

Fig. 12.6 A State Transition Diagram.

Take as a case in point—a gas bill is sent out to a customer who died four years ago—it really happens and it is because a programmer somewhere has not taken care with their state transitions.

As state transitions can be quite complex, the UML provides a syntax to allow us model them.

12.3.5 Package Diagrams

Any non-trivial system needs to be divided up in smaller, easier to understand "chunks", and the UML Package Diagram enables us to model this in a simple and effective way. We'll be looking in detail at this model when we explore large systems in the "System Architecture" chapter.

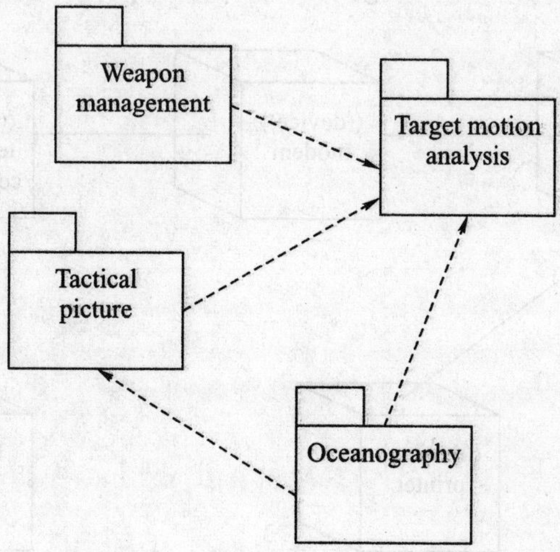

Fig. 12.7 The UML Package Diagram.

12.3.6 Component Diagrams

The Component Diagram is similar to the package diagram—it allows us to notate how our system is split up, and what the dependencies between each module are. However, the Component Diagram emphasizes the physical software components (files, headers, link libraries, executables, and packages) rather than the logical partitioning of the Package Diagram. Again, we'll look at this diagram in more detail in the System Architecture chapter.

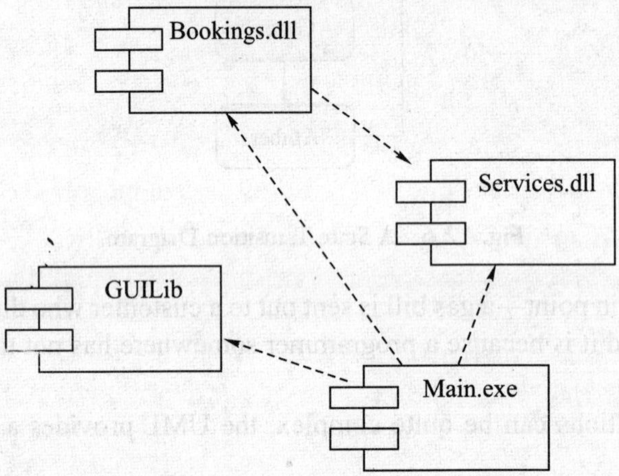

Fig. 12.8 The UML Component Diagram.

12.3.7 Deployment Diagrams

The UML provides a model to allow us to plan how our software is going to be deployed. The diagram shows a simple PC configuration, for example.

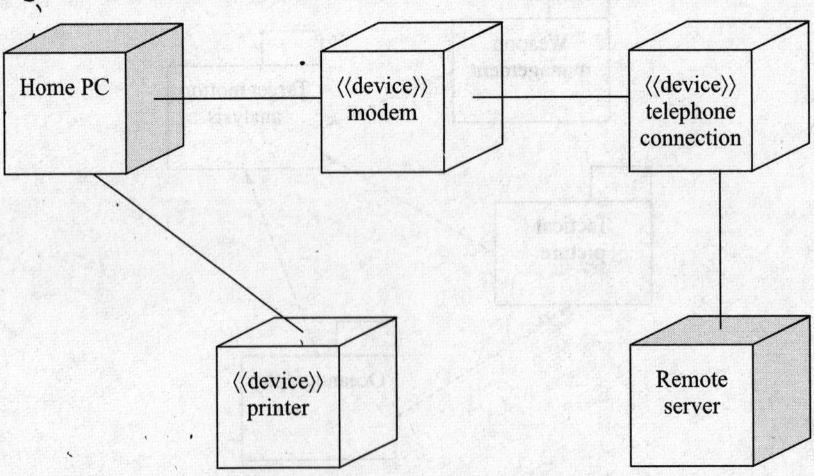

Fig. 12.9 A UML Deployment Diagram.

Summary

The UML provides many different models of a system. The following is a list of them, with a one sentence summary of the purpose of the model:

- **Use Cases**—"How will our system interact with the outside world?"
- **Class Diagram**—"What objects do we need? How will they be related?"
- **Collaboration Diagram**—"How will the objects interact?"
- **Sequence Diagram**—"How will the objects interact?"
- **State Diagram**—"What states should our objects be in?"
- **Package Diagram**—"How are we going to modularize our development?"
- **Component Diagram**—"How will our software components be related?"
- **Deployment Diagram**—"How will the software be deployed?"

CHAPTER 13

UML Notations

UML is popular for its diagrammatic notations. We all know that UML is for visualizing, specifying, constructing and documenting the components of software and non software systems. Here the *Visualization* is the most important part which needs to be understood and remembered by heart.

UML notations are the most important elements in modeling. Efficient and appropriate use of notations is very important for making a complete and meaningful model. The model is useless unless its purpose is depicted properly.

So learning notations should be emphasized from the very beginning. Different notations are available for things and relationships. And the UML diagrams are made using the notations of things and relationships. Extensibility is another important feature which makes UML more powerful and flexible.

The chapter describes the UML Basic Notations in more details. This is just an extension to the UML building block section I have discussed in previous chapter.

13.1 STRUCTURAL THINGS

Graphical notations used in structural things are the most widely used in UML. These are considered as the nouns of UML models. Following are the list of structural things.

- Classes
- Interface
- Collaboration
- Use case
- Active classes
- Components
- Nodes

13.1.1 Class Notation

UML *class* is represented by the diagram as shown Fig. 13.1. The diagram is divided into four parts.

- The top section is used to name the class.
- The second one is used to show the attributes of the class.
- The third section is used to describe the operations performed by the class.
- The fourth section is optional to show any additional components.

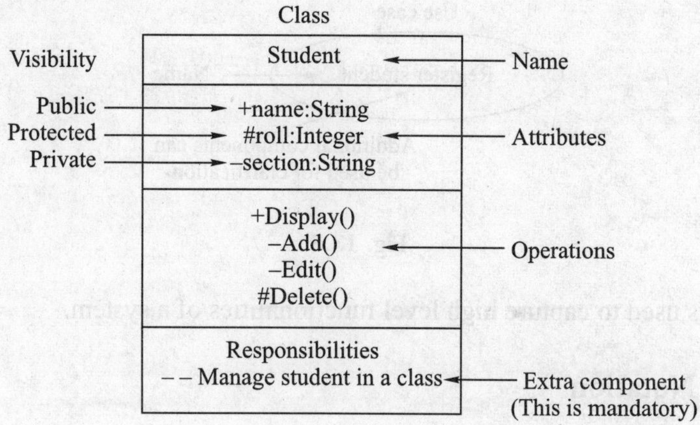

Fig. 13.1

Classes are used to represent objects. Objects can be anything having properties and responsibility.

13.1.2 Object Notation

The *object* is represented in the same way as the class. The only difference is the *name* which is underlined as shown Fig. 13.2.

As object is the actual implementation of a class which is known as the instance of a class. So it has the same usage as the class.

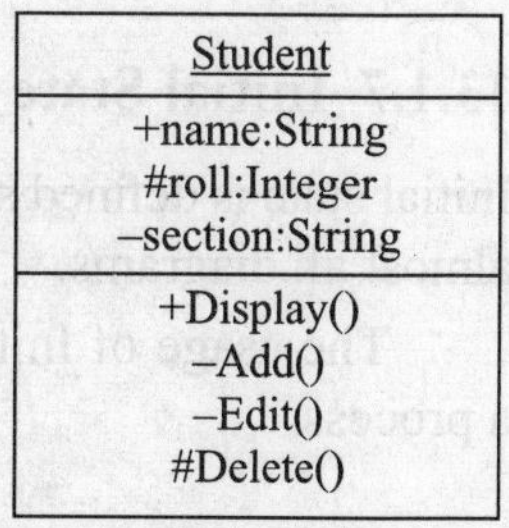

Fig. 13.2

13.1.3 Interface Notation

Interface is represented by a circle as shown Fig. 13.3. It has a name which is generally written below the circle.

Interface is used to describe functionality without implementation. Interface is the just like a template where you define different functions not the implementation. When a class implements the interface it also implements the functionality as per the requirement.

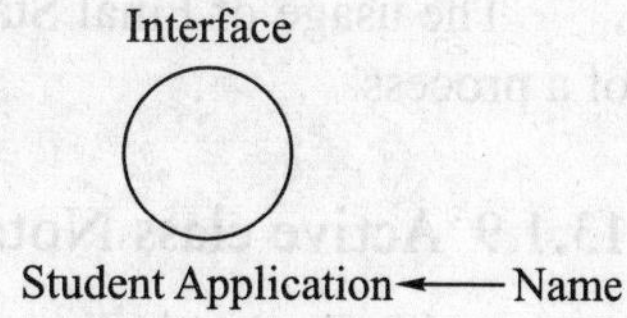

Fig. 13.3

13.1.4 Collaboration Notation

Collaboration is represented by a dotted eclipse as shown Fig. 13.4. It has a name written inside the eclipse.

Collaboration represents responsibilities. Generally responsibilities are in a group.

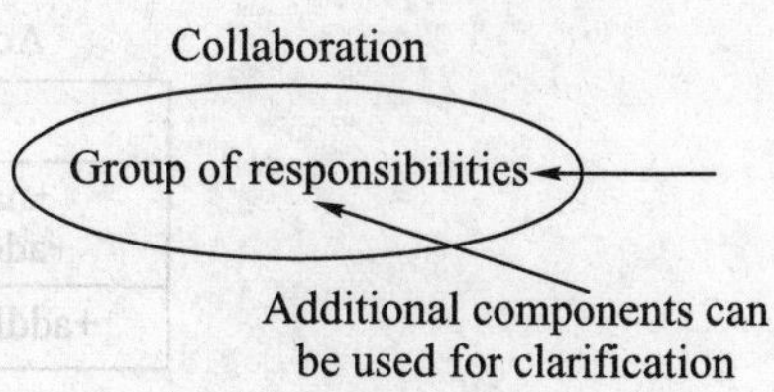

Fig. 13.4

13.1.5 Use case Notation

Use case is represented as an eclipse with a name inside it. It may contain additional responsibilities.

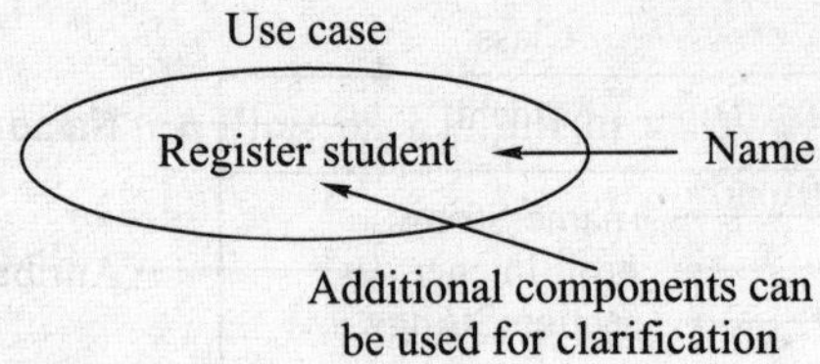

Fig. 13.5

Use case is used to capture high level functionalities of a system.

13.1.6 Actor Notation

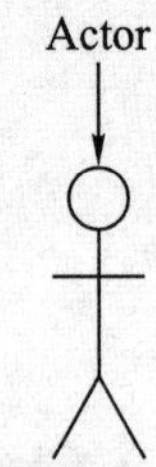

Fig. 13.6

An actor can be defined as some internal or external entity that interacts with the system.

Actor is used in a use case diagram to describe the internal or external entities.

13.1.7 Initial State Notation

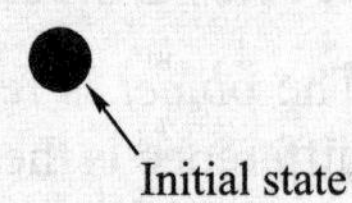

Fig. 13.7

Initial state is defined show the start of a process. This notation is used in almost all diagrams.

The usage of Initial State Notation is to show the starting point of a process.

13.1.8 Final State Notation

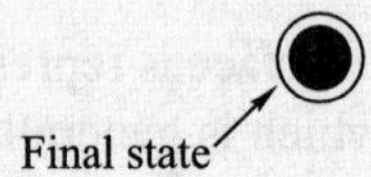

Fig. 13.8

Final state is used to show the end of a process. This notation is also used in almost all diagrams to describe the end.

The usage of Final State Notation is to show the termination point of a process.

13.1.9 Active class Notation

Active class looks similar to a class with a solid border. Active class is generally used to describe concurrent behavior of a system.

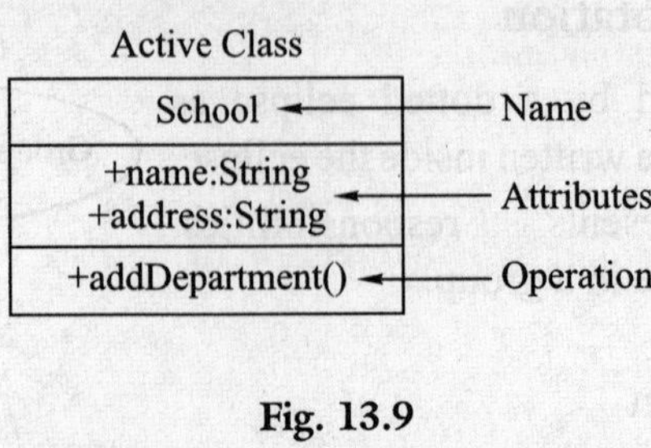

Fig. 13.9

Active class is used to represent concurrency in a system.

13.1.10 Component Notation

A component in UML is shown as in Fig. 13.10 with a name inside. Additional elements can be added wherever required.

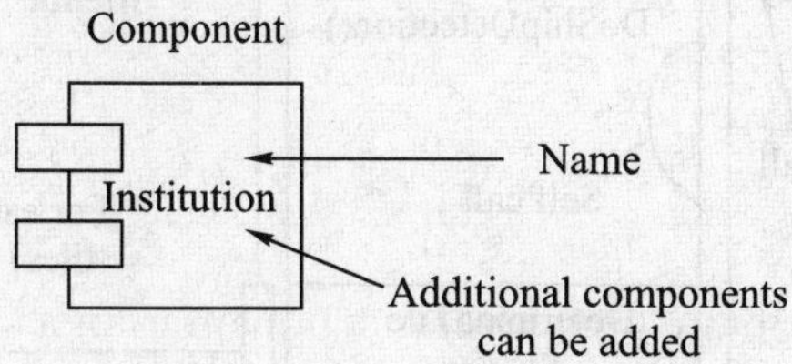

Fig. 13.10

Component is used to represent any part of a system for which UML diagrams are made.

13.1.11 Node Notation

A node in UML is represented by a square box as shown in Fig. 13.11 with a name. A node represents a physical component of the system.

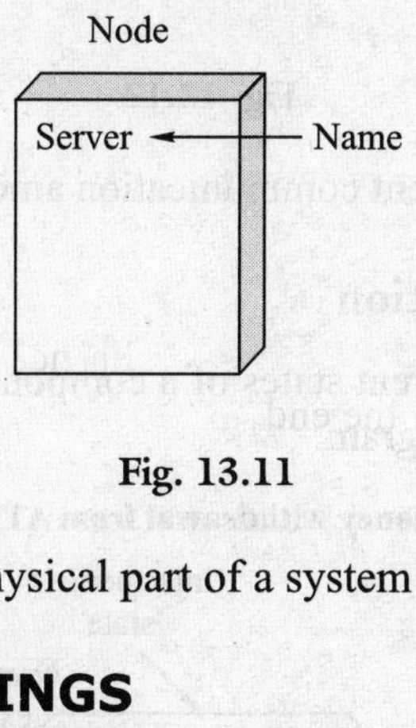

Fig. 13.11

Node is used to represent physical part of a system like server, network etc.

13.2 BEHAVIORAL THINGS

Dynamic parts are one of the most important elements in UML. UML has a set of powerful features to represent the dynamic part of software and non software systems. These features include *interactions* and *state machines*.

Interactions can be of two types:

- Sequential (Represented by sequence diagram)
- Collaborative (Represented by collaboration diagram)

13.2.1 Interaction Notation

Interaction is basically message exchange between two UML components. The following diagram represents different notations used in an interaction.

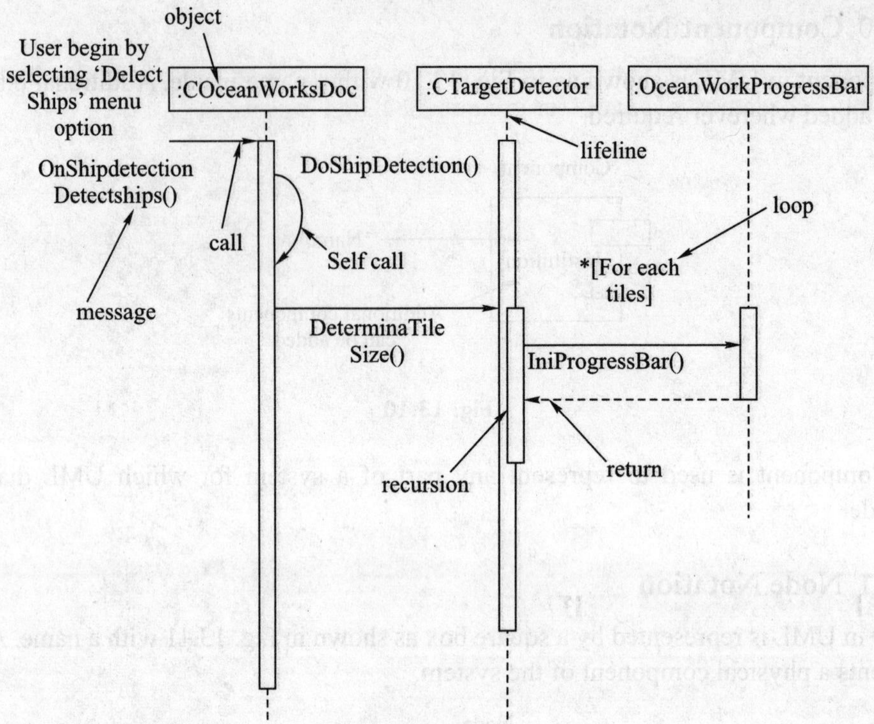

Fig. 13.12

Interaction is used to represent communication among the components of a system.

13.2.2 State Machine Notation

State machine describes the different states of a component in its life cycle. The notations are described in the following diagram.

Money withdrawal from ATM

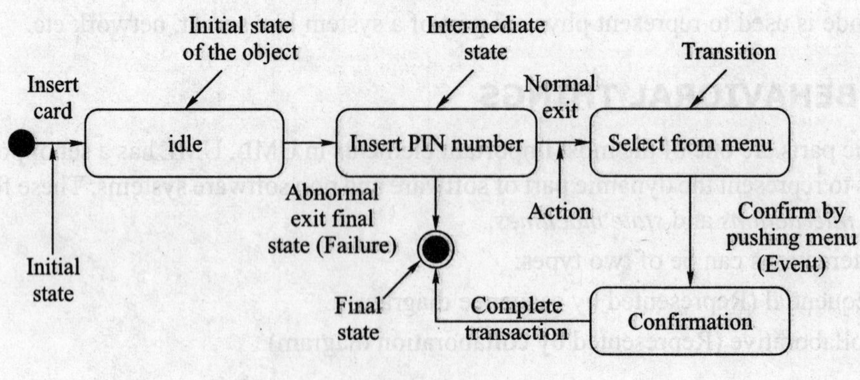

Fig. 13.13

State machine is used to describe different states of a system component. The state can be active, idle or any other depending upon the situation.

13.3 GROUPING THINGS

Organizing the UML models are one of the most important aspects of the design. In UML there is only one element available for grouping and that is package.

13.3.1 Package Notation

Package notation is shown as in Fig. 13.14 and this is used to wrap the components of a system.

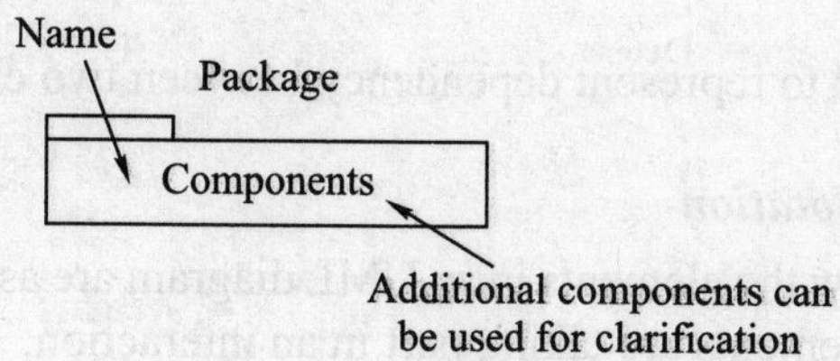

Fig. 13.14

13.4 ANOTATIONAL THINGS

In any diagram explanation of different elements and their functionalities are very important. So UML has notes notation to support this requirement.

13.4.1 Note Notation

This notation is shown as in Fig. 13.15 and they are used to provide necessary information of a system.

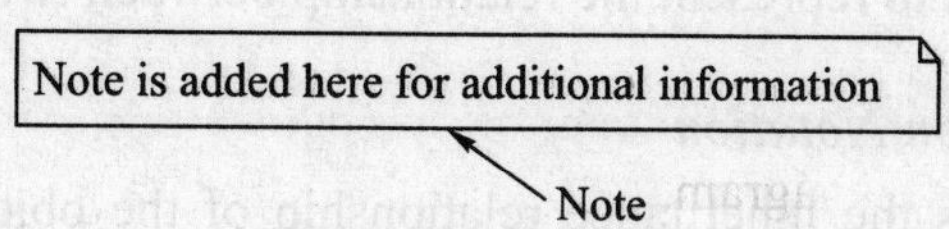

Fig. 13.15

13.4.2 Relationships

A model is not complete unless the relationships between elements are described properly. The *Relationship* gives a proper meaning to an UML model. Following are the different types of relationships available in UML.

- Dependency
- Association
- Generalization
- Extensibility

13.4.2.1 *Dependency Notation*

Dependency is an important aspect in UML elements. It describes the dependent elements and the direction of dependency.

Dependency is represented by a dotted arrow as shown in Fig. 13.16. The arrow head represents the independent element and the other end the dependent element.

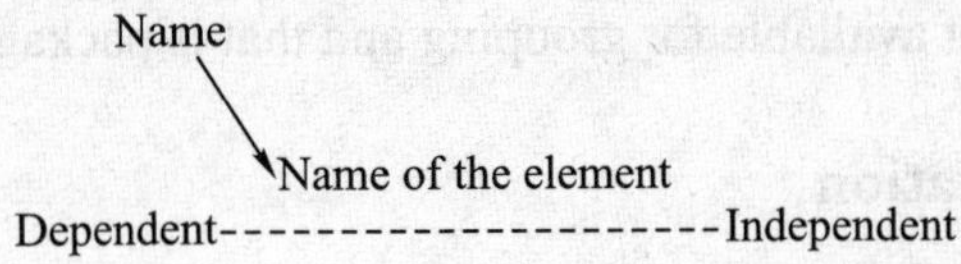

Fig. 13.16

Dependency is used to represent dependency between two elements of a system.

13.4.2.2 *Association Notation*

Association describes how the elements in an UML diagram are associated. In simple word it describes how many elements are taking part in an interaction.

Association is represented by a dotted line with (without) arrows on both sides. The two ends represent two associated elements as shown in Fig. 13.17. The multiplicity is also mentioned at the ends (1, * etc) to show how many objects are associated.

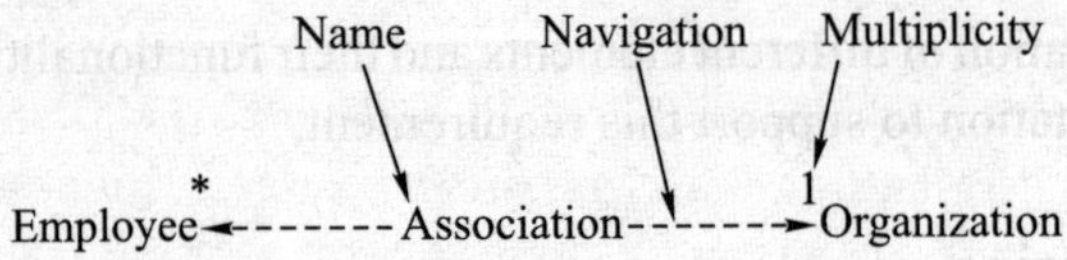

Fig. 13.17

Association is used to represent the relationship between two elements of a system.

13.4.2.3 *Generalization Notation*

Generalization describes the inheritance relationship of the object oriented world. It is parent and child relationship. Generalization is represented by an arrow with hollow arrow head as shown in Fig. 13.18. One end represents the parent element and the other end child element.

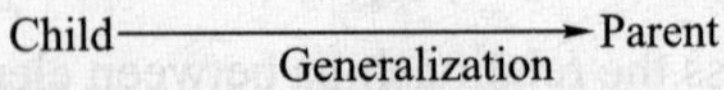

Fig. 13.18

Generalization is used to describe parent-child relationship of two elements of a system.

13.4.2.4 *Extensibility Notation*

All the languages (programming or modeling) have some mechanism to extend its capabilities like syntax, semantics etc. UML is also having the following mechanisms to provide extensibility features:

- Stereotypes (Represents new elements)

- Tagged values (Represents new attributes)
- Constraints (Represents the boundaries)

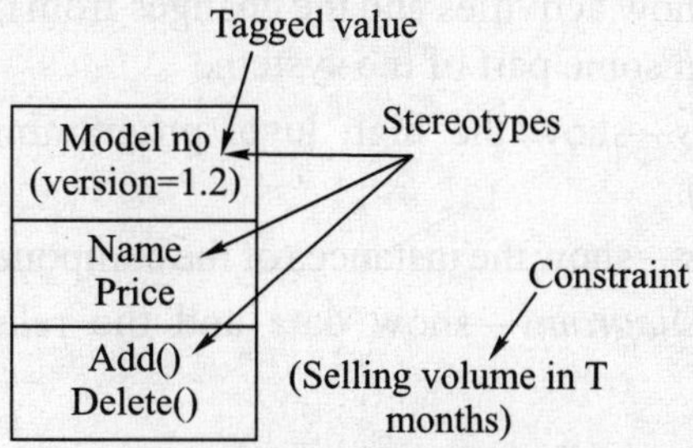

Fig. 13.19

Extensibility notations are used to enhance the power of the language. It is basically additional elements used to represent some extra behavior of the system. These extra behaviors are not covered by the standard available notations.

13.4.3 About UML

This chapter will give you a quick overview of the basics of UML. Keep in mind that this is not a comprehensive tutorial on UML but rather a brief introduction to UML which can be read as a UML tutorial. If you would like to learn more about the Unified Modeling Language, or in general about software analysis and design, refer to one of the many books available on the topic. There are also a lot of tutorials on the Internet which you can take as a starting point.

The Unified Modeling Language (UML) is a diagramming language or notation to specify, visualize and document models of Object Oriented software systems. UML is not a development method that means it does not tell you what to do first and what to do next or how to design your system, but it helps you to visualize your design and communicate with others. UML is controlled by the Object Management Group (OMG) and is the industry standard for graphically describing software.

UML is designed for Object Oriented software design and has limited use for other programming paradigms.

UML is composed of many model elements that represent the different parts of a software system. The UML elements are used to create diagrams, which represent a certain part, or a point of view of the system. The following types of diagrams are supported by Umbrello UML Modeller:

- *Use Case Diagrams*—show actors (people or other users of the system), use cases (the scenarios when they use the system), and their relationships.
- *Class Diagrams*—show classes and the relationships between them.
- *Sequence Diagrams*—show objects and a sequence of method calls they make to other objects.
- *Collaboration Diagrams*—show objects and their relationship, putting emphasis on the objects that participate in the message exchange.

- *State Diagrams*—show states, state changes and events in an object or a part of the system.
- *Activity Diagrams*—show activities and the changes from one activity to another with the events occurring in some part of the system.
- *Component Diagrams*—show the high level programming components (such as KParts or Java Beans).
- *Deployment Diagrams*—show the instances of the components and their relationships.
- *Entity Relationship Diagrams*—show data and the relationships and constraints between the data.

13.4.4 Use Case Diagram

Use Case Diagrams describe the relationships and dependencies between a group of *Use Cases* and the Actors participating in the process.

It is important to notice that Use Case Diagrams are not suited to represent the design, and cannot describe the internals of a system. Use Case Diagrams are meant to facilitate the communication with the future users of the system, and with the customer, and are especially helpful to determine the required features the system is to have. Use Case Diagrams tell, *what* the system should do but do not—and cannot—specify *how* this is to be achieved.

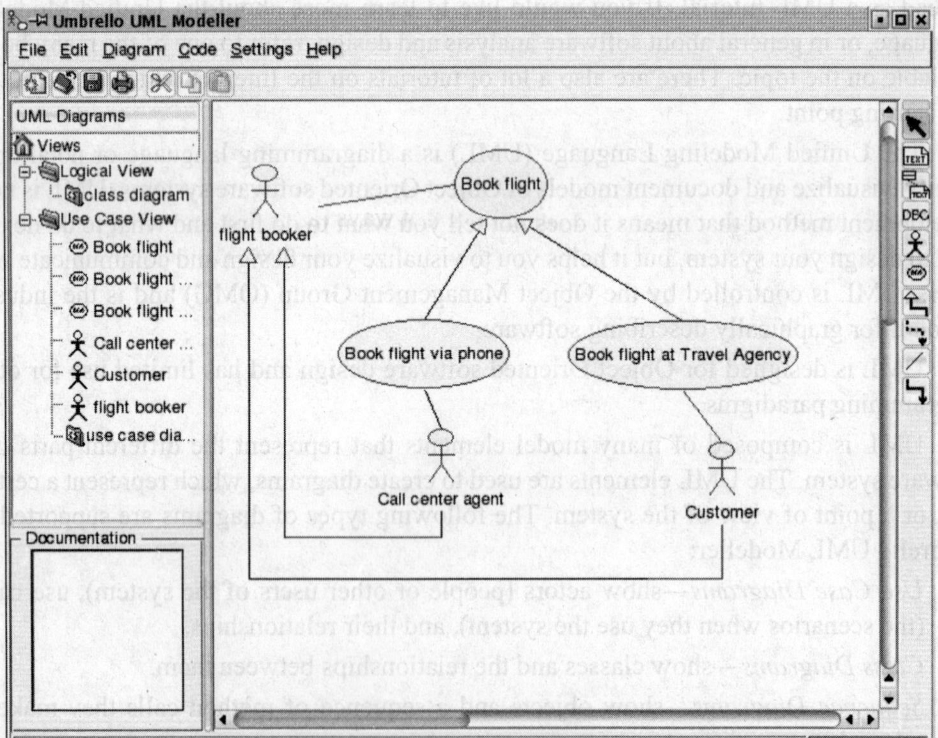

Fig. 13.20 Umbrello UML Modeller showing a Use Case Diagram.

13.4.5 Use Case

A *Use Case* describes—from the point of view of the actors—a group of activities in a system that produces a concrete, tangible result.

Use Cases are descriptions of the typical interactions between the users of a system and the system itself. They represent the external interface of the system and specify a form of requirements of what the system has to do (remember, only what, not how).

When working with Use Cases, it is important to remember some simple rules:

- Each Use Case is related to at least one actor
- Each Use Case has an initiator (*i.e.*, an actor)
- Each Use Case leads to a relevant result (a result with "business value")

Use Cases can also have relationships with other Use Cases. The three most typical types of relationships between Use Cases are:

- ⟨⟨*include*⟩⟩ which specifies that a Use Case takes place *inside* another Use Case.
- ⟨⟨*extends*⟩⟩ which specifies that in certain situations, or at some point (called an extension point) a Use Case will be extended by another.
- *Generalization* specifies that a Use Case inherits the characteristics of the "Super"—Use Case, and can override some of them or add new ones in a similar way as the inheritance between classes.

13.4.6 Actor

An actor is an external entity (outside of the system) that interacts with the system by participating (and often initiating) a Use Case. Actors can be in real life people (for example users of the system), other computer systems or external events.

Actors do not represent the *physical* people or systems, but their *role*. This means that when a person interacts with the system in different ways (assuming different roles) he will be represented by several actors. For example a person that gives customer support by the telephone and takes orders from the customer into the system would be represented by an actor "Support Staff" and an actor "Sales Representative".

13.4.7 Use Case Description

Use Case Descriptions are textual narratives of the Use Case. They usually take the form of a note or a document that is some how linked to the Use Case, and explains the processes or activities that take place in the Use Case.

13.4.8 Class Diagram

Class Diagrams show as in Fig. 13.21, the different classes that make up a system and how they relate to each other. Class Diagrams are said to be "static" diagrams because they show the classes, along with their methods and attributes as well as the static relationships between them: which classes "know" about which classes or which classes "are part" of another class, but do not show the method calls between them.

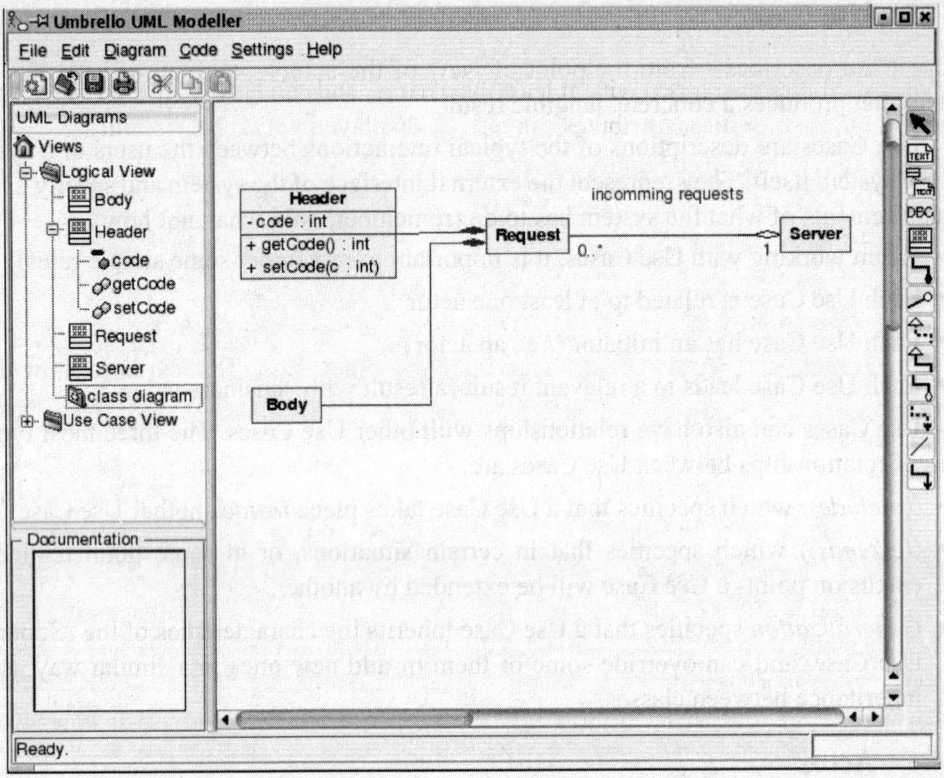

Fig. 13.21 Umbrello UML Modeller showing a Class Diagram.

13.4.9 Class

A Class defines the attributes and the methods of a set of objects. All objects of this class (instances of this class) share the same behavior, and have the same set of attributes (each object has its own set). The term "Type" is sometimes used instead of Class, but it is important to mention that these two are not the same, and Type is a more general term.

In UML, Classes are represented by rectangles, with the name of the class, and can also show the attributes and operations of the class in two other "compartments" inside the rectangle.

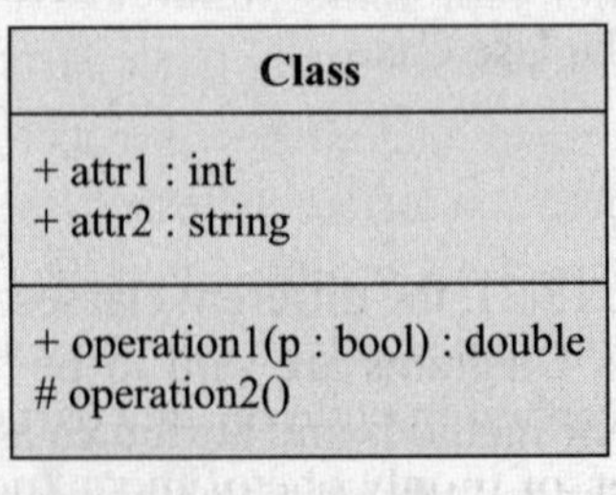

Fig. 13.22 Visual representation of a Class in UML.

13.4.10 Attributes

In UML, Attributes are shown with at least their name, and can also show their type, initial value and other properties. Attributes can also be displayed with their visibility:

- + Stands for *public* attributes
- # Stands for *protected* attributes
- –Stands for *private* attributes

13.4.11 Operations

Operations (methods) are also displayed with at least their name, and can also show their parameters and return types. Operations can, just as Attributes, display their visibility:

- + Stands for *public* operations
- # Stands for *protected* operations
- –Stands for *private* operations

13.4.12 Templates

Classes can have templates, a value which is used for an unspecified class or type. The template type is specified when a class is initiated (*i.e.*, an object is created). Templates exist in modern C++ and will be introduced in Java 1.5, where they will be called Generics.

13.4.13 Class Associations

Classes can relate (be associated with) to each other in different ways:

- **Generalization:** Inheritance is one of the fundamental concepts of Object Oriented programming, in which a class "gains" all of the attributes and operations of the class it inherits from, and can override/modify some of them, as well as add more attributes and operations of its own.

  In UML, a *Generalization* association between two classes puts them in a hierarchy representing the concept of inheritance of a derived class from a base class. In UML, Generalizations are represented by a line connecting the two classes, with an arrow on the side of the base class. (see Fig. 13.23)

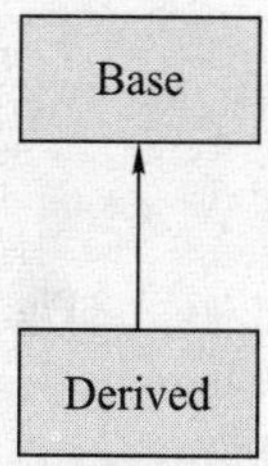

Fig. 13.23 Visual representation of a generalization in UML.

- **Associations:** An association represents a relationship between classes, and gives the common semantics and structure for many types of "connections" between objects.

  Associations are the mechanism that allows objects to communicate to each other. It describes the connection between different classes (the connection between the actual objects is called object connection, or *link*.

  Associations can have a role that specifies the purpose of the association and can be uni- or bidirectional (indicates if the two objects participating in the relationship can send messages to the other, of if only one of them knows about the other). Each end of the association also has a multiplicity value, which dictates how many objects on this side of the association can relate to one object on the other side.

In UML, associations are represented as lines connecting the classes participating in the relationship, and can also show the role and the multiplicity of each of the participants. Multiplicity is displayed as a range [min.max] of non-negative values, with a star (*) on the maximum side representing infinite. (see Fig. 13.24)

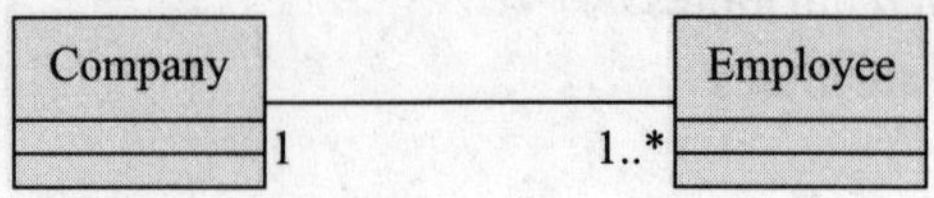

Fig. 13.24 Visual representation of an Association in UML.

13.4.14 Aggregation

Aggregations are a special type of associations in which the two participating classes don't have an equal status, but make a "whole-part" relationship. An Aggregation describes how the class that takes the role of the whole, is composed (has) of other classes, which take the role of the parts. For Aggregations, the class acting as the whole always has a multiplicity of one.

In UML, Aggregations are represented by an association that shows in Fig. 13.25, a rhomb on the side of the whole.

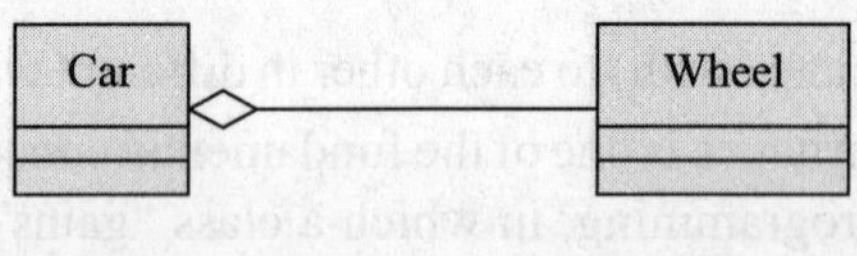

Fig. 13.25 Visual representation of an Aggregation relationship in UML.

13.4.15 Composition

Compositions are associations that represent very *strong* aggregations. This means, Compositions form whole-part relationships as well, but the relationship is so strong that the parts cannot exist on its own. They exist only inside the whole, and if the whole is destroyed the parts die too.

In UML, Compositions are represented by a solid rhomb on the side of the whole. (see Fig. 13.26)

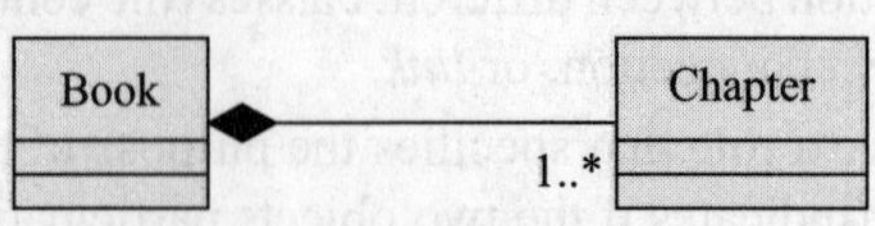

Fig. 13.26

13.5 OTHER CLASS DIAGRAM ITEMS

Class diagrams can contain several other items besides classes.

13.5.1 Interfaces

Interfaces are abstract classes which means instances can not be directly created of them. They can contain operations but no attributes. Classes can inherit from interfaces (through a realization association) and instances can then be made of these diagrams.

13.5.2 Data Types

Data types are primitives which are typically built into a programming language. Common examples include integers and Booleans. They can not have relationships to classes but classes can have relationships to them Enums.

Enums are a simple list of values. A typical example is an enum for days of the week. The options of an enum are called Enum Literals. Like data types they can not have relationships to classes but classes can have relationships to them.

13.5.3 Packages

Packages represent a namespace in a programming language. In a diagram they are used to represent parts of a system which contain more than one class, maybe hundreds of classes.

13.5.4 Sequence Diagrams

Sequence Diagrams show in Fig. 13.27, the message exchange (*i.e.*, method call) between several Objects in a specific time-delimited situation. Objects are instances of classes. Sequence Diagrams put special emphasis in the order and the times in which the messages to the objects are sent.

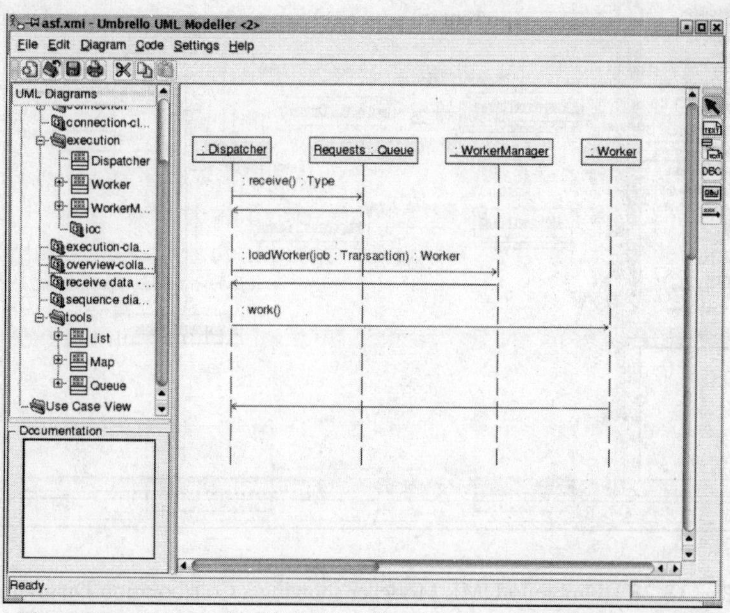

Fig. 13.27 Umbrello UML Modeller showing a Sequence Diagram.

In Sequence Diagrams objects are represented through vertical dashed lines, with the name of the Object on the top. The time axis is also vertical, increasing downwards, so that messages are sent from one Object to another in the form of arrows with the operation and parameters name.

Messages can be either synchronous, the normal type of message call where control is passed to the called object until that method has finished running, or asynchronous where control is passed back directly to the calling object. Synchronous messages have a vertical box on the side of the called object to show the flow of program control.

13.5.5 Collaboration Diagrams

Collaboration Diagrams show in Fig. 13.28, the interactions occurring between the objects participating in a specific situation. This is more or less the same information shown by Sequence Diagrams but there the emphasis is put on how the interactions occur in time while the Collaboration Diagrams put the relationships between the objects and their topology in the foreground.

In Collaboration Diagrams messages sent from one object to another are represented by arrows, showing the message name, parameters, and the sequence of the message. Collaboration Diagrams are especially well suited to showing a specific program flow or situation and are one of the best diagram types to quickly demonstrate or explain one process in the program logic.

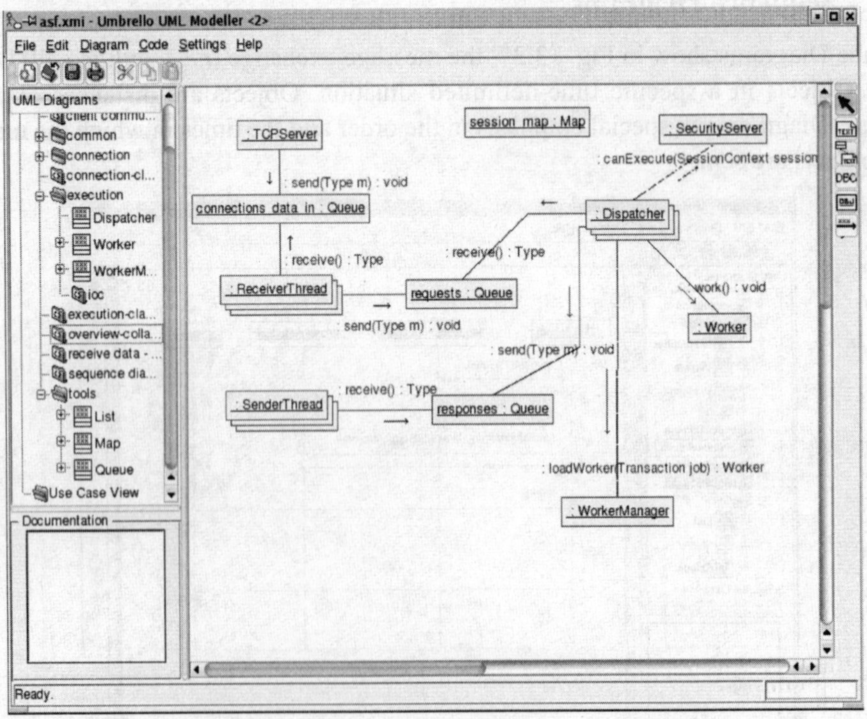

Fig. 13.28 Umbrello UML Modeller showing a Collaboration Diagram.

13.5.6 State Diagram

State Diagrams show in Fig. 13.29, the different states of an Object during its life and the stimuli that cause the Object to change its state.

State Diagrams view Objects as *state machines* or finite automates that can be in one of a set of finite states and that can change its state via one of a finite set of stimuli. For example an Object of type *NetServer* can be in one of following states during its life:

- Ready.
- Listening.
- Working.
- Stopped.

And the events that can cause the Object to change states are:

- Object is created.
- Object receives message listen.
- A Client requests a connection over the network.
- A Client terminates a request.
- The request is executed and terminated.
- Object receives message stop etc.

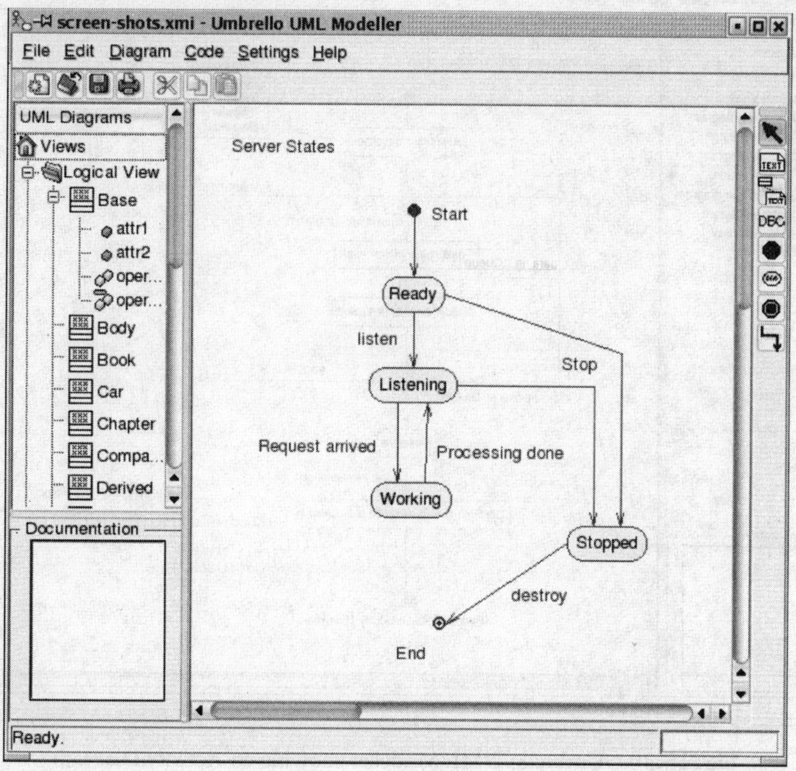

Fig. 13.29 Umbrello UML Modeller showing a State Diagram.

13.5.7 State

States are the building block of State Diagrams. A State belongs to exactly one class and represents a summary of the values the attributes of a class can take. A UML State describes the internal state of an object of one particular class.

Note that not every change in one of the attributes of an object should be represented by a State but only those changes that can significantly affect the workings of the object. There are two special types of States:

- **Start.**
- **End.**

They are special in that there is no event that can cause an Object to return to its Start state, in the same way as there is no event that can possible take an Object out of its End state once it has reached it.

13.5.8 Activity Diagram

Activity Diagrams describe the sequence of activities in a system with the help of Activities. Activity Diagrams are a special form of State Diagrams that only (or mostly) contains Activities.

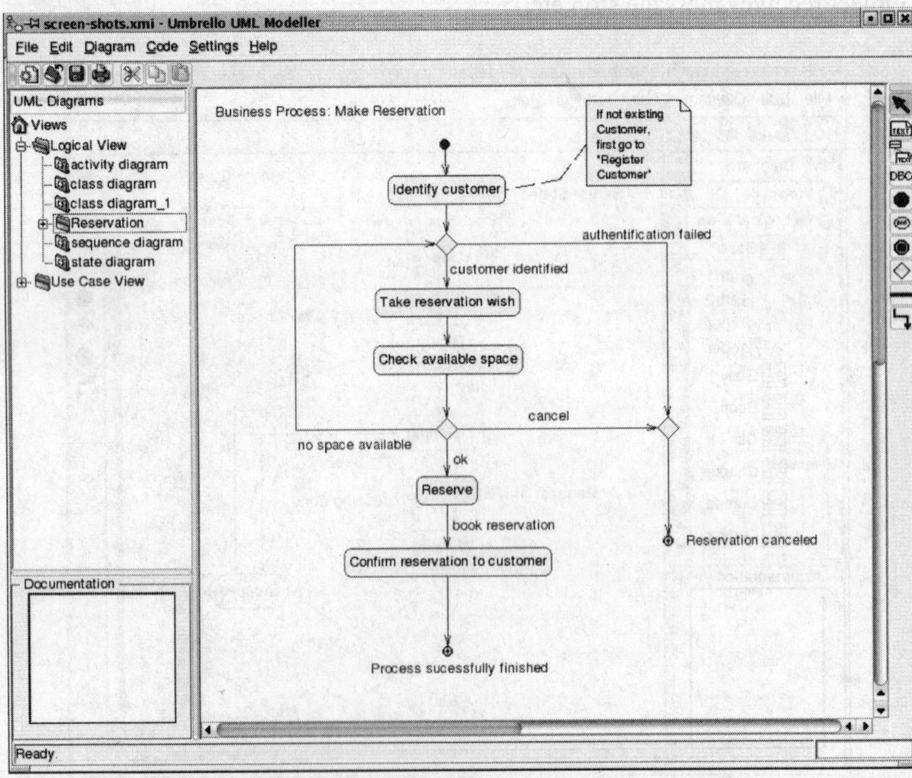

Fig. 13.30 Umbrello UML Modeller showing an Activity Diagram.

Activity Diagrams are similar to procedural Flux Diagrams, with the difference that all Activities are clearly attached to Objects.

Activity Diagrams are always associated to a *Class*, an *Operation* or a *Use Case*.

Activity Diagrams support sequential as well as parallel Activities. Parallel execution is represented via Fork/Wait icons, and for the Activities running in parallel, it is not important the order in which they are carried out (they can be executed at the same time or one after the other).

13.5.9 Activity

An Activity is a single step in a process. One Activity is one state in the system with internal activity and, at least, one outgoing transition. Activities can also have more than one outgoing transition if they have different conditions.

Activities can form hierarchies, this means that an Activity can be composed of several "detail" Activities, in which case the incoming and outgoing transitions should match the incoming and outgoing transitions of the detail diagram.

13.5.10 Helper Elements

There are a few elements in UML that have no real semantic value for the model, but help to clarify parts of the diagram. These elements are:

- Text lines
- Text Notes and anchors
- Boxes

Text lines are useful to add short text information to a diagram. It is free-standing text and has no meaning to the Model itself.

Notes are useful to add more detailed information about an object or a specific situation. They have the great advantage that notes can be anchored to UML Elements to show that the note "belongs" to a specific object or situation.

Boxes are free-standing rectangles which can be used to group items together to make diagrams more readable. They have no logical meaning in the model.

13.5.11 Component Diagrams

Component Diagrams show the software components (either component technologies such as KParts, CORBA components or Java Beans or just sections of the system which are clearly distinguishable) and the artifacts they are made out of such as source code files, programming libraries or relational database tables.

Components can have interfaces (*i.e.*, abstract classes with operations) that allow associations between components.

13.5.12 Deployment Diagrams

Deployment diagrams show the runtime component instances and their associations. They include Nodes which are physical resources, typically a single computer. They also show interfaces and objects (class instances).

13.5.13 Entity Relationship Diagrams

Entity Relationship Diagrams (ER Diagrams) show the conceptual design of database applications. They depict the various entities (concepts) in the information system and the existing relationships and constraints between them. An extension of Entity Relationship Diagrams named 'Extended Entity Relationship Diagrams' or 'Enhanced Entity Relationship Diagrams' (EER), are used to incorporate Object Oriented design techniques in ER Diagrams.

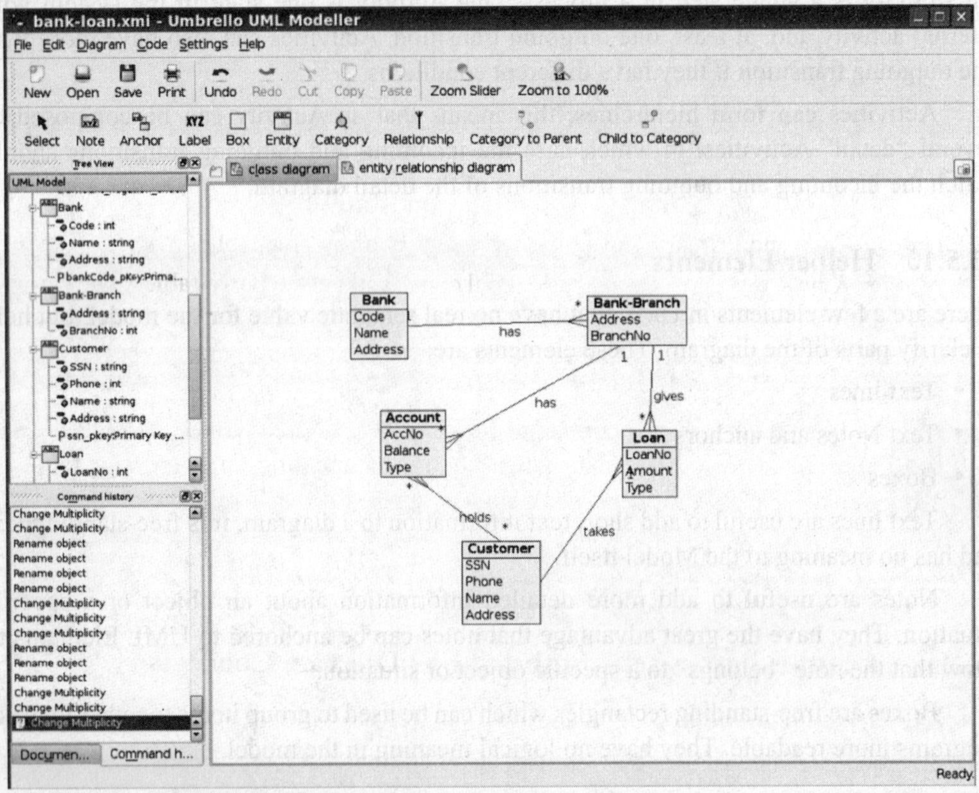

Fig. 13.31 Umbrello showing an Entity Relationship Diagram.

13.6 ENTITY

An *Entity* is any concept in the real world with an independent existence. It may be an object with a physical existence (example, Computer, Robot) or it may be an object with a conceptual existence (eq: University Course). Each entity has a set of attributes which describe the properties of the Entity.

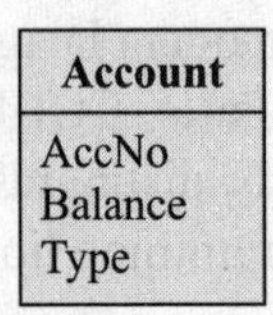

Fig. 13.32 Visual representation of an entity in an ER Diagram.

Note: No standard notations exist for depicting ER Diagrams. Different texts on this subject use different notations. The concepts and notations for EER diagrams used in Umbrello are from the following book: *Elmasri R. and Navathe S. (2004). Fundamentals of Database Systems 4th edn. Addison Wesley.*

In an ER Diagram, Entities are represented by rectangles, with the name of the entity at the top, and can also show the attributes of the entity in another "compartment" inside the rectangle.

13.6.1 Entity Attributes

In ER Diagrams, Entity Attributes are shown with their name in a different compartment of the Entity to which they belong.

13.6.2 Constraints

Constraints in ER Diagrams specify the restrictions on data in the information schema.

There are four types of constraints supported in Umbrello:

- *Primary Key*: The set of attributes declared as *primary key* are unique to the entity. There can be only one primary key in an Entity and none of its constituent attributes can be NULL.
- *Unique Key*: The set of attributes declared as *unique* are unique to the entity. There can be many unique constraints on an Entity. Its constituent attributes can be NULL. Unique Keys and Primary Keys uniquely identify a row in a table (entity).
- *Foreign Key*: A Foreign Key is a referential constraint between two tables. The foreign key identifies a column or a set of columns in one (referencing) table that refers to a column or set of columns in another (referenced) table. The columns in the referenced table must form a primary key or unique key.
- *Check Constraint*: A check constraint (also known as table check constraint) is a condition that defines valid data when adding or updating an entry in a table of a relational database. A check constraint is applied to each row in the table. The constraint must be a predicate. It can refer to a single or multiple columns of the table.

  Example: price >= 0

13.6.3 Extended Entity Relationship (EER) Diagram Concepts

13.6.3.1 *Specialization*

Specialization is a way to form new entities using entities that have already been defined. The new entities, known as derived entities, take over (or inherit) attributes of the pre-existing entities, which are referred to as base entities. It is intended to help reuse existing data with little or no modification.

In Umbrello, one can specify Disjoint and Overlapping Specialization.

13.6.3.2 *Disjoint Specialization*

Disjoint Specialization specifies that the subclasses of the specialization must be disjoint. This means that an entity can be a member of at most one of the derived entities of the specialization.

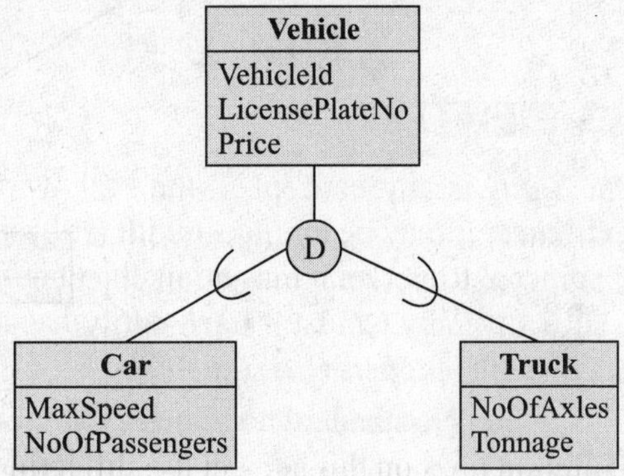

Fig. 13.33 Visual representation of Disjoint Specialization in EER Diagram.

13.6.3.3 *Overlapping Specialization*

When the derived entities are not constrained to be disjoint, their set of entities are said to be in overlapping specialization. This means that the same real world entity may be a member of more than one derived entity of the specialization.

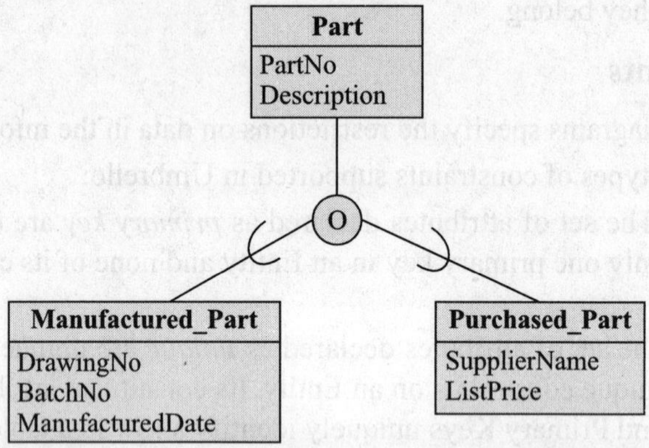

Fig. 13.34 Visual representation of Overlapping Specialization in EER Diagram.

13.6.3.4 *Category*

A derived Entity is said to be a *Category* when it represents a collection of objects that is a subset of Union of the distinct entity types. A Category is modeled when the need arises for a single super class/subclass relationship with more than one super class, where the super classes represent different entity types. (Much like multiple inheritances in Object Oriented Programming).

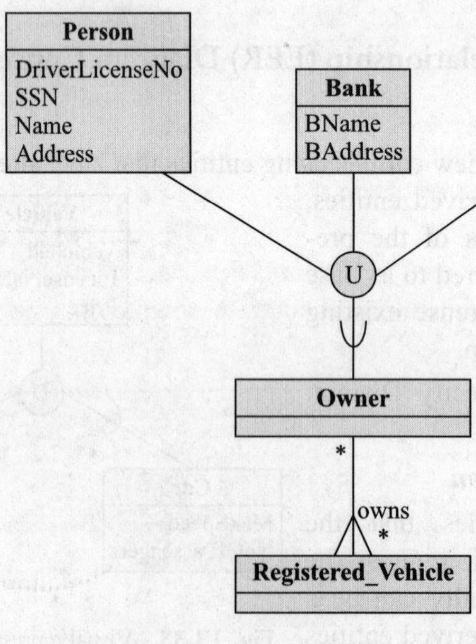

Fig. 13.35 Visual representation of a Category in EER Diagram.

Behavior diagrams capture the varieties of interaction and instantaneous state within a model as it "executes" over time.

13.6.4 Use Case Model

The use case model captures the requirements of a system. Use cases are a means of communicating with users and other stakeholders what the system is intended to do.

13.6.4.1 *Actors*

A use case diagram shows the interaction between the system and entities external to the system. These external entities are referred to as actors. Actors represent roles which may include human users, external hardware or other systems. An actor is usually drawn as a named stick figure, or alternatively as a class rectangle with the ⟨⟨Actor⟩⟩ keyword.

Actors can generalize other actors as detailed in the following diagram:

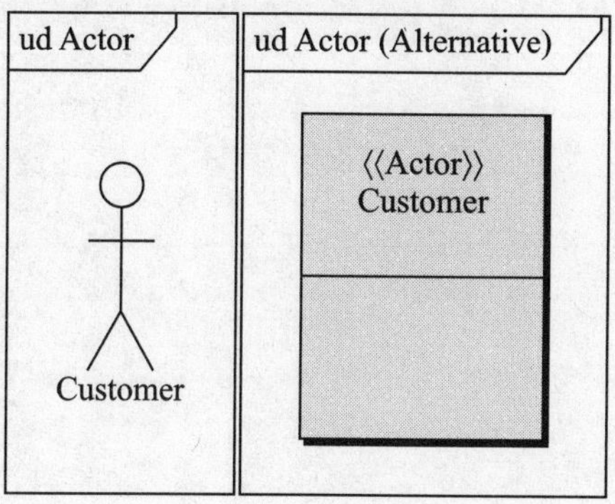

Fig. 14.36

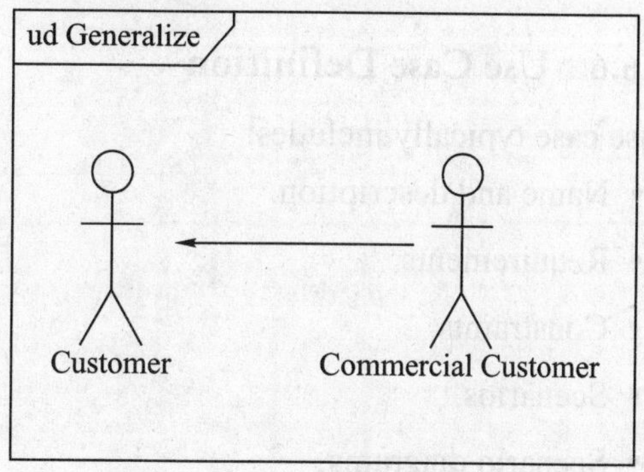

Fig. 14.37

13.6.5 Use Cases

A use case is a single unit of meaningful work. It provides a high-level view of behavior observable to someone or something outside the system. The notation for a use case is an ellipse.

The notation for using a use case is a connecting line with an optional arrowhead showing the direction of control. The following diagram indicates that the actor "Customer" uses the "Withdraw" use case.

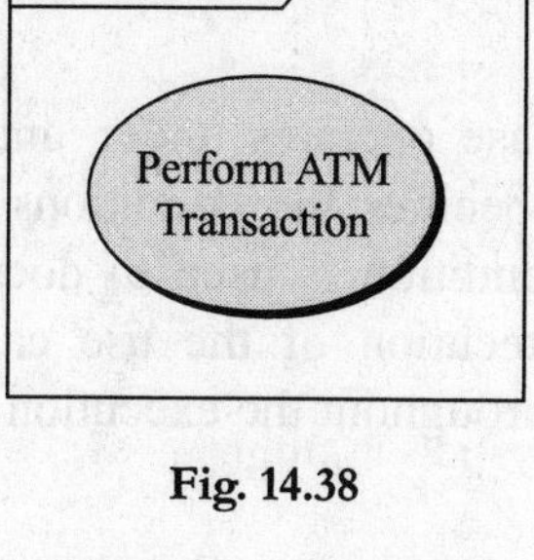

Fig. 14.38

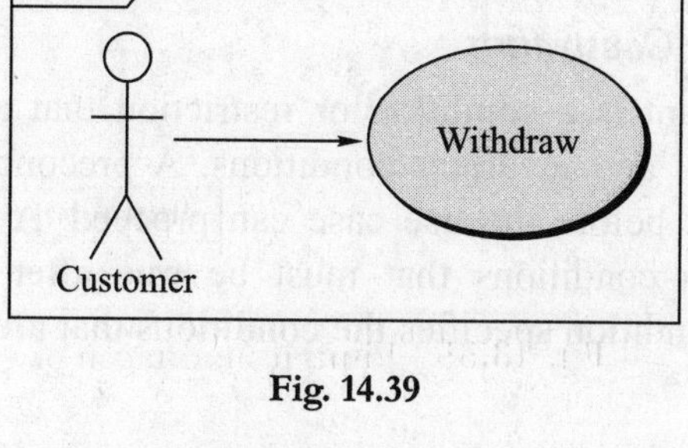

Fig. 14.39

The uses connector can optionally have multiplicity values at each end, as in the following diagram, which shows that a customer may only have one withdrawal session at a time, but a bank may have any number of customers making withdrawals concurrently.

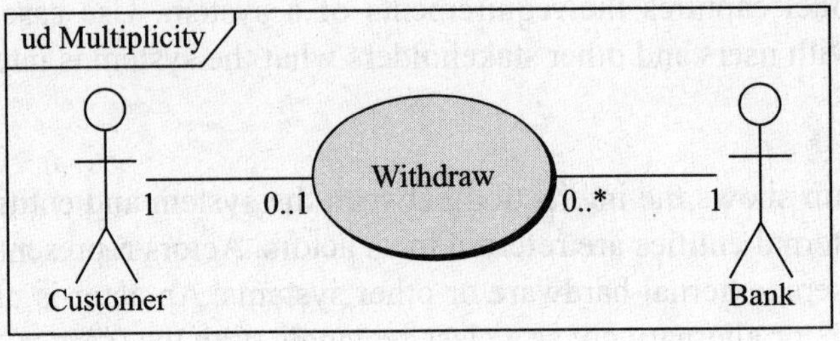

Fig. 13.40

13.6.6 Use Case Definition

A use case typically includes:

- Name and description.
- Requirements.
- Constraints.
- Scenarios.
- Scenario diagrams.
- Additional information.

13.6.6.1 *Name and Description*

A use case is normally named as a verb-phrase and given a brief informal textual description.

13.6.6.2 *Requirements*

The requirements define the formal functional requirements that a use case must supply to the end user. They correspond to the functional specifications found in structured methodologies. A requirement is a contract or promise that the use case will perform an action or provide some value to the system.

13.6.6.3 *Constraints*

A constraint is a condition or restriction that a use case operates under, and includes pre-, post- and invariant conditions. A precondition specifies the conditions that need to be met before the use case can proceed. A post-condition is used to document the change in conditions that must be true after the execution of the use case. An in variant condition specifies the conditions that are true throughout the execution of the use case.

13.6.6.4 *Scenarios*

A scenario is a formal description of the flow of events that occur during the execution of a use case instance. It defines the specific sequence of events between the system and the external actors. It is normally described in text and corresponds to the textual representation of the sequence diagram.

13.6.7 Including Use Cases

Use cases may contain the functionality of another use case as part of their normal processing. In general it is assumed that any included use case will be called every time the basic path is run. An example of this is to have the execution of the use case ⟨Card Identification⟩ to be run as part of a use case ⟨Withdraw⟩.

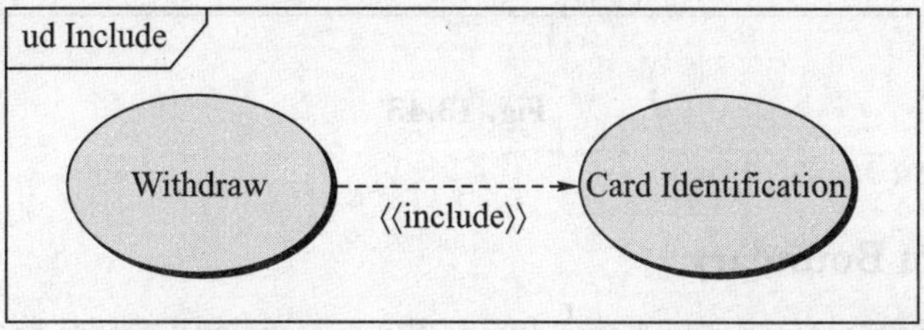

Fig. 13.41

Use Cases may be included by one or more Use Case, helping to reduce the level of duplication of functionality by factoring out common behavior into Use Cases that are re-used many times.

13.6.8 Extending Use Cases

One use case may be used to extend the behavior of another; this is typically used in exceptional circumstances. For example, if before modifying a particular type of customer order, a user must get approval from some higher authority, then the ⟨Get Approval⟩ use case may optionally extend the regular ⟨Modify Order⟩ use case.

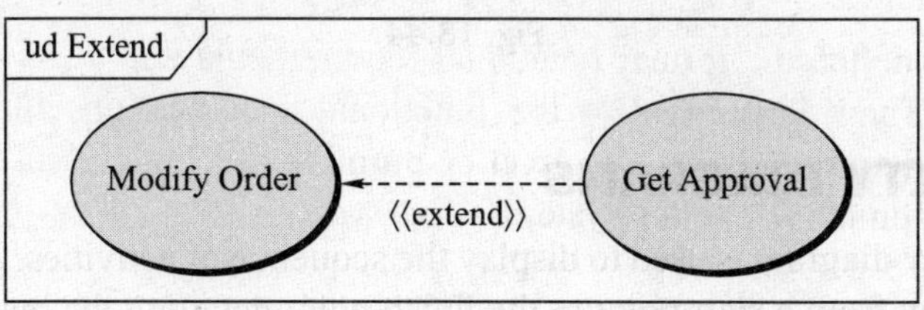

Fig. 13.42

13.6.9 Extension Points

The point at which an extending use case is added can be defined by means of an extension point.

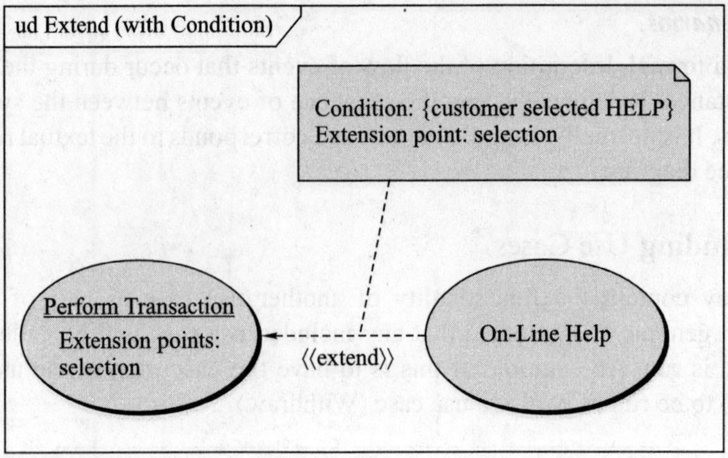

Fig. 13.43

13.6.10 System Boundary

It is usual to display use cases as being inside the system and actors as being outside the system. (see Fig. 13.44)

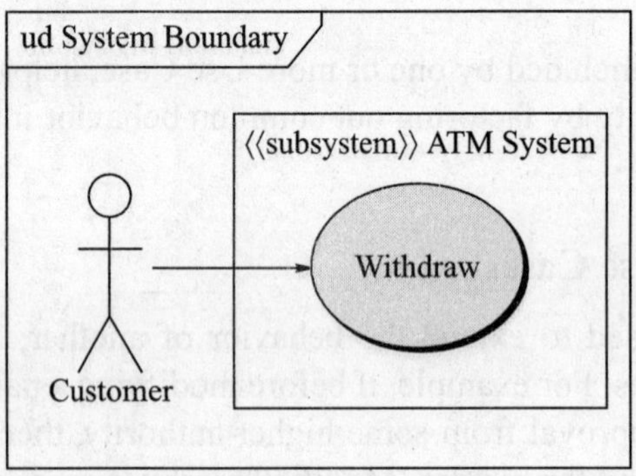

Fig. 13.44

13.7 ACTIVITY DIAGRAMS

In UML an activity diagram is used to display the sequence of activities. Activity diagrams show the workflow from a start point to the finish point detailing the many decision paths that exist in the progression of events contained in the activity. They may be used to detail situations where parallel processing may occur in the execution of some activities. Activity diagrams are useful for business modeling where they are used for detailing the processes involved in business activities.

An example of an activity diagram is shown as in Fig. 13.45.

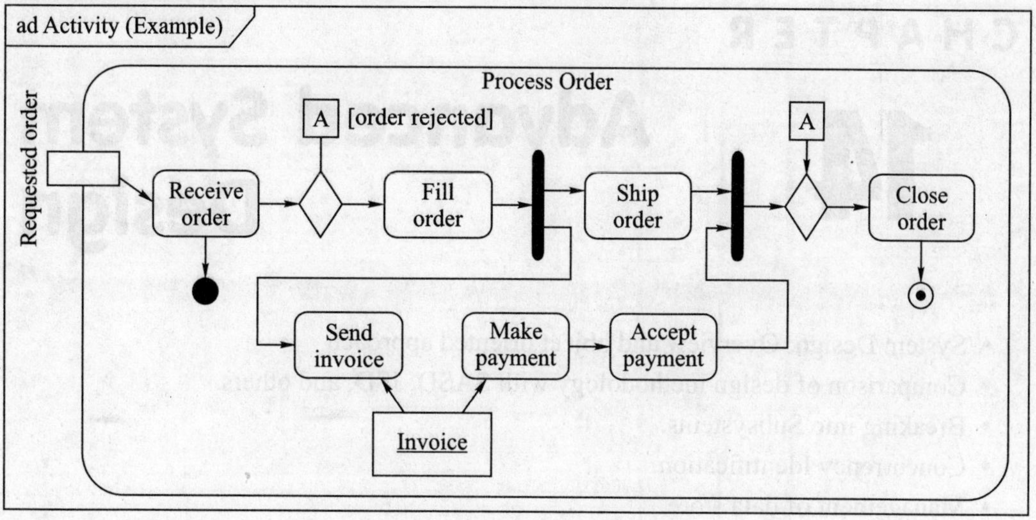

Fig. 13.45

The following sections describe the elements that constitute an Activity diagram:

13.7.1 Activities

An activity is the specification of a parameterized sequence of behavior. An activity is shown as a round-cornered rectangle enclosing all the actions, control flows and other elements that make up the activity.

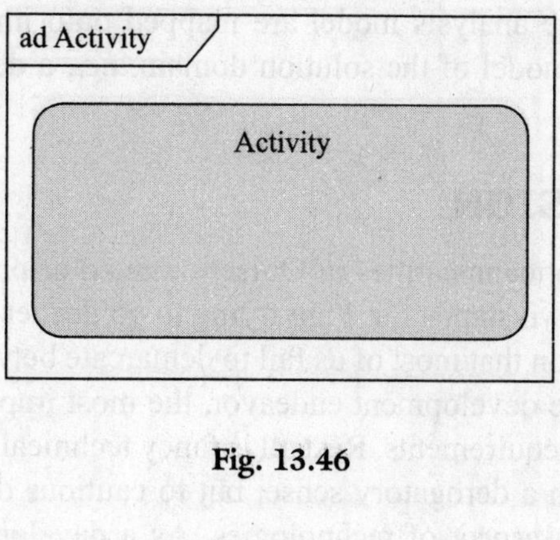

Fig. 13.46

13.7.2 Actions

An action represents a single step within an activity. Actions are denoted by round cornered Rectangles. (see Fig. 13.47)

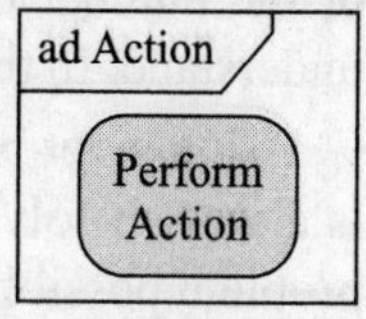

Fig. 13.47

13.7.3 Action Constraints

Constraints can be attached to an action. The following diagram shows an action with local pre- and post-conditions.

CHAPTER

14 Advanced System Design

- System Design: Overview and object oriented approach.
- Comparison of design methodology with SASD, JSD, and others.
- Breaking into Subsystems.
- Concurrency Identification.
- Management of data store.
- Controlling events between Objects.
- Handling Boundary Conditions.

14.1 OBJECT ORIENTED DESIGN

During object-oriented design (OOD), a developer applies implementation constraints to the conceptual model produced in object-oriented analysis. Such constraints could include not only constraints imposed by the chosen architecture but also any non-functional—technological or environmental—constraints, such as transaction throughput, response time, run-time platform, development environment, or those inherent in the programming language. Concepts in the analysis model are mapped onto implementation classes and interfaces resulting in a model of the solution domain, *i.e.*, a detailed description of *how* the system is to be built.

14.2 SYSTEM DESIGN

Before we go deeper into technicalities of Object oriented or procedural, let's understand what "approach" on its own stands for. I am trying to go deeper into the word "approach" because of one plain reason that most of us fail to demarcate between the concept of means and ends. In any software development endeavor, the most important thing is and should be fulfilling of customer requirements. Rest all is fancy technicalities. I am using fancy, not to put the technologies in a derogatory sense, but to cautious developers from indulging into the self glorification aspect of technologies. As a developer we tend to feel proud of the number of frameworks we know or the intricacies of a server administration we understand. In this, many times the customer requirements are fitted on top of technologies.

Let's get back into our discussion on approach. What is an approach? An approach is a way to solve a problem. Approach represents the means and not the ends. The same problem possibly can be solved using number of approaches.

Let's take a simple example of traveling from one city to another. There are many approaches for doing this as such, taking a flight for driving on the highway to cycling.

Now which approach is better for completely problem specific? Now, if the cities are nearby than flight may take longer considering the check in and checkout over heads. Similarly if it is an old city, near to each other with narrow by lanes, cycling would be a better idea. Now let's go into our original topic of Object Oriented Approach. Please look into the further discussion, keeping the discussion on approach we did.

Object oriented approach is one of the ways of solving the problem. We will try to understand why it is a good approach in many cases but also what are the pitfalls you should be aware of while working with this approach.

Object oriented approach takes the notion of object as its center stage. The counterpart of Object oriented approach is the procedural approach. Procedural approach puts procedures/functions as the central theme. The important notions of object oriented approach are abstraction, encapsulation and inheritance. We will not go into the definitions of these as there is enough material on these aspects. Rather let's try to understand how this notions help in building better software's.

A parallel analogy can be drawn, when a certain idea is adapted into a movie or story. For example, if one wants to write a story of how a princess was rescued from an evil demon by a prince. Most of Hindi movies till some time back were of similar nature. Now to bring this story to life, one has to identify the characters and the backdrops in which the story will flow. These are the elements of the movies and the interaction of these elements in certain sequence brings the whole story out. The counterpart of these elements is objects in the software world. Building software is similar to building a story from an idea. Object oriented approach involves in identifying those objects so that they can interact with other objects in some meaningful way. Also Object oriented approach has certain notions which help in characterizing the objects in a better way.

Abstraction is about identifying the elements of a system. For example in finding the elements of our story there are obvious elements like prince and princess. Sometimes the elements are not so obvious. For example who are the friends and associated of prince and of demon. The identification of these elements depends on the context also. In case of software development, the customer requirements will drive the identification of these elements. With abstraction, the other important aspect is granularity. How many elements are used to identify a notion. For example the notion of evil is constructed by one demon or a demon and his Guru.

Encapsulation on the other hand is about characterization of the element. In software terms, we talk about data and behavior when we talk about encapsulation. For example, the mood of the prince may be a data point, which brings out the emotions of a particular moment. Similarly when princess will call for help, the prince has to run for her rescue. This is the behavior. Encapsulation is important from the perspective of characterization of the element.

Inheritance is very specific to software world. This one can realize by noticing that you never discuss the inheritance aspect with the customer. But one does discusses Abstraction and Encapsulation elements. (May not be using the terms themselves). Inheritance is mostly a design issue driven more by the need of reusability.

In the discussion we have avoided using the word class and completely relied on the word object to build the discussion. The reason is because class is again specific to software world. It's a means to build the representation of the real world using objects.

Also another important aspect which is specific to object oriented world is use of interfaces. Use of interfaces is related to the notion of indirection it provides to the system. The interaction of the system is build around the notion of expected behavior and not how the behavior is implemented. The underlying behavior can change as per the context. This is also known as polymorphism.

The most popular principals of object oriented programming approach are:

- Open close principle: Open for extension but closed for change. This means that design in such a way that new behavior can be added, but the existing behavior cannot be modified by mistake also. It boils down to using the right access modifiers and also to allow a class to be inherited or not.
- Liskov Substitution principle: This means that working against an interface, it should not matter which underlying implementation is working. The agent interacting with the above element should not have to acquire the knowledge of the specific type. This also drives to Design by contract.
- Dependency Inversion Principle: The different layers of an application should depend on the contracts (in terms of interfaces).

The main advantage of using object oriented approach is that it provides a neat design approach and the maintainability and reusability of the elements is higher. Also by deploying design by contract approach the parts of the systems can be changed without impacting the whole system.

On the disadvantage side, the learning curve for mastering object oriented approach is steeper. Developer often does mistakes by assuming that by knowing how to write a class they know the object oriented approach. It's more about developing the capability to abstract and encapsulate elements in the system and building right contracts between them.

A data model can be derived from a JSD specification. Data is associated with actions (events) of an entity process; the data constitutes the state vector of the entity process. Although data models, such as the relational model, can be taught independently of systems development, database design is properly understood, not as a starting point for modeling an information system, but rather as part of the implementation phase of system development. In the Spring of 1991 I explored object-oriented design with some students. I had the intuition that JSD entities and actions were closely related to object-oriented objects and methods, and I used this seminar to implement a JSD specification in Smalltalk.

JSD is an object-based method of analysis. A JSD specification can be seamlessly implemented using an object-oriented programming language: entities, actions, and attributes of a JSD specification map into objects, methods and instance variables of an OOP language. I have termed the method of implementing a JSD specification using an OOP language "JSDOOP".

JSD is object-based, that is, JSD models the behavior of the objects of interest in a user's problem domain. A JSD specification is not some set of abstractions that only programmers and analysts can understand, but consists of the same objects that the users of the system know from their day-to-day activities. This is the essence of what object based means. The third part of these lectures deals with coupling a JSD specification with object-oriented implementation—what I have termed JSDOOP. We present examples mapping a

JSD specification into an implementation using the object-oriented programming language Smalltalk.

Michael Jackson invented JSP from 1972–74 and JSD with John Cameron and other colleagues who worked for Michael Jackson Systems, LTD during the late 1980s.

Jackson has written two books, "Principles of Program design" in 1975, which describes JSP and System Development in 1983 which describes JSD. Another primary source material for JSP and JSD is "JSP & JSD: The Jackson Approach to Software Development" by John Cameron (1983 and 1989). Other sources on JSP and JSD may be found in the bibliography.

Jackson's writing excels in clarity and expository approach. If you are interested in understanding Jackson methodology, you cannot do better than others.

Structured Analysis and Structured Design (SASD) was developed in the 1970's with emphasis on easing the management task of the software development project by dividing the system into smaller partitions and understanding what each component does and the relationship between each component. This in turn leads to reduced development time.

14.2.1 Background

SASD was developed in the late 1970s by De Marco, Yourdon, and Constantine after the emergence of structured programming. Then IBM incorporated SASD into their development cycle in the late 1970s and early 1980s. In 1989, Yourdon publicized SASD after he published his book "Modern Structured Analysis". Classical SASD was enhanced to improve its ability to represent real-time systems. The resulting technique is now called Modern SASD.

14.2.2 The Essential Model

Structured Analysis in SASD is made up of the Environmental Model and the Behavioral Model. ***The Environmental Model*** defines the boundary and interaction between the system and the outside world. It is composed of the Statement of Purpose, the Context Diagram, and Event List:

- **The Statement of Purpose** is a clear and concise textual description of the purpose for the system and it is must be deliberately vague.
- **The Context Diagram** is a graph that highlights the boundary between the system and the outside world. It highlights the people, organizations, and outside systems that interact with the system under development.
- **The Event List** is similar to "use-cases". It is a list of the events outside of the system to which it must respond.

The Behavioral Model consists of the Data Flow Diagram (DFD), process specification, the Data Dictionary, the Entity Relationship diagram (ERD), and the State Transition Diagram (STD):

- **The Data Flow Diagram** is graphical technique the highlights the information movement between processes in the system from input to output. It helps the developer understand what the functions of the system do, and the interaction between these functions. The DFD's can be decomposed into smaller lower level partitions in a top-down approach.

- **Process Specification** is a description of each process/function in the DFD. It is usually in Pseudo code. It describes the input, the algorithm of the process, and the output.
- **The Data Dictionary** is a repository containing details about each data item that appears on the DFD.
- **The Entity Relationship Diagram** is a graphical model of the relationships between the data entities in the system. It gives further details about the data stores that were presented in the DFD.
- **The State Transition Diagram** is a graphical technique to highlight the time-dependent behavior of the system. It describes **what** happens **when** [Yourdon, 1989]. The sequence of events can be complex for real-time systems. The STD's can also be partitioned and leveled as needed.

14.2.3 The Implementation Model

Finishing the Essential Model means that we have analyzed all the customer requirements. After approving the customer requirements, the basis is available to start designing the system. *The Implementation Model* is the Structured Design portion of SASD. There is one tool that is used in this model, **The Structure Chart**. It is a tool that models the synchronous hierarchy of modules in a system. It is extensively used for program design. [Yourdon, 1989]

The Structure chart is based on the HIPO concept. HIPO stands for the Hierarchal Input Process and Output. The system is broken down into modules that are well defined using the HIPO concept. The structure chart shows the top-down hierarchy of the modules and the data interfaces between them [Yourdon, 1989]. The function of the modules is defined but the internal procedure of processing inside the modules are not defined in the structure chart. The "black-box" concept is used. The input and the output of the modules is clearly defined as well. The arrows connecting the modules indicate subroutine calls.

14.2.4 Critique

SASD has been around for over 30 years. So it has become a mature software design technique. It has wide range of skilled users all over the world. It is used extensively today in database design. Process-oriented techniques like SASD appeal to many people because it is the natural way of thinking.

SASD doesn't focus too much on user participation which raises a concern. The lack of user involvement in SASD can result in project failure because it might develop a product that doesn't meet the user expectations. SASD does provide a complete software life cycle, but it can be used in combination with different RE techniques like JAD. When comparing SASD with other techniques, I found that OOAD is the closest technique to SASD. The interest of the software community is shifting towards OOAD. One of the reasons OOAD is gaining popularity over SASD is that OOAD is more "well-rounded" to the different aspects of the business. Also there is a shortage of modern CASE tools that support SASD.

14.2.5 Comparison with Other Techniques

14.2.5.1 *SASD Vs OOAD*

Both SASD and OOAD had started off from programming techniques. The roots of SASD came from structured programming, and the roots of OOAD came from object-oriented programming. Both techniques use graphical design and graphical tools to analyze and model the requirements. Both techniques provide a systematic step-by-step process for developers. Both techniques focus on documentation of the requirements.

There are many differences between SASD and OOAD. SASD is Process-Oriented. It considers the processes to be the primary driver of the system. But OOAD is Data-Oriented; it considers the data to be the primary driver of the system. Another difference is that OOAD encapsulates as much of the systems' data and processes into objects, while SASD separates between them.

14.2.5.2 *SASD Vs JAD*

Both techniques require the user to review the models developed. JAD requires good communication between user and analysts while SASD focuses more on analysis and design without much interaction with users. JAD focuses on Customer satisfaction while SASD focuses on quality design.

JAD is good for making decisions at the requirements elicitation phase, and SASD is good at analysis and design of the system. They make a good combination if used together.

14.2.5.3 *SASD Vs CSE*

Both use decomposition to analyze the system, and they use diagrams to demonstrate different components of the system. The tools used by both techniques share the same idea: Context Diagram VS. Black Box, State Transition Diagram VS. State Box, Data Flow Diagram VS. Clear Box. The differences are that CSE uses formal specifications, while SASD doesn't. CSE contains its own iterative life cycle model, while SASD may fit in waterfall life cycle model or iterative life cycle. CSE uses statistical testing. CSE uses usage model to exhaust all input possibilities to get a complete system, while SASD uses event lists to get a complete system. CSE uses the box structure method for specification and design, while SASD uses more graphical data flow diagrams.

14.2.5.4 *SASD Vs QFD*

Both are used in requirements analysis. Both Support facilitated meetings with customers. Both use problem-solving strategies.

QFD uses HOQ to produce a prioritization of requirements. SASD doesn't use prioritization. QFD requires user participation in almost all the stages but SASD requires user participation in requirements elicitation only. SASD takes us a step further than QFD into building an implementation model. QFD is used mostly for competitor analysis for generic products, while SASD is used to build user-specific systems.

14.2.5.5 *SASD Vs Agile Methods*

There are no similarities that I can think of between SASD and Agile Methods. SASD focuses on building a design model, or software plan. Agile methods don't allow for too much planning. Agile methods use prototyping with short iterative life cycles. SASD requires longer life cycles because of the analysis and design involved. SASD requires great effort in the analysis and design which leads to a more stable system and makes maintenance easier later on, but Agile methods might make maintenance impossible in later stages. SASD is good for for long term planning while Agile Methods is good for short term quick software releases. Agile methods require frequent user interaction, and group works, while SASD doesn't.

14.2.6 Breaking a System into Sub-systems

In system design the first step for all except the smallest applications is to break the system into subsystems. In subsystems classes share common properties, have similar functionality, have the same physical location, or execute on the same hardware. A subsystem is a package of classes, associations, operations, events and constraints that are interrelated and have a reasonably well defined interface to the rest of the system. The interface specifies all interactions with the subsystem to allow independent subsystem design. Relationships between subsystems may be client supplier or per to per. A system may be broken into layers and partitions. Layers define an abstract world and work like a client of services for layers below and as a supplier of services for layers above it. Layers may be of opened or closed architecture. In opened architecture a layer knows of all layers below it and in closed architecture a layer only knows about the immediate lower layer. Layers do not know of layer above them. Partitions vertically divide systems into independent or weakly coupled subsystems. Each partition provides a particular service. Simple system architectures as pipelines and stars are used to reduce the complexity of the system.

Concurrency is a way to think about programs as being composed of separate processes that can run all at the same time.

I am most familiar with the concept as it relates to **Erlang**. In this model processes are logically separated from each other. The *only* way that two processes can communicate is by "message passing". That is, object (or module, or process) A wants to tell process B that B should compute the product of two numbers. I'll sketch the procedure here, each line below will represent a step, and parenthetical items are the messages passed.

A –> (3 * 4) –> B
B computes 3 * 4 = 12
A <– (12) <– B

In a real system, you often have to add some more info, let's do that below:

A –> ("A", "multiply", 3, 4) –> B
B computes 3 * 4 = 12
A <– (12) <– B

This time, A sent more information about what it wanted done. A told B four things, where to send the result (back to "A"), what operation A wanted done "multiply", and the two arguments (3 and 4) to be used. Notice here that there is more flexibility in the communication. We could imagine that the two processes could even be on different computers:

A –> ("http://example.com:8080", "multiply", 3, 4) –> B

A addressed B over the internet (I'm just making this up, there isn't necessarily any need to go over HTTP, though there is XML-RPC, if you're interested).

CHAPTER 15

Functional Modeling

15.1 INTRODUCTION

The functional model describes computations and specifies those aspects of the system concerned with transformations of values—functions, mappings, constraints, and functional dependencies. The functional model captures what the system does, without regard to how or when it is done.

The functional model uses a hierarchy of data flow diagrams (DFDs) in a similar fashion to the Yourdon method. However, the DFDs are not very well integrated with the object and dynamic models and it is difficult to imagine many projects making extensive use of the functional model.

Some aspects of the functional model are, however, quite useful. For example, the context diagram is vital for defining the scope of the system. Also, it may be possible to strengthen the real-time aspects of the method by introducing the concept of a processor and task model using DFDs.

Data Flow Diagrams are commonly used during problem analysis. They are quite general and are not limited to problem analysis for software requirements specification. DFDs are very useful in understanding a system and can be effectively used during analysis.

15.2 OBJECTIVES

In this chapter, you will learn what is functional model and DFDs. The chapter discusses how to draw a DFD, what is data dictionary and metadata. It also introduces concepts of candidate keys.

15.3 PRESENTATION OF CONTENTS

15.3.1 Functional Modeling

The functional model describes computations and specifies those aspects of the system concerned with transformations of values—functions, mappings, constraints, and functional dependencies. The functional model captures what the system does, without regard to how or when it is done.

The functional model is represented graphically with multiple data flow diagrams, which show the flow of values from external inputs, through operations and internal data stores, to external outputs. Data flow diagrams show the dependencies between values and the computation of output values from input values and functions. Functions are invoked as actions in the dynamic model and are shown as operations on objects in the object model. The data flow diagram should adhere to OMT's notation and exploit the capabilities of OMT, such as nesting, control flows, and constraints.

15.3.1.1 *Data Flow Diagram (DFD)*

Data Flow Diagrams are commonly used during problem analysis. They are quite general and are not limited to problem analysis for software requirements specification. DFDs are very useful in understanding a system and can be effectively used during analysis.

A DFD shows the flow of data through a system. It views a system as a function that transforms the inputs into desired outputs. Any complex system will not perform this transformation in a "single step", and a data will typically undergo a series of transformations before it becomes the output. The DFD aims to capture the transformations that take place within a system to the input data so that eventually the output data is produced. The agent that performs the transformation of data from one state to another is called a process. So a DFD shows the movement of data through the different transformation or process in the system.

DFDs are basically of 2 types: Physical and logical ones. Physical DFDs are used in the analysis phase to study the functioning of the current system. Logical DFDs are used in the design phase for depicting the flow of data in a proposed system.

In a nutshell, a data flow diagram is a graph showing the flow of data values from their sources in objects through processes that transform them to their destinations in other objects.

Data Flow Diagrams are composed of the four basic symbols—external entities, processes, data stores and data flow—as discussed below:

- The External Entity symbol represents sources of data to the system or destinations of data from the system.
- The Process symbol represents an activity that transforms or manipulates the data (combines, reorders, converts, etc.).
- The Data Store symbol represents data that is not moving (delayed data at rest).
- The Data Flow symbol represents movement of data.
- Any system can be represented at any level of detail by these four symbols. Now, these four elements of DFD are discussed in detail.

15.3.1.1.1 *External Entity*

The External Entity symbol represents sources of data to the system or destinations of data from the system. They determine the system boundary. They are external to the system being studied. They are often beyond the area of influence of the developer. They can represent another system or subsystem. These go on margins/edges of data flow diagram. They are represented by a rectangle symbol and are named with appropriate name as shown in below:

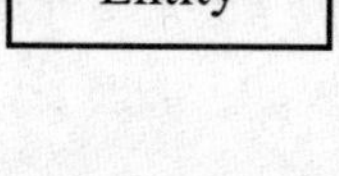

Some authors call them actors as they are active objects that drive the data flow diagram by producing or consuming values. Actors are attached to the inputs and outputs of a data flow diagram. Actors are also called as terminators as they act as source and sink for data.

15.3.1.1.2 *Process*

Processes are work or actions performed on incoming data flows to produce outgoing data flows. These show data transformation or change. Data coming into a process must be "worked on" or transformed in some way. Thus, all processes must have inputs and outputs. In some cases, data inputs or outputs will only be shown at more detailed levels of the diagrams. Each process is always "running" and ready to accept data. Major functions of processes are computations and making decisions. Each process may have dramatically different timing: yearly, weekly, daily etc.

A process is depicted by a circle as shown below:

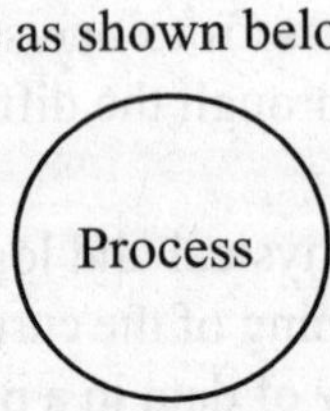

Every process is named. Processes are named with one carefully chosen verb and an object of the verb. There is no subject. Name is not to include the word "process". Each process should represent one function or action. If there is an "and" in the name, you likely have more than one function (and process). For example, get invoice, update customer and create Order. Processes are numbered within the diagram as convenient. Levels of detail are shown by decimal notation. For example, top level process would be Process 4, next level of detail Processes 4.1, and so on. Processes should generally move from top to bottom and left to right.

15.3.1.1.3 *Data Store*

Data stores are repository for data that are temporarily or permanently recorded within the system. It is an "inventory" of data. These are common link between data and process models. Only processes may connect with data stores.

There can be two or more systems that share a data store. This can occur in the case of one system updating the data store, while the other system only accesses the data. Data stores are represented by open rectangle or two parallel lines as shown below:

Data stores are named with an appropriate name, not to include the word "file", Names should consist of plural nouns describing the collection of data. Like customers, orders, and products. These may be duplicated.

They store data for later use. They do not generate any operation on its own but can respond to request. That is why they are passive objects in a data flow diagram.

15.3.1.1.4 *Data Flow*

Data flow represents the input (or output) of data to (or from) a process, data store or an actor. Data flow only data, not control. Represent the minimum essential data the process needs. Using only the minimum essential data reduces the dependence between processes. Data flows must begin and/or end at a process.

Data flows are always named. Name is not to include the word "data". It should be given unique names. Names should be some identifying noun. For example, marks, order, payment, complaint, registration no.

A data flow is represented by an arrow as shown in below:

—— Data Flow ——→

An arrow between the producer and the consumer of the data value represents a data flow. Arrow is labeled with description of data. Data can be elementary or aggregate. Input arrow indicates storing data in the data store and output arrow indicates accessing of data from data store.

Elementary data can not be decomposed into its meaningful constituents. For example, roll no, pin code, and quantity. Aggregate data can be decomposed into its meaningful constituents. For example, name can be decomposed into first name, middle name and last name. Sometimes an aggregate value is split into its constituents, each of which goes to a different process. A fork in the path as shown below is used to do this. Reverse can also be done. That is elementary data coming from different sources can be aggregated. This is done by reversing the arrows in the Fig. 15.1.

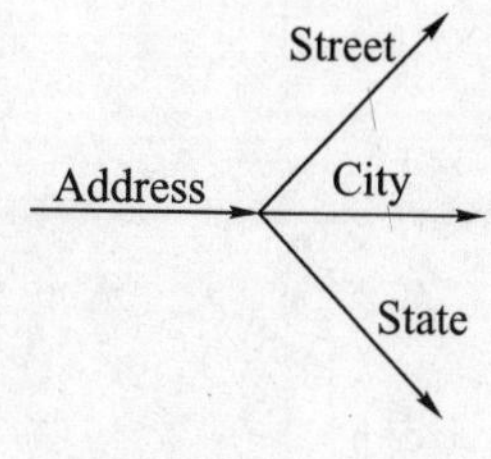

Fig. 15.1

15.3.1.2 *Control Flow*

Control flow is a Boolean value in the DFD that affects whether a process is evaluated or not. The control flow is not an input value to the process. It is represented by a dotted line from a process originating the Boolean value to the process being controlled as shown in fig below. This DFD is for a withdrawal from a bank account. The customer supplies a password and an amount. The update (withdrawal) can occur only when password is OK, which is shown as control flow in the Fig. 15.2.

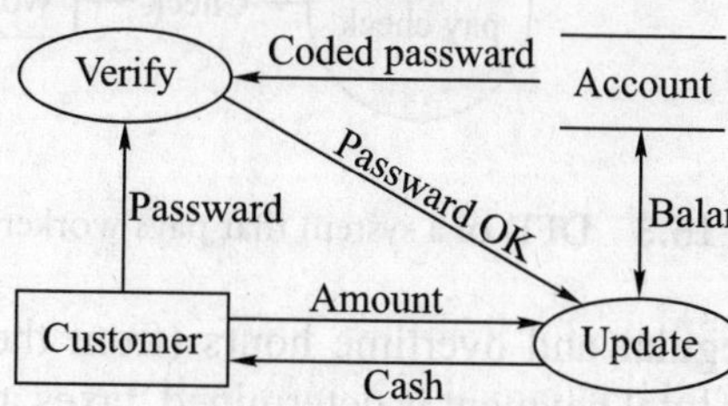

Fig. 15.2 Control flow

15.3.1.3 *Examples of DFDs*

Example 1: An example of a Data Flow Diagram—DFD for a system that pays workers is shown in the Fig. 15.3. In this DFD there is one basic input data flow, the weekly time sheet, which originates from the source worker. The basic output is the pay check, the sink for which is also the worker. In this system, first the employee's record is retrieved, using the employee ID, which is contained in the time sheet. From the employee record, the rate of payment and overtime are obtained.

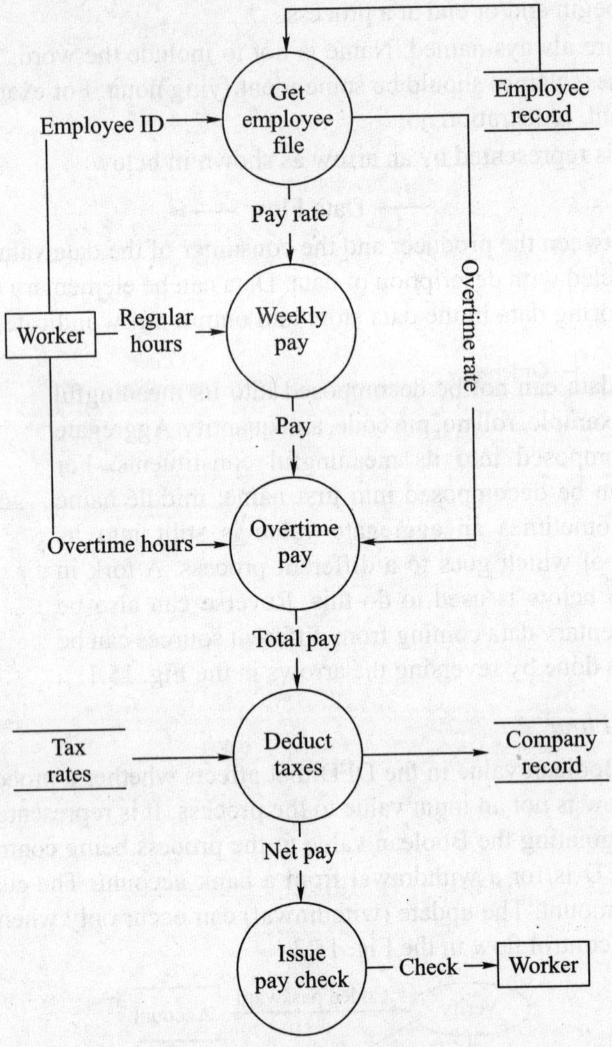

Fig. 15.3 DFD of a system that pays workers

These rates and the regular and overtime hours (from the time sheet) are used to complete the payment. After total payment is determined, taxes are deducted. To computer the tax deduction, information from the tax rate file is used. The amount of tax deducted is recorded in the employee and company records. Finally, the paycheck is issued for the net pay. The amount paid is also recorded in company records.

Following are the set of DFDs drawn for the General model of publisher's present ordering system.

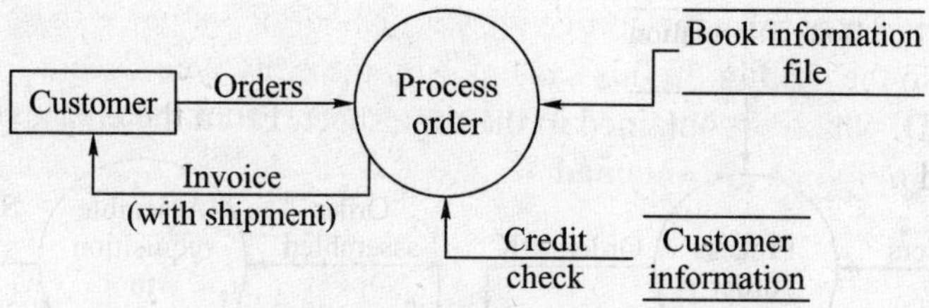

Fig. 15.4 First Level DFD

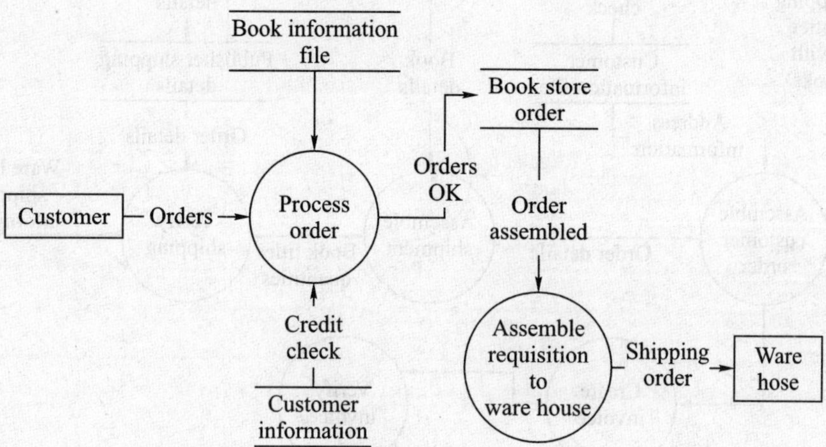

Fig. 15.5 Second Level DFD—Showing Order Verification & credit check

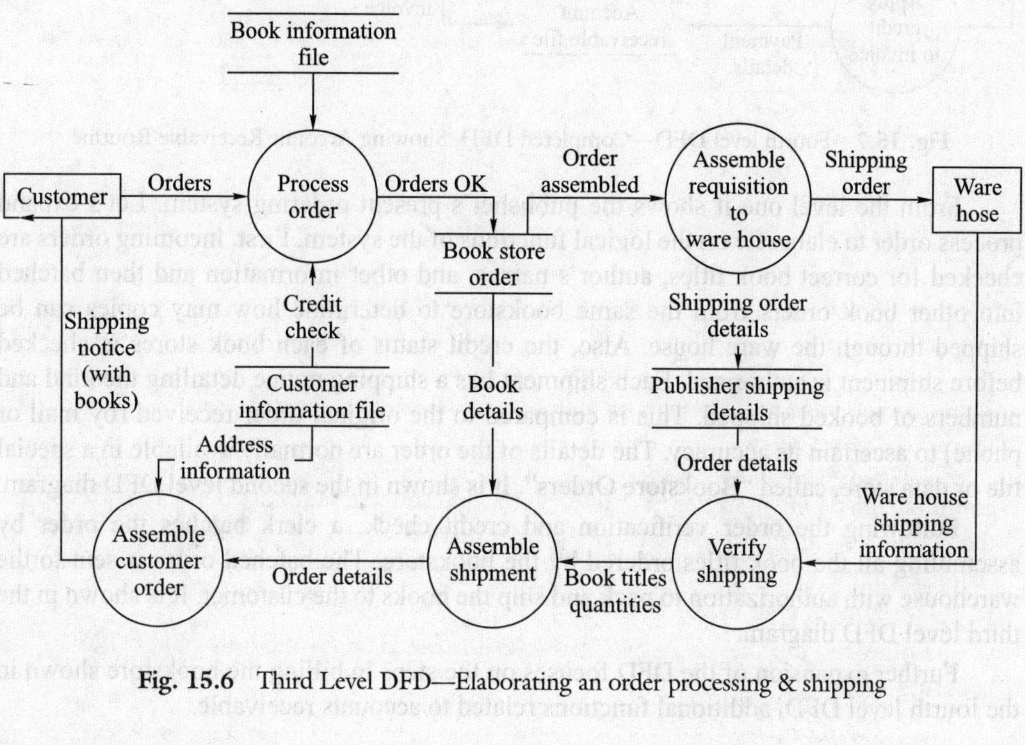

Fig. 15.6 Third Level DFD—Elaborating an order processing & shipping

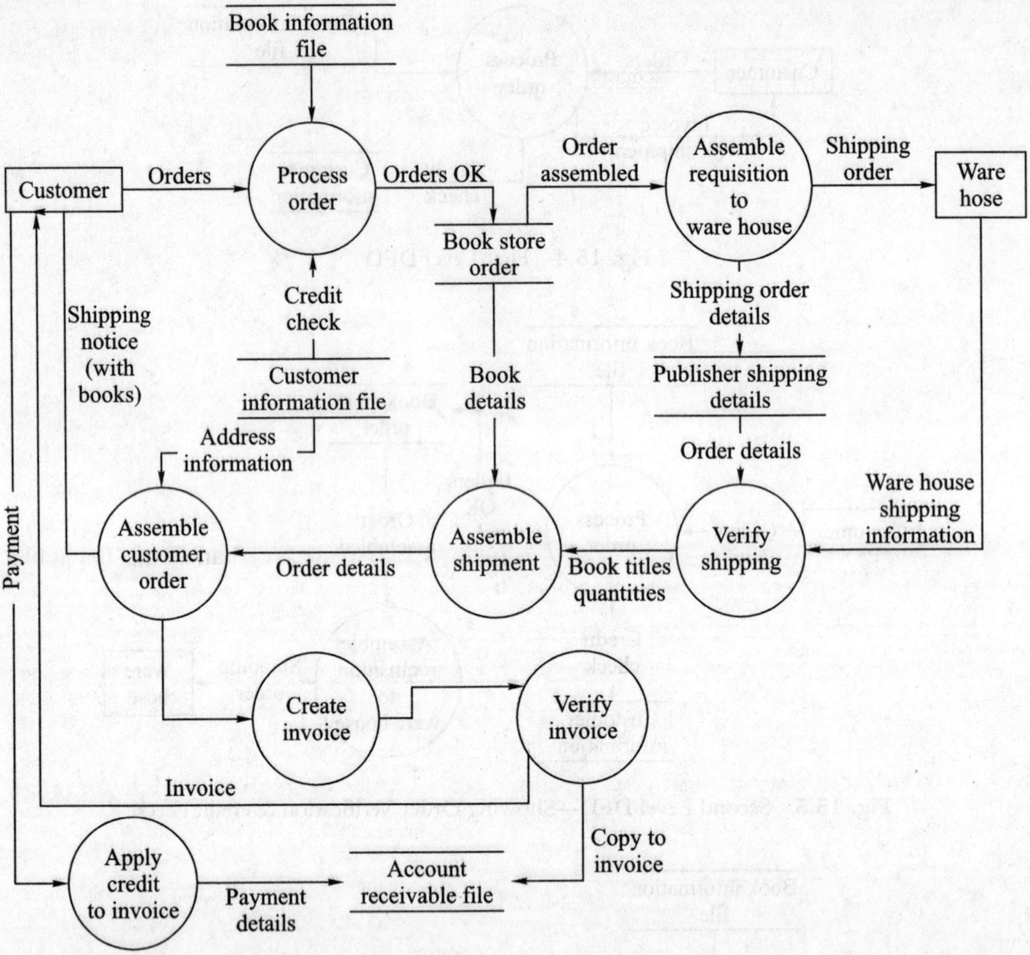

Fig. 15.7 Fourth level DFD—Completed DFD, Showing Account Receivable Routine

From the level one it shows the publisher's present ordering system. Let's expand process order to elaborate on the logical functions of the system. First, incoming orders are checked for correct book titles, author's names, and other information and then batched into other book orders from the same bookstore to determine how may copies can be shipped through the ware house. Also, the credit status of each book stores is checked before shipment is authorized. Each shipment has a shipping notice detailing the kind and numbers of booked shipped. This is compared to the original order received (by mail or phone) to ascertain its accuracy. The details of the order are normally available in a special file or data store, called "Bookstore Orders". It is shown in the second level DFD diagram.

Following the order verification and credit check, a clerk batches the order by assembling all the book titles ordered by the bookstore. The batched order is sent to the warehouse with authorization to pack and ship the books to the customer. It is shown in the third level DFD diagram.

Further expansion of the DFD focuses on the steps in billing the bookstore shown in the fourth level DFD, additional functions related to accounts receivable.

Example 3: DFD below shows updation of a bank account in a banking system.

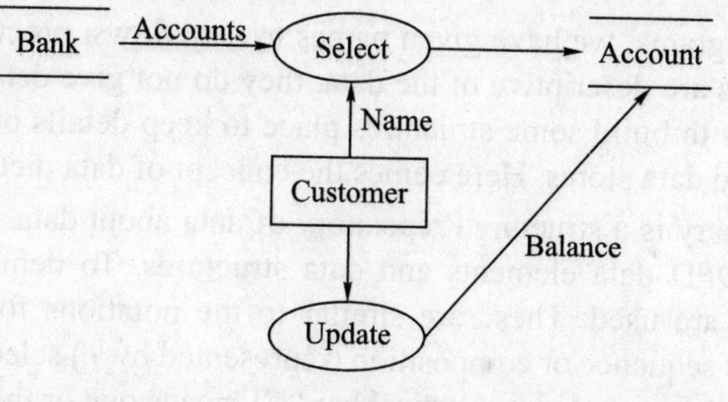

Fig. 15.8

Example 4: DFD below shows the purchase order processing system. There are four actors involved in this system - Purchasing Officer, Vendor, Purchaser 1 and Purchaser 2. Purchasing Officer creates purchase orders on receiving the purchase acquisition requests from the perspective purchasers. Purchasers approve orders and they can verify the status of the orders. All order details are kept in a database.

This functional model represents:

- Functions. For example, create order and approve order.
- Data flows. For example, purchasing data flows from the purchasing officer to the create order function.
- External entities. For example, a vendor is an entity external to the system. Data stores. For example, orders are kept in an order data store.

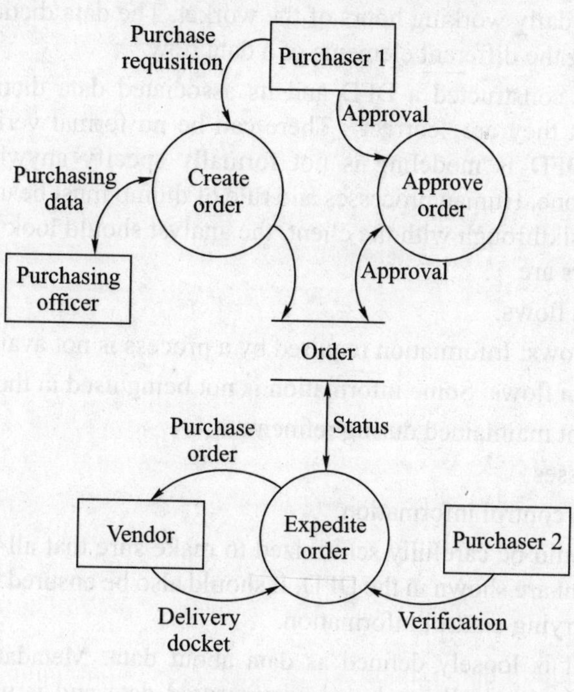

Fig. 15.9

15.3.2 Data Dictionary and Meta Data

In the data flow diagrams, we have given names to data flows, processes and data stores. Although the names are descriptive of the data, they do not give details. So following the DFD, the interest is to build some structures place to keep details of the contents of data flows, processes and data stores. Here comes the concept of data dictionary.

A data dictionary is a structured repository of data about data. It is a set of rigorous definitions of all DFD data elements and data structures. To define the data structure, different notations are used. These are similar to the notations for regular expression. Essentially, besides sequence or composition (represented by +) selection and iteration are included. Selection (represented by vertical bar "|") means one or the other, and repetition (represented by "*") means one or more occurrences.

The data dictionary for the DFD of system that pays to workers given above is created as shown below:

Weekly timesheet = Employee_Name + Employee_ID + {Regular_hours + overtime_hours}

Pay_rate = {Horly | Daily | Weekly} + Rupees_amount

Employee_Name = Last + First + Middle_Initial

Employee_ID = digit + digit + digit + digit

Most of the data flows in the DFD are specified here. Some of the most obvious ones are not shown here. The data dictionary entry for weekly timesheet specifies that this data flow is composed of three basic data entities - the employee name, employee ID and many occurrences of the two—tuple consisting of regular hours and overtime hours. The last entity represents the daily working hours of the worker. The data dictionary also contains entries for specifying the different elements of a data flow.

Once we have constructed a DFD and its associated data dictionary, we have to somehow verify that they are "correct". There can be no formal verification of a DFD, because what the DFD is modeling is not formally specify anywhere against which verification can be done. Human processes and rule of thumb must be used for verification. In addition to the walkthrough with the client, the analyst should look for common errors. Some common errors are

- Unlabeled data flows.
- Missing data flows: Information required by a process is not available.
- Extraneous data flows: Some information is not being used in the process.
- Consistency not maintained during refinement.
- Missing processes.
- Contains some control information.

The DFDs should be carefully scrutinized to make sure that all the processes in the physical environment are shown in the DFD. It should also be ensured that none of the data flows is actually carrying control information.

Meta Data: It is loosely defined as data about data. Metadata is a concept that applies mainly to electronically archived or presented data and is used to describe the: (*a*) definition, (*b*) structure and (*c*) administration of data files with all contents in context to ease the use of the captured and archived data for further use. For example, a web page may include metadata specifying what language it's written in, what tools were used to create it, where to go for more on the subject and so on.

Metadata is defined as data providing information about one or more other pieces of data, such as:

- means of creation
- purpose of the data
- time and date of creation
- creator or author of data
- placement on a network (electronic form) where the data was created
- What standards used etc.

For example: A digital image may include metadata that describes how large the picture is, the color depth, the image resolution, when the image was created, and other data. A text document's metadata may contain information about how long the document is, who the author is, when the document was written, and a short summary of the document.

Metadata is data. As such, metadata can be stored and managed in a database, often called a registry or repository. However, it is impossible to identify metadata just by looking at it. We don't know when data is metadata or just data.

Metadata is structured data which describes the characteristics of a resource. It shares many similar characteristics to the cataloguing that takes place in libraries, museums and archives. The term "meta" derives from the Greek word denoting a nature of a higher order or more fundamental kind. A metadata record consists of a number of pre-defined elements representing specific attributes of a resource, and each element can have one or more values. Below is an example of a simple metadata record:

Element name	**Value**
Title	Web catalogue
Creator	Raj Nath
Publisher	G.GS Jambeshwar
Identifier	www.gju.ac.in.metadata.html
Format	Text/html
Relation	Distance Education Web site

Each metadata schema will usually have the following characteristics:

- a limited number of elements
- the name of each element
- the meaning of each element

Typically, the semantics is descriptive of the contents, location, physical attributes, type (*e.g.*, text or image, map or model) and form (*e.g.*, print copy, electronic file). Key metadata elements supporting access to published documents include the originator of a work, its title, when and where it was published and the subject areas it covers. Where the information is issued in analog form, such as print material, additional metadata is provided to assist in the location of the information, *e.g.*, call numbers used in libraries. The resource community may also define some logical grouping of the elements or leave it to the encoding scheme. For example, Dublin Core may provide the core to which extensions may be added.

In a nutshell, metadata is structured information that describes, explains, locates, or otherwise makes it easier to retrieve, use, or manage an information resource. Metadata is often called data about data or information about information.

There are three main types of metadata: Descriptive metadata: It describes a resource for purposes such as discovery and identification. It can include elements such as title, abstract, author, and keywords. Structural metadata: It indicates how compound objects are put together, for example, how pages are ordered to form chapters.

Administrative metadata: It provides information to help manage a resource, such as when and how it was created, file type and other technical information, and who can access it.

15.3.3 Steps to Produce a DFD

- Identify and list external entities providing inputs/receiving outputs from system.
- Identify and list inputs from/outputs to external entities.
- Draw a context DFD.

  Defines the scope and boundary for the system and project
- Think of the system as a container (black box).
- Ignore the inner workings of the container.
- Ask end-users for the events the system must respond to.
- For each event, ask end-users what responses must be produced by the system.
- Identify any external data stores.
- Draw the context diagram:
  - (*i*) Use only one process.
  - (*ii*) Only show those data flows that represent the main objective or most common inputs/outputs.
- identify the business functions included within the system boundary.
- identify the data connections between business functions.
- confirm through personal contact sent data is received and vice-versa.
- trace and record what happens to each of the data flows entering the system (data movement, data storage, data transformation/processing).
- Draw an overview DFD:
  - o Shows the major subsystems and how they interact with one another - Exploding processes should add detail while retaining the essence of the details from the more general diagram.
  - o Consolidate all data stores into a composite data store.
- Draw middle-level DFDs:
  - o Explode the composite processes.
- Draw primitive-level DFDs:
  - o Detail the primitive processes.
  - o Must show all appropriate primitive data stores and data flows.

- verify all data flows have a source and destination;
- verify data coming out of a data store goes in;
- review with "informed";
- Explode and repeat above steps as needed.

Balancing DFDs:

- Balancing: child diagrams must maintain a balance in data content with their parent processes.
- Can be achieved by either:
    - o exactly the same data flows of the parent process enter and leave the child diagram,
    - o the same net contents from the parent process serve as the initial inputs and final outputs for the child diagram, or
    - o the data in the parent diagram is split in the child diagram.

Rules for Drawing DFDs:

- A process must have at least one input and one output data flow.
- A process begins to perform its tasks as soon as it receives the necessary input data flows.
- A primitive process performs a single well-defined function.
- Never label a process with an IF-THEN statement.
- Never show time dependency directly on a DFD.
- Be sure that data stores, data flows, data processes have descriptive titles. Processes should use imperative verbs to project action.
- All processes receive and generate at least one data flow.
- Begin/end data flows with a bubble.

Rules for Data Flows:

- A data store must always be connected to a process.
- Data flows must be named.
- Data flows are named using nouns Customer ID, Student information.
- Data that travel together should be one data flow.
- Data should be sent only to the processes that need the data.

Use the following additional guidelines when drawing DFDs:

- Identify the key processing steps in a system. A processing step is an activity that transforms one piece of data into another form.
- Process bubbles should be arranged from top left to bottom right of page.
- Number each process (1.0, 2.0, etc.). Also name the process with a verb that describes the information processing activity.
- Name each data flow with a noun that describes the information going into and out of a process. What goes in should be different from what comes out.
- Data stores, sources and destinations are also named with nouns.
- Realize that the highest level DFD is the context diagram. It summarizes the entire system as one bubble and shows the inputs and outputs to a system.

- Each lower level DFD must balance with its higher level DFD. This means that no inputs and outputs are changed.
- Think of data flow not control flow. Data flows are pathways for data. Think about what data is needed to perform a process or update a data store. A data flow diagram is not a flowchart and should not have loops or transfer of control. Think about the data flows, data processes, and data storage that are needed to move a data structure through a system.
- Do not try to put everything you know on the data flow diagram. The diagram should serve as index and outline. The index/outline will be "fleshed out" in the data dictionary, data structure diagrams, and procedure specification techniques.

15.3.4 Different Types of Keys

This concept is related to relational data base management systems. A relation is two dimensional table that has rows called tuples and columns called domains. There are different types of keys, namely Primary keys, alternate keys, etc., which are described below:

- **Primary key:** Within a given relation, there can be one attribute with values that are unique within the relation that can be used to identify the tuples of that relation. That attribute is said to be primary key for that relation. For example, in a Student relation roll no is a primary key.
- **Composite primary key:** Not every relation will have a single-attribute primary key. There can be a possibility that some combination of attributes when taken together have the unique identification property. These attributes as a group is called composite primary key. A combination consisting of a single attribute is a special case.

  Existence of such a combination is guaranteed by the fact that a relation is a set. Since sets don't contain duplicate elements, each tuple of a relation is unique with respect to that relation. Hence, at least the combination of all attributes has the unique identification property.

  - o In practice it is not usually necessary to involve all the attributes-some lesser combination is normally sufficient. Thus, every relation does have a primary (possibly composite) key.
  - o Tuples represent entities in the real world. Primary key serves as a unique identifier for those entities.
- **Candidate key:** In a relation, there can be more than one attribute combination possessing the unique identification property. These combinations, which can act as primary key, are called candidate keys.

Table 15.1. Having "EmpNo" and "SocSecurityNo" as candidate keys

EmpNo	*SocSecurityNo*	*Name*	*Age*
1011	2364236	Harry	21
1012	1002365	Sympson	19
1013	1056300	Larry	24

- **Alternate key:** A candidate key that is not a primary key is called an alternate key. In if EmpNo is primary key then SocSecurityNo is the alternate key.

Summary

- The functional model describes computations and specifies those aspects of the system concerned with transformations of values - functions, mappings, constraints, and functional dependencies.
- The functional model is represented graphically with multiple data flow diagrams, which show the flow of values from external inputs, through operations and internal data stores, to external outputs.
- DFDs play a major role in designing of the software and also provide the basis for other design-related issues. Some of these issues are addressed in this chapter. All the basic elements of DFD are further addressed in the designing phase of the development procedure.
- Metadata is structured information that describes, explains, locates, or otherwise makes it easier to retrieve, use, or manage an information resource. Metadata is often called data about data or information about information.
- Within a given relation, there can be one attribute with values that are unique within the relation that can be used to identify the tuples of that relation. That attribute is said to be primary key for that relation.

QUESTIONS

1. What is functional model of OMT? How is it related to other models of OMT? Explain.
2. What is DFD? What are elements of DFD? Explain the purpose of DFD with a suitable example.
3. Distinguish between control flow and data flow.
4. Discuss the steps to draw a DFD systematically.
5. What is metadata? Explain its usefulness.
6. What is data dictionary? How is it created?
7. What is a key? Explain different types of keys with suitable examples.

CHAPTER

16 Object and Dynamic Model

The OMT uses three models to describe the system being created. The three models used to describe the system are;

- The Object model.
- The Dynamic model.
- The Functional model.

The three models are initially developed during the analysis phase of the system and are subsequently used and added to during all stages of development. This three pronged approach to application design and development is important as each model enables the designer to view the system from different perspectives. The object model identifies and describes the objects used to build the system, the dynamic model represents the interactions between the various objects, and the functional model identifies the data transformations of the system.

Chonoles & Quatrani (1996) describes OMT as a set of activities that need to be performed to construct a system. The activities can be performed in several different orders as well as simultaneously, depending on the needs of the project at hand. When the activities are performed there is a considerable amount of overlap and iteration. When developing this project, a modified version of them will be performed in an iterative fashion. The first stage of the software development process is analysis.

16.1 THE OBJECT MODEL

The main model of the system is the object model, as it will identify all the objects that will make up the system, their attributes and relationships with other objects. Derr (1995) identifies guidelines that are followed when developing an object model, they have been modified slightly to suit the scale of this project as follows:

1. Develop a problem statement.
2. Identify the object classes and their attributes and associations.
3. Discard unnecessary and incorrect classes, attributes and associations.
4. Use inheritance to share common structure.

The object model describes the structure of the objects in the system—their identity, their relationships to other objects, their attributes, and their operations. The object model depicts the primary view of how the real world in which the system interacts is divided and the overall decomposition of the system. The object model provides the framework into which the other models are placed.

The object model is represented graphically with an object diagram. The object diagram contains classes interconnected by association lines. Each class represents a set of individual objects. The association lines establish relationships among classes. Each association line represents a set of links from the object of one class to the object of another class. Now we discuss the concepts of object, class and relationships between objects and/or classes. We also introduce the notations and symbols of OMT used for object, class and relationships.

16.2 OBJECT AND CLASS

A class describes a collection of similar objects. It is a template where certain basic characteristics of a set of objects are defined. A class defines the basic attributes and the operations of the objects of that type. Defining a class does not define any object, but it only creates a template. For objects to be actually created, instances of the class are to be created as per the requirement of the case.

Classes are built on the basis of abstraction, where a set of similar objects is observed and their common characteristics are listed. Of all these, the characteristics of concern to the system under observation are taken and the class definition is made. The attributes of no concern to the system are left out. This is known as abstraction. So, the abstraction is the process of hiding superfluous details and highlighting pertinent details in respect to the system under development. It should be noted that the abstraction of an object varies according to its application. For instance, while defining a pen class for a stationery shop, the attributes of concern might be the pen color, ink color, pen type etc., whereas a pen class for a manufacturing firm would be containing the other dimensions of the pen like its diameter, its shape and size etc. Each application-domain concept from the real world that is important to the application should be modeled as an object class. Classes are arranged into hierarchies sharing common structure and behavior and are associated with other classes. This gives rise to the concept of inheritance. Through inheritance, a new type of class can be defined using a similar existing class with a few new features. For instance, a class vehicle can be defined with the basic functionality of any vehicle and a new class called car can be derived out of it with a few modifications. This would save the developers time and effort as the classes already existing are reused without much change.

In OMT, classes are represented by a rectangular box which may be divided into three parts as shown in Fig. 16.1. The top part contains the name of the class written in bold, middle part contains a list of attributes and bottom part contains a list of operations.

ClassName
Attribute-name1:data-type1=default-val1 Attribute-name2:data-type2=default-val2
Operation-name1(argument1):result-type1 Operation-name2(argument2):result-type2

Fig. 16.1

An attribute is a data value held by objects in a class. Each attribute has a value for each object instance. This value should be a pure data value, not an object. Attributes are listed in the second part of the class box. Attributes may or may not be shown; it depends on the level of detail desired. Each attribute name may be followed by the optional details such as type and default value.

An object model should generally distinguish independent base attributes from dependent derived attributes. A derived attribute is that which is derived from other attributes. For example, age is a derived attribute, as it can be derived from date-of-birth and current-date attributes.

An operation is a function or transformation that may be applied to or by objects in a class. Operations are listed in the third part of the class box.

Operations may or may not be shown; it depends on the level of detail desired. Each operation may be followed by optional details such as argument list and result type. The name and type of each argument may be given. An empty argument list in parentheses shows explicitly that there are no arguments. All objects in a class share the same operations. Each operation has a target object as an implicit argument. An operation may have arguments in addition to its target object, which parameterize the operation.

The behavior of the operation depends on the class of its target. An operation may be polymorphic in nature.

A polymorphic operation means that the same operation takes on different forms in different/same classes. Overloading of operators, overloading of functions and overriding of functions provided by object-oriented programming languages are all examples of polymorphic operations. A method is the implementation of an operation for a class. The method depends only on the class of the target object.

Now, we present a number of examples of classes to clarify what we have discussed above. Figure 16.2 shows the class Book. Attributes of Book are title, author, publisher along with their data types. Operations on Book areopen(), close(), read().

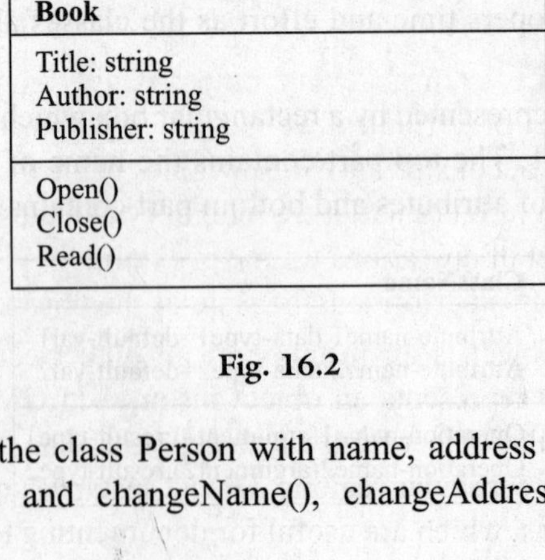

Fig. 16.2

Figure 16.3 shows the class Person with name, address & phone along with their data types as attributes and changeName(), changeAddress() & changePhone() as operations.

Person
Name: string Address: string Phone: number
ChangeName() ChangeAddress() ChangePhone()

Fig. 16.3

Figure 16.4 shows the class Window with xMin, yMin, xMax, yMax along with their data types as attributes and draw(), cut(), erase() & move() as operations.

Window
xMin: integer yMin: integer xMax: integer yMax: integer
Draw() Cut() Erase() Move()

Fig. 16.4

Now, let us formally define an object. An object is a concept, abstraction, or thing with crisp boundaries and meaning for the problem at hand. An object has the following four main characteristics:

- Unique identification
- Set of attributes
- Set of states
- Set of operations (behavior)

Unique identification, we mean every object has a unique name by which it is identified in the system. Set of attributes, we mean every object has a set of properties in which we are interested in. Set of states we mean values of attributes of an object constitute the state of the object. Every object will have a number of states but at a given time it can be in one of those states. Set of operations we mean externally visible actions an object can perform. When an operation is performed, the state of the object may change.

In other words, an object is an instance of an object class. Figure 16.2 (rounded box) represents an object instance in OMT. Object instance is a particular object from an object class. The box may/may not be divided in particular regions. Object instances can be used in instance diagrams, which are useful for documenting test cases and discussing examples.

(ClassName)
Object name

Fig. 16.5

Now we give three examples of objects of class Book shown in Figures 1.2, which are shown in Fig. 16.6 (*a*), (*b*) and (*c*) respectively.

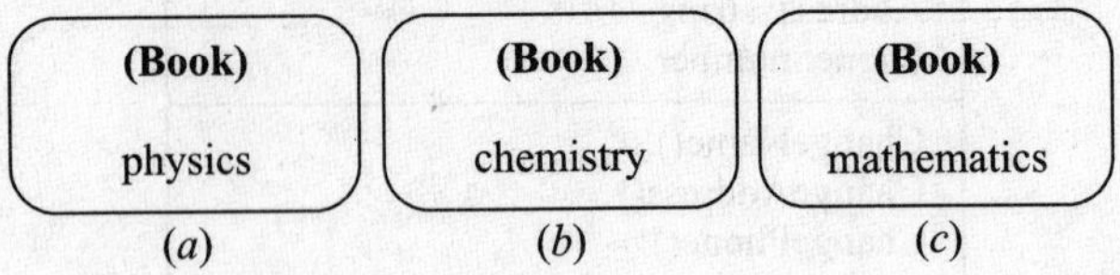

Fig. 16.6

Here we give three examples of objects of class Person shown in Figures 1.3, which are shown in Fig. 16.7 (*a*), (*b*) and (*c*) respectively.

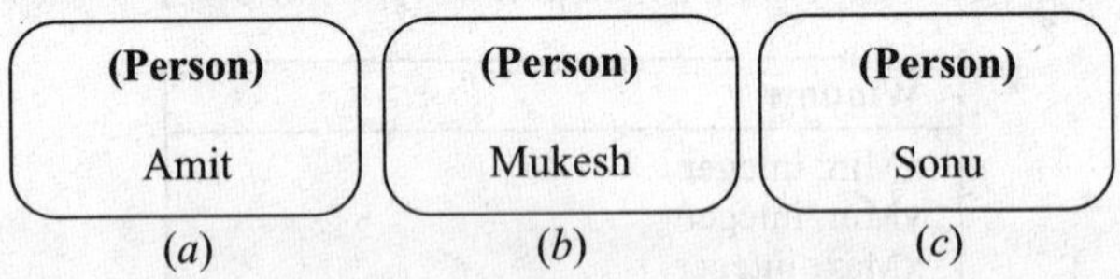

Fig. 16.7

Next we give three examples of objects of class Window shown in Figures 1.4, which are shown in Fig. 16.8 (*a*), (*b*) and (*c*) respectively.

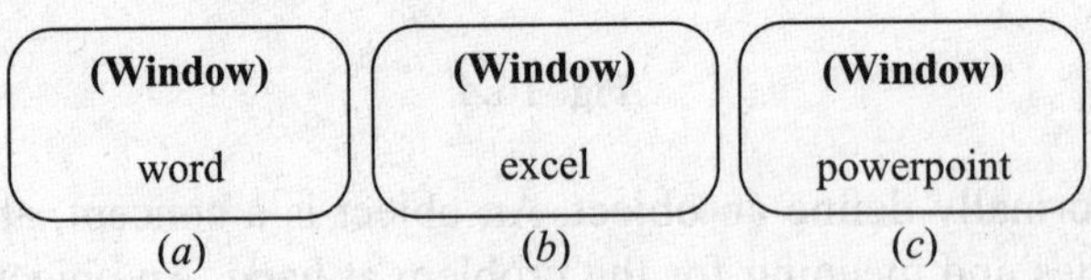

Fig. 16.8

Let us introduce the concept of derived object. It is defined as a function of one or more objects. It is completely determined by the other objects. Derived object is redundant but can be included in the object model. After having discussed the concepts of objects and their classes, let us discuss relationships between objects and between classes.

Links and Associations

A link is a physical or conceptual connection between object instances. In OMT, link is represented by a line labeled with its name as shown in Fig. 16.9.

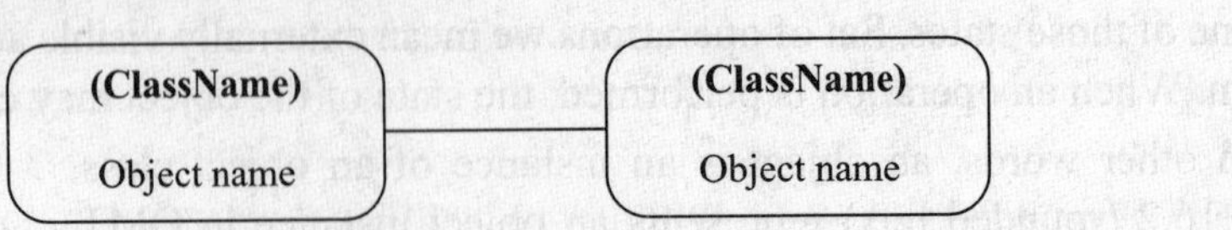

Fig. 16.9

For example Mohit flies Spice. So 'flies' is a link between object instance Mohit of class Person and object instance of class spice Airplane as shown in Fig. 16.10. Sumit reads

Physics. Here reads is a link between object instance Sumit of class Person and object instance.

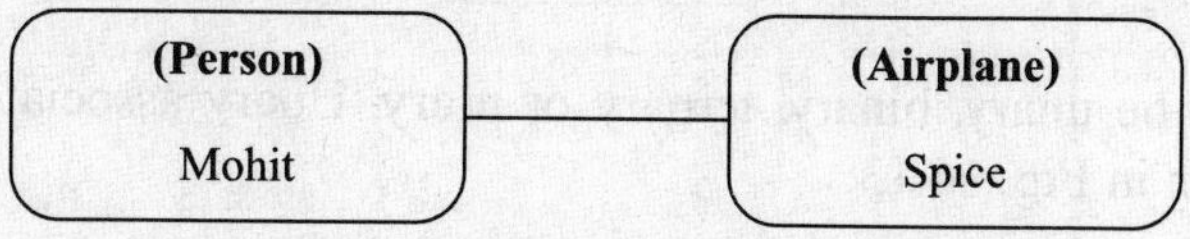

Fig. 16.10

Physics of class Book as shown in Fig. 16.11.

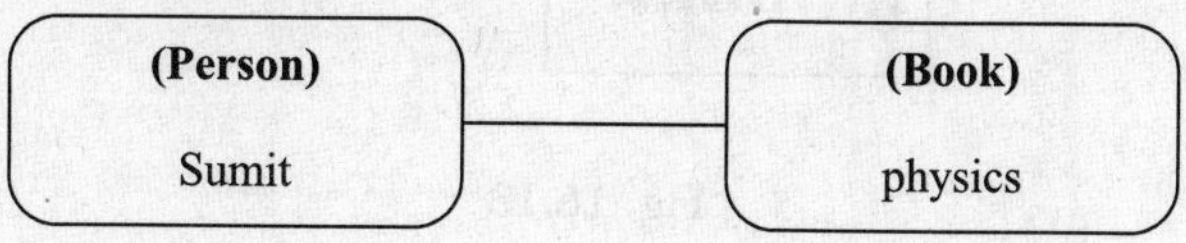

Fig. 16.11

An association describes a group of links with common structure and common semantics between two or more classes. Association is represented by a line labeled with the association name in italics as shown in Fig. 16.12.

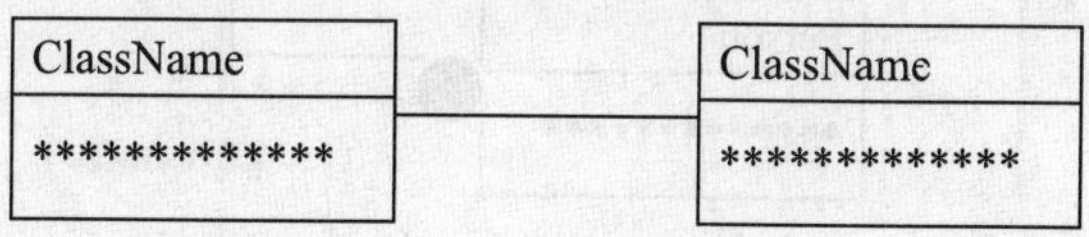

Fig. 16.12

Association names are optional. If the association is given a name, it should be written above the line. Association names are initialized. In case of a binary association, the name reads in a particular direction (*i.e.*, left to right), but the binary association can be traversed in either direction. For example, a pilot flies an airplane or an airplane is flown by a pilot. All the links in an association connect objects from the same classes. Associations are bidirectional in nature.

Multiplicity: It specifies how many instances of one class may relate to a single instance of an associated class. Multiplicity constrains the number of related objects.

There are special line terminators to indicate certain common multiplicity values. A solid ball is the symbol for "many", meaning zero, one or more. A hollow ball indicates "optional", meaning zero or one. The multiplicity is indicated with special symbols at the ends of association lines. In the most general case, multiplicity can be specified with a number or set of intervals. If no multiplicity symbol is specified that means a one-to-one association. The rules of multiplicity are summarized below:

- Line without any ball indicates one-to-one association.
- Hollow ball indicates zero or one.
- Solid ball indicates zero, one or more.

- Numbers written on solid ball such as 1, 2, 6 indicates 1 or 2 or 6.
- Numbers written on solid ball such as 1+ indicates 1 or more, 2+ indicates 2 or more etc.

An association can be unary, binary, ternary or n-ary. Unary association is between the same class as shown in Fig. 16.13.

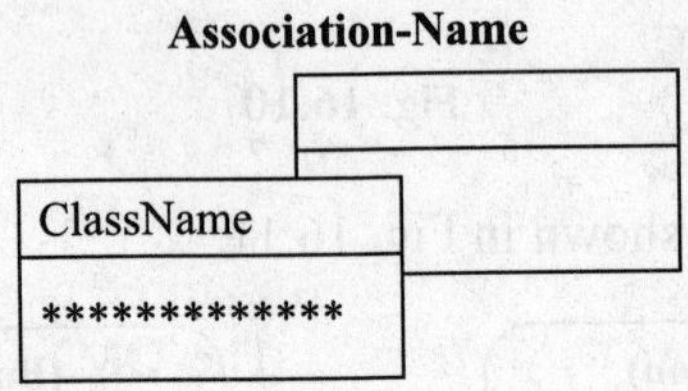

Fig. 16.13

Example of unary association is Person teaches Person as shown in Fig. 16.14. Other examples of unary association can be Person marries a Person, Person manages Person etc.

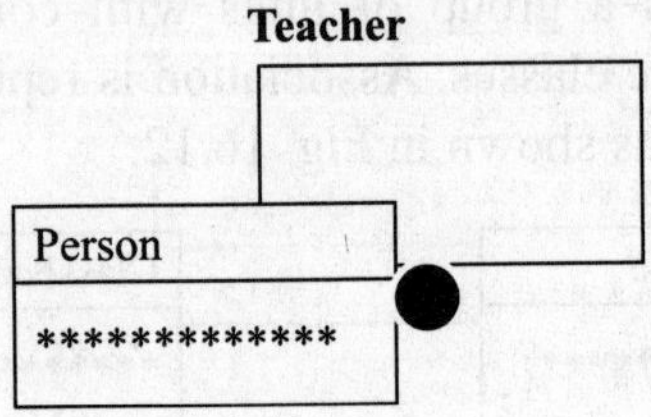

Fig. 16.14

A binary association is an association between two classes as shown in Fig. 1.15.

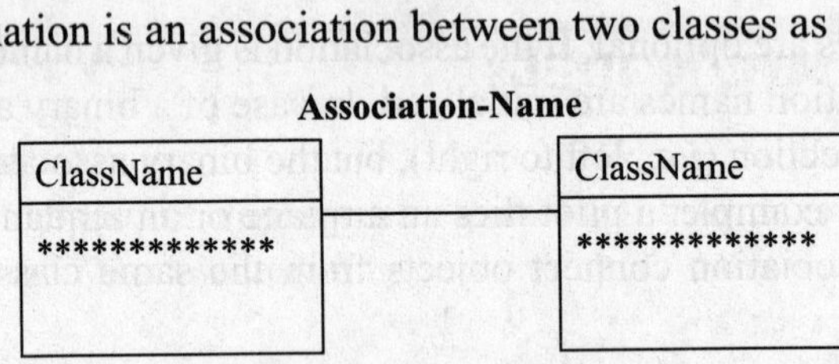

Fig. 16.15

Example of a binary association is "Person sits on a Chair". One person can sit at one chair. So multiplicity of this association is one-to-one as shown in Fig. 16.16.

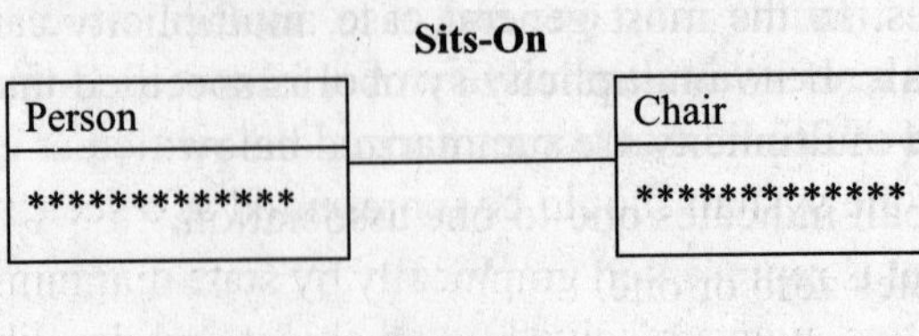

Fig. 16.16

Example of a binary association is "Supplier supplies Parts". One supplier can supply many parts or one part can be supplied by many suppliers. So multiplicity of this association is many-to-many as shown in Fig. 16.17.

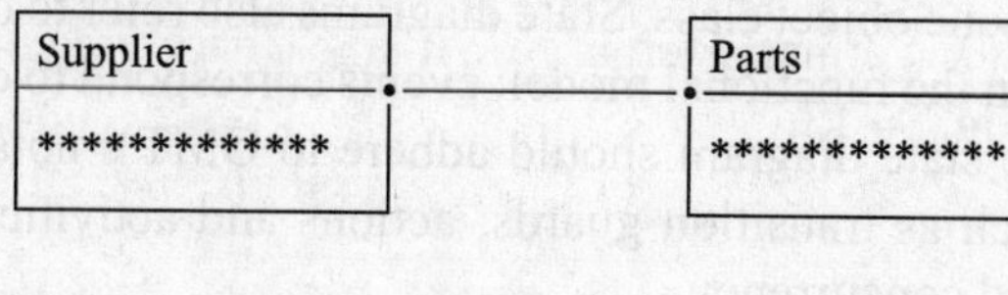

Fig. 16.17

Ternary association is an association among three classes. On the same line, n-ary association is an association among n classes. The OMT symbol for ternary and n-ary associations is a diamond with lines connecting to related classes as shown in Fig. 16.18. A name for the association is optional and is written next to the diamond. An n-ary associations cannot be subdivided into binary associations without losing information.

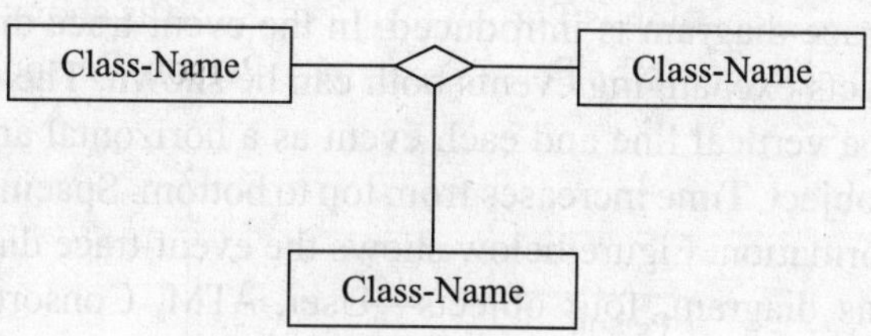

Fig. 16.18

There are many other concepts related to associations such as link attribute, link class, role names, qualifiers etc.

16.3 THE DYNAMIC MODEL

The dynamic model reflects the changes to objects and their relationships over time, demonstrating possible control flows through the system. Rumbaugh (1991) verifies this: "*The dynamic model shows the time independent behaviour of the system and the objects in it*".

The dynamic model is important for interactive and real time systems. It is vital for applications that depend on collecting information from the user.

Dynamic model describes those aspects of the system that changes with the time. It is used to specify and implement control aspects of the system. It depicts states, transitions, events and actions. The dynamic model includes event trace diagrams describing scenarios. An event is an external stimulus from one object to another, which occurs at a particular point in time. An event is a one-way transmission of information from one object to another. A scenario is a sequence of events that occurs during one particular execution of a system. Each basic execution of the system should be represented as a scenario.

The dynamic model is represented graphically by state diagrams. A state corresponds to the interval between two events received by an object and describes the "value" of the object for that time period. A state is an abstraction of an object's attribute values and links, where sets of values are grouped together into a state according to properties that affect the general behavior of the object. Each state diagram shows the state and event sequences permitted in a system for one object class. State diagrams also refer to other models: actions correspond to functions in the functional model; events correspond to operations on objects in the object model. The state diagram should adhere to OMT's notation and exploit the capabilities of OMT, such as transition guards, actions and activities, nesting (state and event generalization), and concurrency.

The outcomes of dynamic modeling are scenario, event-trace diagram and state diagram.

16.4 EVENT-TRACE DIAGRAM

The limitation of scenario is that it is not clear from scenario, how many objects are involved and which object generates an event and which object receives an event. To overcome this limitation, an event-trace diagram is introduced. In the event-trace diagram, the sequence of events and the objects exchanging events both can be shown. The diagram (Fig. 16.19) shows each object as a vertical line and each event as a horizontal arrow from the sender object to the receiver object. Time increases from top to bottom. Spacing between horizontal arrows carries no information. Figure below shows the event-trace diagram for interaction with the ATM. In this diagram, four objects—User, ATM, Consortium and Bank—are involved, which are shown with four vertical lines. User generates an event "insert card" which is shown as horizontal arrow from user to ATM. That means source of the event is User object and destination of the event is ATM. In response to this event, the ATM generates the "request password" event to the User. Spacing between these two arrows is insignificant but the event "insert card" occurs before the event "request password" and so on.

16.4.1 State Machine

A state machine is a behavior which specifies the sequence of states an object visits during its lifetime in response to events, together with its responses to those events. Now, we describe the various concepts related to state machine in the following subsections.

16.4.2 State

A state is a condition during the life of an object during which it satisfies some condition, performs some activity, or waits for some external event. A state corresponds to the interval between two events received by an object and describes the "value" of the object for that time period. A state is an abstraction of an object's attribute values and links, where sets of values are grouped together into a state according to properties that affect the general behavior of the object. For instance, stack is empty or stack is full are different states of the object stack. As state corresponds to interval between two events received by an object so it has duration. A sub state is a state that is nested in another state. A state that has sub states is called a composite state. A state that has no sub states is called a simple state. Sub states may be nested to any level.

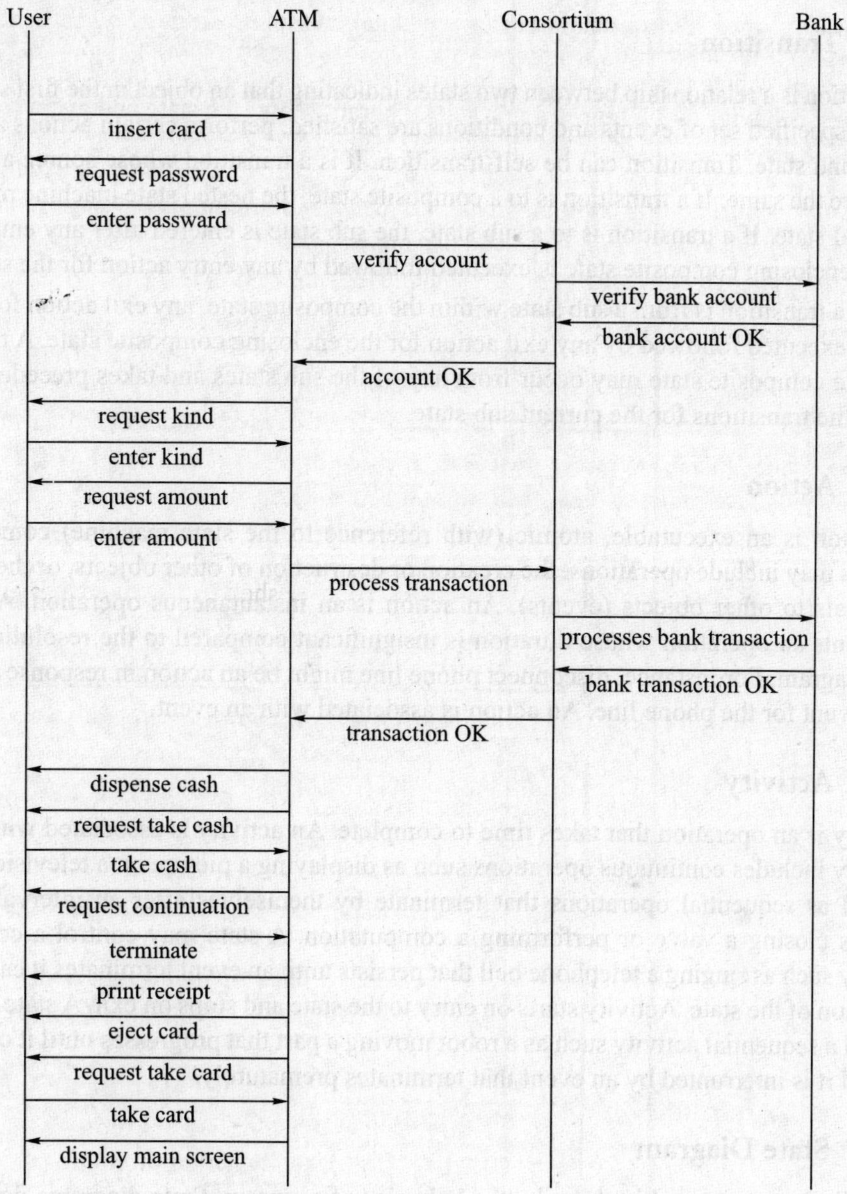

Fig. 16.19

16.4.3 Event

An event is the specification of a significant occurrence. For a state machine, an event is the occurrence of a stimulus that can trigger a state transition. In other words, we can say an event is something that happens at a point in time. An event does not have duration. An individual stimulus from one object to another is an event. Press a button on mouse, airplane departs from an airport are examples of events.

16.4.4 Transition

A transition is a relationship between two states indicating that an object in the first state will, when a specified set of events and conditions are satisfied, perform certain actions and enter the second state. Transition can be self-transition. It is a transition whose source and target states are the same. If a transition is to a composite state, the nested state machine must have an initial state. If a transition is to a sub state, the sub state is entered after any entry action for the enclosing composite state is executed followed by any entry action for the sub state.

If a transition is from a sub state within the composite state, any exit action for the sub state is executed followed by any exit action for the enclosing composite state. A transition from the composite state may occur from any of the sub states and takes precedence over any of the transitions for the current sub state.

16.4.5 Action

An action is an executable, atomic (with reference to the state machine) computation. Actions may include operations, the creation or destruction of other objects, or the sending of signals to other objects (events). An action is an instantaneous operation. An action represents an operation whose duration is insignificant compared to the resolution of the state diagram. For instance, disconnect phone line might be an action in response to an on-hook event for the phone line. An action is associated with an event.

16.4.6 Activity

Activity is an operation that takes time to complete. An activity is associated with a state. Activity includes continuous operations such as displaying a picture on a television screen as well as sequential operations that terminate by themselves after an interval of time such as closing a valve or performing a computation. A state may control a continuous activity such as ringing a telephone bell that persists until an event terminates it causing the transition of the state. Activity starts on entry to the state and stops on exit. A state may also control a sequential activity such as a robot moving a part that progresses until it completes or until it is interrupted by an event that terminates prematurely.

16.4.7 State Diagram

State diagrams are used to describe the behavior of a system. State diagrams describe all of the possible states of an object as events occur. Each diagram usually represents objects of a single class and tracks the different states of its objects through the system. It relates events and states. A change of state caused by an event is called a transition. Transition is drawn as an arrow from the receiving state to the target state. A state diagram is graph whose nodes are states and whose directed arcs are transitions labeled by event names. State diagram specifies the state sequence caused by an event sequence.

16.4.8 When to use State Diagrams

Use state diagrams to demonstrate the behavior of an object through many use cases of the system. Only use state diagrams for classes where it is necessary to understand the behavior of the object through the entire system. Not all classes will require a state diagram and state diagrams are not useful for describing the collaboration of all objects in a use case. State diagrams are combined with other diagrams such as interaction diagrams and activity diagrams.

16.4.9 How to draw State Diagrams

State diagrams have very few elements. The basic elements are rounded oxes representing the state of the object and arrows indicting the transition to the next state. The activity section of the state symbol depicts what activities the object will be doing while it is in that state as shown Fig. 16.20.

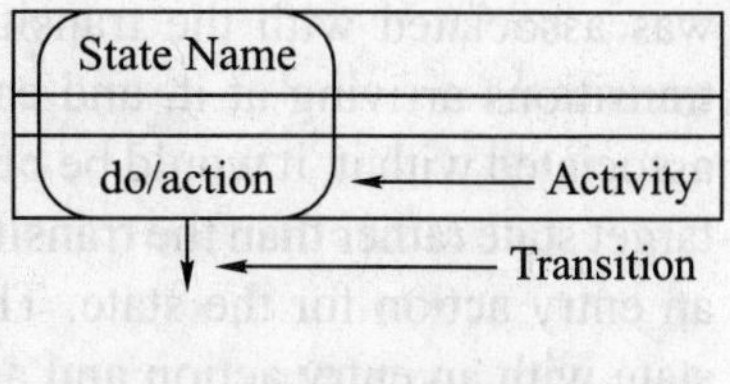

Fig. 16.20

Initial and Final States: All state diagrams being with an initial state of the object as shown in Fig. 16.21. This is the state of the object when it is created. After the initial state the object begins changing states. Conditions based on the activities can determine what the next state the object transitions to.

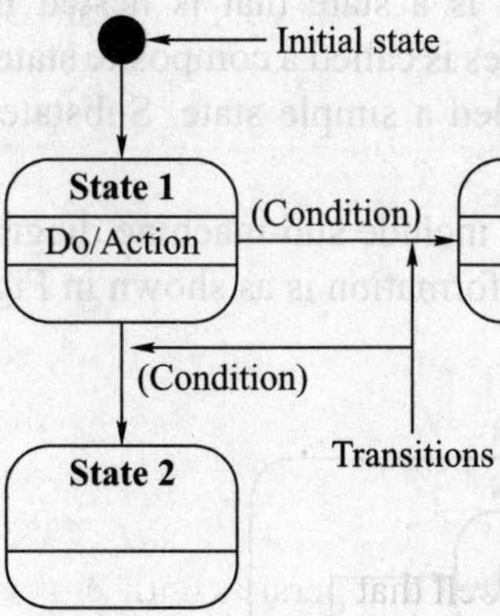

Fig. 16.21

The initial state is denoted by a filled black circle and may be labeled with a name. The final state is denoted by a circle with a dot inside and may also be labeled with a name as shown in Fig. 16.22.

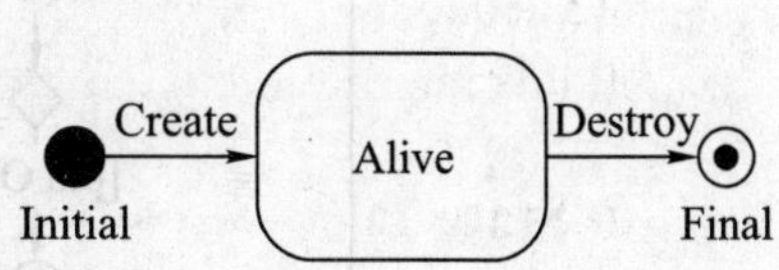

Fig. 16.22

Transitions: Transitions from one state to the next are denoted by lines with arrowheads. A transition may have a trigger, a guard and an effect, as shown in Fig. 16.23.

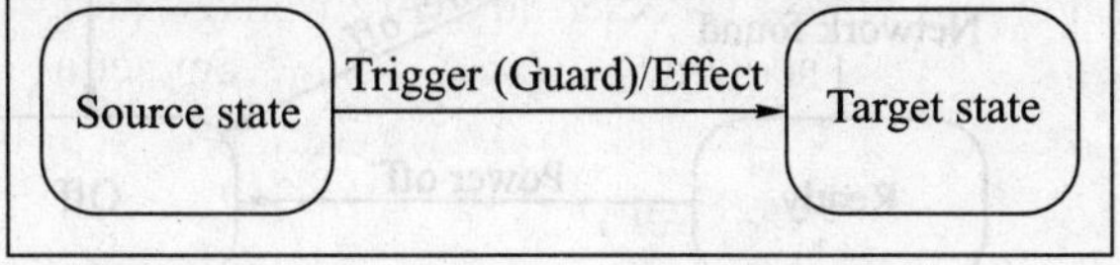

Fig. 16.23

"Trigger" is the cause of the transition, which could be a signal, an event, a change in some condition, or the passage of time. "Guard" is a condition which must be true in order for the trigger to cause the transition. "Effect" is an action which will be invoked directly on the object that owns the state machine as a result of the transition.

State Actions: In the transition example above, an effect was associated with the transition. If the target state had many transitions arriving at it, and each transition had the same effect associated with it, it would be better to associate the effect with the target state rather than the transitions. This can be done by defining an entry action for the state. The diagram in Fig. 16.24 shows a state with an entry action and an exit action. It is also possible to define actions that occur on events, or actions that always occur. It is possible to define any number of actions of each type.

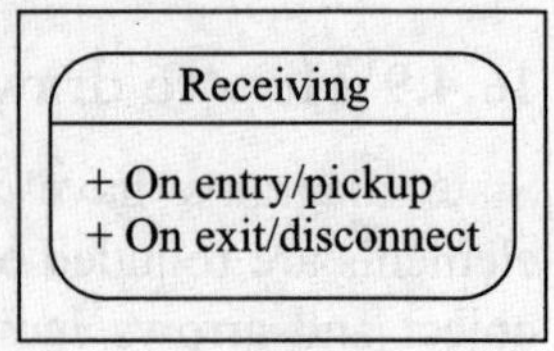

Fig. 16.24

Self-Transitions: A state can have a transition that returns to itself, as shown in the Fig. 16.25. This is the most useful when an effect is associated with the transition.

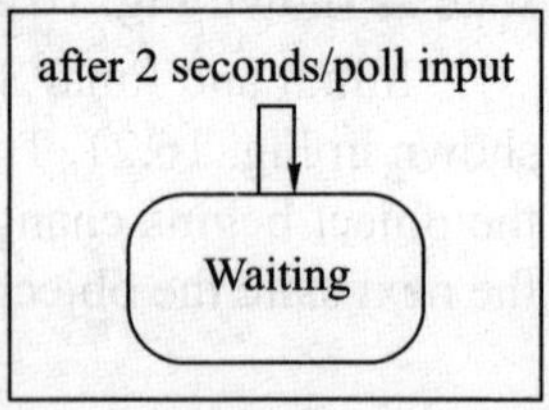

Fig. 16.25

Compound States: A substate is a state that is nested in another state. A state that has substates is called a composite state. A state that has no substates is called a simple state. Substates may be nested to any level.

A state machine diagram may include sub-machine diagrams, as in Fig. 16.26. The alternative way to show the same information is as shown in Fig. 16.27.

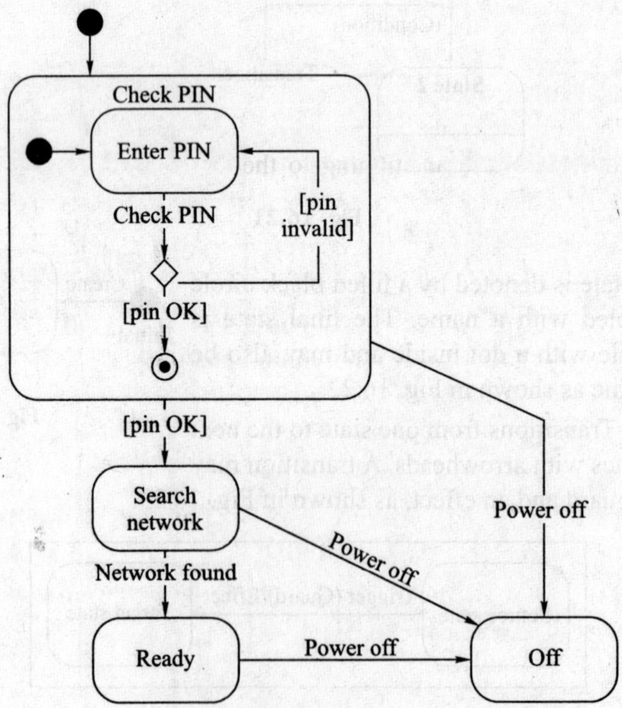

Fig. 16.26

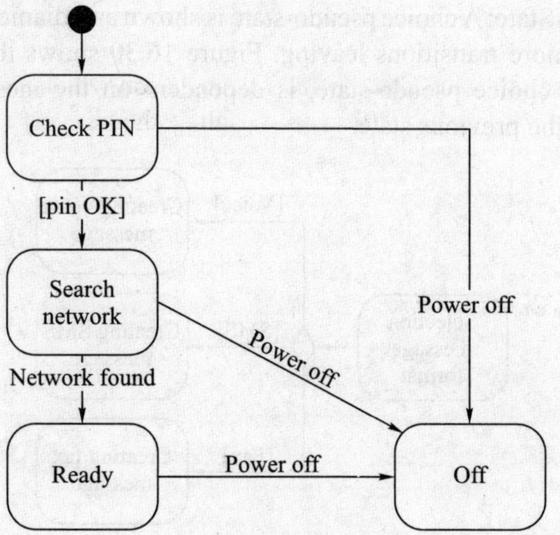

Fig. 16.27

The notation in the above version indicates that the details of the Check PIN submachine are shown in a separate diagram.

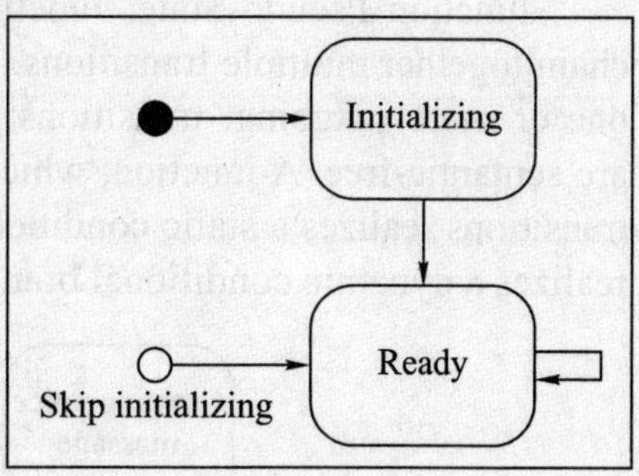

Fig. 16.28

Entry Point: Sometimes you won't want to enter a sub-machine at the normal initial state. For example, in the sub-machine shown in Fig. 16.28, it would be normal to begin in the "Initializing" state, but if for some reason it wasn't necessary to perform the initialization, it would be possible to begin in the "Ready" state by transitioning to the named entry point.

Exit Point: In a similar manner to entry points, it is possible to have named alternative exit points. Figure 16.29 gives an example where the state executed after the main processing state depends on which route is used to transition out of the state.

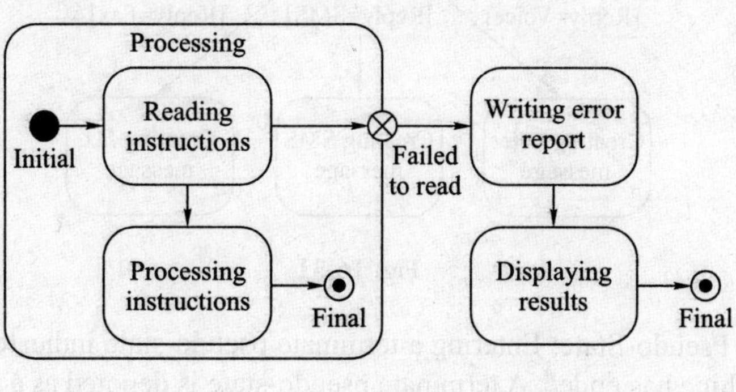

Fig. 16.29

Choice Pseudo-State: A choice pseudo-state is shown as a diamond with one transition arrives and two or more transitions leaving. Figure 16.30 shows that whichever state is arrived at, after the choice pseudo-state, is dependent on the message format selected during execution of the previous state.

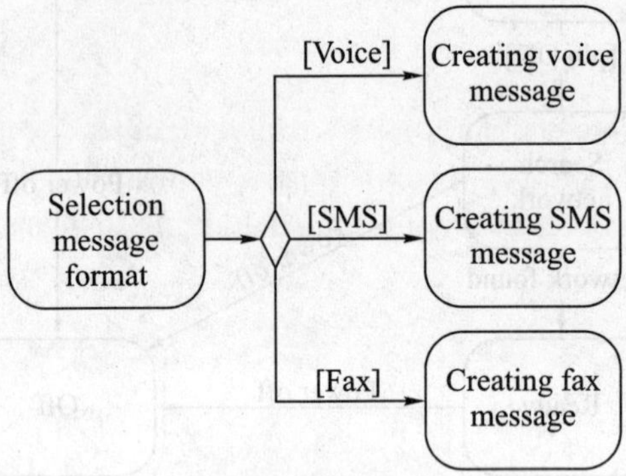

Fig. 16.30

Junction Pseudo-State: Junction pseudo-states as shown in Fig. 16.31 are used to chain together multiple transitions. A single junction can have one or more incoming, and one or more outgoing, transitions; a guard can be applied to each transition. Junctions are semantic-free. A junction, which splits an incoming transition into multiple outgoing transitions realizes a static conditional branch, as opposed to a choice pseudo-state which realizes a dynamic conditional branch.

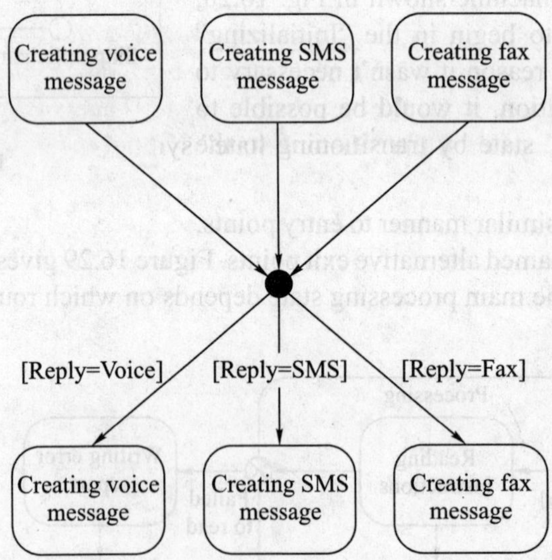

Fig. 16.31

Terminate Pseudo-State: Entering a terminate pseudo-state indicates that the lifeline of the state machine has ended. A terminate pseudo-state is denoted as a cross as shown in Fig. 16.32.

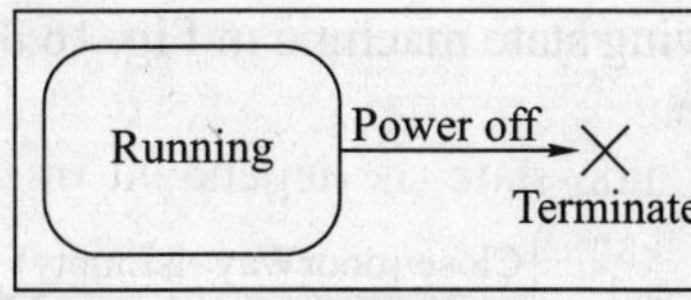

Fig. 16.32

History States: A history state is used to remember the previous state of a state machine when it was interrupted. The diagram shown in Fig. 16.33 illustrates the use of history states. The example is a state machine belonging to a washing machine.

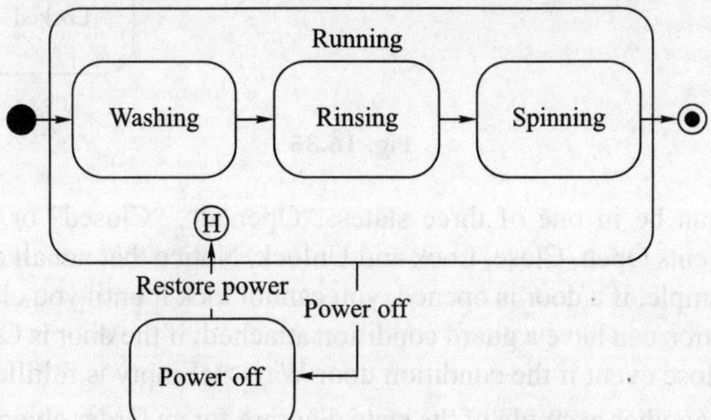

Fig. 16.33

In this state machine, when a washing machine is running, it will progress from "Washing" through "Rinsing" to "Spinning". If there is a power cut, the washing machine will stop running and will go to the "Power Off" state. Then when the power is restored, the Running state is entered at the "History State" symbol meaning that it should resume where it last left-off.

Concurrent Regions: A state may be divided into regions containing sub-states that exist and execute concurrently. Figure 16.34 shows that within the state "Applying Brakes", the front and rear brakes will be operating simultaneously and independently. Notice the use of fork and join pseudo-states, rather than choice and merge pseudo-states. These symbols are used to synchronize the concurrent threads.

A state machine diagram models the behavior of a single object, specifying the sequence of events that an object goes through during its lifetime in response to events.

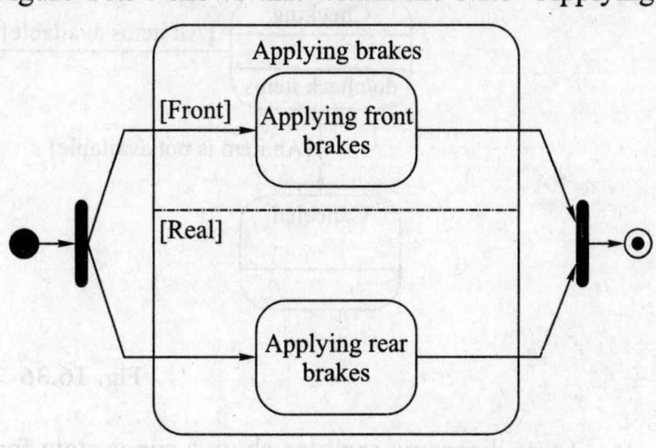

Fig. 16.34

As an example, the following state machine in Fig. 16.35 shows the states that a door goes through during its lifetime.

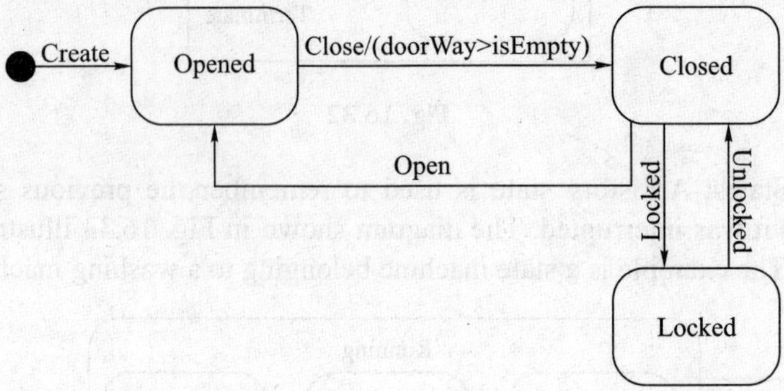

Fig. 16.35

The door can be in one of three states: "Opened", "Closed" or "Locked". It can respond to the events Open, Close, Lock and Unlock. Notice that not all events are valid in all states; for example, if a door is opened, you cannot lock it until you close it. Also notice that a state transition can have a guard condition attached: if the door is Opened, it can only respond to the Close event if the condition door Way->isEmpty is fulfilled.

Let us take another example of the state diagram for an Order object as shown in Fig. 16.36. When the object enters the Checking state it performs the activity "check items." After the activity is completed the object transitions to the next state based on the conditions [all items available] or [an item is not available]. If an item is not available the order is canceled. If all items are available then the order is dispatched. When the object transitions to the Dispatching state the activity "initiate delivery" is performed. After this activity is complete the object transitions again to the Delivered state.

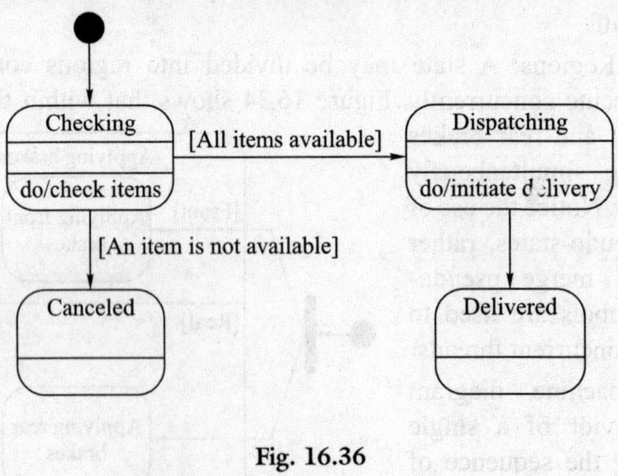

Fig. 16.36

State diagrams can also show a super-state for the object. A super-state is used when many transitions lead to a certain state. Instead of showing all of the transitions from each state to the redundant state a super-state can be used to show that all of the states inside of the super-state can transition to the redundant state. This helps make the state diagram easier to read.

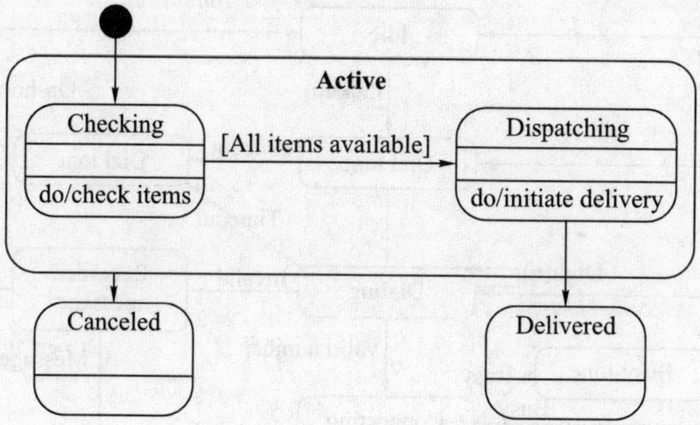

Fig. 16.37

Figure 16.38 shows a super-state. Both the Checking and Dispatching states can transition into the Canceled state, so a transition is shown from a super-state named Active to the state Cancel. By contrast, the state Dispatching can only transition to the Delivered state, so we show an arrow only from the Dispatching state to the Delivered state.

Another illustrative example of state diagram is shown in Fig. 16.38. It shows the bank transaction and verification of bank account. Activities are shown in the state such as do: update account, do: verify card number and do: verify password. Diagram also shows initial and final states.

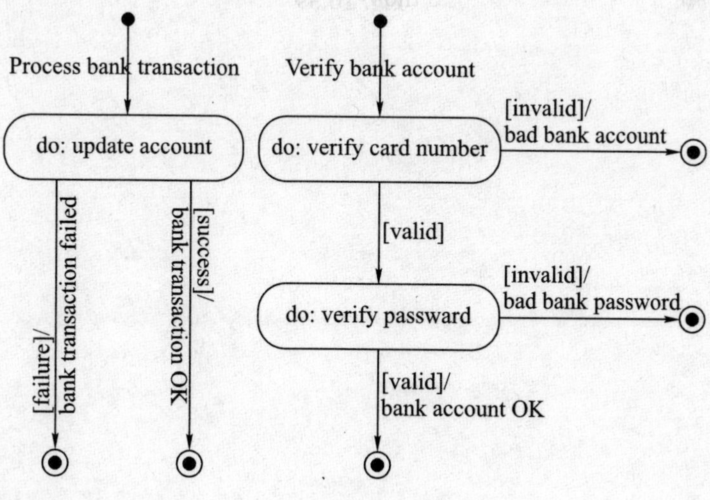

Fig. 16.38

Now, we consider one more example of state diagram for phone line is shown Fig. 16.39. A phone can have many states such as idle, dial tone, dialing, connecting ringing etc. various states and events are shown in Fig. 16.39.

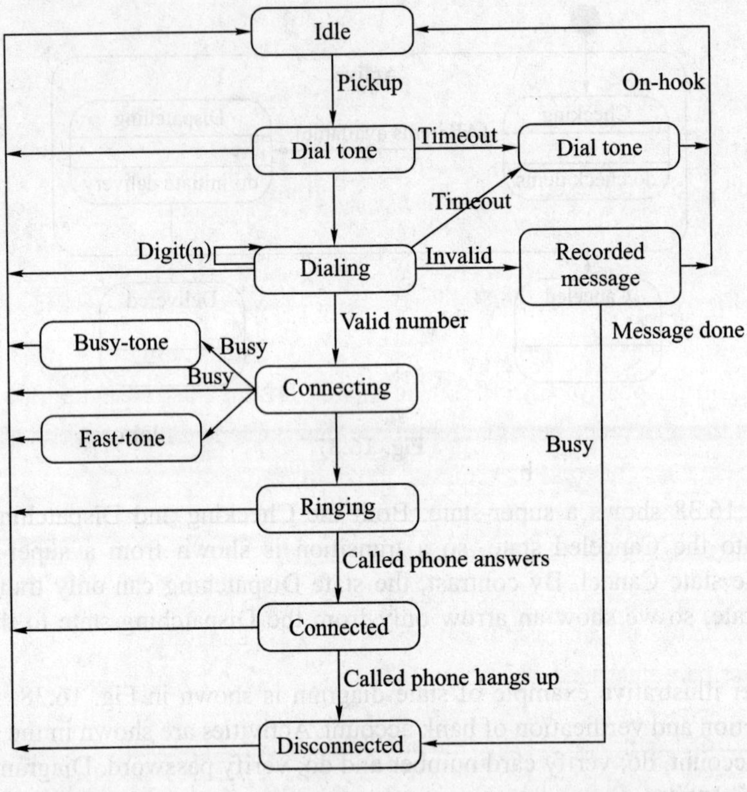

Fig. 16.39

ASSIGNMENT-1

QUESTIONS

1. What are the uses and application of UML diagrams?
2. What do Actors represent in a Use case diagram?
3. What is a use case and how is it connected to the outside world?
4. What is the difference between scenario and a use case?
5. Explain the following terms:
   (*a*) Use case (*b*) Actor (*c*) Transaction
6. What is the purpose of EXTEND and INCLUDE in a use case diagram?
7. What is the difference between Sequence diagram and collaboration diagram?
8. Can a Sequence diagram be replaced by a collaboration diagram?
9. How do you add an object to already existing interaction diagram?
10. Explain Logical view of Rational Rose Model?
11. What is the purpose of a class diagram?
12. Give the names of various components of a Class Diagram?
13. What are parameterised classes in UML?
14. How do you identify strong aggregation (composition) relationship between classes?
15. Classify the following as standard aggregation, composition or association:
    (*a*) A telephone and its handset (*b*) A school and its teacher
    (*c*) A book and its chapters
16. Create a list of use cases for:
    (*a*) A telephone answering machine (*b*) A video-cassette recorder
17. Develop a complete set of use cases for the Small Hotel Reservation System.
18. Model a simple vending machine that can be in four states: Waiting, Receiving money, Returning money.
19. What is basic relation between an object and a class?
20. Differentiate between a Package, Component Diagram and Deployment diagram.
21. Write a note on Class diagram taking library system as an example.
22. For the following entities develop class and object:
    (*a*) Book (*b*) Teacher
23. Compare and contrast between Static model and dynamic model.
24. Differentiate between State chart diagram and activity diagram.
25. What is difference between Sequence diagram and Activity diagram?

26. What is an actor ? How is it different from a user?
27. What is an event class?
28. What is the purpose of Sequence diagram and Collabration diagram?
29. What is the significance of use case diagram from modeling prospective? Consider a Hospital Management System and draw the use case diagram and the class diagram after enlisting the requirements for the system.

ASSIGNMENT-2

QUESTIONS

1. Classify the following as standard aggregation, composition or association:
   (*a*) A telephone and its handset (*b*) A school and its teacher
   (*c*) A book and its chapters
2. Create a list of use cases for:
   (*a*) A telephone answering machine (*b*) A video-cassette recorder
3. Develop a complete set of use cases for the Small Hotel Reservation System.
4. Model a simple vending machine that can be in four states: Waiting, Receiving money, Returning money.
5. What is basic relation between an object and a class?
6. Differentiate between a Package, Component Diagram and Deployment diagram.
7. Write a note on Class diagram taking library system as an example.
8. For the following entities develop class and object:
   (*a*) Book (*b*) Teacher
9. Compare and contrast between Static model and dynamic model.
10. Differentiate between State chart diagram and activity diagram.
11. What is difference between Sequence diagram and Activity diagram?
12. What is an actor? How is it different from a user?
13. What is an event class?
14. What is the purpose of Sequence diagram and Collabration diagram?
15. What is the significance of use case diagram from modeling prospective? Consider a Hospital Management System and draw the use case diagram and the class diagram after enlisting the requirements for the system.

ASSIGNMENT–3

QUESTIONS

1. Differentiate between Object Oriented design and Function oriented design?
2. Give the advantages of Object Oriented Design.
3. Describe the difference between Structured Analysis and Object Oriented Analysis.
4. What is the purpose of Domain Analysis?
5. For the following classes develop attributes and methods:
   (*a*) Account Voucher (*b*) Order
   (*c*) Computer
6. Draw use case models for the following scenarios:
   (*a*) Payment for Video library (*b*) Withdrawl of money from Atm
7. Compare and contrast the following terms:
   (*a*) Static model versus Dynamic model
8. Explain the following terms:
   (*a*) Association (*b*) Generalization
   (*c*) Aggregation
9. Who are actors in a Use case Scenarios? How would you identify them? How is the actor different From user?
10. Explain the following terms in context of use cases:
    (*a*) Use case (*b*) Actor
    (*c*) Transaction
11. Consider a Library system each book in a library cotains bibliography, each bibliography consists consistes of a no of references to other books. A book will be refered to in many cases and Therefore a reference can appear in more than one bibliography. Draw a Class Diagram for this situation and discuss the possible uses of aggregation in the Diagram.
12. Explain the three types of Objects in Analysis Model.
13. What is the importance of Construction phase?
14. Which UML diagrams are useful for analysis modeling? Provide an example of each.
15. Describe the weaknesses of use-cases as part of the requirements engineering process.

ASSIGNMENT-4

QUESTIONS

1. Define conceptual model of UML?
2. Explain common and extensible mechanisms of UML using examples?
3. UML is a language for visualizing, constructing, documenting and specification. Suppose your college director hires you to make a software for your institution. Elaborate how will you use the above mentioned feature of the UML for developing the software for your institute.
4. Explain the keywords in "Unified Modelling Language".
5. Whether unified method and unified modeling language are same or different?
6. Describe some techniques for expressing business rules/constraints in UML.
7. State true or false: UML means one can handle object oriented analysis and design.
8. Name five object oriented methods except UML and compare any three mentioning the strength and weaknesses while modeling the various aspects of a system.
9. What are the different views that are considered when building an object oriented software system?
10. Compare three prominent object oriented methods except UML, considering static, functional and dynamic aspects of the system to be modeled?

ASSIGNMENT–5

QUESTIONS

1. What is System Development Life Cycle (SDLC)? Explain briefly about the stages in SDLC according to Waterfall Life Cycle Model?
2. Write short note on:
   (*a*) Spiral Model
   (*b*) Prototype Model
3. What is the purpose of the class in a system? How does roles, responsibilities, attributes and Methods help in achieving the purpose?
4. Describe the role of risk analysis in evolutionary process models like the spiral model.
5. Explain the term "System Development is model Building" emphasising on the various models in system development.
6. What are the different stages of system development life cycle?
7. Why can you not describe boundary use cases during requirement illicitation or analysis?
8. Briefly explain the various Requirement Elicitation Techniques.
9. Discuss in brief the strength and weakness of the following life cycle models:
   (*i*) Evolution model
   (*ii*) Iterative model
   (*iii*) Code and fix
   (*iv*) Waterfall model
   (*v*) Spiral model
10. Explain the process of requirements elicitation in detail and the activities to be performed by stakeholders in the review of gathered requirements?

APPENDIX

1. Draw a Usecase Diagram, Activity Diagram, Analysis Model and Sequence Diagram (for each usecase). Write description of each use case for a Simple Answering Machine given below.

- Use Case: Leave a Message
  - o Actor: Caller
  - o Pre-condition: Room on Tape
  - o Post-condition: New Message
- Use Case: Review Messages
  - o Primary Path: Review New Messages
  - o Alternate Path: No New Messages
  - o Actor: Owner
- Use Case: Review Messages Locally
  - o Primary Path: Review New Messages
  - o Alternate Path: No New Messages
  - o Extends: Review Messages
- Use Case: Review Messages Remotely
  - o Primary Path: Review New Messages
  - o Alternate Path: No New Messages
  - o Extends: Review Messages
  - o Uses: Authorize Access
- Use Case: Authorize Access
  - o Primary Path: User Authorized
  - o Alternate Path: User Not Authorized

USECASE DIAGRAM

See Fig. App. 1.

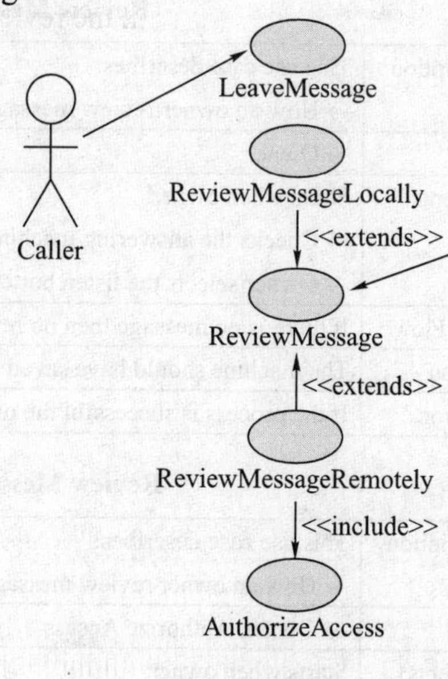

App. 1

USE CASE DESCRIPTION

Leave Message

Brief Description	This use case describes: → How a caller leaves a message onto the machine when owner is not present.
Actors	→ Caller
Flow of Events	Starts when caller calls the owner: → The caller dials the number. → When the owner doesn't pick the call the call is routed to the answering machine. → The answering machine logs the voice onto the tape.
Alternative Flow	No
Pre-condition	The owner must have a simple answering machine.
Post-condition	If the process is successful the message is saved onto the machine.

Review Message

Brief Description	This use case describes: → How an owner review a message from the machine.
Actors	→ Owner
Flow of Events	Starts when owner: → Checks the answering machine for the message. → Owner selects the listen button to listen to the logged messages.
Alternative Flow	If there is no message then no reviewing
Pre-condition	The machine should have saved messages.
Post-condition	If the process is successful the message is reviewed.

Review Message Locally

Brief Description	This use case describes: → How an owner review messages locally.
Actors	→ Owner
Flow of Events	Starts when owner: → Checks the answering machine for the message. → Owner selects the listen button to listen to the logged messages.
Alternative Flow	If there is no message then no reviewing will take place.
Pre-condition	The machine should have saved messages.
Post-condition	If the process is successful the messages are reviewed.

Review Message Remotely

Brief Description	This use case describes: → How an owner review messages globally.
Actors	→ Owner, Authorize Access
Flow of Events	Starts when owner:
	→ Checks the answering machine for the message.

	→ Owner inputs the secret userid and pin number at the terminal. → Owner then selects the listen button to listen to the logged messages.
Alternative Flow	No
Pre-condition	The owner must have access to remote terminal.
Post-condition	If the process is successful the message is reviewed by the owner remotely.

2. Draw Usecase Diagram, Activity Diagram and Sequence Diagram (for each usecase) for Movie Ticket Machine problem given below. Write description of each usecase.

Implement a simple movie ticket vending machine. The movie theater that will use the machine has only one movie and one show time each day. Every morning, the theater manager will turn on the ticket machine, and it will ask him for the name of the movie and the ticket price that day. It will also ask how many seats are in the theater (so it won't sell too many tickets). When a customer walks up to the ticket machine, he will see the name of the movie, the time, and the ticket price displayed. There is a slot to insert money, a keypad of buttons to enter a number into the "Number of Tickets" field, and a "Buy" button. Printed tickets come out of a slot at the bottom of the machine. Above the ticket slot is a message display (for error messages like "Please enter more money or request fewer tickets" or "SOLD OUT!"). An additional display shows the customer's balance inside the machine. Finally, there is a "Return Change" button so the customer can get his unspent money back.

The ticket machine might look like Fig. App. 2.

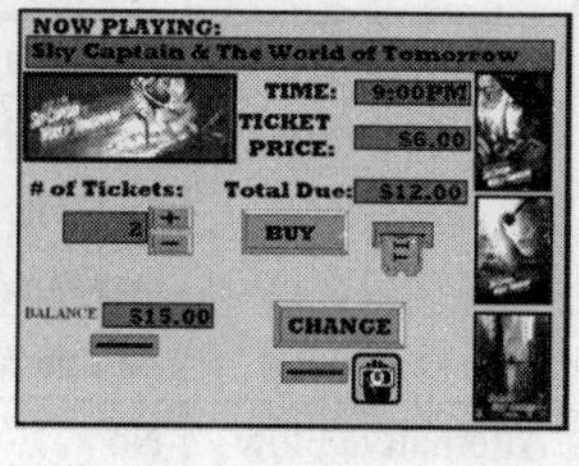

App. 2

USE CASE DIAGRAM

See Fig. App. 3.

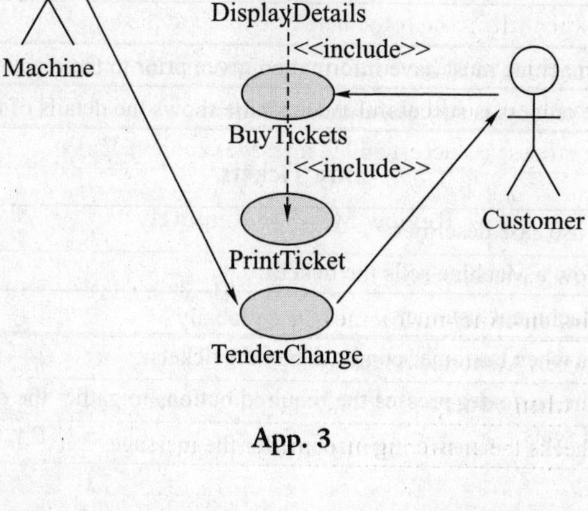

App. 3

USE CASE DESCRIPTION

Turn On

Brief Description	This use case describes: → How a Manager turn on the machine.
Actors	→ Manager, Machine
Flow of Events	Starts when Manager: → Switch on the machine to start the ticket selling placed at the theatre.
Alternative Flow	No
Pre-condition	No
Post-condition	If the process is successful the machine is now operational.

Set Details

Brief Description	This use case describes: → How a Manager input the details of the movie into the machine.
Actors	→ Manager, Machine
Flow of Events	Starts when Manager: → Switch on the machine to start the ticket selling placed at the theatre. → Machine will ask for the movie details, time, no of seats etc. → The manager inputs the details and saves the configuration.
Alternative Flow	No
Pre-condition	The machine must be turned on and must be functional (without an error).
Post-condition	Now the machine has been configured to sell the tickets.

Display Details

Brief Description	This use case describes: → How a Machine displays the information.
Actors	→ Machine, Customer
Flow of Events	Starts when machine: → Has been configured to display the details of the movie. → Customer will come and check out the details of the movie.
Alternative Flow	No
Pre-condition	The machine must have information given prior to the displaying details.
Post-condition	If the process is successful the machine shows the details of the movie.

Buy Tickets

Brief Description	This use case describes: → How a Machine sells the tickets.
Actors	→ Machine, Customer
Flow of Events	Starts when customer comes to buy the tickets: → The customer presses the required buttons to gather the details and to select the no of seats.

	→ Customer then inserts the money and takes the printed tickets.
Alternative Flow	→ If customer doesn't want the tickets he/she cancel the process. → If money is insufficient cancel the tickets → If no of tickets are not available request fewer tickets → If all the tickets are sold out, cancel the process.
Pre-condition	The machine must have information given prior to selling the tickets.
Post-condition	Now machine is again in ready state to sell the tickets.

Print Tickets

Brief Description	This use case describes: → How a Machine prints the tickets.
Actors	→ Machine, Customer
Flow of Events	Starts when customer comes to buy the tickets: → The customer buys the ticket. → In return the machine generates the printed tickets. → Customer then takes the tickets to enter into the hall.
Alternative Flow	If customer doesn't want the tickets he/she cancel the process.
Pre-condition	Customer must buy the tickets.
Post-condition	Now machine is again in ready state to sell the tickets.

Tender Change

Brief Description	This use case describes:
	→ How a Machine returns the unspent money.
Actors	→ Machine, Customer
Flow of Events	Starts when customer comes to buy the tickets:
	→ The customer buys the ticket.
	→ He inserts the money, if money is more than sufficient the machine returns the change after deducting the ticket amount.
Alternative Flow	No
Pre-condition	Customer must buy the tickets, and money must be more than the amount.
Post-condition	Now machine is again in ready state to sell the tickets.

3. Draw Usecase Diagram and Analysis Model for Movie Ticket Machine problem given below. Write description of each usecase. Draw the Class Diagram and Generate Code for the same.

Implement a simple movie ticket vending machine. The movie theater that will use the machine has only one movie and one show time each day. Every morning, the theater manager will turn on the ticket machine, and it will ask him for the name of the movie and the ticket price that day. It will also ask how many seats are in the theater (so it won't sell too many tickets). When a customer walks up to the ticket machine, he will see the name of the movie, the time, and the ticket price displayed. There is a slot to insert money, a keypad of buttons to enter a number into the "Number of Tickets" field, and a "Buy" button. Printed tickets come out of a slot at the bottom of the machine. Above the ticket slot is a message display (for error messages like "Please enter more money or request fewer tickets" or "SOLD OUT!"). An additional display shows the customer's balance inside the machine. Finally, there is a "Return Change" button so the customer can get his unspent money back.

The ticket machine might look like Fig. App. 4.

App. 4

USE CASE DIAGRAM

See Fig. App. 5.

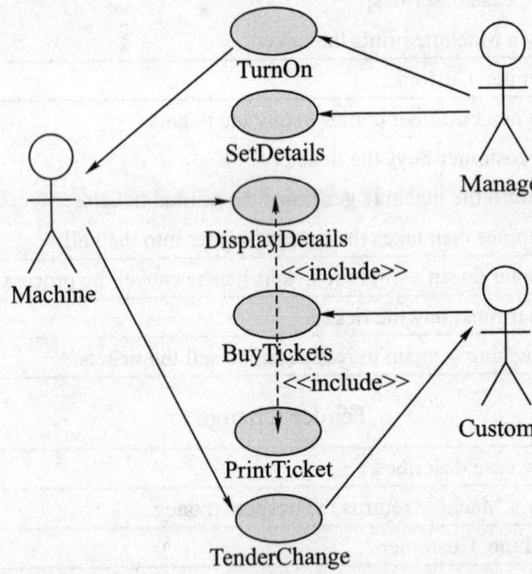

App. 5

CLASS DIAGRAM

See Fig. App. 6.

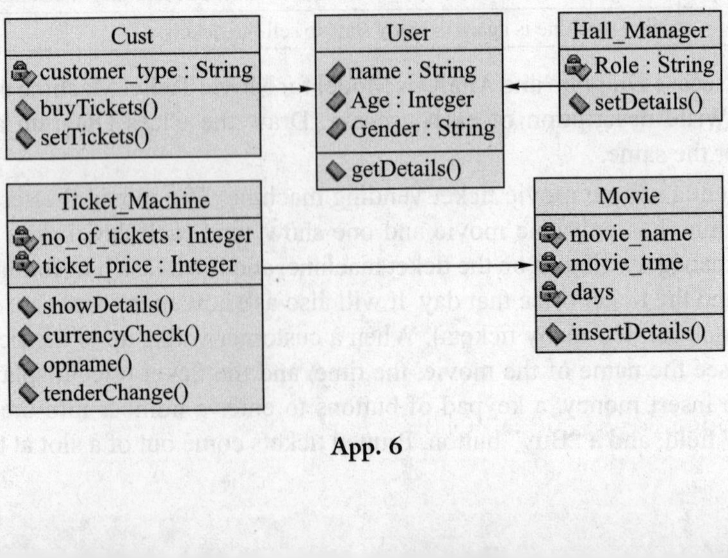

App. 6

CODE GENERATION FOR TICKET MACHINE

```
#include "Cust.h"

//##ModelId=5120C36201C8
Cust::buyTickets()
{
}

//##ModelId=5120C36201C9
Cust::setTickets()
{
}

#include "Hall_Manager.h"

//##ModelId=5120C36201CF
Hall_Manager::setDetails()
{
}

#include "Movie.h"

//##ModelId=5120C36201DE
Movie::insertDetails()
{
}

#include "Ticket_Machine.h"

//##ModelId=5120C36201D5
Ticket_Machine::showDetails()
{
}

//##ModelId=5120C36201D6
```

```
Ticket_Machine::currencyCheck()
{
}

//##ModelId=5120C36201D7
Ticket_Machine::opname()
{
}

//##ModelId=5120C36201D8
Ticket_Machine::tenderChange()
{
}

//##ModelId=5120C36201D9
Integer Ticket_Machine::no
_of_tickets;
```

4. Consider an Online Airline Reservation System.

- Identify actors for Online Airline Reservation System. Explain the relevance of each actor.
- One use case is to make a Flight Reservation. List four additional use cases at a comparable level of abstraction. Describe each use case with exceptional flow.
- Prepare a Usecase Diagram for an online airline reservation system. Write Usecase description of each usecase.
- Draw Class Diagram. Elaborate ticket class and Generate Code for the same.
- Identify at least four states of Ticket object and draw the State Transition Diagram for the same.

USECASE DIAGRAM

See Fig. App. 7.

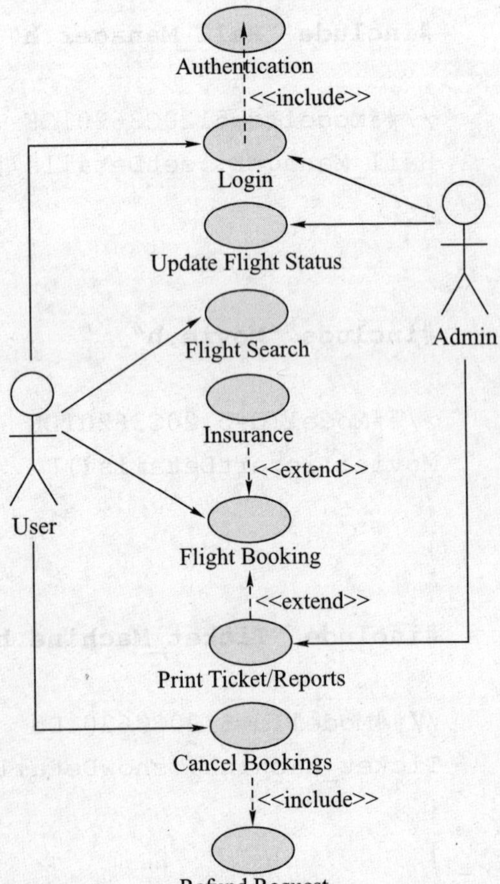

App. 7

USECASE DESCRIPTION

Log in

Brief Description	This use case describes: → How a user or an admin logins into the "Airline reservation system".
Actors	→ User, Admin
Flow of Events	Starts when user wants to login into the system: → The system requests the actors to their username, password, and role. The role can be anyone of the administrator, clerk, travel agent or passenger. → The Actors enter their username, password and role. → The system validates the entered username, password, role from the database and logs actor into the system.
Alternative Flow	If user enters the wrong username or password the system logs the event and sends a error message to the user, then user can select to try again or cancel the dialog with the system.
Pre-condition	User must have a username, password, and role, created for them in the system, prior to start of the use case.
Post-condition	If the process is successful the actor is logged into the system. If not, the system state remains unchanged.

Update Flight Details

Brief Description	→ Allows the admins to maintain flight information. This includes adding and updating flight information.
Actors	→ Admin
Flow of Events	Starts when the clerk adds or changes the flight information. → System prompts for the flight ID and airline details to update the information into the system. → If new flight is added the details are fed into the system by executing the sub flow to add new flight. → If existing flight ID is provided then the existing details are updated with new information.
Alternative Flow	If in sub flow of updation or adding a flight, admin select to cancel the process he can cancel and exit from the process.
Pre-condition	Admin must have the username and password to enter into the system
Post-condition	If the process is successful, the flight information is added or updated from the system. Otherwise, the system state remains unchanged.

Flight Search

Brief Description	Allows the user to view flight information.
Actors	User
Flow of Events	This process starts when user logs in into the system and search for the required flights.
Alternative Flow	None
Pre-condition	Flight details must be updated.
Post-condition	Required flight ticket is booked or user cancels the process.

Flight Booking

Brief Description	Allows the user to book the flight tickets.
Actors	User
Flow of Events	Starts when the passenger wants to book the tickets. → Enters name → Enters Flight name → Date of travel → Number of passengers
Alternative Flow	If seat is not available then the booking is not completed *i.e.*, cancelled.
Pre-condition	Flight search process.
Post-condition	Tickets are booked or process is cancelled if the tickets are not available.

Cancel Booking

Brief Description	Allows the user to cancel the booked tickets.
Actors	User
Flow of Events	Starts when the user wants to cancel the tickets. → Enters details → Select the tickets booked → Cancel the selected booking
Alternative Flow	If date or time for the flight had passed then the cancelling of ticket is not allowed and the process is cancelled.
Pre-condition	Flight is already booked.
Post-condition	Money is refunded back to the customer's bank or in cash.

Generate Report

Brief Description	This use case allows the clerk to generate report of flight and passenger details.
Actors	Reservation Clerk
Flow of Events	This use case starts when the clerk want to generate reports of the flights → Enter flight details → Enter passenger details → Maintain records
Alternative Flow	None
Pre-condition	Updated System
Post-condition	Print reports

Print

Brief Description	This use case is included with the GENERATE REPORT use case to print the ticket.
Actors	Reservation Clerk
Flow of Events	Clerk generates report and takes its print if required.
Alternative Flow	None
Pre-condition	Generate Report
Post-condition	None

CLASS DIAGRAM FOR AIRLINE RESERVATION SYSTEM

See Fig. App. 8.

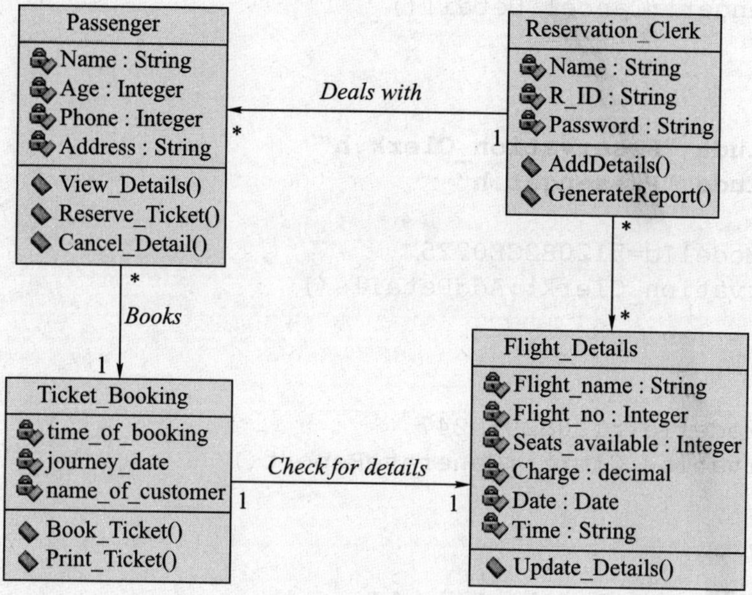

App. 8

CODE GENERATION

```
#include "Flight_Details.h"

//##ModelId=5120B3590281
Flight_Details::Update_Details()
{
}

#include "Passenger.h"

//##ModelId=5120B2440079
Passenger::View_Details()
{
}

//##ModelId=5120B2370079
Passenger::Reserve_Ticket()
{
```

```
}

//##ModelId=5120B24D01D2
Passenger::Cancel_Detail()
{
}

#include "Reservation_Clerk.h"
#include "Passenger.h"

//##ModelId=5120B2CE0225
Reservation_Clerk::AddDetails()
{
}

//##ModelId=5120B2D60247
Reservation_Clerk::GenerateReport()
{
}

#include "Ticket_booking.h"

//##ModelId=5120BEB40024
Ticket_booking::Book_Ticket()
{
}

//##ModelId=5120BEC900A6
Ticket_booking::Print_Ticket()
{
}
```

5. Consider a software system for supporting a Public Library.

- Identify actors for Library System. Explain the relevance of each actor.
- One use case is to borow a library item. List three additional use cases at a comparable level of abstraction. Describe each use case with exceptional flow.
- Prepare a **Usecase Diagram** for a library system. Describe each use case with exceptional flow.
- Elaborate **Library Item as an abstract class with concrete classes class. Generate the code** for the same using **forward engineering** in Rational Rose.
- Identify at least four states of Library item and draw the **State Transition Diagram** for the same.

USECASE DIAGRAM

See Fig. App. 9.

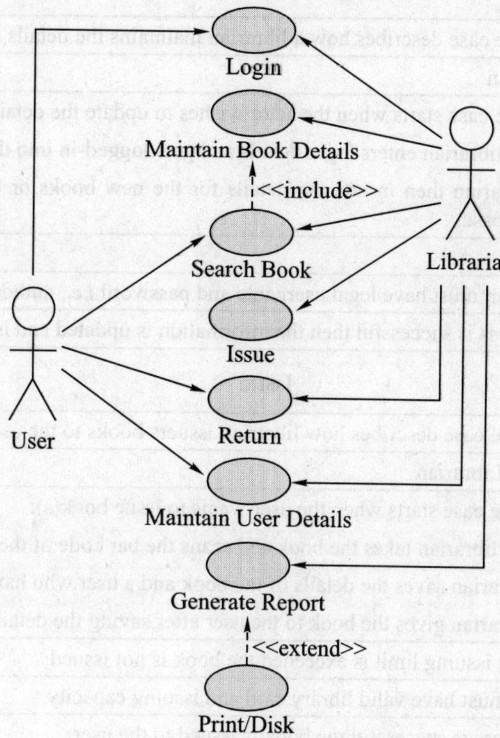

App. 9

USECASE DESCRIPTION

Log in

Brief Description	This use case describes how user or librarian login into the system
Actors	Users, Librarian
Flow of Events	This use case starts when the actor wishes to login → The system requests that the actors enter their username, password → The actors enter their username, password → The system validates the entered username, password and logs actor into the system
Alternative Flow	If the actor enters an invalid name, password → The system displays an error message, and then actor can choose to either return to the beginning of the basic flow or cancel the login.
Pre-conditions	All users must have user name and password created for them in the system prior to use case

Post-conditions	If use case got successful then users are logged on to the system else system state is unchanged

Maintain Book Details

Brief Description	This use case describes how a librarian maintains the details of the books
Actors	Librarian
Flow of Events	This use case starts when the actor wishes to update the details: → The librarian enters login details and gets logged-in into the system. → Librarian then inserts the details for the new books or the existing books in the database.
Alternative Flow	No
Pre-conditions	Librarian must have legal username and password *i.e.*, authority.
Post-conditions	If process is successful then the information is updated and is consistent.

Issue

Brief Description	This use case describes how librarian issuers books to the users.
Actors	Users, Librarian
Flow of Events	This use case starts when the user wants to issue book(s): → The librarian takes the book and scans the bar code of the book. → Librarian saves the details of the book and a user who have issued it. → Librarian gives the book to the user after saving the details.
Alternative Flow	If users issuing limit is exceeded the book is not issued.
Pre-conditions	Users must have valid library card and issuing capacity.
Post-conditions	If process is successful the book is issued to the user.

Maintain user Details

Brief Description	This use case describes the maintenance of user details.
Actors	Librarian
Flow of Events	This use case starts when the librarian updates the user details in system: → Librarian checks the validity of the user in contrast with his ID. → Inputs the details and set the maximum issuing capacity. → Updates the user details if any.
Alternative Flow	If users issuing limit is exceeded the book is not issued.
Pre-conditions	Users must have valid library card and issuing capacity.
Post-conditions	If process is successful the book is issued to the user.

Generate Report

Brief Description	This use case describes the generation of reports.
Actors	Librarian
Flow of Events	This use case starts when the librarian wants to generate the report: → Librarian login into the system.

	→ Select the report generation tool and enters the monthly, yearly or daily format reports. → Then he/she reviews the details.
Alternative Flow	If librarian is not authorized the process will be cancelled.
Pre-conditions	Librarian must have valid credentials.
Post-conditions	If process is successful the report is generated and print out is taken (if needed).

6. Consider a Computer Email System.
   - Identify actors for email system. Explain the relevance of each actor.
   - One use case is to get email. List four additional use cases at a comparable level of abstraction. Describe each use case with exceptional flow.
   - Prepare a Usecase Diagram for a computer email system. Write Description for each use case.
   - Draw Class Diagram and Generate Code.
   - Identify at least four states for an email object and draw the State Transition Diagram for the same.

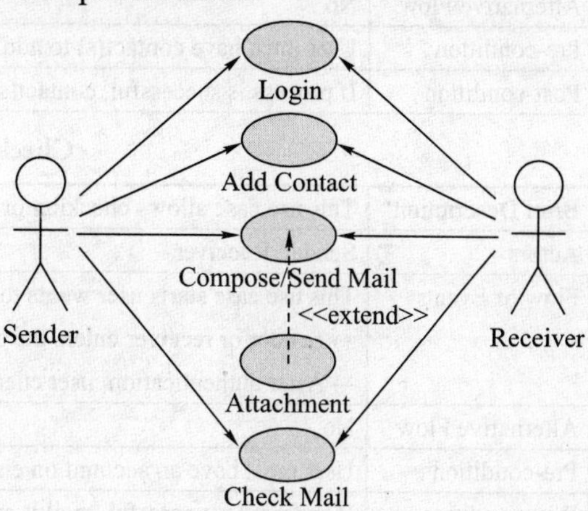

App. 10

USECASE DIAGRAM

See Fig. App. 10.

USECASE DESCRIPTION

Log in

Brief Description	This use case allows to login into the system.
Actors	Sender, Receiver
Flow of Events	This use case starts when user wants to logs into the system: → Sender or receiver enters the username and password. → After authentication the users will get their space on email servers. → Now users can send or receive the mails.
Alternative Flow	If user is not authorized the process is cancelled and rolled back.
Pre-condition	User must have legal username and password *i.e.*, he must have a account.
Post-condition	If process is successful, users can now send or receive the mails.

Compose/Send Mail

Brief Description	This use case allows composing and sending of mails.
Actors	Sender, Receiver
Flow of Events	This use case starts user wants to send or receive the mails: → Sender or receiver enters the username and password. → After authentication, user writes and sends the mails.

Alternative Flow	No
Pre-condition	User must have an account on email server.
Post-condition	If process is successful, sent or written mail is saved.

Add Contact

Brief Description	This use case allows users to add contacts.
Actors	Sender, Receiver
Flow of Events	This use case starts user wants save the contact: → Sender or receiver logins into the system. → Sender or receiver inputs the details of the contact into the contact box and save.
Alternative Flow	No
Pre-condition	User must have contact(s) to add.
Post-condition	If process is successful, contact(s) are saved.

Check Mail

Brief Description	This use case allows checking or receiving of mails.
Actors	Sender, Receiver
Flow of Events	This use case starts user wants to check or receive the mails: → Sender or receiver enters the username and password. → After authentication, user checks the mails.
Alternative Flow	No
Pre-condition	User must have an account on email server.
Post-condition	If process is successful, mail is received and reviewed.

CLASS DIAGRAM FOR COMPUTER EMAIL SYSTEM

See Fig. App. 11.

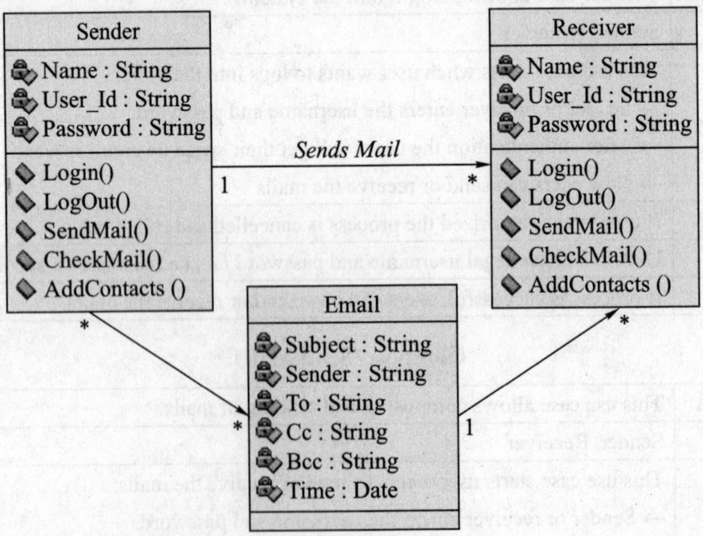

App. 11

CODE GENERATION

```
#include "Sender.h"

//##ModelId=5120FF2003AA
Sender::LogIn()
{
}


//##ModelId=5120FF24036C
Sender::LogOut()
{
}


//##ModelId=5120FF290213
Sender::SendMail()
{
}


//##ModelId=5120FF370077
Sender::CheckMail()
{
}

//##ModelId=5120FF2E01C1
Sender::AddContacts()
{
}

#include "Receiver.h"

//##ModelId=5120FF6C02A6
Receiver::LogIn()
{
}


//##ModelId=5120FF75025A
Receiver::LogOut()
```

```
{
}

//##ModelId=5120FF780333
Receiver::ReceiveMail()
{
}

//##ModelId=5120FF800248
Receiver::LogOut()
{
}

//##ModelId=5120FF8700B4
Receiver::AddContacts()
{
}
```

7. Draw a Use Case Diagram (write description of each use case), Activity Diagram and Sequence Diagram (for each usecase) for Hurry's Store Stock Control System.

Hurry's require a new point of sale and stock control system for their many stores throughout the UK to replace their ageing mini based systems. A sales assistant will be able to process an order by entering product numbers and required quantities into the system. The system will display a description, price and available stock. In-stock products will normally be collected immediately by the customer from the store but may be selected for delivery to the customer's home address for which there will be a charge. If stock is not available the sales assistant will be able to create a backorder for the product from a regional warehouse. The products will then either be delivered direct from the regional warehouse to the customer's home address, or to the store for collection by the customer. The system will allow products to be paid for by cash or credit card. Credit card transactions will be validated via an online card transaction system. The system will produce a receipt. Order details for in-stock products will be printed in the warehouse including the bin reference, quantity, product number and description. These will be collected by the sales assistant and given to the customer. The sales assistant will be able to make refunds, provided a valid receipt is produced. The sales assistant will also be able to check stock and pricing without creating an order and progress orders that have been created for delivery. The store manager will be able at any time to print a summary report of sales in the store for a given period, including assignment of sales to sales assistants in order to calculate weekly salesbonuses. The stock manager will be able to monitor stock levels and weekly run-rates in order to set minimum stock levels and requisition products which fall below the minimum stock levels or for which demand is anticipated. When the stock arrives it will be booked in by the warehouse person. Stock that has been backordered for collection from the store is held in a separate area and the store manager advised of its arrival. The catalogue of available products will be maintained remotely by marketing from head office. Marketing will also be able to access sales information from each store system.

USECASE DIAGRAM

See Fig. App. 12.

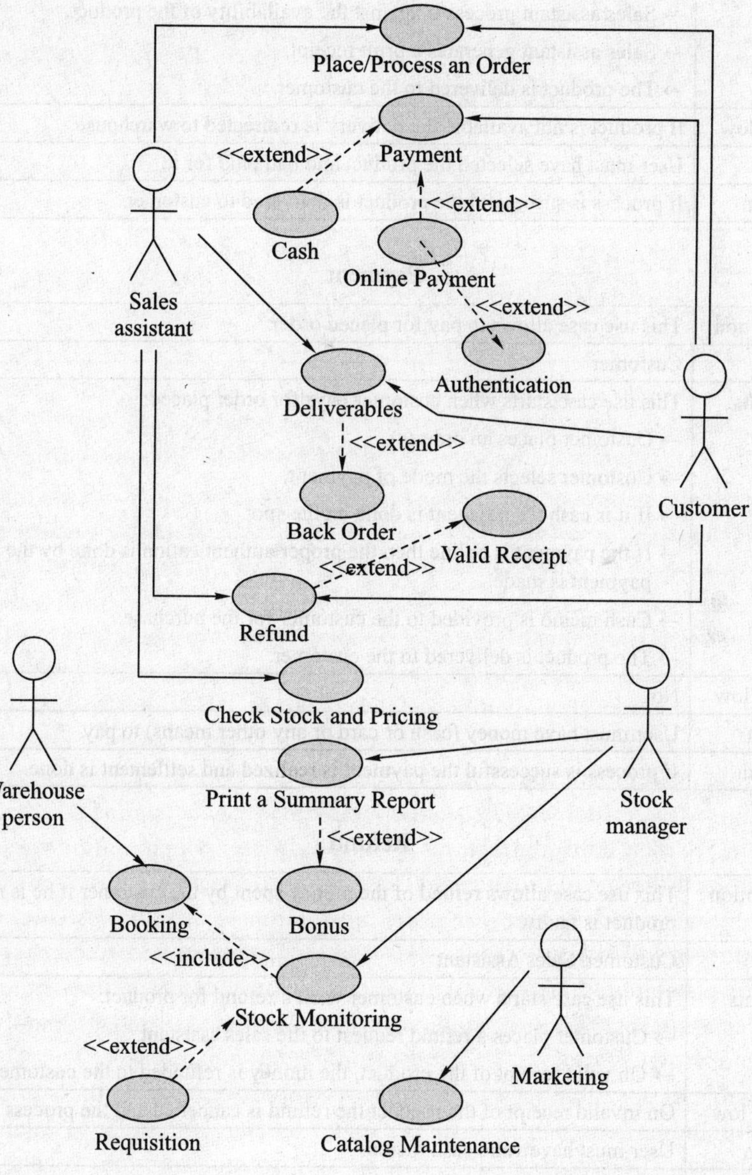

App. 12

USECASE DESCRIPTION

Place/Process an Order

Brief Description	This use case allows to place or process an order.
Actors	Sales Assistant, Customer
Flow of Events	This use case starts when customer places an order and assistant process it: → Customer places an order(s). → Customer defines no of products, its quantity ets. → Sales assistant process it against the availability of the product. → Sales assistant generates a print receipt. → The product is delivered to the customer.
Alternative Flow	If product is not available the delivery is redirected to warehouse.
Pre-condition	User must have selected the product and had paid for it.
Post-condition	If process is successful the product is delivered to customer.

Payment

Brief Description	This use case allows to pay for placed order.
Actors	Customer
Flow of Events	This use case starts when customer pays for order placed: → Customer places an order(s). → Customer selects the mode of payment. → If it is cash the payment is done on the spot. → If the payment is online then the proper authentication is done by the bank and then payment is made. → Cash memo is provided to the customer for the purchase. → The product is delivered to the customer.
Alternative Flow	No
Pre-condition	User must have money (cash or card or any other means) to pay.
Post-condition	If process is successful the payment is realized and settlement is done.

Refund

Brief Description	This use case allows refund of the money spent by the customer if he is not satisfied or product is faulty.
Actors	Customer, Sales Assistant
Flow of Events	This use case starts when customer want a refund for product: → Customer places a refund request to the sales assistant. → On valid receipt of the product, the money is refunded to the customer.
Alternative Flow	On invalid receipt of the product the refund is cancelled and the process ends.
Pre-condition	User must have valid cash memo.
Post-condition	If process is successful the refund is done to customer.

Check Stock and Pricing

Brief Description	This use case allows sales assistant to maintain the details and pricing of product.
Actors	Sales Assistant
Flow of Events	This use case starts when sales assistant checks for product pricing: → Sales assistant logs-in to the system. → He then checks the product price and stock availability. → If product is going under stock a request is done to warehouse to update the stock. → He also changes the price if authority allows for better sale of the product. → The information is then successfully saved onto the system.
Alternative Flow	No
Pre-condition	Sales assistant must have proper authority to access the databases to manipulate the pricing of the product(s).
Post-condition	If process is successful the information is saved.

Catalogue Maintenance

Brief Description	The catalogue of the available products is maintained into the system.
Actors	Marketing
Flow of Events	→ The catalogue of available products is maintained remotely by marketing from head office.
Alternative Flow	None
Pre-condition	None
Post-condition	None

8. Identify the Usecases, Not everything is specified in these initial requirements. When you need make assumptions, put them explicitly in the document. Draw the **Usecase Diagram, Class Diagram and Generate Code** using Rational Rose.

The drawing editor is an interactive graphics editor. With it, users can create and edit drawings composed of lines, rectangles, ellipses and text Tools control the mode of operation of the editor. Exactly one tool is active at any one time. Two kinds of tools exist: the selection tool and creation tools. When the selection tool is active, existing drawing elements can be selected with the cursor. One or more drawing elements can be selected and manipulated; if several drawing elements are selected, they can be manipulated as if they were a single element. Elements that have been selected in this way are referred to as the current selection. The current selection is indicated visually by displaying the control points for the element. Clicking on and dragging a control point modifies the element with which the control point is associated.

When a creation tool is active, the current selection is empty. The cursor changes in different ways according to the specific creation tool, and the user can create an element of the selected kind.

The text creation tool: the position of the first character of the text is determined by where the user clicks the mouse button. The creation tool is no longer active when the user clicks the mouse button outside the text element. The control points for a text element are at the four corners of the region within which the text is formatted. Dragging the control points changes this region.

The other creation tools allow the creation of lines, rectangles and ellipses. The appropriate element starts to be created when the mouse button is pressed, and is completed when the mouse button is released. These two events create the start point and the stop point.

The line creation tool creates a line from the start point to the stop point. These are the control points of a line. Dragging a control point changes the end point.

The rectangle creation tool creates a rectangle such that these points are diagonally opposite corners. These points and the other corners are the control points. Dragging a control point changes the associated corner.

The ellipse creation tool creates an ellipse fitting within the rectangle defined by the two points described above. The major radius is one half the width of the rectangle, and the minor radius is one half the height of the rectangle. The control points are at the corners of the bounding rectangle. Dragging a control point changes the associated corner.

The specification states nothing about the environment in which the diagram editor will run. We will assume that the program should provide a graphical display of the diagram being created, and that a mouse and keyboard will be used as input devices.

USECASE DIAGRAM

See Fig. App. 13.

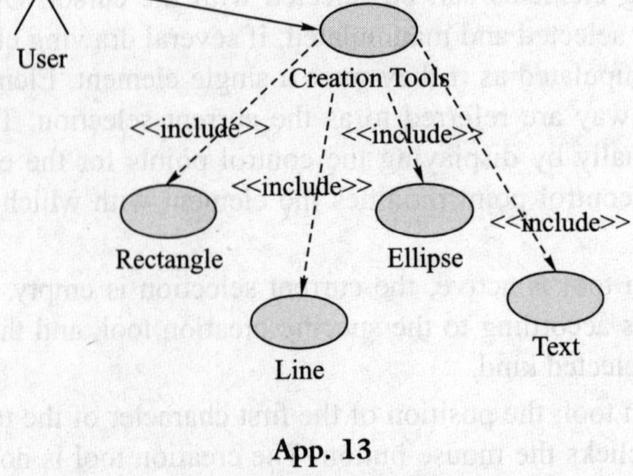

App. 13

CLASS DIAGRAM

See Fig. App. 14.

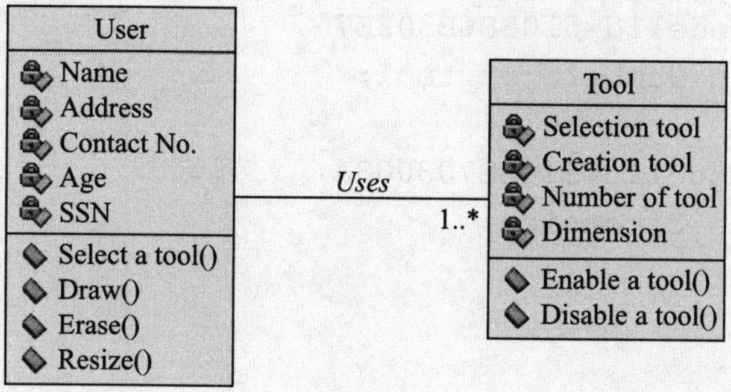

App. 14

CODE

Tool.h

```
#ifndef TOOL_H_HEADER_INCLUDED_AEF4168E
#define TOOL_H_HEADER_INCLUDED_AEF4168E
class User;

//##ModelId=510BB66C023C
class Tool
{
  public:
    //##ModelId=510BB6D50108
    static Enable a tool();

    //##ModelId=510BB6E9002B
    static Desable a tool();

    //##ModelId=510BB7300002
    static User *Uses;

  private:
    //##ModelId=510BB69F024E
    static Selection tool;
```

```
    //##ModelId=510BB6A801A8
    static Creation tool;

    //##ModelId=510BB6B302E7
    static Number  of tool;

    //##ModelId=510BB703008A
    static Dimension;

};


#endif /* TOOL_H_HEADER_INCLUDED_AEF4168E */
```

Tool.cpp

```
#include "Tool.h"
#include "User.h"

//##ModelId=510BB6D50108
Tool::Enable a tool()
{
}

//##ModelId=510BB6E9002B
Tool::Desable a tool()
{
}

//##ModelId=510BB7300002
User *Tool::Uses;

//##ModelId=510BB69F024E
Tool::Selection tool;

//##ModelId=510BB6A801A8
Tool::Creation tool;

//##ModelId=510BB6B302E7
```

```
Tool::Number  of tool;

//##ModelId=510BB703008A
Tool::Dimension;
```

User.h

```
#ifndef USER_H_HEADER_INCLUDED_AEF4737B
#define USER_H_HEADER_INCLUDED_AEF4737B

//##ModelId=510BB5D400D7
class User
{
  public:
    //##ModelId=510BB63101D7
    static Select a tool();

    //##ModelId=510BB64500CB
    static Draw();

    //##ModelId=510BB64C0068
    static Erase();

    //##ModelId=510BB651036B
    static Resize();

  private:
    //##ModelId=510BB5E80279
    static Name;

    //##ModelId=510BB5FB0007
    static Address;

    //##ModelId=510BB6010033
    static Contact NO;

    //##ModelId=510BB5EA0211
    static Age;
```

```
    //##ModelId=510BB61702C3
    static SSN;

};

#endif /* USER_H_HEADER_INCLUDED_AEF4737B */
```

User.cpp

```
#include "User.h"

//##ModelId=510BB63101D7
User::Select a tool()
{
}

//##ModelId=510BB64500CB
User::Draw()
{
}

//##ModelId=510BB64C0068
User::Erase()
{
}

//##ModelId=510BB651036B
User::Resize()
{
}

//##ModelId=510BB5E80279
User::Name;

//##ModelId=510BB5FB0007
User::Address;

//##ModelId=510BB6010033
User::Contact NO;
```

```
//##ModelId=510BB5EA0211
User::Age;

//##ModelId=510BB61702C3
User::SSN;
```

9. Draw a **Use Case Diagram** (with **usecase description**), that shows the system that the requirements are specifying and any interactions with external systems/users, **Anlaysis Model and class diagram** based on a set of requirements for a HD TV System. Watch Out! Some of the requirements are non-functional and so won't become use cases. Also, some of the requirements may result in more than one use case.

(*i*) Requirement 1. The user shall be able to turn the system on at the press of a button either on the system itself, or by means of a remote control.

(*ii*) Requirement 2. The user shall be able to change the channel at the press of a button either on the system itself, or by means of a remote control.

(*iii*) Requirement 3. The System shall be tunable to any broadcast channel at the press of a button either on the system itself, or by means of a remote control.

(*iv*) Requirement 4. The System shall have a built-in tuner as well as being capable of connecting to an external tuner.

(*v*) Requirement 5. The System shall be able to display HD 1080 progressive scan content at 1,920 × 1,080 resolution in wide-screen mode.

(*vi*) Requirement 6. The System shall be able to display HD 1080 interlaced scan content at 1,920 × 1,080 resolution in wide-screen mode.

(*vii*) Requirement 7. The System shall be able to display HD 720 progressive scan content at 1,280 × 720 resolution in wide-screen mode.

(*viii*) Requirement 8. The System shall be able to display Wide-screen 480 progressive scan content (from DVDs for example) at 852 × 480 resolution in wide-screen mode.

(*ix*) Requirement 9. The System shall be able to display Regular Up to 480 line content.

(*x*) Requirement 10. The System shall be connectable to a surround sound system.

(*xi*) Requirement 11. The System shall provide an output connection that can be connected to recording equipment, such as a HD-DVD recorder when such systems become available.

(*xii*) Requirement 12. The System shall be operable for a minimum of 10,000 hours before maintenance is required.

(*xiii*) Requirement 13. The System shall be ready for market by the middle of 2020, when there will finally be some decent HD content available.

(*xiv*) Requirement 14. The System shall abide by the constraints of the Digital Rights Management policies as placed upon it by the.

USECASE DIAGRAM

See Fig. App. 15.

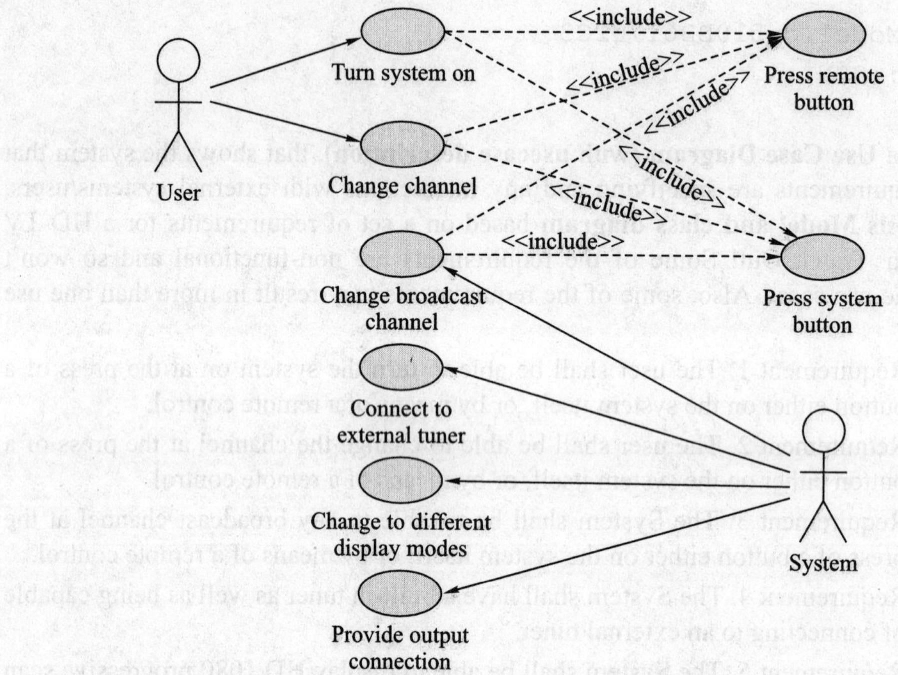

App. 15

CLASS DIAGRAM

See Fig. App. 16.

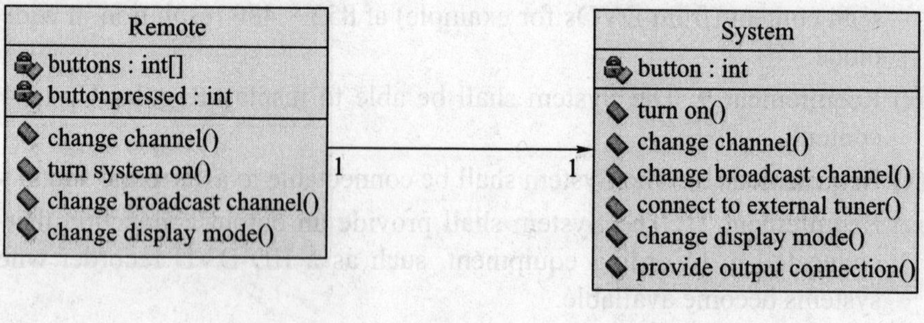

App. 16

CODE GENERATION

```
#include "System.h"
  //##ModelId=4F7B018A030D
```

```
System::turn on()
{
}
//##ModelId=4F7B019102FD
System::change channel()
{
}

//##ModelId=4F7B0195036B
System::change broadcast channel()
{
}
//##ModelId=4F7B019E031C
System::connect to external tuner()
{
}
//##ModelId=4F7B01A5029F
System::change display mode()
{
}
//##ModelId=4F7B01AA03A9
System::provide output connection()
{
}
#endif /* SYSTEM_H_HEADER_INCLUDED_B084BBFA */
#include "Remote.h"
//##ModelId=4F7AFF9C01D4
Remote::change channel()
{
}
//##ModelId=4F7AFFA200EA
Remote::turn system on()
{
}
//##ModelId=4F7AFFA50399
Remote::change broadcast channel()
{
}
//##ModelId=4F7AFFB60157
```

```
Remote::change display mode()
{
}
#ifndef REMOTE_H_HEADER_INCLUDED_B0849404
#define REMOTE_H_HEADER_INCLUDED_B0849404
//##ModelId=4F7AFF7A038A
class Remote
{
  public:
    //##ModelId=4F7AFF9C01D4
    change channel();
    //##ModelId=4F7AFFA200EA
    turn system on();
    //##ModelId=4F7AFFA50399
    change broadcast channel();
    //##ModelId=4F7AFFB60157
    change display mode();
  private:
    //##ModelId=4F7AFF82000F
    int buttons[];
    //##ModelId=4F7AFF910186
    int buttonpressed;
};
#endif /* REMOTE_H_HEADER_
INCLUDED_B0849404 */
```

ANALYSIS DIAGRAM

See Fig. App. 17.

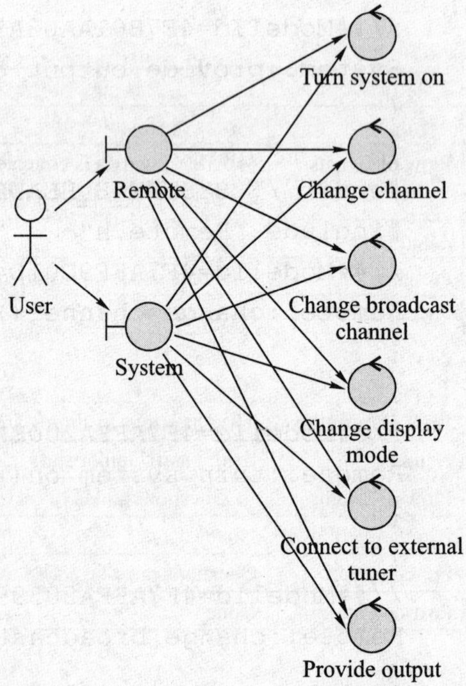

App. 17

10. Draw **Usecase Diagram**, **Activity Diagram**, **Analysis Model** and **write usecase description** for the **Survey Management System**. Draw the **Class Diagram** and **Generate Code** for the same.

A Survey Institution that performs/ manages public surveys. After the raw survey data is collected, a senior staff adds a survey header into the database;

senior or junior staff add questions into the survey, may categorize questions, or add a question category. Questions with sensitive content are restricted to senior staff.

USECASE DIAGRAM

See Fig. App. 18.

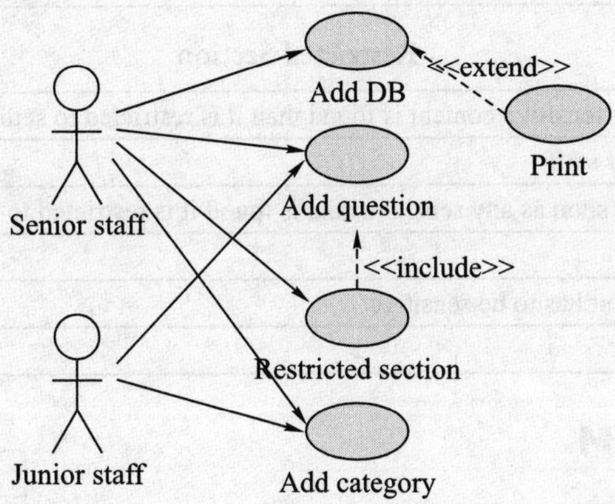

App. 18

USECASE DESCRIPTION

Add Question

Brief Description	The staff adds questions to survey sheet.
Actors	Senior staff, junior staff
Flow of Events	→ After raw data is collected senior staff adds header to database. → Then the questions are added to survey by the actors.
Alternative Flow	None
Pre-condition	Raw data needs to be collected
Post-condition	None

Add Category

Brief Description	The Questions in survey are categorized
Actors	Senior staff, Junior staff
Flow of Events	→ Questions added to survey are categorized
Alternative Flow	None
Pre-condition	Questions must be added to survey
Post-condition	None

Add Database

Brief Description	The senior staff adds Header to DB as raw data is collected

Actors	Senior staff, Junior staff
Flow of Events	→ Raw data is collected from surveys and then Header is added to the DB by senior staff.
Alternative Flow	None
Pre-condition	Raw data must be collected
Post-condition	None

Restricted Section

Brief Description	If any sensitive content is found than it is restricted to senior staff
Actors	Senior staff
Flow of Events	→ As soon as any sensitive data is found it is restricted to senior staff.
Alternative Flow	None
Pre-condition	Content has to be sensitive
Post-condition	None

CLASS DIAGRAM

See Fig. App. 19.

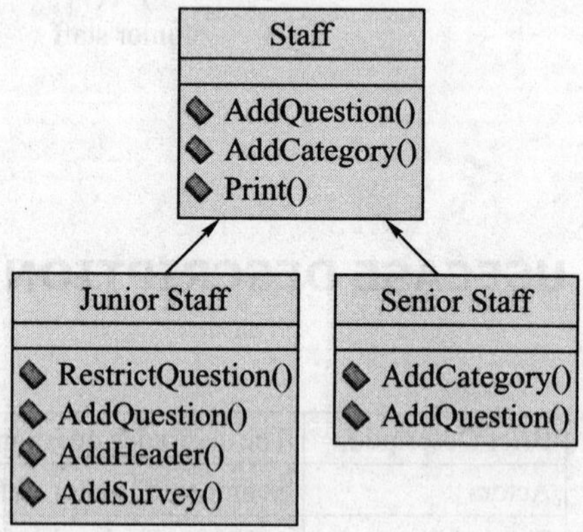

App. 19

CODE

```
#include "JuniorStaff.h"
//##ModelId=4F7AAA7500F6
JuniorStaff::RestrictQuestion()
{ }
//##ModelId=4F7AAA87038A
JuniorStaff::AddQuestion()
{ }
//##ModelId=4F7AAABB0222
JuniorStaff::AddHeader()
{ }
//##ModelId=4F7AAAF70006
JuniorStaff::AddSurvey()
{ }
#include "SeniorStaff.h"
//##ModelId=4F7AAACA0272
SeniorStaff::AddCategory()
{ }
//##ModelId=4F7AABBC0132
SeniorStaff::AddQuestion()
{ }
```

```
#include "Staff.h"
//##ModelId=4F7AAA8D00C4
Staff::AddQuestion()
{ }
//##ModelId=4F7AAAC20178
Staff::AddCategory()
{ }
//##ModelId=4F7AAB210380
Staff::Print()
{ }
```

ACTIVITY DIAGRAM

See Fig. App. 20.

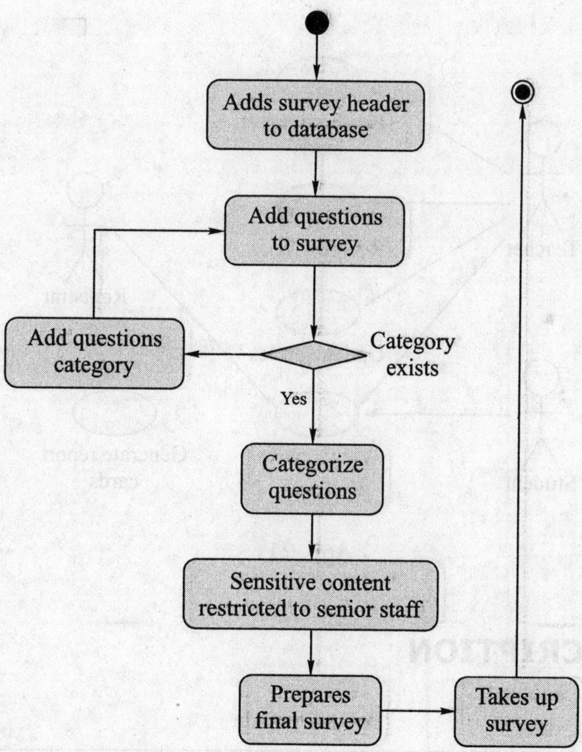

App. 20

11. Consider a system with which teachers can record and update grades of students. Teachers should also be able to distribute report cards. Here is a complete list of the requirements for the system:

- A teacher can record grades. Whenever grades are recorded, they are also saved to disk.

- A teacher can update grades. Whenever grades are updated, the existing grade is loaded. Then the updated grade is saved to disk.
- A teacher, a registrar, and/or a student can view grades.
- Whenever any of these people view grades, they must always log on to the system. If their log on fails, they must re-authenticate their user name and password.
- A part-time student is a kind of student.
- A registrar can generate report cards.
- A teacher can distribute report cards.

Draw **Use Case diagram**, including all actors, Use Cases, and relationships. Be sure to use the correct notation for all actors, Use Cases, and relationships. Also be sure to label each and every actor, Use Case, and relationship. Draw **Analysis Model**, **Class Diagram** and **Generate Code**. Write **description of each usecase**.

USECASE DIAGRAM

See Fig. App. 21.

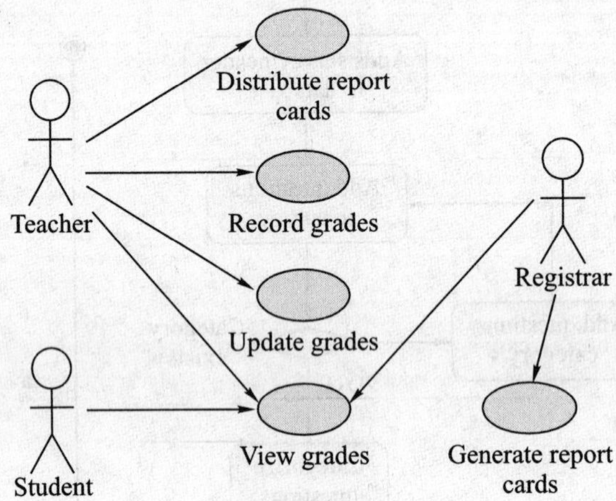

App. 21

USECASE DESCRIPTION

Record Grade

Brief Description	This helps to store grades of the student
Actors	Teacher
Pre-conditions	None
Post-conditions	Grades are stored on the disk
Flow of Events	→ This use case starts when the teacher wishes to record the grades of the students, for doing so data is saved to the disk.
Alternative Flow	None

Save to Disk

Brief Description	This helps to store data on the disk
Actors	None
Pre-conditions	Data is present to be saved
Post-conditions	Data is saved
Flow of Events	→ This use case starts when there is data to be saved on the disk, after saving the data use case terminates.
Alternative Flow	None

Load Grades

Brief Description	This loads data from the disk
Actors	None
Pre-conditions	Data is present to be restored
Post-conditions	Data is loaded in the memory from the disk
Flow of Events	→ This use case starts when there is data to be restored from the disk, after loading the data use case terminates.
Alternative Flow	None

Update

Brief Description	This helps to update grades of the students
Actor	None
Pre-conditions	Data is present to be updated
Post-conditions	Data is updated
Flow of Events	→ This use case starts when there is data to be updated, for doing so data from the disk is loaded in to the memory, changes are made and then saved back to the disk.
Alternative Flow	None

Login

Brief Description	This will allow users to login the system
Actors	Student, Teacher and Registrar
Pre-conditions	All users must have user name and password created for them in the system prior to use case
Post-conditions	If use case got successful then users are logged on to the system else system state is unchanged
Flow of Events	This use case starts when the actor wishes to login: → The system requests that the actors enter their username, password. → The actors enter their username, password. → The system validates the entered username, password and logs actor into the system.
Alternative Flow	If in the basic flow, the actor enters an invalid name, password the system displays an error message. The actor can choose to either return to the beginning of the basic flow or cancel the login, at which point the use case ends.

CLASS DIAGRAM

See Fig. App. 22.

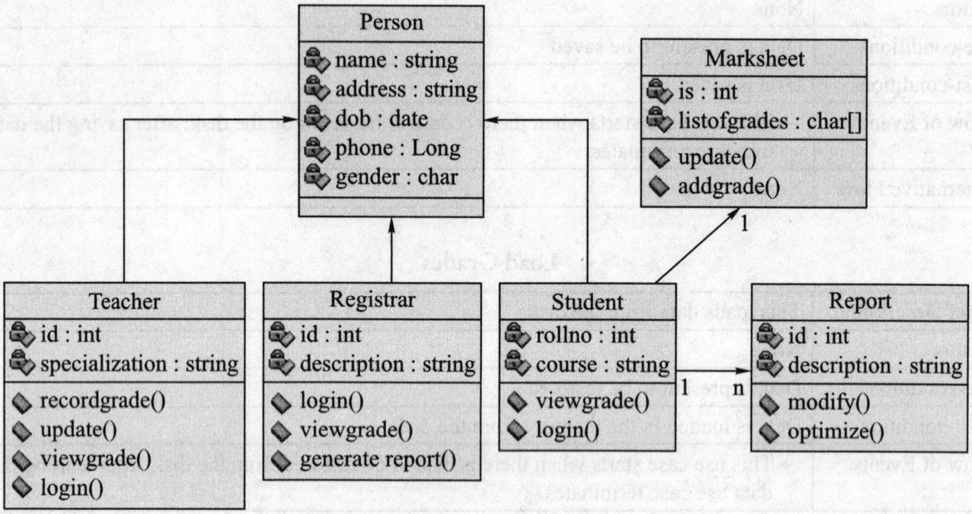

App. 22

CODE GENERATION

```
#include "Marksheet.h"

//##ModelId=4F7AB4AA0203
Marksheet::update()
{
}

//##ModelId=4F7AB4AC0186
Marksheet::addgrade()
{
}
#ifndef MARKSHEET_H_HEADER_INCLUDED_B0850CF8
#define MARKSHEET_H_HEADER_INCLUDED_B0850CF8

//##ModelId=4F7AB46C005D
class Marksheet
{
  public:
```

```
    //##ModelId=4F7AB4AA0203
    update();

    //##ModelId=4F7AB4AC0186
    addgrade();

  private:
    //##ModelId=4F7AB477038A
    int is;

    //##ModelId=4F7AB47A034B
    char listofgrades[];

};
#endif /* MARKSHEET_H_HEADER_INCLUDED_B0850CF8 */
#ifndef PERSON_H_HEADER_INCLUDED_B0851932
#define PERSON_H_HEADER_INCLUDED_B0851932

//##ModelId=4F7AB43C02BF
class Person
{
    //##ModelId=4F7AB442003E
    string name;

    //##ModelId=4F7AB4450251
    string address;

    //##ModelId=4F7AB4480399
    date dob;

    //##ModelId=4F7AB44E03B9
    Long phnno;

    //##ModelId=4F7AB46300CB
    char gender;

};
#endif /* PERSON_H_HEADER_INCLUDED_B0851932 */
#include "Registrar.h"
```

```
//##ModelId=4F7AB50E0109
Registrar::login()
{
}

//##ModelId=4F7AB510005D
Registrar::viewgrade()
{
}

//##ModelId=4F7AB51302CE
Registrar::generate report()
{
}
#ifndef REGISTRAR_H_HEADER_INCLUDED_B08562A8
#define REGISTRAR_H_HEADER_INCLUDED_B08562A8
#include "Person.h"

//##ModelId=4F7AB4FC03A9
class Registrar : public Person
{
  public:
    //##ModelId=4F7AB50E0109
    login();

    //##ModelId=4F7AB510005D
    viewgrade();

    //##ModelId=4F7AB51302CE
    generate report();

  private:
    //##ModelId=4F7AB50202EE
    int id;

    //##ModelId=4F7AB5060242
    string desciption;
```

```
};
#endif /* REGISTRAR_H_HEADER_INCLUDED_B08562A8 */
#include "report.h"

//##ModelId=4F7AB53D00CB
report::modify()
{
}

//##ModelId=4F7AB54000BB
report::optimize()
{
}
#ifndef REPORT_H_HEADER_INCLUDED_B0855F9D
#define REPORT_H_HEADER_INCLUDED_B0855F9D

//##ModelId=4F7AB51C030D
class report
{
  public:
    //##ModelId=4F7AB53D00CB
    modify();

    //##ModelId=4F7AB54000BB
    optimize();

  private:
    //##ModelId=4F7AB52E00CB
    int id;

    //##ModelId=4F7AB5310119
    string descrption;

};
#endif /* REPORT_H_HEADER_INCLUDED_B0855F9D */
#include "student.h"

//##ModelId=4F7AB4EF0251
student::viewgrade()
```

```
{
}

//##ModelId=4F7AB4F60138
student::login()
{
}
#ifndef STUDENT_H_HEADER_INCLUDED_B085349B
#define STUDENT_H_HEADER_INCLUDED_B085349B
#include "Person.h"

//##ModelId=4F7AB4DE0271
class student : public Person
{
  public:
    //##ModelId=4F7AB4EF0251
    viewgrade();

    //##ModelId=4F7AB4F60138
    login();

  private:
    //##ModelId=4F7AB4E3034B
    int rollno;

    //##ModelId=4F7AB4E900DA
    string course;
};
#endif /* STUDENT_H_HEADER_INCLUDED_B085349B */
#include "Teacher.h"

//##ModelId=4F7AB4CF007D
Teacher::recordgade()
{
}

//##ModelId=4F7AB4D500CB
Teacher::update()
{
```

```
}

//##ModelId=4F7AB4D700AB
Teacher::viewgrade()
{
}

//##ModelId=4F7AB4DA00BB
Teacher::login()
{}
#ifndef TEACHER_H_HEADER_INCLUDED_B0855609
#define TEACHER_H_HEADER_INCLUDED_B0855609
#include "Person.h"

//##ModelId=4F7AB4B302EE
class Teacher : public Person
{
 public:
    //##ModelId=4F7AB4CF007D
    recordgade();

    //##ModelId=4F7AB4D500CB
    update();

    //##ModelId=4F7AB4D700AB
    viewgrade();

    //##ModelId=4F7AB4DA00BB
    login();

 private:
    //##ModelId=4F7AB4BE0167
    int id;

    //##ModelId=4F7AB4C0031C
    string specialisation;

};
#endif /* TEACHER_H_HEADER_INCLUDED_B0855609 */
```

ANALYSIS DIAGRAM

See Fig. App. 23.

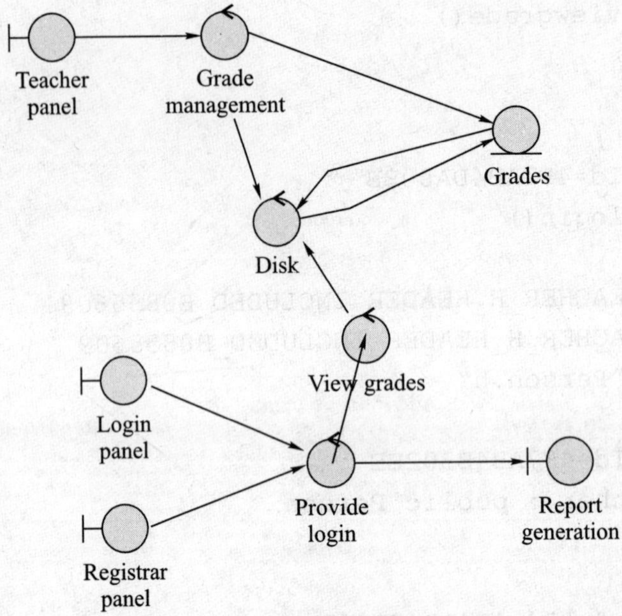

App. 23

12. Consider a Social Networking Website. The aim of the site is to let people network socially over the Internet. A user can register with the site. On doing so, he is connected with all other registered users of this site. To begin networking, he must search for names through a general search. The system will display the public record of the user under the name. He can select a particular user and invite him to become a friend. On acceptance of the request, the latter's record will be visible in the Friends List of the user and vice versa. The user can send and receive messages that can be of two types: public and private. A public message, when sent, will be visible to all the registered users browsing the public message list, whereas a private message will be visible only to the recipient. A registered user can upload his photographs and delete previously uploaded photographs. For the persons who do not have any knowledge of this site, an email can be sent, providing information of this site. User can also delete an already added friend from his friend list. He is also allowed to send group messages to a group of friends.

Consider only client side functional requirements and answer the followings. Draw **Usecase Diagram** and **Analysis Model** using Rational Rose. Write **description for each usecase**.

USECASE DIAGRAM

See Fig. App. 24.

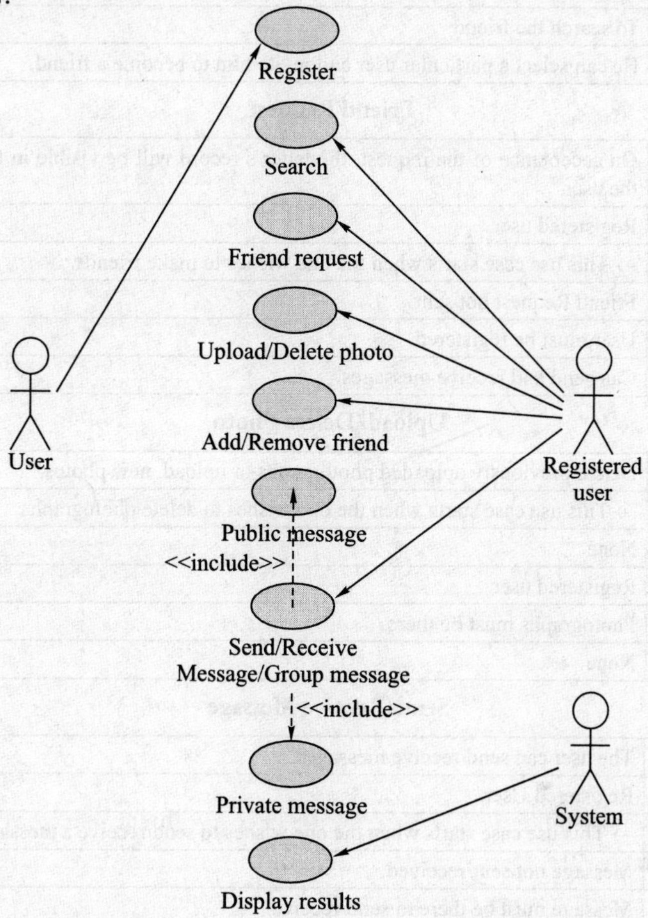

App. 24

USECASE DESCRIPTION

Register

Brief Description	A user can register with the site. On doing so, he is connected with all other registered users of this site.
Actors	User
Flow of Events	→ This use case starts when the one wishes to become registered user.
Alternative Events	Not registered user.
Pre-conditions	User must be available to the network
Post-conditions	To become registered user

Search

Brief Description	To begin networking, he must search for names through a general search.
Actors	Registered User.

Flow of Events	→ This use case starts when the one wishes to search the person on site.
Alternative Events	Search function not used.
Pre-conditions	To search the friend
Post-conditions	He can select a particular user and invite him to become a friend.

Friend Request

Brief Description	On acceptance of the request, the latter's record will be visible in the Friends List of the user.
Actors	Registered user.
Flow of Events	→ This use case starts when the one wishes to make friends.
Alternative Events	Friend Request not sent.
Pre-conditions	User must be registered.
Post-conditions	Can send and receive messages.

Upload/Delete Photo

Brief Description	Delete previously uploaded photographs or upload new photos.
Flow of Events	→ This use case starts when the one wishes to delete photographs.
Alternative Events	None
Actors	Registered user.
Pre-conditions	Photographs must be there.
Post-conditions	None

Send/Receive Message

Brief Description	The user can send/receive messages.
Actors	Registered User.
Flow of Events	→ This use case starts when the one wishes to send/receive a message.
Alternative Events	Message not sent/received.
Pre-conditions	Message must be there to send/receive.
Post-conditions	Message must be send/received.

ANALYSIS MODEL

See Fig. App. 25.

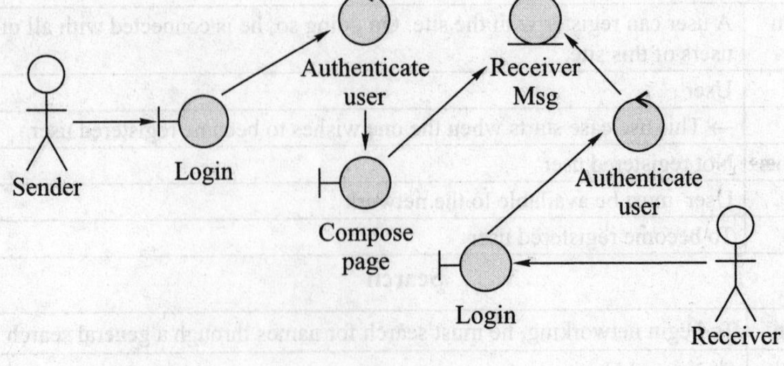

App. 25

13. Draw **Use Case Diagram**, **Sequence Diagram (for each usecase)** and **Analysis Model** for ESU University. Extend the analysis model to the **Class Design** and **Generate Code**.

- The ESU University wants to computerize their registration system.
- The Registrar sets up the curriculum for a semester.
  - o One course may have multiple course offerings.
- Students select 4 primary courses and 2 alternate courses.
- Once a student registers for a semester, the billing system is notified so the student may be billed for the semester.
- Students may use the system to add/drop courses for a period of time after registration.
- Professors use the system to receive their course offering rosters.
- Users of the registration system are assigned passwords which are used at logon validation.

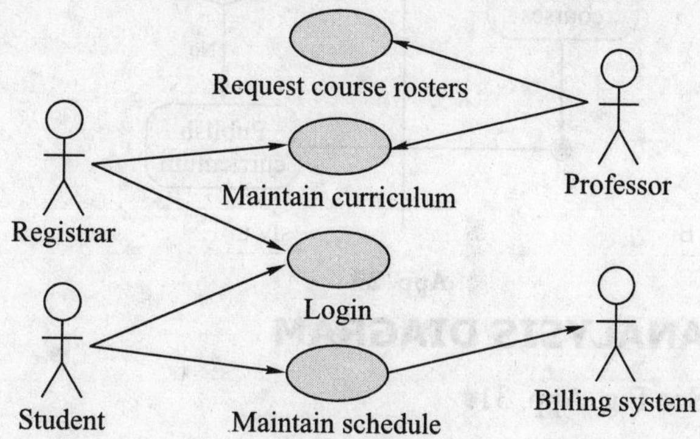

App. 26

USECASE DIAGRAM

See Fig. App. 26.

SEQUENCE DIAGRAM

See Fig. App. 27, 28, 29, 30 and 31.

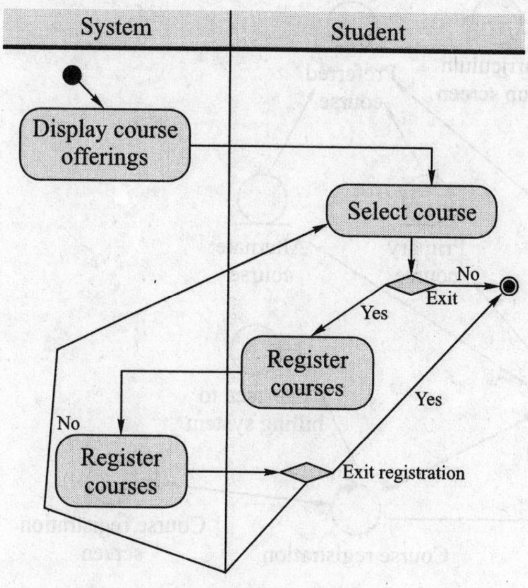

App. 27

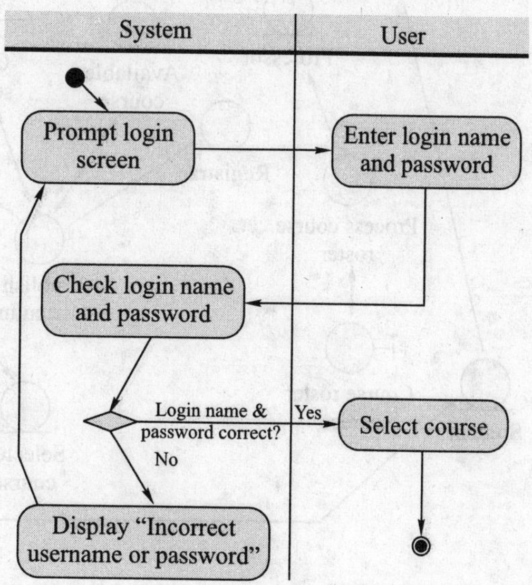

App. 28

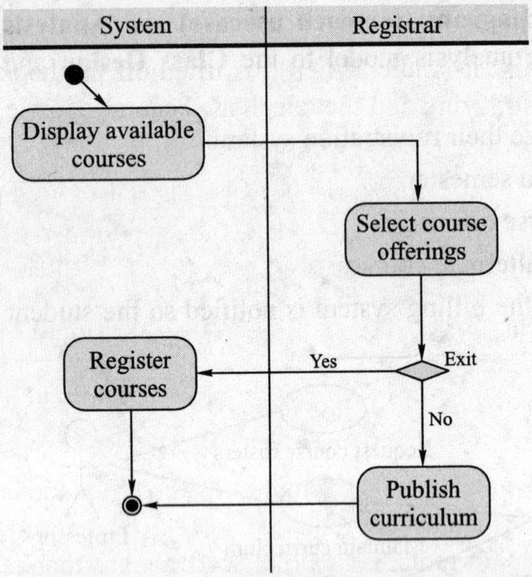

App. 29

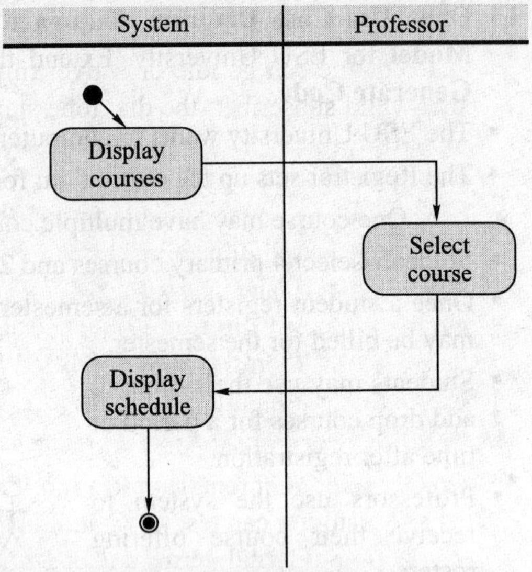

App. 30

ANALYSIS DIAGRAM

See Fig. App. 31.

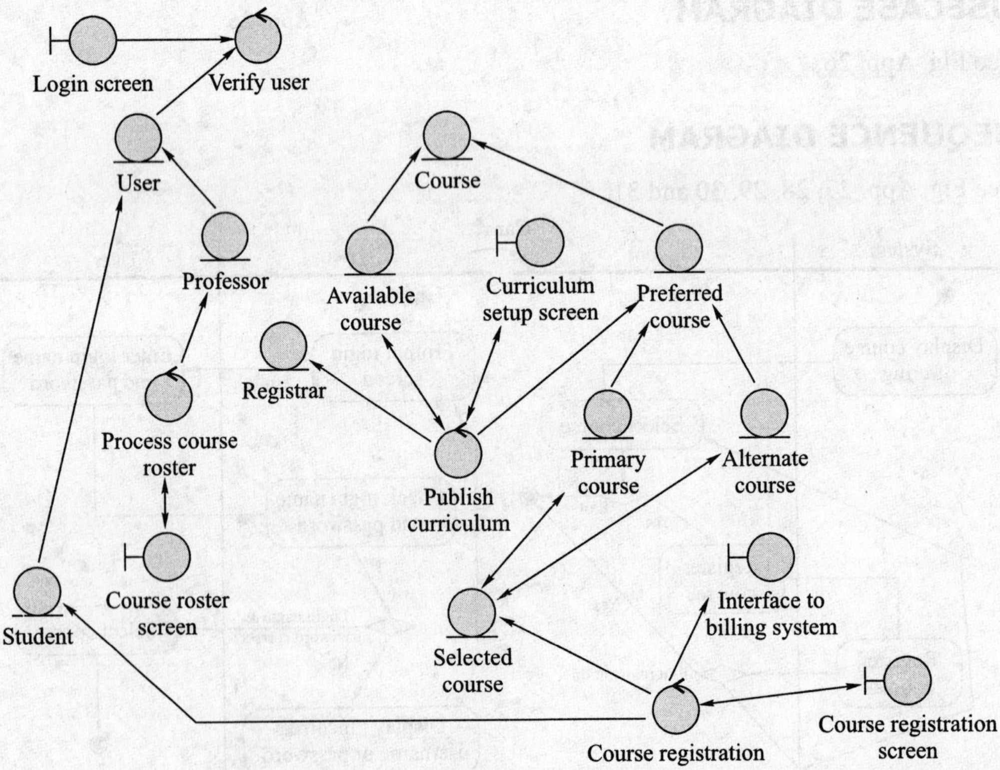

App. 31

14. Draw a State Transition Diagram to depict the following:

A telephone can be idle or active. Initially it is idle. When it is lifted off the hook by a valid subscriber, the dial tone starts playing and the telephone becomes active. When it is active, the dial tone plays, or it can be in the midst of dialing, or in the midst of connecting, or in the midst of talking. When the first digit is punched, the dial tone stops playing and the process of dialing begin. When all digits are punched it starts to connect. When the phone is lifted by the other party, both parties can talk.

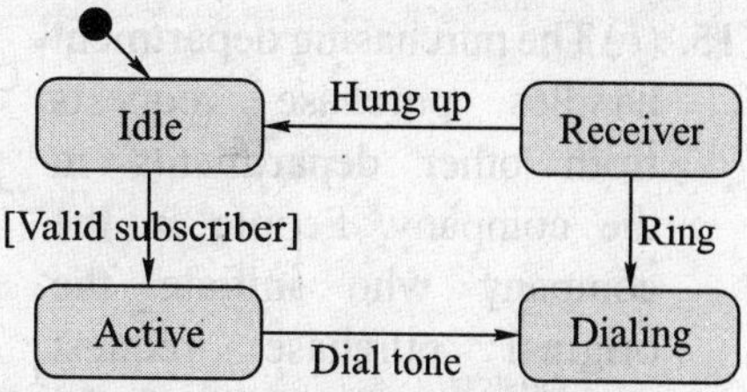

App. 32 State Transition Diagram.

Solution: See Fig. App. 32.

15. (*a*) Consider a car rental application. The rental agency has multiple offices/ locations where customer can test drive and then select a car for rental (local or to outstation). The period of rental, terms and conditions for rental is flexible. Software has to take responsibility for loaning cars, keeping track of availability of cars, return of cars, billing, maintenance activities for cars and keeping track of driver's availability and assignment in case of chauffeur driver car rentals.

Draw **use case diagram and Analysis model** for above application taking advantage of full UML notation for use case diagrams.

USECASE DIAGRAM

See Fig. App. 33.

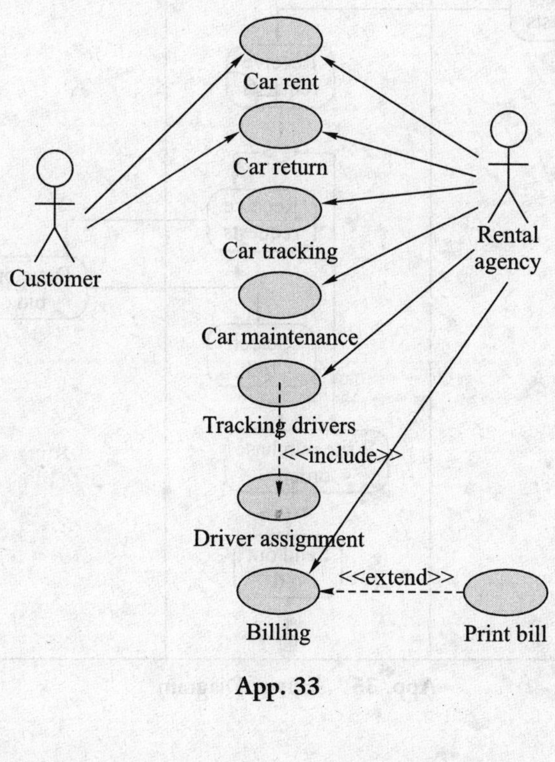

App. 33

ANALYSIS MODEL

See Fig. App. 34.

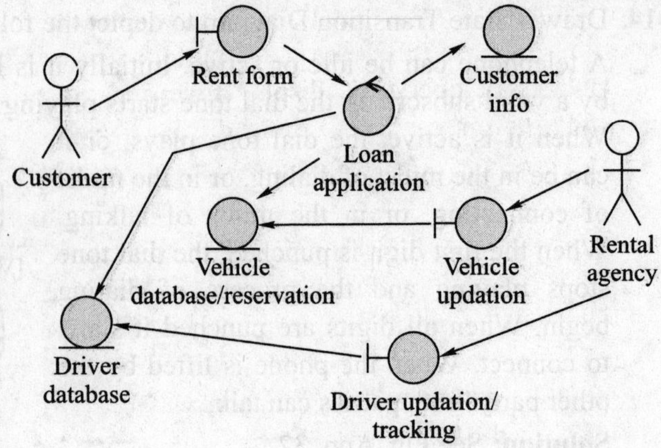

App. 34

15. (*b*) The purchasing department handles purchase requests from other departments in the company. People in the company who initiate the original purchase request are the "customers" of the purchasing department. A case worker within the purchasing department receives that request and monitors it until it is ordered and received. Case workers process the requests for purchasing products under $ 1,500, write a purchase order, and then send it to the approved vendor. Purchase requests over $ 1,500 must first be sent out for a bid from the vendor that supplies the product. When the bids return, the case worker selects one bid. Then, the case worker writes a purchase order and sends it to the approved vendor. Draw (see Fig. App. 35) **Activity Diagram** for the case study given above.

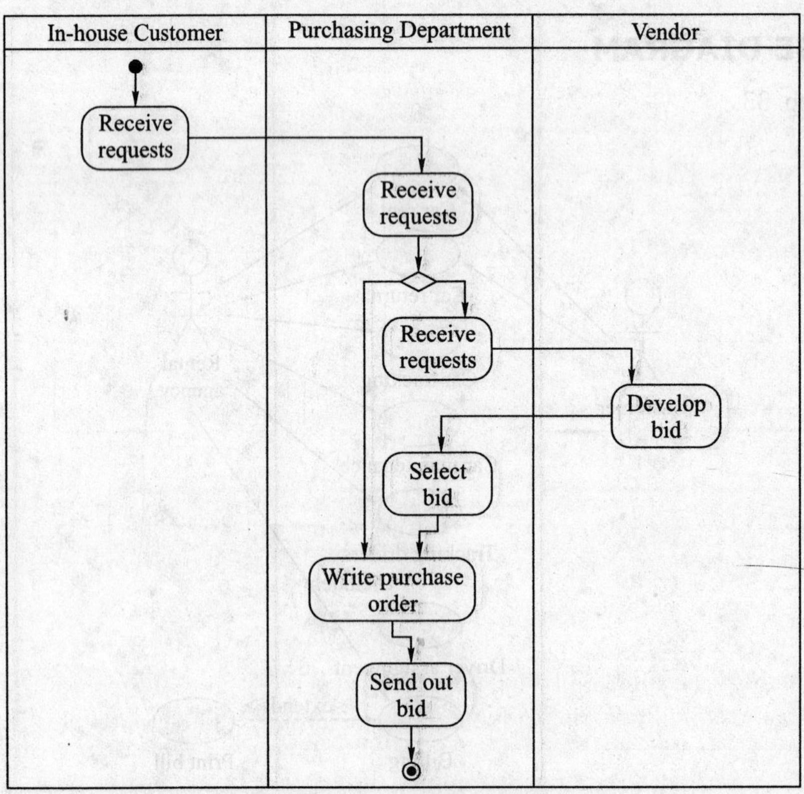

App. 35 Activity Diagram

16. A simple digital watch has a display and two buttons to set it, the A button and the B button. The watch has two modes of operation, display time and set time. In the display time mode, the watch displays hours and minutes, separated by a flashing colon. The set time mode has two sub modes, set hours and set minutes. The A button selects modes. Each time it is pressed, the mode advances in the sequence: display, set hours, set minutes, display, etc. Within the sub modes, the B button advances the hours or minutes once each time it is pressed. Buttons must be released before they can generate another event. Prepare a state diagram of the watch.

Solution: See Fig. App. 36.

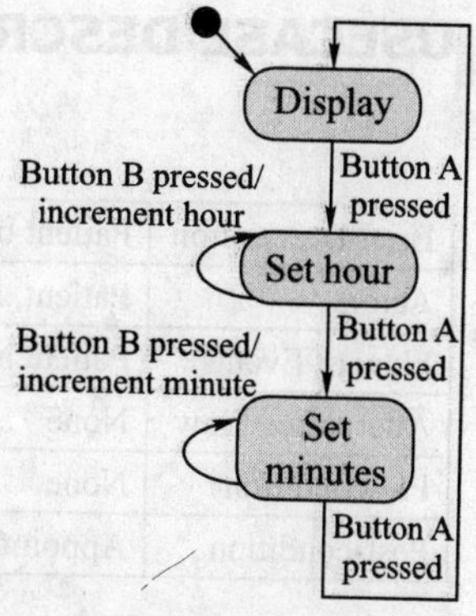

App. 36 State Transition Diagram

17. Draw **Usecase Diagram**, **Class Diagram** and **Generate Code** for **Health Care Center**. Write **usecase description for each usecase**. Patient Can arrange and cancel appointment with physician using scheduler. Physician decides to Prescribe Medication for Patient. Physician Specifies Drug Info: Medication Name, Dosage Amount, Number Doses & Refills. Computer Cross-Checks for Conflict Between Medication and Current Medications/Medical History Prescription Forwarded Electronically to Pharmacy or Else Printed for Patient.

USECASE DIAGRAM

See Fig. App. 37.

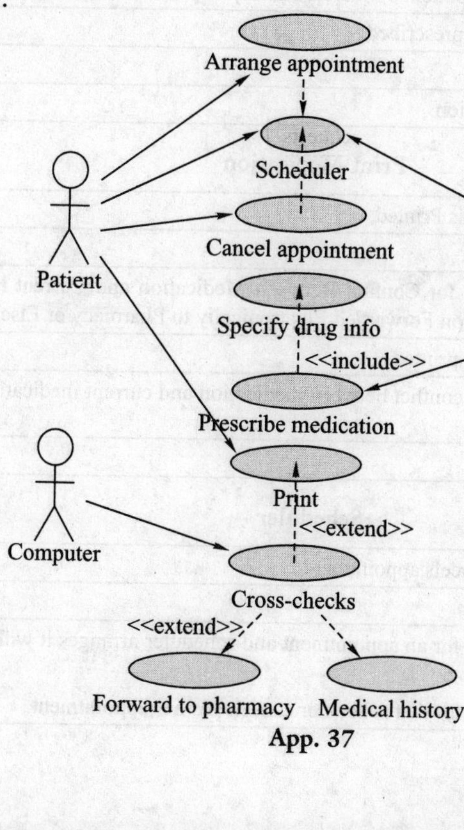

App. 37

USECASE DESCRIPTION

Arrange Appointment

Brief Description	Patient use Scheduler to get appointment with Physician using.
Actors	Patient, Physician.
Flow of Events	Patient arranges appointment with physician using scheduler.
Alternative Flow	None
Pre-condition	None
Post-condition	Appointment is made.

Cancel Appointment

Brief Description	Patient use Scheduler to cancel appointment with Physician.
Actors	Patient, Physician.
Flow of Events	Patient cancels appointment with physician using scheduler.
Alternative Flow	None
Pre-condition	None
Post-condition	Appointment is cancelled.

Medical History

Brief Description	Physician checks medical History to Prescribe Medication.
Actors	Patient, physician .
Flow of Events	Physician checks patient's Medical History to prescribe Medication.
Alternative Flow	Medication is not prescribed.
Pre-condition	None
Post-condition	Prescribe medication.

Print Medication

Brief Description	Final Medication is Printed.
Actors	Patient, computer.
Flow of Events	As Cross-Checks for Conflict Between Medication and Current Medications/Medical History Prescription Forwarded Electronically to Pharmacy or Else Printed for Patient.
Alternative Flow	Medication is not printed.
Pre-condition	Cross-checks for conflict between medication and current medications/Medical History prescription.
Post-condition	None

Scheduler

Brief Description	Arranges and cancels appointment.
Actors	Patient, Physician.
Flow of Events	1. If patient asks for an appointment and scheduler arranges it with physician when he/ she is free. 2. If patient asks for that scheduler cancels his/her appointment.

Alternative Flow	None
Pre-condition	None
Post-condition	None

Cross check for conflict

Brief Description	Computer checks the Medication and Current Medication/Medical history prescription.
Actors	Computer.
Flow of Events	Computer Cross-Checks for Conflict Between Medication and Current Medications/ Medical History Prescription Forwarded Electronically to Pharmacy or Else Printed for Patient.
Alternative Flow	None
Pre-condition	None
Post-condition	Forward to pharmacy.

Forward to pharmacy

Brief Description	If cross-check performed by computer result's is positive than this use is executed.
Actors	Computer.
Flow of Events	If cross-check performed by computer result's is positive than patient is forwarded to pharmacy.
Alternative Flow	None
Pre-condition	None
Post-condition	Medication is provided.

CLASS DIAGRAM

See Fig. App. 38.

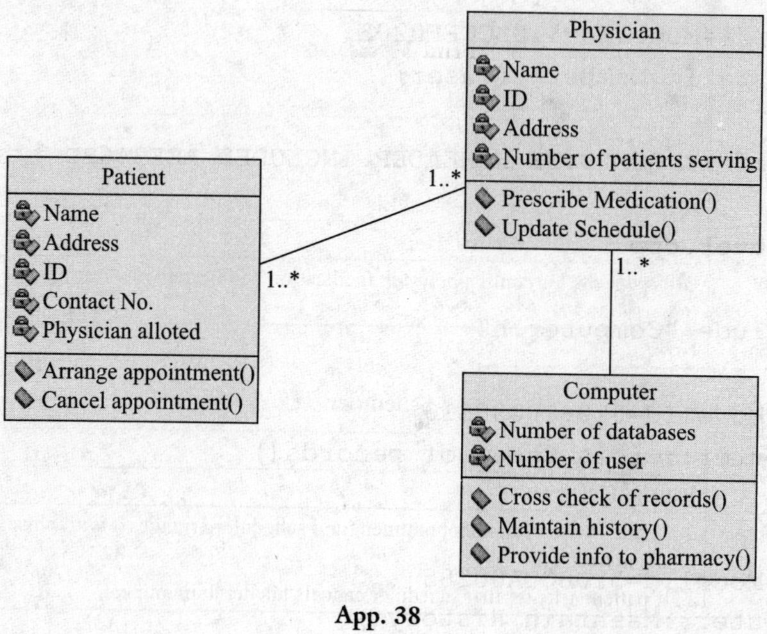

App. 38

CODE

Computer.h

```
#ifndef COMPUTER_H_HEADER_INCLUDED_AEF346BD
#define COMPUTER_H_HEADER_INCLUDED_AEF346BD

//##ModelId=510BCCDF01FF
class Computer
{
  public:
    //##ModelId=510BCD850310
    static Cross Check of records();

    //##ModelId=510BCDA00285
    static Maintain History();

    //##ModelId=510BCDB9028E
    static Provide info to pharmacy();

  private:
    //##ModelId=510BCCEC00D9
    static Number of databases;

    //##ModelId=510BCCFF020F
    static Number of user;
};
#endif /* COMPUTER_H_HEADER_INCLUDED_AEF346BD */
```

Computer.cpp

```
#include "Computer.h"

//##ModelId=510BCD850310
Computer::Cross Check of records()
{
}
//##ModelId=510BCDA00285
Computer::Maintain History()
```

```
{
}
//##ModelId=510BCDB9028E
Computer::Provide info to pharmacy()
{
}

//##ModelId=510BCCEC00D9
Computer::Number of databases;

//##ModelId=510BCCFF020F
Computer::Number of user;
```

Patient.h

```
#ifndef PATIENT_H_HEADER_INCLUDED_AEF35BD1
#define PATIENT_H_HEADER_INCLUDED_AEF35BD1

//##ModelId=510BCB8700CB
class Patient
{
  public:
    //##ModelId=510BCBF200A8
    static Arrange appointment();

    //##ModelId=510BCC060025
    static Cancel appointment();

  private:
    //##ModelId=510BCBA30253
    static Name;

    //##ModelId=510BCBAE0071
    static Address;

    //##ModelId=510BCBB60339
    static ID;
    //##ModelId=510BCBBA0236
    static Contact NO;
    //##ModelId=510BCBDE0033
    static Physician Alloted;
};
```

```
#endif /* PATIENT_H_HEADER_INCLUDED_AEF35BD1 */
```

Patient.cpp

```
#include "Patient.h"

//##ModelId=510BCBF200A8
Patient::Arrange appointment()
{
}
//##ModelId=510BCC060025
Patient::Cancel appointment()
{
}
//##ModelId=510BCBA30253
Patient::Name;

//##ModelId=510BCBAE0071
Patient::Address;

//##ModelId=510BCBB60339
Patient::ID;

//##ModelId=510BCBBA0236
Patient::Contact NO;

//##ModelId=510BCBDE0033
Patient::Physician Alloted;
```

Physician.h

```
#ifndef PHYSICIAN_H_HEADER_INCLUDED_AEF37D1D
#define PHYSICIAN_H_HEADER_INCLUDED_AEF37D1D

//##ModelId=510BCC28001E
class Physician
{
  public:
    //##ModelId=510BCCA601C2
    static Prescribe Medication();

    //##ModelId=510BCCBD023C
    static Update Schedule();
```

```
   private:
      //##ModelId=510BCC3802A6
      static Name;

      //##ModelId=510BCC3A025A
      static ID;

      //##ModelId=510BCC4A0213
      static Address;

      //##ModelId=510BCC5A009D
      static Number of Patients serving;
};

#endif /* PHYSICIAN_H_HEADER_INCLUDED_AEF37D1D */
```

Physician.cpp

```
#include "Physician.h"

//##ModelId=510BCCA601C2
Physician::Prescribe Medication()
{
}

//##ModelId=510BCCBD023C
Physician::Update Schedule()
{
}

//##ModelId=510BCC3802A6
Physician::Name;

//##ModelId=510BCC3A025A
Physician::ID;

//##ModelId=510BCC4A0213
Physician::Address;

//##ModelId=510BCC5A009D
Physician::Number of Patients serving;
```